ו or before

THE WEBBS IN ASIA

The Webbs in Asia

The 1911–12 Travel Diary

Introduced and Edited by

George Feaver

Professor of Political Science
University of British Columbia

First published 1992 by
THE MACMILLAN PRESS LTD
Houndmills, Basingstoke, Hampshire RG21 2XS
and London
Companies and representatives
throughout the world

ISBN 0-333-55027-7

A catalogue record for this book is available
from the British Library

Copy-edited and typeset by Povey–Edmondson
Okehampton and Rochdale, England

Printed in Hong Kong

Contents

Preface

In readying the Webbs' account of their 1911–12 Asian tour for publication, I have consulted both the holograph diaries and the typescript copies of the originals now housed with the rest of the Passfield Papers at the British Library of Political and Economic Science, London School of Economics (LSE). Notwithstanding Sidney's and Beatrice's evident enthusiasm for Japan, and their sympathy with Indian nationalism, readers of these diaries will be struck, in many derogatory remarks scattered throughout the text, by the Webbs' robust capacity for snobbishness, and even, where the Chinese and Koreans are concerned, for palpable racism. These might appear, with the passage of time, notable faults in convinced socialists (one of them a future Colonial Secretary), joint founders, moreover, of the LSE, an institution of higher learning intimately connected with the preparation for rule of the emergent political elites of many newly-independent Third World nations. I need hardly disclaim any association with such views where they occur. Nor has it been my intent, with the publication of materials not fully readied for publication by Beatrice herself, to embarrass in any way the Webbs' already received reputations. Like all of us, they were products of their age; and if the Webbs' Asian tour diaries contain these disconcerting faults, they contain much that is of undeniable value and interest to successor generations. That they are here printed as they were left, without excisions, is due solely to an editor's determination to be faithful to the integrity of the originals.

In other respects, since the contents of the holograph notebooks were left in somewhat ramshackle form, it early became clear that an interventionist editorial policy was required. Obvious punctuation and spelling errors have been set right as have the usually minor misreadings that occur in the typescript copies; and I have taken the further liberty of breaking up into separate paragraphs many of the longer unbroken diary entries as these occur in the original notebooks. Whenever the Webbs, as they frequently do, emphasize terms or report conversations by placing them within double quotation marks, I have replaced these with single quotation marks. And I have set in italics matter that is underlined in the original, as I have certain foreign terms not, of course, italicised by the Webbs. A more important and rather challenging task, given the Webbs' commendable insistence throughout their travels on not restricting their contacts to Europeans, has been that of tracking down and correcting the many instances in which a diary entry identifying some local Asian notable is at best a more-or-less imaginative approximation in English. In the main, my approach has been eclectic rather than systematic in rendering Asian terms in English. Certain modern place names have been substituted throughout the diaries for the Webbs' own usages, as have standard modern usages for other words, such as 'Hindu' and 'Muslim' rendered variously in the originals (though I have departed from this rule in using *'jinricksha'* in the Japan section, and *'ricksha'* otherwise). Generally, the Hepburn system of romanisation has been used in rendering Japanese terms in English, while with Chinese words I have relied on the old Wade-Giles system of transliteration rather than the more recent *pinyin* conventions favoured in the People's Republic of China. In the India section, there are both older Anglo-Indian and newer post-independence English spellings. In the Japan section, I have followed the Japanese convention of placing surnames first. And in the main place and date entries, where the form of entry, reflecting the originals, varies, I have added an element of uniformity by adopting as a standard usage throughout the text the Webbs' own periodic recourse to a superscript suffix following the entry of abbreviated months and calendar dates.

I have followed the practice of identifying the starting-point of entries in the original holograph diary in the respective hands of Sidney and Beatrice with the symbols [SW→] and [BW→]. Inserts within entries by one or the other are identified by the symbols [SW: ...] and [BW: ...]. Throughout the whole, I have sought wherever possible (but not with uniform success) to provide brief biographical entries for the personalities encountered by the Webbs in the course of their Asian sojourn. Other reference notes have been added in hopes of clarifying allusions to historical, political and other matters not otherwise self-explanatory in the manner of their entry in the text.

This volume has been some time in the making. I am indebted for their assistance to many not here singled out for individual mention. But I do wish to acknowledge the encouragement of Professor Ian Nish and the Publications Committee of The London School of Economics, and expressly to record my gratitude to Mr. Patrick Davis, the School's recently retired Publications Officer, who stoically shepherded this project through its various ups and downs. Further thanks are due to Dr. Angela Raspin and her colleagues in the Manuscripts and Special Collections Division of the British Library of Political and Economic Science, and to the LSE's Government Department, which has so hospitably provided me with an academic home from home over the years. At Macmillan, Tim Farmiloe and Steven Gerrard deserve thanks for being so patiently supportive, as do Keith Povey and Elaine Towns for their assiduous and constructive copy-editing. And here at UBC, my Asian-area departmental colleagues Pete Chamberlain, Frank Langdon and John Wood have been most helpful, though any faults remaining are entirely my own. Finally, the award of a University of British Columbia Humanities and Social Sciences Research Grant helped to defray the costs of travel to and from London in conjunction with this project.

Vancouver GEORGE FEAVER

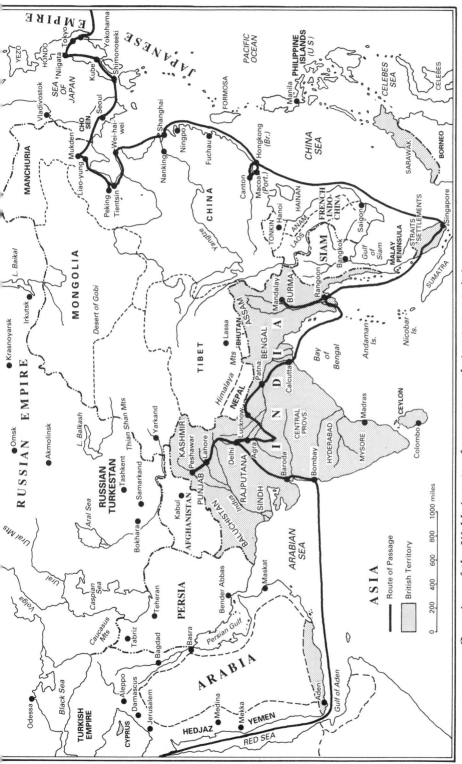

Overview of the Webbs' route of passage on their 1911–12 Asian tour

Introduction: A Pilgrim's Progress in the Far East

THE WEBBS AND ASIA

The awakening of modern Asia in the early years of the twentieth century was a time of promise and portent. Japan emerged as a muscular power of large ambition. There was an epochal revolution in China. Incipient nationalism coursed beneath the deceptive surface calm of British India. Such developments were to have profound implications, not only for the British Empire, but for the further course of Western civilisation itself. Yet there are few published accounts by non-official Western observers recording their first-hand impressions of Asia in these momentous times. It is thus the more surprising that this remarkable diary, so unlike anything else written by the Webbs, should have remained in manuscript form all these years. It was composed at the dawn of a millennial century in which global and regional warfare would make much unrecognisable in both East and West. Today, the waning century's two world wars cast a shrinking shadow. Yet the sense of the world as a smaller place ushered in by them has led a once less-attentive Western audience to a keener interest in the multifarious goings-on of contemporary Asia; just as, throughout a still rapidly-modernising Asia itself, there is everywhere a fascination with the West and with Western perceptions of the East. In such circumstances, the Webbs' Asian tour diary, providing intelligent and frankly opinionated touristic impressions of a world so near to ours in historic time, and yet now largely lost, has much to recommend it even if considered merely as a contribution to early-twentieth-century travel literature.

The further fact that it is a product of the famous intellectual partnership of Sidney and Beatrice Webb should itself guarantee an interested reception. The two social reformers and founders of The London School of Economics, shortly to celebrate its centenary, remain intriguing biographical figures. And, quite aside from its intrinsic interest as a travel diary, this overlooked document throws light on the influences at work in the fermentative years preceding the First World War that contributed to shaping the further course of their eventful lives. They were long lives. The Asian diary was written when Beatrice (1858–1943) and Sidney (1859–1947) were in their early

1

fifties; both were to live on well into their eighties. Born into a world of mid-Victorian progress and *laissez-faire* Empire, their deaths would coincide with the effective demise of British and European imperialism and the rise of the Welfare State. With the benefit of hindsight, we can discern in the pages of this Asian diary the faint beginnings of a doctrinal conversion, with implications for the Webbs' joint biography as far-reaching as these larger background changes in the received assumptions of the mainstream European political world of their day. It would be an exaggeration to suggest that their year-long sojourn in Asia was the definitive influence triggering this conversion. It is perhaps better seen as one of several mutually reinforcing considerations that led the two by stages to abandon the trademark political moderation of their original and very British Fabian Society precepts, and to substitute for them a commitment to the revolutionary promise, as they came so controversially to believe in old age, of Soviet Russia.

Another retrospective interest of this 1911–12 Asian travel diary is that Beatrice Webb actually intended it to form an integral part of her never-completed autobiography. She struggled with the shape of this larger, multi-volume work, to be based upon her manuscript diaries, until very near the end of her long life, when she eventually lost the strength to continue with it. The Asian diary thus remained unpublished. Yet Beatrice wrote in a draft preface to the volume that was to have been based upon this diary, reproduced below, that 'This year's sojourn in strange worlds acted as a powerful ferment, altering and enlarging our conception of the human race, its past, its present and its future.' She added: 'Speaking for myself, I was never again quite the same person after this exciting journey. Our [Asian] diaries are in fact predominantly autobiographical.'

BEATRICE WEBB AS DIARIST AND AUTOBIOGRAPHER

In restoring this Asian travel diary to its proper place, we need to bear in mind just how reliant has been our generally received view of the Webbs' famous partnership on the testimony of Beatrice Webb's diary. Though extensive extracts from the full diary have been published over the years, these still constitute only part of a larger whole.[1] We need also to consider the connection between the full diary and various schemes of autobiography long-projected by Beatrice, but of which only two volumes were ever published. Strictly speaking, the first of these alone, *My Apprenticeship* (1926), was actually completed and published in her lifetime. The second, *Our Partnership* (1948), appeared posthumously as an edited volume based upon draft materials intended for a larger, uncompleted work. It concludes with a postscript, written by Beatrice when she was eighty, indicating the general outline of the much fuller autobiography she realised by then she would not live to complete.

Whatever the Webbs' joint achievements, Beatrice was in her own right one of England's most accomplished diarists this century. It has been said that the most propitious kind of intellectual biography is the intellectual autobiography; but the generalisation requires modification if it is to fit the case of Sidney and Beatrice Webb. So central was the habit of diary-making to Beatrice's sense of self that her intellectual biography really involved *two* quite distinct partnerships, one with her diary and another with Sidney Webb. Looked at in this way, her own most propitious intellectual biography is really her full diary itself, whereas the intellectual biography she shared with Sidney is to be found in the product of their working lives together and as an aspect of her projects of autobiography considered as separate from her practice of the diarist's craft as such.[2]

She had begun to keep a diary while accompanying her father on a visit to America; she would continue making entries in it until only days before her death. At its girlhood outset, she explained, her diary-making was a substitute form of conversation with 'some mysterious personification'[3] of her own identity, drawing her to solitudinous reflection on the ultimate questions of life. And throughout her long life, in fact, belying a public persona that was assured and even imperious, these reflections involved her in recurring struggles to contain bouts of despondency and doubt. Of course, her tenacious habit (the original diary, covering the period 13 September 1873 – 19 April 1943, survives in some fifty-seven exercise books of various sizes) also served a more varied purpose. It was thus that, following her marriage to Sidney Webb in 1892, writing in her diary was to provide a more self-expressive outlet than did the dreary works of historical, institutional and sociological scholarship she was destined to undertake with him.

Beatrice first gave serious thought to the idea of preparing an autobiography based on her diaries when Sidney became distracted from their joint work by the exigencies of Labour Party reconstruction planning in the midst of the First World War. Almost five years had then elapsed since their return from Asia. On 3 January 1917, she noted in her diary that she had 'bought a small cheap typewriter and . . . am using up some of my spare hours in the afternoon in copying out and editing my MSS diaries so as to make a "Book of My Life"'.[4] She gave to the project the tentative title '*My Craft and My Creed*'. Its first fruit was *My Apprenticeship*, which took much longer to write than she expected. Nearly six years later, she was still reassuring herself that she had 'done so much drudgery that I think I have a right to let myself go on a work of art!'[5] But it was not until the early morning hours of 29 October 1925 that she was able to record: '*Done it*: and never before have I been so relieved to see the last words of a book; for never before have I been so utterly and painfully uncertain as to its value.'[6] But when favourable reviews greeted the book's publication in the early summer of 1926, she started in immediately on a sequel. Sidney had by then again set aside their joint work to enter Parliament in 1924 as a member of the first Labour Cabinet. 'What troubles me,' she mused, 'is that before I die I should like to work out more completely than I have done in *My Apprenticeship* my conception of the place of religion in the life of man.'[7] Her first instalment of autobiography had told the story of her life from its earliest years up to her marriage in 1892, when she was thirty-four; the new work, begun when she was sixty-eight, would treat her partnership with Sidney in a similar fashion. She quickly prepared a short typescript, '*Prologue: Sidney Webb*', adding to it a marginal note in her distinctive hand: 'An attempt at a portrait written mostly in the night and early morning during July 1926.'[8] But after that, work on the new book, *Our Partnership*, proceeded slowly.

My Apprenticeship owed something of its success to Beatrice's reliance on a 'development of character' theme reminiscent of George Eliot's novels. The book's story, chronicling the triumphant emergence from a privileged milieu of a once lonely and purposeless young woman, has an uplifting ending. In the early part, the featured character, the eligible if headstrong Miss Beatrice Potter, comes to terms with the emotional disaster of an unrequited passion for the dashing Liberal politician Joseph Chamberlain – though more is made of this searing experience in Beatrice's manuscript diary itself than in the printed text of *My Apprenticeship*. She has also to deal with the wrenching trauma of her beloved father's lingering demise. These challenges are met and overcome when, abjuring the idle security of the social set in which a daughter of the wealthy Richard Potter had an assured place, Beatrice rededicates her life to the service of her fellows, against a backdrop of East London slums. Lingering doubts vanish before a newly-won belief in the promise of social science. At the book's end, she converts to 'socialism' and enters upon a comradely marriage to Sidney Webb, an unlikely suitor whose chief attraction to our heroine, as is made clear, lies in his advanced views. The now unfolded story is thus one of acute personal anguish overcome and reason triumphant over emotion. Here was the literary testament of a new breed of 'politically correct' late-Victorian woman.

In composing *My Apprenticeship*, then, Beatrice had had the advantage of looking back upon a concluded chapter of her life, some years after the fact, and of seeing in it a settled victory of affirmation over despair. But when she set to work on her sequel, she still had no really very clear idea where the joint biographical adventure upon which she had embarked with Sidney some thirty-four years before might end. After his arrival on the scene, her diary featured a good deal of matter concerned with the topical intellectual and political preoccupations of their crowded public life together. And her diarist's verdict on the various fruits of their collaboration, at least for the years from 1892 down to their departure for Asia in 1911, did not lack for justificatory direction. But there had also persisted in Beatrice's diary that essentially private conversation with herself which pre-dated her relationship with Sidney. Their complementary intellectual and marital union had not stilled her attraction to deep thoughts. In fact, the inception of *Our Partnership* in 1926 owed not a little to a vague idea that in the further exercise of her powers of creative artifice, she might come to grasp just how the joint-partnership stage of her life's journey, as distinct from the apprenticeship stage, itself fitted into the larger design of a still unfinished quest. But in the years since their return from Asia in the Spring of 1912, Beatrice had grown increasingly perplexed by the turbulent direction of public affairs: the slide into the First World War, with its horrendous consequences for the sanguine assumptions of nineteenth century advanced thought, had been bad enough; and she was writing, after all, midway through the 1920s, itself a freakish decade that was to end in global depression and political disaster for Britain's Labour Party. And so, at first, she could not see her authorial way clearly forward beyond the sketch she had drawn of Sidney.

It was not until the decade's end, when the Webbs began to be seriously interested in Russia, that things changed. It was only then that Beatrice took up anew the *Our Partnership* project and recorded that she was making definite progress with it. Their interest in Russia, and Beatrice's in particular, very quickly became all-consuming, the more so after May 1932 when the two made a brief visit to see Russia under Stalin for themselves. Their minds were already made up; and, not alone amongst Western intellectuals at the time, seeing what they wanted to see, they came home brimming with enthusiasm. What remained of their joint mid-septuagenarian energies were harnessed to prepare *Soviet Communism: A New Civilisation* (1935), 'in two ponderous volumes', as Beatrice admitted. It was a frankly eulogistic work in which their powers of critical judgement were so largely suspended as to threaten their reputations, even allowing the excuse of their advanced years and the very real moral and political confusion of the day. Yet Beatrice was to pay tribute to *Soviet Communism* as 'the final and certainly the most ambitious task of "Our Partnership"'. Her words occur near the conclusion of the postscript mentioned earlier, composed in 1938 and placed at the end of the typescript chapters of *Our Partnership* she had actually completed by then. These had, in fact, carried her account of her career with Sidney up to June 1911. 'First,' the postscript noted, 'on our return from our Far Eastern tour in June 1912, we discovered that our propaganda of a national minimum of civilised life within the capitalist system was out of date.' There was the impact on their thinking of militant labour unrest and capitalist intransigence in the years immediately preceding the First World War. There was the war itself, and the 'still more disastrous peace'. Then there was the Great Depression which began in 1929; and then, she declared dramatically, there was the rise 'out of a tumultuous but successful revolution [of] a new social order' in Russia.[9]

The conversion to communism in the early 1930s yielded what otherwise had eluded Beatrice's halting pen – an *Our Partnership* parallel to the edifying conclusion of *My Apprenticeship*. As much may be inferred from the 1938 postscript's hortative tone, leaving readers in no doubt that some larger meaning had after all informed her shared quest with Sidney and, by implication, her continuing personal pilgrimage in its partnership stage. But if there was this benefit to the Webbs' political conversion, there was also a cost: the long middle period of Beatrice's autobiography remained unwritten, a state of affairs poignantly illustrated by her practice, in sporadic attempts late in life to return to its composition, of using as typing paper the reverse sides of discarded galley sheets from *Soviet Communism*!

Quite aside from encroaching old age and her protracted hesitancy about a firm narrative direction, Beatrice also had to cope with a daunting practical problem. How was she going to compress her ever more extensive manuscript diaries? She had at first thought of a single *Our Partnership* volume for the entire period 1892–1932. But this she turned into two, covering the years 1892–1911 and 1912–1932 respectively. The first of these would conclude with a chapter entitled 'The Far East, 1911–12', so bridging the gap between the essentially hopeful Fabian atmosphere of Volume One and the somewhat less sanguine mood of the projected Volume Two. But by the time she was ready to begin the actual composition of the 'Far East' chapter, she had already written some 900 pages. Why not make this the basis of two separate volumes for 1892–98 and 1899–1912, with 1912–32 now making a third volume? Under this freshly modified plan, she would conclude Volume One with a bridging chapter based on an earlier travel diary, kept during the Webbs' tour of America and Australasia in 1898, just as the projected Asia chapter would conclude the volume for 1899–1912. But upon a careful re-examination of the uncut Asian diaries, she persuaded herself that they really ought to be published in their entirety as a separate volume entitled *The Far East*. And this, assuming the retention of the further volume for 1912–32, now meant *four* volumes of *Our Partnership* instead of three, or two, or the original one! And it was not only old age, the search for a satisfactory narrative device, and the unwieldiness of her materials that contributed to a situation in which, like a retreating horizon, a finally settled scheme eluded her. There was still the problem of how she might best inform any successor volumes to *My Apprenticeship* with that sense that her continuing intellectual biography thereafter embraced two overlapping but distinct partnerships, one with her diary and the other with Sidney Webb.

A consideration not unrelated to this last point might at this juncture have weighed in Beatrice's thoughts. By 1938, she had arrived at the stage of reconnoitring the 1911–12 Asia matter, and had even managed, as we earlier saw, to draft a preface to it in which she indicated that 'Speaking for myself, I was never again quite the same person after this exciting journey. Our [Asian] diaries are . . . predominantly autobiographical.' But the fact is that a good deal of the Asia tour diary was actually written by Sidney rather than by herself – the only instance of such a practice, except for the appearance of entries by him in the pages of the earlier 1898 travel diary and the Soviet tour diary of 1932, in the entire holograph diary. Why he should have written so much of this portion of the full diary is not entirely clear, though Beatrice indicates that she was out of sorts in the course of their tour. It was fully three months after their return to England before she made a fresh diary entry, explaining that she needed the time 'to get over the effect of the tropical climate and perpetual journeyings – my nerves were all to pieces, and waves of depression and panic followed each other'.[10] It is worth recollecting here that on the Webbs' return from their earlier 1898 tour, Beatrice had experienced a similar interruption in her habitual diary-making, though the reason she then gave was both different and instructive. 'Since we returned to England I have been disinclined to write in my diary', she noted at the time, 'having lost the habit of intimate confidences impossible in a joint diary such as we have kept together during our journey around the world. One cannot run on into self-analysis, family gossip, or indiscreet and hasty descriptions of current happenings, if someone else, however dear, is solemnly to read one's chatter then and there. I foresee the kind of kindly indulgence, or tolerant boredom, with which Sidney would decipher this last entry! And this feeling would, in itself, make it impossible to write whatever came into my head at the time of writing without thought of his criticism.'[11]

But even allowing that Sidney's participation in the writing of the Asia diary might have impeded Beatrice's further progress with her autobiography, it does not detract from the interest or value of the diary to us, at the least illustrating the intimacy of the Webbs' working union. On occasion, as she hints was the case in 1898, Sidney appears in the 1911–12 diary to serve as a kind of amanuensis, so that what is entered in his uncluttered schoolboy's hand may really be Beatrice's words. Elsewhere, the reader encounters substituted or overwritten matter in his handwriting amidst passages otherwise rendered in her own crabbed script, or finds him doggedly filling in the spaces for places and persons left blank in entries by her. And throughout, there are numerous instances of one taking over the writing from the other, in the middle of a page, a paragraph or even a sentence. Generally, their separate contributions to the Asia diary bear out our received biographical views of the two. Though Sidney occasionally unburdens himself of vivid passages of general touristic observation, as in his account of their mountain walk from Ikao or his interview with the Japanese prostitute at Nagano – or of the *Magh Mela* at Allahabad – he seems most comfortable with 'institutions', with collecting social facts and details of governmental, educational, industrial and agricultural organisation, his speculative horizons perhaps purposely restricted to these. Beatrice's entries, in comparison, have about them something of the atmosphere of the frustrated novelist that she was,[12] dwelling on the close observation of individual character and private lives. And she is altogether more ruminative than Sidney, musing at length upon the plight of women in East and West, or brooding about the religious life of Asia.

On New Year's Eve, 1938, Beatrice mentions that she had been mulling over a literary adventure entirely separate from *Our Partnership*. She at first called her new project 'Our Testament' or 'Our Pilgrimage', then changed it to *The Three Stages of Our Pilgrimage, 1892–1941, By Sidney and Beatrice Webb*. Early in that same year (the year too, remember, of the *Our Partnership* postscript), Sidney had suffered a severely incapacitating stroke, and Beatrice had entered a blunt, underlined query in her diary: 'The End of Our Partnership?'[13] She meant its definitive end and the prospect of having to continue on alone, now an aged and lonely pilgrim embarked on yet a further stage of life's mysterious journey. The aim of *Our Pilgrimage*, which she would compose on her own, but unlike *Our Partnership* she would issue in their joint names, would be to provide a final summary of the Webbs' views on man's relation to man, 'with just a word on my part – about man's relation to the universe'.[14] In a conscious borrowing from Bunyan, she scribbled atop a draft typescript of 'Chapter I, Volume I', 'The First Stage of the Pilgrim's Progress', indicating her intent to tell the story of '[a] Pilgrim's Progress . . . not of one individual, but of two in one: a sort of Siamese twin . . . joined together, not in the middle of one body, but in the middle of two lives'.[15] But work on *Our Pilgrimage* was to prove itself no less a struggle than the oft-modified *Our Partnership* schemes of unfinished autobiography. Certainly, the crowded years of her unusually close intellectual partnership with Sidney, including their controversial homage to Soviet Russia, were in Beatrice's view suitable for celebration as a political pilgrim's progress. But she also seemed to see, near the end, that their union had been itself only an aspect of a still more encompassing lifelong pilgrimage, an ultimately personal striving towards a union of faith and science in a new social order rising upon the wreckage of nineteenth-century liberal civilisation she had wanted to believe in for as long as she could remember.

Denied Sidney's steadying companionship, daily 'brain-work' through her autobiographical diarist's pen helped her to muster the strength to keep the faith. Striving every morning 'to do a mite of work on the book, and hoping that if I persist, the daily inch will eventually become a yard, and a consecutive yard' had become a kind of personal measure of progress for this 'religious-minded agnostic'.[16] She felt compelled to go on by a '*mania* for heaping up materials for future conclusions about what is happening in the world I live in'. Authorship, she confided, 'seems to be a profession from which you cannot retire – you long to carry on, however unfit you may be to do so . . . And I shall die with my diary, pen and ink, in a drawer by the side of my bed'.[17] She was 'dead tired'; and completion of even the first part of *The Three Stages of Our Pilgrimage* seemed a far-off goal. In a diary entry for 24 November 1939, she had reasoned she could still carry it off in 'a volume of 400 pages'. A year later, the book had instead expanded into three 'parts' rather than 'stages', and she acknowledged her failure to complete even the first of these. By the close of 1941, the 'parts' had become three 'volumes', with the first of these still some way from completion. During 1942, the tortured diary entries of the 'aged and decrepit' autobiographer began to confuse *Our Pilgrimage* with *Our Partnership*.

The last mention of the two works, which between them had occupied a persistent place in Beatrice's plans of authorship over a period of some sixteen years, occurred on 25 September 1942. 'It is clear,' she then allowed, 'that I shall not be able to finish either the one or the other for publication, either before or after my disappearance from the scene.'[18] Barbara Drake was invited down to Passfield Corner to spend the night and discuss what was to be done with the unfinished drafts. But Beatrice's chief concern was that her complete holograph diaries be typed, with spare copies in case the originals were somehow destroyed. There is something touching and revealing in this. She had seized upon the idea in her final unrealised plan of autobiography of completing an account of her years with Sidney conceived allegorically as a joint pilgrim's progress. Yet all the while, the monumental diaries she assiduously crafted for posterity had been infused with a not dissimilar underlying spirit, one perhaps more personal than comradely, more spiritual than political. And she had achieved in them what she was never to achieve as a conscious autobiographer, the true recording of a pilgrim's progress.[19]

THE AUTOBIOGRAPHY AND THE TRAVEL DIARIES

One result of Beatrice's failure to complete a full autobiography separate from her diaries was that the travel journals compiled by the Webbs during their two world tours were never to be published in the format she had envisaged for them. At the very least, she had planned to issue substantial selections from these diaries, with accompanying commentary in the style of *My Apprenticeship*. The impressions the two had recorded in the course of these 'busman's holidays', she was convinced, provided a useful complement to their formal sociological studies. Besides, travel abroad had made them aware of alternatives to democratic capitalism with the potential to modify its excesses, or even to supplant it.

Beatrice did complete 'Round the Anglo-Saxon World', the chapter intended to conclude the 1892–98 volume, and sent it for comment to Felix Frankfurter. But when the American jurist responded with 'a courteously expressed but wholly unfavourable criticism', urging upon her that its contents were 'far too unfavourable to American civilisation even in 1898', she dismissed his views as the testimony of an apologist for American capitalism. When Sidney took a somewhat different tack in observing that the related 1898 Australian material seemed to him to fall between two stools – 'too laboured and technical to interest the general reader, and too casual and incomplete for the research student' – his objection was likewise overridden.[20] The value of the 'Anglo-Saxon' matter, she insisted, was precisely that it had drawn upon 'a prolonged change of scene, a sort of sabbatical year' from the Webbs' usual sociological studies. Informal touristic observation yielded a supplement to the more methodical and narrow perspective of the professional social investigator. 'After all,' she averred, 'it is, at worst, as good a basis to build on as the "contemporaneous literature" of books and journals, novels and poems, pamphlets and sermons, plays and newspapers, that we have described as a valuable auxiliary to the official records. It is, at least, open to the investigator, on his holiday, to write some "contemporaneous literature" for his own use, and even for consultation by those who come after him.' What the partners had learned from travel abroad, she suggested, was not so much scientific knowledge of the institutions of other lands as 'suggestions and hypotheses for the investigation of those amid which we lived'. There was a further important purpose served by these travel journals. 'They make the investigator aware of the limits to be set to his generalisations. For centuries prior to Captain Cook, the European naturalists had described the swan as invariably having, among other attributes, that of whiteness. When travellers at last got to Australia, they saw, for the first time, a swan that was black.'

It was, in fact, Barbara Drake and Margaret Cole who made the eventual decision to omit 'Round the Anglo-Saxon World' from the single volume version of *Our Partnership* published after Beatrice's death. Acknowledging that the chapter contained much interesting matter, they judged it to have had 'little or no bearing on the main concerns of the present volume'.[21] A similar fate befell Beatrice's modified plan to publish the Asian travel diaries as a separate third volume of *Our Partnership* entitled *The Far East*. She did actually make some headway with this project. But when Margaret Cole, herself a prominent socialist intellectual of the successor generation to the Webbs, eventually published two further volumes of selections from Beatrice's diaries for the years 1912–24 and 1924–32, she decided to exclude this matter in its entirety, giving as her reason that the Asian diaries were 'almost entirely written by Sidney and [are], as might be expected, monumentally dull'.[22] Her disregard of their travels abroad is a consistent feature of Mrs. Cole's extensive writings on the Webbs. 'It cannot be said that [the Webbs'] travels were of much importance to the outside world,' she explained. 'They were too British to assimilate easily non-British habits of thought.' But she saw no inconsistency between this rather dismissive judgement and the dubious further claim that 'Only in the case of the USSR, where they had already an eager appreciation and desire to understand, did they bring back anything that was of great value to the British to learn.'[23]

More recently, the editors of an authorised edition in four volumes of extracts from the diary, Norman and Jeanne MacKenzie, have

acknowledged of the 1911–12 Asia tour that 'this was an important
year for both of them and the diary records significant changes in
attitude.'[24] But, like Beatrice herself, faced with the daunting task of
reducing the full manuscript diary, the MacKenzies decided to exclude
the Asia materials — even though, long before their decision was taken,
the 1898 travel journals, which Beatrice had drawn upon to make a
single 'Round the Anglo-Saxon World' chapter, had been published in
their entirety as three separate books. The New Zealand portion was
the first to appear, in 1959, followed in 1963 by the American diary
and, in 1965, by its Australian counterpart.[25] From beyond the grave,
and more expansively than she had herself intended, Beatrice was to
have her way over the publication of the 1898 travel diaries. But the
1911–12 Asian diaries remained unpublished, even though their
publication, holus-bolus, she fully intended — having indicated, in her
1938 *Our Partnership* postscript, that the Asian tour in particular had
marked the close of one phase of her joint quest with Sidney and the
opening of another.

Then, in 1987, Oxford University Press brought out in New Delhi
the India section, about half the complete Asian diary.[26] But this
effective separation of the Indian matter from the rest of the Asian
diary, which, besides providing accounts of the specific countries
visited by the Webbs, includes periodic comparisons of a more general
nature concerning the character and prospects of the historic Asian
civilisations of Japan, China and India, flies in the face of Beatrice's
express view that the only way to do justice to the 1911–12 tour was
to publish the entire diary intact. Japan especially struck their fancy as
leading the way in Asia towards an emergent 'new social order'; and
Japan loomed large in the narrative background for the remainder of
their stay in the East. 'The Land of the Rising Sun' in fact had a
fermentative influence upon their thinking that in certain respects was
surpassed only by that made many years later by Soviet Russia. There
is, then, more than one irony in the posthumous fate of the Webbs'
travel diaries, not the least of which is that the New Zealand diary,
which had no apparent bearing on the Webbs' intellectual biography,
was the first to be published, while what is easily the most significant
of them, the Japan diary, has until now remained unpublished.

When the Webbs embarked on their world travels,[27] the intellectual
influences which had chiefly shaped their views of the world beyond
British shores were a combination of Positivism, Fabianised Darwinism,
and Liberal Imperialism. They had chosen the itinerary of their first
tour in 1898 because 'in spite of differences in magnitude of territory,
in climate, in natural resources, and in an admixture of races, the
political and economic structure and social habits of the U.S.A., New

Zealand and Australia were varieties of the British species, expressed in the same language and embedded in the same cultural traditions'. All shared in a common inheritance of beliefs and practices, a species *trilogia* — the Christian religion, capitalist profit-making and political democracy — that was synonymous with Western civilisation. And so the Webbs believed at the time that the eventual, and, as it seemed to them, inevitable achievement of a socialist international order would be best secured by promoting the world-wide hegemony of a reformist 'Anglo-Saxon' Empire as preferable to the inevitable practical alternative, a throw-back imperial dictatorship.

This accounts for the sometimes superior tone of the 1898 travel diary. In it, the Webbs had judged the political life of the United States of the day to have fallen short of the institutional evolution of the 'Anglo-Saxon' parent stock from which it had sprung, in its neglect of industrial democracy, the inefficiency of its municipal institutions and the corruption of its party politics. The Australians were indicted for their vulgar materialism and 'uncoordinated individualism'. The leading politicians of New Zealand were dismissed as unscientifically collectivist. And yet, the Webbs had attempted to balance these criticisms of the 'Anglo-Saxon' progeny of the world in 1898: in the initiative and efficiency of her profit-making enterprise, as in 'public welfare by private persons', the well-mannered American was unsurpassed by any nation; the Australian, like the Briton, was to be found ' "Muddling on", with a high standard of honour' (though higher perhaps in public life than in the sphere of ordinary business); New Zealand's class moderation and social egalitarianism was so appealing, according to Beatrice, that 'if I had to bring up a family outside of Great Britain I would chose New Zealand as its home'. Underlying the Webbs' basically hopeful view of these countries in 1898 was their belief that, as members of the species 'Anglo-Saxon', all shared in that hopeful and redeeming quality of adherence to political democracy. Modified to embrace a greater element of social democracy along the lines of the gradualist 'socialism' indigenous to Great Britain and propagandised by the Fabian Society, it was the feature of their 'Anglo-Saxon' heritage that rendered them, or so the Webbs thought as the nineteenth century ended, demonstrably the family of nations morally fittest to survive.

When Beatrice and Sidney left for Asia at the outset of their second world tour in the early summer of 1911, they still clung to their belief in 'Anglo-Saxon' imperialism. Looking back at the time, Beatrice was of the view that the Minority Report on the Poor Law and the Anti-Destitution Campaign based upon it that had engaged the partners' main propagandistic energies in the half-dozen years before their Asian tour, forming the high-water mark of the Fabian stage of their joint pilgrimage, had been 'a great success'. But in the last diary entry prior to embarkation she also noted that she had reached 'a tag end of a period of my life'.[28] The time had arrived for 'a genuine Socialist Party with a completely worked out philosophy and very detailed programme'.[29] And certainly, circumstances had changed by the date of their return to England. Once more looking back, but now some twenty-seven years later when writing the 1938 postscript to *Our Partnership*, Beatrice's best recollection, as we have seen, was that by 1912 their old ideas were 'out of date'. Their own proposals for eradicating poverty and ushering in an era in which Britons would enjoy 'a national minimum of civilised life within the capitalist system' had been effectively dished while they were still away. Britain erupted with an epidemic of militant strikes by transport workers, railwaymen, miners and others. Lloyd George's Liberal Government announced a pioneering (and unsocialistic) social insurance scheme and minimum wage law. Meantime, they had discovered abroad, particularly in Japan, arresting alternatives to the tripartite 'Anglo-Saxon' values of Christianity, profit-making capitalism, and political democracy.

In their Liberal Imperialist phase, the Webbs had envisaged the British Empire as a world-wide workshop in which the able-bodied unemployed, who idled away their hours in the labour exchanges of Britain's major cities, might be more productively deployed — a vision in which any purely compassionate concerns were wedded to Sidney's predilection for social efficiency and Beatrice's puritanism. This theme is still amply evidenced in the Canadian diary for the first leg of the 1911–12 tour, the contents of which belong both topically and in mood with the 1898 'Anglo-Saxon' diary. With an expanding economy crying out for additional workers, the Northern Dominion seemed the perfect laboratory for a grand sociological experiment that would 'fit the Anglo-Saxon Unemployable to the Canadian life, and the Canadian life to the Anglo-Saxon Unemployed'. In the unpublished 'Anglo-Saxon' chapter, Beatrice urged that 'If our Empire is to mean anything, it ought at least to mean the salvation of our own race', though, influenced by the American example, so many of the new immigrants to Canada in the early years of the new century seemed to be drawn from 'the lower races of Europe' rather than from Britain.[30]

Beatrice's argument here points to the importance of what we might term race-thinking in the Webbs' pre-First World War writings — important because it constitutes a link in their joint intellectual biography between an initial and optimistic Fabian 'stage' and that extended and increasingly pessimistic middle 'stage' of their intellectual pilgrimage in which prominence came to be accorded to Western decadence and decline, as is so strikingly instanced in their post-war polemic, *The Decay of Capitalist Civilisation*. While still clinging to Liberal Imperialism at the outset of their 1911–12 travels, their hopes for Britain's evolutionary role as a morally superior society had already begun by then to be eroded. In their social scientific analyses of domestic British trends in this period, they worried that the British class system, bad enough in its old incarnation, was now in danger of ossifying into a 'money system' rather than a 'natural selection system' for marital matching, with an attendant weakening of the vital racial stock. They were disturbed by the decline of middle-class birth rates, and the concomitant growth in numbers of the eugenically-inferior poor.[31] In a more general sense, consistent with their nineteenth century intellectual formation, the Webbs subscribed to an old-fashioned idea of race, now perhaps less intellectually credible but amply illustrated in these Asian diaries, in which it was not so much the genetic attributes of individuals or classes but rather a range of cultural considerations bearing on the evolution of the 'character' of nations writ large that commanded the interest of these restless intellectual pilgrims. And the frustration of their political plans at home only seemed to reinforce a growing realisation that Britain's status as a world leader was in decline.

ASIA AND THE WEBBS

Certainly it was an adventure – these two habitual social investigators become world travellers, their usual London routine (enacted within a geographical expanse no greater than the distance separating their Millbank home from the LSE and the Fabian Society and National Committee meeting rooms nearby) left far behind for the better part of a year. Now the Webbs were temporarily transformed into tourists, exploring the Japanese temples of Kyoto, Ise, Koyasan and Miyajima, the tombs of the Ming and Manchu, the Great Wall of China and 'the beauty of Peking with its walls and gates and its picturesque grey-tiled roofs embedded in trees, and here and there, relieved by the golden, green and blue-tiled edifices of the Imperial Palaces and the Temple of Heaven and other ceremonial buildings'. They found the Indian temples of Khajuraho 'very wonderful', those of Dilwara and Achil-garh 'fantastically beautiful'; and they marvelled at Agra and the Taj Mahal and the Sikh Golden Temple, and much besides.

But the Webbs were not the usual sort of tourist. With Sidney in frock-coat and tall silk hat, for instance, they interviewed the Japanese Prime Minister, Prince Katsura, at his private residence, Beatrice noting that he 'talked of "civilisation" as a disagreeable medicine which the country had to take, & was willing to acquiesce in anything it entailed'. They were shown the *geisha* 'beauties of Niigata' by a wealthy banker, visited the greatest landlord in Japan and dined with the Mitsuis. They toured Seoul in one of the Governor's state carriages, mixed with Morrison of *The Times* and the financial set in Peking's Legation Quarter, stayed at Hong Kong's Government House as guests of the Governor, had audiences with the Sultan of Perak and the Begum of Bhopal, with Maharajas and Gaekwars. And everywhere they went, they were entertained by well-placed former students of their then still-fledgling London School of Economics, by government functionaries and civil servants, assorted educators and socialist intellectuals. But, even in the midst of their varied touristic and social activities, they investigated: schools and colleges, prisons, brothels and factories, slums and forests and the agricultural countryside. And all this tourism, socialising and investigating, of 'coloured peoples speaking unknown languages, inspired by strange mythologies, practising unfamiliar rites; belonging in fact to ancient civilisations outside our ken', was conducted against a backdrop of bizarre discoveries, of officialdom and intrigue and moments of high drama. They were in Peking, after all, on the very eve of the fall of the Manchu dynasty — calamitous events recently recounted anew in the Hollywood film *The Last Emperor*[32] — making a narrow escape, as the two colourfully recount in the diary and in their *Crusade* article on China, from a city and regime in disarray.

Nowhere in their extensive Asian travels were the Webbs more profoundly impressed than in Japan. 'Who would have foreseen,' Beatrice mused retrospectively, that the 'little yellow men and women' depicted by Gilbert and Sullivan's *Mikado*, 'with their fantastic rites and ceremonies and flippant and even naughty ways',[33] would by the first decade of the century have militarily humbled Imperial China and Tsarist Russia alike. In certain respects the Webbs found Japan strikingly reminiscent of England. Both nations were peopled by energetic island races of remarkably pure racial stock, though it seemed to the Webbs that the Japanese were more intent than their 'Anglo-Saxon' counterparts on maintaining the distinction. Both the English and the Japanese, as Beatrice explained to her sister Kate Courtney, were 'by nature "exploiters of other people", but with different standards of what is permissible — hence their mutual dislike'.[34] And the 'governing class' of Japan struck them as 'exactly like that at Downing Street, except [Beatrice wrote home] I should think they worked rather longer hours and they don't take holidays — also they are more matter-of-fact and inclined to work entirely through the Experts'.[35] The Webbs, at least, felt rather that there was a case for mutual admiration; for the longer they remained in Japan, the more they found themselves becoming persuaded that Japan's admirable blending of traditional and modern institutions posed an impressive Oriental challenge to the purported supremacy of the 'Anglo-Saxon' way of life which, despite its blemishes, they had still been prepared to celebrate in the 1898 travel diaries.

In rural Japan, where democratic institutions were largely unknown and seemingly unwanted, there was everywhere evidenced in practice, as Beatrice wrote approvingly, 'an immense amount of Social Democracy as distinguished from Political Democracy'.[36] The system worked because there was an expert bureaucracy with high standards of dedication to public service to oversee its operation. But the appeal of rural Japan was only half the story. The Webbs realised that Japan was a nation in dramatic transition, undertaking to accomplish in a matter of decades a degree of social evolution greater than that of the preceding three centuries, and thus, analogous to the situation of Britain in the years following the Industrial Revolution.

With the development of a native Japanese capitalism, the traditional focus of life in the village community was bound to give way to large industrial cities with a wage-earning proletariat. As industrial growth proceeded, the challenge would be to preserve an underlying sense of community and spiritual purpose in a world increasingly dominated by the rationalist ascendancy of science and technology. The pitfalls were many, the outcome problematic: but the Webbs were confident on the basis of what they saw of Japan that its 'alert and open-minded' bureaucracy would realise in time 'the precipice down which capitalist exploitation . . . is hurrying the nation'.[37] Yet the Fabian pilgrims, and Beatrice in particular, wondered whether in view of the relentless pressures of modernisation, Buddhism had any future in Japan. Told that the educated Japanese felt they could do without religion, she responded by noting that 'hooliganism' was on the increase in Japan's cities. 'If,' she asked, 'all the old reverence and sense of domestic and social obligation which have been associated for centuries with Shinto shrines and Buddhist temples falls away, and if all supernaturalism becomes an absurdity, will any new philosophy other than agnosticism or materialism rise to give noble purpose to the life of the individual and the race?' What buttressed her optimism on this score was her evident admiration for a certain Japanese capacity to link the spirit of administrative efficiency to the communal religious impulse. 'The innovative collectivism . . . the idealism, the self-abnegation of all classes of the community to a common cause', Beatrice felt, was the strength of the Japanese. 'What makes Japan great,' she observed in a letter to Lady Betty Balfour, 'is her practical mysticism – the spiritual significance which she attaches to so many of the relations of life – to that of parent and child, teacher and student, the officer and the private soldier, the Emperor and his people.'[38] It was this 'practical mysticism' which confirmed the Webbs in their belief that Japan in 1911 was 'still the Land of the Rising Sun'.

The Webbs' pro-Japanese sentiments were only reinforced by their further travels in Asia. Long before the post-Second World War and post-Korean War era had familiarised Westerners with the notions of Japan and China as the 'Great Dragons', and Taiwan, Korea, Singapore and Malaysia as the 'Little Dragons' of a highly energised economic advance throughout the region, the two found Korea and China especially corrupt and even degenerate. They were particularly upset by what they took to be the rampancy in China of the 'unnatural vice' of homosexuality.[39] And while the Japanese way of life might indeed offer an appealing alternative to the 'Anglo-Saxon', contemporary Korea and China seemed to be lacking entirely in any living traditions of communal religiosity, enlightened governance or rational political economy. The Koreans struck them as 'a horrid race – idle, dirty, and quarrelsome, with sullen and suspicious look . . . The whole race seems to have gone into decay – by centuries of mismanagement and oppressive taxation.'[40] It was the Webbs' stern judgement, though admittedly harsh medicine, that Korea stood in present circumstances only to benefit from its recent annexation by the progressive, if ruthless, Japanese. As for the Chinese, they were 'very difficult to like or respect . . . the strange combination of cowardice & cruelty & corruption in the ruling class, & the lack of loyalty or faith in the people at large, is very distasteful'.[41] This 'so-called great race' was in 1911 'by all the available evidence, capable of nothing'. It followed that China's best hopes for future improvement lay in the success of the republican revolution that was unfolding in the very course of the Webbs' sojourn there.[42]

It was in British India that they spent the longest time of any of the Asian countries they visited. 'We are immensely glad we came to India,' Beatrice assured her sister, 'especially now that we can compare it with Japan and China.'[43] The Webbs were not only confirmed in their admiration of the Japanese; they were also converted to the view that the easy assumptions of racial superiority they encountered among the 'Anglo-Saxon' administrators of India did not stand in especially favourable comparison with their own first-hand impressions of the subjugated Hindus and Muslims it was the administrators' task to govern. They arrived at this disturbing conclusion after traversing the length and breadth of the Indian sub-continent. 'The more we saw of India, the more we learned about the Government and the officials, and the longer we lived among the people,' Sidney sombrely noted in the diary as the Webbs sailed home to England, *the graver became our tone*, and the more subdued our optimism. At first, after China, India seemed hopeful . . . But as our acquaintance with the Indian bureaucracy has increased, and as we have more and more appreciated its alliance in the main with reactionary imperialism and commercial selfishness in England, we are less confident. Three months' acquaintance has greatly increased our estimate of the Indians, and greatly lessened our admiration for, and our trust in, this Government of officials.'

What frustrated the Webbs about the Anglo-Indian bureaucracy was that its objectives seemed so amateurish – so narrow and so limited. Its conception of government was simply to put down internal war and violent crime, to decide civil suits and maintain order, 'and for the rest, to leave people alone'. The Webbs felt that the British should *do something* to bring a fuller sense of common purpose to this hopelessly uncoordinated land (it was Beatrice's view that an Indian version of the Boy Scouts would be a useful beginning).[44] Their diary entries make clear their impatience with the 'complete and almost fatuous ignorance' of most British officials of their 'essential inferiority in culture, charm and depth of intellectual and spiritual experience', compared to the Indian 'aristocracy of intellect' they governed. In the circumstances, they feared that friction between the 'actual alien governor' and the 'potential native governor' was bound to increase. Instead of driving India's intellectuals into an underground nationalist movement, the British should take them into civic partnership, so that 'the British race might pride themselves on having been the finest race of schoolmasters, as well as the most perfect builders of an empire'.

Near the completion of their Asian tour, Beatrice was to reflect at length in a diary entry on the similarities and differences of the races with which they had come in contact. All shared such common institutions as the joint family and the small-scale cultivator, and displayed alike a 'certain community of religious experiences'. But there remained a 'deep-down unlikeness' in the three major races. 'The Japanese,' she mused, 'are a race of idealists, but these ideals are fixed and amazingly homogeneous and are always capable of being translated into immediate and persistent action. They are in fact perhaps the most *executive* race in the world – the most capable of discovering the means to the end – and the most self-contained and self-disciplined in working out these means, and therefore in attaining their ends.' What she found so uncongenial in the Chinese was 'on the one hand, the absence of the idealism of the Japanese and Indian races, and on the other, their present lack of capacity for the scientific method and for disciplined effort of the Japanese'. The Hindu too was an idealist, but lacked the political efficiency of the Japanese. His ideals were ' "all over the place", and frequently he lacks the capacity to put them into practice – he can neither discover the means nor work at them with unswerving persistency.' Besides which, the Indian aristocracy was 'dragged down by a multitude of lower castes and lower races – embedded in a population which seems strangely childish in intellect and undisciplined in conduct'.

Visiting the temples of Benares and at the *Magh Mela* of Allahabad, and especially at the Khajuraho temples, Beatrice had been dismayed in India by 'the incontinence of the popular religion – the strange combination of almost hysterical and certainly promiscuous idolatry . . . and behind it all, the sinister background of revolting lasciviousness and gross exudity'. But this was 'only one side of the shield'. In the austere and pious domesticity of *purdah*, with its 'almost fanatical idealisation of wifely devotion', Beatrice discerned elements of an alternative tradition of self-abnegation in Hinduism at its best, even sympathising with the idea of reintroducing *suttee* (though, socialist that she was, she felt the practice should apply to widower and widow alike!). Another and more inspiring vision was that of the so-called New Hinduism. In organisations such as the *Arya Samaj*, the religious impulse was 'combined with a sincere and powerful self-discipline, a self-discipline with the express object of maintaining the mind and body in the fittest condition for the most perfect service of the community'. One must balance the superstition and incontinence of the populace with 'the healthy, virile and free service of religious orders self-dedicated to the progress of the race'. She felt the Westerner could learn much from this Eastern conception of social service rendered by an aristocracy of birth and intellect, with its restricted democracy of a 'community of social equals'.[45]

India, then, presented a situation which struck the British pilgrims as the very antithesis of what they had encountered in Japan, where the pious religiosity of the common man was the strength of the Japanese national character, the contemporary decadence of the Buddhist priests its shame. What was needed was somehow to combine the best features of the Japanese and Indian racial traits to yield a reverential social order in which a unifying political religion was practiced by leader and follower alike. And that is just what the Webbs were eventually to find so appealing about Soviet Russia. There, they were to discover, the 'priests' of Marxism-Leninism practised a tradition of service as impressive as that of the *Arya Samaj*, an energetic co-ordination of national purpose every bit as effective as that of the

Japanese bureaucracy. And there, the masses, so unlike the Hindu population of India, shared (or so the Webbs were naïvely prepared to believe in the 1930s) the political faith of their leaders.

THE WEBBS AS PILGRIMS

The Webbs' discovery of a possible cultural alternative to the 'Anglo-Saxon' way on their Asian tour was to lead them, in the upheavals of the decade that followed their return to England in 1912, to the pessimistic middle 'stage' of their life's journey. Their pilgrims' route of passage was thus to land them in The Slough of Despond. In Asia, though, seed had been sown that would bear fruit in their eventual passage beyond this, to a third and final 'stage' of their intellectual pilgrimage, in the USSR. Less than a year after its original publication in London in 1923, their *The Decay of Capitalist Civilisation* was to be translated into Japanese; and it was perhaps more than mere coincidence that, a decade later, the Webbs would praise the Communist Party of the USSR for its 'Samurai vocation of leadership' in their *Soviet Communism, A New Civilisation*.

Of course, the Webbs' boundless 1911 enthusiasm for the promise of Japan was to cool in time. A 1938 diary entry notes that Beatrice had lately read 'with interest, because the next chapter of *Our Partnership* will include our stay in Japan 27 years ago', D. C. Holton's *The National Faith of Japan*. How things had changed, she mused. Intrigued in 1911 with the potential in the Japanese example for combining into a new social creed 'Western enlightened agnosticism' and 'Buddhist mysticism', by 1938 State Shintoism and insistence on Japanese racial dominance had turned Japan into a state 'very similar in its religious, political and economic creeds to Italian Fascism and German Nazism'.[46] She would not live long enough to have a similar opportunity to re-examine her estimate of the full political, economic and spiritual record of Russia and Eastern Europe under Soviet Communism. Had she done so, living on in the world as it has evolved since her demise at mid-century, might Beatrice have felt a certain chagrin at her misplaced faith in the promise of Soviet Communism? Might she and Sidney have found solace in the manner in which, purged of militarism by her decisive defeat at the hands of the Western democracies, Japan would prove herself, as they had long ago predicted she would, an emergent twentieth century state full of future promise? Might they have acknowledged a renewed respect for the staying power of the 'Anglo-Saxon' political institutions they early championed but tended later to disparage?

Beatrice was to suggest at the conclusion of the Asian tour that 'A traveller, especially an elderly traveller, is liable to come back from his travels with his own general ideas confirmed'. Certainly she had found much food for thought in Asia. The well-being of civilisation in a secular age, she had long believed, required that means be devised to combine the undoubted blessings of science with those deeply-rooted communal and spiritual impulses of humankind it tended to disregard. Only then might the world see the emergence of a social order with a higher nobility of purpose than any hitherto attained. Uncertain of the way forward, she confessed to her diary aboard ship, steaming for Suez: 'I come back as mystified as ever'. But with the benefit of hindsight, we can see better perhaps than she could herself at the time, that the Asian tour had indeed served to further the course of the joint pilgrimage she shared with Sidney, as it had her own more personal journey of self-discovery. And in the personage of 'Our Guide – Nishi', who so enchanted these intrepid socialist pilgrims in Japan, one might be forgiven for seeing a sort of Intourist Guide two decades before the fact.

The word 'pilgrim' has two shades of meaning, one of them signifying a wayfarer in alien lands, the other, more purposive, a traveller to a distant shrine or holy place as a devotee. And there is something of both these senses of 'pilgrim' in Beatrice Webb. But if, as a diarist, the first of these meanings is never far from view, the second was uppermost in her mind as the would-be autobiographer of her famed union with Sidney. She came, as we have seen, to apply just such an imagery of purposive pilgrimaging to her unfinished account of her partnership with him, in which they had journeyed together on a kind of political *Pilgrim's Progress*, struggling, like Bunyan's Christian on his allegorical journey to spiritual salvation, towards the Wicket-Gate through which they must pass from the spiritual emptiness of capitalism and its secular city of Mansoul.

But as we know from the diaries of this 'religious-minded agnostic', her personal quest for such certainty as this, however devoted her yearning for it, continued to the end to elude her grasp. 'We sail straight to our port over a sunlit sea,' she allowed, 'But the point we make for seems sometimes an unconscionable way off!'[47] Many years before she wrote these words, traversing Japan, China and India on her 1911–12 journey to Asia with Sidney, Beatrice thought she had detected the faint outlines of her new social order, speaking alike to the needs of the political quest she shared with Sidney and to her own more personal spiritual journey, something like a combined regime of scientific administration and spiritual affirmation. Addressing a letter to Beatrice sent out from England to Asia, Lady Betty Balfour had been more prescient than she appreciated in employing the striking salutation, *'Dear Pilgrim'*.[48]

Notes

1. In addition to *My Apprenticeship*, *Our Partnership*, and the travel diaries for New Zealand, America, Australia and India (see below), the published extracts include Margaret Cole (ed.), *Beatrice Webb's Diaries, 1912–24* (London, 1952) (in the following Notes referred to as (1)) and *Beatrice Webb's Diaries, 1924–32* (London, 1956) (in these Notes referred to as (2)); and Norman and Jeanne MacKenzie (eds), *The Diary of Beatrice Webb*, Volume One, 1873–1892, *Glitter Around and Darkness Within* (London, 1982); Volume Two, 1892–1905, *All the Good Things of Life* (London, 1983); Volume Three, 1905–1924, *The Power to Alter Things* (London, 1984); and Volume Four, 1924–1943, *The Wheel of Life* (London, 1985). In addition, there is a microfiche edition of *The Diary of Beatrice Webb, 1873–1943* (Cambridge: Chadwyck-Healey, 1978). This reproduces the holograph diary itself, running to over two million words, and an incomplete typed transcript of it of some 7500 pages. A separate *Index to the Diary of Beatrice Webb, 1873–1943* includes essays by Geoffry Allen, 'The Text of the Diary'; Margaret Cole, 'Historical Introduction'; and Norman MacKenzie, 'The Diary as Literature'.

2. For discussions of Beatrice Webb as autobiographical diarist see F. R. Leavis, 'Mill, Beatrice Webb and the "English School" ', *Scrutiny*, vol. XVI (June 1949) pp. 104–26; Shirley Letwin, *The Pursuit of Certainty* (Cambridge, 1965) pp. 352–57; Samuel Hynes, 'The Art of Beatrice Webb', in his *Edwardian Occasions* (New York, 1972) pp. 153–72; George Feaver, 'Introduction' to the 1976 Cambridge reprint of *Our Partnership*, pp. ix–xlvii; and Deborah Epstein Nord, *The Apprenticeship of Beatrice Webb* (Amherst, Mass., 1985).

3. Beatrice Webb, *My Apprenticeship* (London, 1926) pp. 280–81 and MacKenzie vol. 1, p. 120. Her diary was 'an old friend', 'a phantom of myself'.

4. MacKenzie, vol. 2, pp. 273–4.

5. 'New Year's Eve' [1922]. Cole (1), p. 232.

6. MacKenzie, vol. 4, p. 61. '5 a.m.'

7. Ibid.

8. *Passfield Papers* (LSE), Section VII, 2 (14), Box 1.

9. Cf. Barbara Drake and Margaret Cole (eds), *Our Partnership* (London, 1948) pp. 489–91.

10. MacKenzie, vol. 3, p. 178. The MacKenzies' view (p. 163) is that the 1911–12 world tour diary 'was not, in fact, a proper personal part of Beatrice's diary'.

11. MacKenzie, vol. 2, p. 156. On the last point, note the entry when writing *My Apprenticeship* that 'I don't think Sidney quite likes it . . . there is something about it that he not exactly resents, but to which he is unsympathetic. In his heart he feels I am overvaluing it, especially the extracts from the diaries; the whole thing is far too subjective, and all that part which deals with "my

creed" as distinguished from "my craft" seems to him the sentimental scribblings of a woman, only interesting just because they are feminine.' 19 March [1925], MacKenzie, vol. 4, p. 49.

12. See Norman MacKenzie, 'Beatrice Webb: The Novelist Who Never Was', in Sir Angus Wilson (ed.), *Essays by Divers Hands*, vol. XLIII (London, 1984) pp. 104–16.

13. MacKenzie, vol. 4, p. 407.

14. 3 January 1939. She added: ' "Why waste time on the unknowable?", Sidney might say.'

15. *Passfield Papers* (LSE), Section VII, 2 (XV), Boxes A–F, G–J, *Our Pilgrimage*. In this latest literary project, begun following Sidney's 1938 stroke, the *Pilgrim's Progress* imagery is applied to the Webbs' joint pilgrimage; but earlier, in *My Apprenticeship*, it had been used to describe Beatrice's personal pilgrimage. There she refers to 'that slough of despond' into which she had been slowly sinking from 1884 onward, 'the deepest and darkest pit being my father's catastrophic illness in the winter of 1885–86' (p. 284). See also MacKenzie, vol. 4, p. 408.

16. 28 May 1940, '*3:30 a.m.*'

17. MacKenzie, vol. 4, p. 485.

18. MacKenzie, vol. 4, p. 487.

19. Norman MacKenzie writes perceptively in 'The Diary as Literature', *Index to the Diary*, that it is 'a creative enterprise with as much internal unity of feeling and structure as if it had been deliberately conceived as a large scale literary work'. In more general terms, on the significance of the diary as a substitute for the confessional, see William Haller, *The Rise of Puritanism* (New York, 1938) p. 96 *passim*.

20. *Passfield Papers* (LSE), Section VII, 2 (XV), A–F, 'Round the Anglo-Saxon World' materials, from which the other quotes in this paragraph also derive. For a brief overview of the 1898 tour, see MacKenzie, vol. 2, pp. 137–49.

21. Barbara Drake and Margaret Cole, *Our Partnership.*, p. v.

22. Cole (2), p. xvii.

23. Margaret Cole, *Beatrice Webb* (London, 1946) pp. 78, 110.

24. Cf. MacKenzie, vol. 3, pp. 163–74 for this observation and a brief overview of the 1911–12 tour, 'a journey that was at once more ambitious and more adventurous than their previous sabbatical voyage'. Earlier, in the course of his three-volume edition of *The Letters of Sidney and Beatrice Webb*, Volume 2, *Partnership, 1892–1912* (Cambridge, 1978) p. 371, Norman MacKenzie had suggested that although Beatrice later claimed that the trip to Asia had 'a powerful influence on the partnerships' conception of the past, present and future of the human race', and though it 'certainly preceded a change of political direction as decisive as the shift in attitude which followed the Australian visit in 1898 and the expedition to the Soviet Union in 1932', the total impact on the Webbs might best be described as 'one of curious detachment . . . They seldom afterwards referred to their experiences or made any serious effort to evaluate them', adding that 'In retrospect the journey seems to have been a long ante-room to the next phase of the partnership'.

25. *Visit to New Zealand in 1898: Beatrice Webb's Diary With Entries By Sidney Webb* (Wellington, 1959); David Shannon (ed.), *Beatrice Webb's American*

Diary, 1898 (Madison, Wis., 1963); and A. G. Austin (ed.), *The Webbs' Australian Diary, 1898* (Melbourne, 1965).

26. Niraja Gopal Jayal (ed.), *Sidney and Beatrice Webb, India Diary* (New Delhi, 1987) (reissued London, 1991).

27. George Feaver, 'The Webbs as Pilgrims', *Encounter*, vol. L (March 1978) pp. 23–32.

28. *Our Partnership*, p. 476.

29. MacKenzie, vol. 3, p. 154.

30. George Feaver, 'The Webbs in Canada: Fabian Pilgrims on the Canadian Frontier', *The Canadian Historical Review*, vol. LVIII, no. 3 (September 1977) pp. 263–276.

31. See, for example, Sidney Webb, *The Decline of the Birth Rate* (London, 1907); Sidney and Beatrice Webb, *The Prevention of Destitution* (London, 1911); their *The Decay of Capitalist Civilisation* (London, 1923); and 'The Guardianship of the Non-Adult Races', *New Statesman*, 2 August 1913. More generally, see David Cannadine, *The Decline and Fall of the British Aristocracy* (London, 1990).

32. Based on Arnold C. Brackman's *The Last Emperor* (New York, 1975), itself indebted to *From Emperor to Citizen: The Autobiography of Aisan-Gioro Pu Yi* (Peking, 1964–5) 2 vols. See also Paul Kramer (ed.), *The Last Manchu: The Autobiography of Henry Pu Yi, Last Emperor of China* (New York, 1967).

33. For background, see Toshio Yokoyama, *Japan in the Victorian Mind* (London, 1987) and Hugh Cortazzi, *Victorians in Japan* (London, 1987).

34. *Passfield Papers* (LSE), II.e.33, Beatrice Webb to Kate Courtney, 9 October 1911.

35. Ibid., II.e.25, Beatrice Webb to Mary Playne, 30 August 1911.

36. Ibid., II.e.27, Beatrice Webb to Clifford Sharp, 13 September 1911.

37. See Appendix, 'The Social Crisis in Japan', *The Crusade* (January 1912).

38. *Passfield Papers*, II.e.48, Beatrice Webb to Lady Betty Balfour, 28 November 1911.

39. Western travellers had for centuries decried the ubiquity of 'the abominable vice of sodomy' in China. The Webbs' own evidence for their sweeping indictment appears to have been largely anecdotal. They note in letters home, for instance, the corroborating authority of the French financial agent Monsieur Cazenave, whose acquaintance they had made at Peking. In a recent study, Bret Hinsch, *Passions of the Cut Sleeve: The Male Homosexual Tradition in China* (Berkeley, Calif., 1990), explores the surviving literary evidence of a 'male homosexual tradition' in China from the Bronze Age until the end of the Ching dynasty, 'when it fell victim to a growing sexual conservatism and the Westernisation of morality'. Today the situation has in a sense been reversed, with many Chinese regarding the West, though materially strong, as a cesspool of sexual and moral decadence.

40. *Passfield Papers*, II.e.36, Beatrice Webb to Clifford Sharp, [?] October 1911.

41. Ibid., II.e.40, Beatrice Webb to Kate Courtney, 4 November 1911.

42. See Appendix, 'China in Revolution', *The Crusade* (March 1912).

43. *Passfield Papers*, II.f.10, Beatrice Webb to Kate Courtney, 3 March 1912.

44. 'Would you please send particulars of the Boy Scout movement – some easy description of its uses and how to begin it & anything else on the same lines that you think of – to Her Highness, The Begum of Bhopal, Ahmadabad

Palace, Bhopal, Central India', Beatrice wrote to her sister, Mary Playne, *Passfield Papers*, II.f.7, 19 February 1912. She wrote separately to Clifford Sharp wondering 'whether a Boy Scout movement would lead to a warrant of deportation for an Indian Baden-Powell', reporting that when she mentioned her scheme to a local British Agent, 'he looked quite scared'. Ibid., II.f.6(a), 14 February 1912.

45. 'The movement,' she wrote approvingly to Kate Courtney of the *Arya Samaj*, 'is really a Protestant Puritan revival of ancient Hinduism, with the same crude faith in the book of the ancient scriptures and with the same hatred of idolatry and yearning for political freedom as our 17th century Roundheads. At present its teaching is chiefly religious and moral: but undoubtedly its ultimate objective is a virile political self-government of a highly aristocratic type'. Ibid., II.f.10, 3 March 1912. At first defensive, upholding Hinduism against Christian influence, movements such as the *Arja Samaj*, as *The Cambridge Encyclopedia of India* (Cambridge, 1989) p. 345 notes, came to be 'increasingly confident, a confidence which was only increased by a pronounced European admiration for the Hindu achievement and by the new pride generated by the Indian nationalist movement. As the twentieth century progressed, Hindu cults became a notable South Asian export to the West'.

46. 24 August 1938.

47. *Our Partnership*, p. 177.

48. *Passfield Papers*, II.e.44, Lady Betty Balfour to Beatrice Webb, 10 November 1911.

1
Japan

Long before our journey to the Far East in 1911 the Japanese had seemed to us certainly the most arresting, and perhaps the most gifted of the coloured races belonging to the ancient civilisations of the Asiatic continent. What struck us was their curiously combined but contrasted characteristics. Who would have foreseen that the little yellow men and women pictured in Gilbert and Sullivan's popular musical comedy *The Mikado*, with their fantastic rites and ceremonies and flippant and even naughty ways, would not only defeat the Chinese multitudinous armies, but would beat back decisively and once for all, in 1905, the steam roller of Tsarist Russia, reputed to be one of the great powers of the European continent. Why did the Conservative Government, as Mr. Arthur Balfour told me, remain in office without dissolving Parliament, in order to carry out a defensive alliance with this far-off island,[2] no bigger than our own Great Britain? Moreover, we had heard about Japan from our friend Sir Charles Eliot, after his visit in 1907, and he, after all, with his knowledge of Eastern languages, was an authority on the subject.

In his *Letters From the Far East*, he gives in measured terms the impression that he left on our minds in conversation. 'The enormous strides which were being made by Japan were long not appreciated at their true value, because she was thought to be an Oriental country, and as such unable to overstep the limits which European ideas thought probable for Oriental progress; and at the present day the gist of much criticism of the reform movement in China is that the Chinese are not likely to change, because Eastern countries are unchanging. It is noticeable, too, that the Californian objections to the Japanese generally contains the word "Oriental" used in a reproachful sense. "We do not want our children to be educated with Orientals" or "We do not want these people in our country, because they are Orientals", is the burden of their complaint . . . Any absolute dichotomy of the Old World into East and West is misleading. Europe

27

has indeed a certain homogeneity in spite of many differences, but even superficial uniformity is wanting in Asia.' 'The Empire of China,' he continues, 'has existed in its present form for more than 2000 years, and, neglecting the legendary beginnings of Japan, the House of the Mikado has certainly been about 1400 years on the throne. This continuity and stability contrast remarkably with the ephemeral states and dynasties of India, which have rarely lasted more than a few generations; nor have the Muhammadan Caliphates had long lives. Then one notices that the people of the Far East are neither aggressive nor fanatical . . . Japan presents a good many special features, which will be considered shortly, but differs from China above all in its strong military spirit of a feudal type, which in some points resembles the institutions of mediaeval Europe . . . In the moral sphere there is one special difference between the Chinese and Japanese. Whereas the former give the first place to filial piety in the literal sense, the Japanese lay more stress on the obligation of loyalty to a feudal superior, and ultimately to the sovereign. As the feudal system has now been abolished, only loyalty to the throne and patriotism remain. Patriotism is, like feudalism, a rare emotion and motive in Asia. The willingness of self-sacrifice is indeed frequent, but it is more commonly associated with religious movements than with love for any one religion. This loyalty preserved the House of Mikado from the dawn of Japanese history till the present day, in spite of the grave danger which continually threatened it from ambitious nobles . . . Yet there was not, as is so often the case in Asia, any personality, book or priesthood which cramped the national mind. Shintoism was vague and easy-going, Buddhism and Confucianism were both imported systems. Therefore, though the Japanese were by no means lacking in national pride, and as ready as the Chinese to believe themselves self-sufficient, there was not the same mass of codified prejudice and obstruction to be overcome . . . What future are we to predict for the Japanese? They are not an aggressive people. Their reserve and moderation in international matters deserve the highest praise, and there is probably no other nation which would have kept its head so well after the Russian wars. But though their character is compounded with so large a dose of sanity and moderation . . . yet they will hardly be able to withstand the pressure of the many influences, geographical, social, political, military and commercial, which urge them towards expansion.'[3]

There was another characteristic about the Japanese of which we had had already some personal experience; their amazing desire to get authoritative information about Western civilisation. The Japanese Embassy for instance, which was a comparatively recent arrival at the Court of St. James, was not content, as most embassies were, to limit their acquaintances to the diplomatic circle. They sent out emissaries into capitalist and even socialist circles to find out what exactly was happening. Whether as a girl or as a married woman, I had never frequented the very exclusive diplomatic circle. But far back in the 'seventies I remember an intelligent attaché of the Japanese Embassy seeking us out, and, in spite of my mother's prejudice against coloured people, was our guest at house parties in Gloucestershire; and a few months before our departure to the Far East the Japanese Ambassador, Kato, begged a mutual friend to introduce him to the Webbs − partly, we understood, because his Government had recently executed a dozen Japanese socialists guilty of possessing bombs, and he wanted to discover whether the British socialists were of the same temperament. After he and we had discussed the difference between British, Continental and Japanese socialism, I observed casually that we were presently going for a year's tour in the Far East, and that we intended to visit Japan. 'What for?' he asked hurriedly. 'Oh,' I answered, 'merely on a holiday. We have just brought out a big book and we want a complete change of scene.' 'I'll look after you,' he answered pleasantly. The next day there arrived eighteen introductions in Japanese characters, with a list which started with the Prime Minister and the Foreign Secretary, and extended tó business men, among them the Mitsuis. As will be apparent from the diary entries, these introductions were of untold value in giving us the entrée into Japanese official circles . . .

[BW→] AUG[t] 14th [1911] ON THE PACIFIC

We are voyaging in the *Inama Maru*, a Japanese liner of 6000 tons belonging to the Nippon Co. − one of the largest shipping companies of the world − heavily subsidised by the Japanese Government. We preferred it to the C.P.R. steamers[4] because it was cheaper and there was the chance of seeing something of Japanese management and Japanese passengers.

In the latter object we are somewhat disappointed. Out of the twenty saloon passengers, only four are Japanese and only two of these frequent the saloon. The other two are a couple of mysterious relationship − a Seattle jeweller and a rather common and coarse-looking Japanese lady − travelling under the protection of what she styles her 'husband's friend'. These two have cabins which they seem to inhabit, somewhat promiscuously, having their food together in the larger cabin − they are intimate with some of the Japanese steerage and they enjoy the luxury of a gramophone. When I suggested to the Chief Engineer that they were husband and wife he said 'She no husband'. But their ways are obviously not a scandal. And they are well-behaved, even considerate, moderating in their use of the gramophone directly they hear that I did not like it. And on deck their behaviour is of the most discreet.

The other two are distinguished-looking, tall Naval Commanders. Unfortunately, they are at the other table and they quite unmistakably do not care to talk to women. Sidney, who is accustomed to merely second my social excursions, at first hardly addressed them — now he has casual conversations about things Japanese and finds them extremely intelligent, well-informed men — both returning from Europe after making special studies of technical naval questions. One is of aristocratic family, the other has worked his way up from poor connections. Both compared favourably, I think, with the English naval officer in openness of mind and intellect — they are in fact more like Engineers than members of a 'swagger service'.

The rest of the company are not very agreeable persons. There is an American widow and daughter — *rentiers* living in Paris who, through sheer boredom, are coming to live a year in Japan. The girl is pleasant and well-dressed — the usual style of cosmopolitan American flirt. She walks arm-in-arm with a young American lawyer whose acquaintance she has made on board — there is an American honeymoon couple who read aloud to each other in rasping accent and voice — the man going out as agricultural professor to some Japanese educational institution — [and] there is the aforesaid young American lawyer and a younger American medical man. All these Americans are tall, spare and with the usual thin-nosed, clear-cut faces. It is when they speak that their monotonous, commonplace conceit appears, giving the impression of bad manners in their somewhat impertinent conversation with the Japanese Commanders. The English are represented by a solid Baptist missionary and his Scotch wife, quiet and unattractive, by two 'well-sinkers' who have made some sort of livelihood in the States — also quiet and self-respecting men — and [by] a bounder of a commercial traveller for a telephone company with a distinctly common wife. Not an invigorating company!

The ship is well managed, with an atmosphere of courtesy and consideration by officers and stewards. Everyone is efficient without being bound down by rules and there is much less visible restraint than on an English steamer — the second-class coming occasionally on to the first-class deck and the whole of the passengers wandering over other parts of the ship. But there is no abuse of this freedom, except perhaps by the American and English ladies, who will take possession of the smoking-room! Altogether, there is more democracy and better manners than on a Canadian, American or English liner.

[SW→] 23rd AUGUST 1911 TOKYO

We have now been a week in Japan, in an almost constant perspiration, and intellectual interest. On reaching the harbour of Yokohama we found a letter from Mrs. and Miss Fairchild, old Boston friends,[5] temporarily resident in Japan, pressing us not to stay in the hot and Europeanised treaty port, but to come at once to Kamakura, a pleasant seaside resort, an hour away, where they were sojourning for a week. They had engaged for us a trustworthy and educated guide, who came out to meet our steamer. We at once accepted this advice and help, and handed over all cares relating to luggage, tickets, money, etc. to this factotum, who is guide, courier and servant at 8/- a day. Such a person is clearly indispensable in this country, if one wishes to get outside the Europeanised hotels, which are still rare.[6]

We have seen endless temples and picturesque views, and watched the doings of these teeming multitudes of yellow-brown people, going about in every variety of costume, from the absolute nudity of many children, and the nudity relieved by the narrowest possible loin cloth (covering only what *has* to be covered) of the labouring men, up to the conventional European dress of the Japanese Club or civil servant. It so happened also that we had to stand by the bathing and swimming and breathing exercises, done from start to finish to the sound of a bugle, under the military order of a one-armed, ex-regimental doctor, of a couple of hundred boys of 'the Peers' School',[7] and a hundred or more youths of a military academy, on the shore at Enoshima (we had to wait for an 'omnibus boat'). So that we feel we know the outward form of the Japanese pretty well! The aristocratic boys were well-made, handsome figures, at that age seemingly of what we should deem full height, startlingly like a company of Assyrians or Egyptians stepping off the old tombs. The common people seem to be of very varied types of face − some almost negroid in lips and nose, some almost Caucasian in form and even colour − although I believe they are historically less mixed than any other nation. We were struck by the almost invariable absence of hair on the trunk and limbs of the men; and by the very deep dark-brown that the skin was tanned by the sun when continually exposed. The women uncover freely their legs up to above the knee, but (except some very old women)[8] were careful not to expose to view their breasts or bodies. (We found that the women were less careful as to the breast in more remote parts of the country and in the poor

quarters of the towns.) The men may uncover everything except what
the thinnest loincloth can cover back and front; and (as in mediaeval
Europe) may reveal the form even of that by a sort of pocket (the old
'cod-piece point' of mediaeval Europe). But what is noticeable is the
invariableness with which these limits of decency are (apart from
children) observed in this land of nudity.

We were asked to dinner, in the Japanese hotel at Kamakura at
which he happened to be staying, by Viscount Suematsu; a Member of
the Upper House, an important political personage, who had come to
London during the late war on some special diplomatic mission; and
who had been in his early manhood at Cambridge University, and
attaché in London.[9] We took off our shoes to walk on the mats of the
Japanese hotel, and were received by the Viscount and his wife, in
Japanese dress; but they gave us a conventional European dinner, the
Japanese man-servant handing sherry, hock and claret at the right
moment, clearing away the crumbs and so on, all in perfect style. The
Viscount and his wife were on familiar conversational terms with the
servants, whether of the hotel or their own.

He, to our surprise, was a burly, hairy, rather rough-mannered
person, frank, cordial and abrupt; understanding English well but
speaking with a little difficulty. She understood and spoke less, but
followed intelligently, and was frequently appealed to by him.

We talked Japan. His standpoint was that of a *laissez-faire* individualist, recognising the evils of industrial change, but seeing no way of
avoiding them. He thought England was becoming dangerously
democratic and collectivist (Lloyd George).[10] He conveyed the
impression that enlightened Japan was entirely agnostic, and the rest
of the people little interested in religion, but confirmed the statement
that more interest was being taken in Buddhist writings, and that men
did go into retreat to study them. He wrote out, then and there on the
Japanese roll of paper, a letter of introduction to the great Abbot of the
western sect (Otani)[11] whom he said we ought to meet at Kyoto. He
did not approve of women's education altogether, thinking it unfitted
them for wifely duties.

The only other person of interest whom we saw at Kamakura was a
Norwegian commercial man, Herr Aall, staying in the hotel, of the
vice-consular sort, who had been for years at Yokohama, and had been
formerly at Johannesburg. He proved to be well up in English politics,
including the latest personalities; and it turned out that he read
habitually fifty newspapers as his distraction during exile. He described the European society at Yokohama as supremely uninteresting,
the women thinking of nothing but dress and housekeeping and the
men mostly drinking! He had the usual local European dislike of the

Japanese, and the usual accusations of duplicity. But on cross-examination, his chief grievance turned out to be that they refused to grant any concessions or business opportunities to foreigners; and rather than say no, took refuge in polite evasions. He described the Government as unbribable in such matters, so far as all influential officials were concerned, in marked contrast with China, Turkey, etc. But he was quite unconscious that he was really giving great credit to a Government of which this could be said.

We lunched at Yokohama with an English businessman (Scott of Strauss & Co., married to an uninteresting sister of William Archer),[12] who equally disliked and despised the Japanese, but left much of the same impression on us. He said that he had heard that foremen and suchlike minor officials had to be conciliated with presents, but could allege nothing worse. The English seemed to know nothing of the Japanese. It must be difficult, living amid an alien people whom one never gets to know at all, and whom one begins by despising, to avoid being lowered in tone and character, or at any rate narrowed and strengthened in racial prejudices.

At Tokyo, in our first stay of two days, we have seen (1) Uehara, the young author of *The Political Development of Japan*, who had written that book at The London School of Economics; (2) his friend Dr. Kuwata, virtual author of last year's Factory Act, and a Member of the Upper House, elected by the 15 biggest taxpayers in his district; (3) Ishii, the Vice-Minister of Foreign Affairs on behalf of Marquis Komura, the Minister, who is indisposed; (4) Baron Shibusawa, a wealthy industrial magnate; (5) Prince Katsura, the Prime Minister, who is just resigning office; (6) Professor Tanaka, of Waseda University; (7) Mr. Sansom, a junior at the British Embassy, left in charge; and (8) a Japanese newspaper reporter! These have involved eight or nine *jinricksha* rides through this bewildering maze of small, low, detached houses along narrow streets, all apparently engaged in the humblest of businesses, relieved now and then by tall stone and brick banks and government offices, and two or three European hotels in a city covering something like 100 square miles, or nearly as much as London, and containing a couple of millions of people.

Uehara is of the awkward, ugly type of Europeanised Japanese, speaking English with some difficulty, after five or six years at Washington and London, but apparently very well instructed in political science, open-minded and intelligent.[13] He has a brother with some means, but has himself next to nothing, and is at present teaching in the Engineering College. He is mainly engaged in writing another book on Japanese politics, and thinks of going into Parliament. His attitude is very critical of the Government and somewhat despairing of parliamentary institutions. He explains the present change of Ministry as involving no principle, and as merely a shifting from one set to another, by friendly arrangement, reversing a similar change made a few years ago, probably merely to prevent a seeming permanent monopoly of office.[14] We are told also that there are two difficult questions to be dealt with, one, the change of gauge of the Government railways, and the other the need of increasing the cost of the army and navy, both of which Prince Katsura would prefer his friendly rivals to deal with.[15]

Uehara was plainly very relieved to find that we had brought introductions from Kato[16] to the Government officials. He and his friends, in the guise of a society for the study of social questions, had been rather concerned lest we, as known socialists, should find all doors closed to us, at any rate so far as official things were concerned; and also, perhaps, lest it might be inconvenient or dangerous for the society to invite us. He conveyed to us the impression that the Government has been very autocratic and tyrannical with regard to all who called themselves socialists (we gather otherwise that they are under police supervision and our guide tells us that no educated person would profess himself a socialist).[17] With regard to those who were tried under such extraordinary forms of secrecy, etc., and condemned, twelve to death and as many more to imprisonment for life, Uehara professed ignorance of the real facts, but said that he believed that there was a dynamite plot, directed not against the Emperor but against the Katsura Cabinet *en bloc*; but that it was possible that Kotoku was a follower of Rousseau, with some leanings towards Tolstoy; he had suffered suppression of his newspaper some years ago, and had fallen into the use of extreme language, especially as regards the autocracy of the Katsura administration; and it was probable that the Government, without much scruple, had used the opportunity to implicate him in the dynamite plot, and thus to rid themselves of a dangerous and outspoken critic, whom they did not understand. This is the theory that we form from what we have learnt so far. But we shall hear more by and by.[18]

Dr. Kuwata, Uehara's friend, was a plainly philanthropic enthusiast, of wealth and goodwill, with a certain characteristic futility.[19] Of him, too, we are to see more.

Certainly, the Government has been most polite and cordial to us. Our letters to Prince Katsura and Marquis Komura, the Prime Minister and Foreign Secretary, brought prompt and courteous invitations for interviews.

For these we put on our best clothes (S.W. in frock-coat, and tall silk hat), and went off in *jinrickshas* in the hot sun. At the Foreign Office,

Marquis Komura was indisposed,[20] and, with many apologies, deputed the Vice-Minister (just made Baron Ishii)[21] to receive us. He, with the Private Secretary as interpreter, received us in a banal Early Victorian drawing-room style of reception room, and conversed with us for half an hour or so. We had concerted to ask him for introductions to officials at Seoul, Korea, and Mukden, Manchuria, which were most freely and willingly promised. The Vice-Minister, who corresponds, we understood, to our Permanent Under-Secretary of State, was exactly like, in dress, bearing, training and apparently character, an Under-Secretary in Downing Street, and the Private Secretary (Sakai) was like our Civil Servant class.

The next morning we drove in our ceremonial attire, as before, to the Prime Minister's private residence, in a locality corresponding to Holland Park in London. We found a comfortable, detached villa in its own grounds, the ground floor, which alone we saw, being furnished in the worst possible taste, a combination of Early Victorian and Second Empire barbarisms, with no trace of the East except the tray of fans placed in the midst of the party, for each to take one and use it constantly. Katsura,[22] in frock-coat, etc., proved to be a round-headed, blunt-featured man, of quiet determination and executive force, alert and wideawake, but not revealing any intellectual distinction. He spoke no English (but is said to know German), and used Sakai, whom we had seen the day before (and who, by the way, had called three times at our hotel on the day of our arrival, to welcome us), as interpreter. After preliminaries, we deliberately turned the conversation on to the great scheme of 'charity organisation', which we had learnt that Katsura had been deputed by the Emperor to carry out; and this proved a fortunate line, as Katsura delighted to talk about it. The Emperor had given a large sum from his private purse, and had directed attempts to be made to raise more. In the course of a few months, no less than 25 million yen (two and a half million sterling) had been subscribed by the rich all over the country; and Katsura had within the past few days formed the governing committee with a Royal Prince as Hon. President, Katsura as Executive-President, and Baron Shibusawa as Vice-President.[23] We noted that Katsura somewhat explicitly stated that they had been delighted at the 'willingness' with which everybody had subscribed; the explanation being subsequently given to us by our caustic guide, who said that every Governor of a province had been ordered to invite to dinner or otherwise see every rich man in his province, and press him for a subscription of a certain sum according to his means.

It was, in fact, an extorted 'benevolence', of the kind used by the Tudor sovereigns. Our guide went so far as to say that anyone who refused would find things made very unpleasant for him – we could not gather exactly what was to be done with the money, beyond that the Emperor had expressed a desire that they should begin with the sick poor, and that it was hoped to secure a unification of charitable effort somehow.[24] We asked to see over the institutions in September, and the Prime Minister, then and there, instructed Sakai, the Secretary, to do all that we might want. We asked also for introductions to the Governors of Nagano and Niigata provinces, to which we had decided to go; and these were at once ordered to be written officially.

The Prime Minister was continually referring to 'civilisation', the inevitable incoming of which he constantly alleged as an explanation of every suggested evil or drawback. He seemed always to assume that everything Western was 'civilisation', and that there was no Japanese 'civilisation' of another kind.[25]

We saw also Baron Shibusawa, to whom Kato had given us a letter, a leading financial magnate (Katsura said he was not so very wealthy himself, but was concerned in the administration of many great enterprises).[26] We found him a sort of Sir Charles Tennant,[27] friendly and talkative (through an able secretary-interpreter); but not really able to convey much information to us. We tried to discuss banking, but only elicited his opinion that the Government could do nothing to control it. We asked for facilities to see over factories at Osaka, etc., including the places where the workers were boarded and lodged, and also for introductions to the two provinces of Nagano and Niigata that we were visiting; and he gave us half-a-dozen to local banks and oil works. He suggested that our guide should come to see him at noon on the following day to get these letters and instructions. (The guide went, and was given the letters, and was somewhat sharply warned by the Baron not to cheat us, and also not to show us anything 'miserable', or discreditable to Japan!)

Prof. Tanaka, to whom Kato had written, called to see us — a handsome, refined and distinguished-looking man; understanding English but speaking only in prepared sentences.[28] He professes political science at Waseda University, the private foundation, which Kato's rich father-in-law, Baron Iwasaki,[29] is reported to have helped. He rather embarrassed us by announcing that he had actually engaged *two* students to travel with us at our expense — we had rashly said to Kato that we should like to pick up a student to do this — and we had some difficulty in convincing him that, now that we had found a good guide, we preferred the latter companion. We professed our deep gratitude and regret at the misunderstanding, and promised to mitigate the disappointment of the two students somehow, later on. He asked S.W. to address his students when the session opened. He said they read Mill, Marshall, Taussig,[30] and the German economists, apparently in originals, but as to that we are not convinced. Our impression was that the political economy was that of the text-books, and hardly in definite relation to the facts of Japan.

We dined with Sansom, a Secretary of the Embassy, whom we had heard of from the Fairchilds, and met at lunch at Yokohama. He was a modest and sensible man of thirty or so, who had spent some years in the Consular Service in China and Korea, before being transferred to the Diplomatic Service.[31] He had just set up a bachelor household of his own to which we journeyed by *jinricksha* in the dark, and which we found a charming bungalow, with the Japanese mats and paper walls but with chairs, tables and bookcases. He gave us a simple, well-served meal, without alcohol; and we smoked and talked, until it was time, in the dark, to go home through the endless maze of streets, in his own *jinricksha*, by his own two men (this he said was customary).

He lent us some books on Japan (learned papers read before *The Asiatic Society of Japan*); and we lent him Uehara's book, which he had never heard of.

It was he who had looked after Sidney Ball,[32] and sent him home in the S.S. Yorck. Ball (of St. John's, Oxford), had been given an A.K. Travelling Scholarship to go round the world; and on reaching Japan had had a nervous breakdown, getting manias about losing his luggage, and behaving so strangely that they took away his razors. He was so unfit to travel alone across the U.S., that he was persuaded to go home by direct steamer, and his relations were communicated with to meet him at Port Said. We are still unaware whether he has reached them safely. Sansom seems to have taken endless trouble and some responsibility to help him.

IKAO[33]

On Thursday, 24th August, we started off for our mountain walk, leaving our luggage behind, and contenting ourselves with a Japanese basket, which a hired coolie carried. We went by rail to Nikko, 2000 feet (90 miles), stayed there one day for the gorgeous tombs and temples; then walked to Yumoto, 5000 ft. (12 miles, plus 3 by boat across Lake Chuzenji); then over the Konsei-toge (6770 ft.) to Higashi-gawa (17 miles); and then over another high pass to Takahara (16 miles), whence we took a carriage to Numata (6 miles), a horse tram-car to Shibukawa (12 miles) and an electric tram-car up to Ikao (7 miles), arriving very tired at 8:30 p.m. on the Monday night. A most magnificent walk, favoured by perfect weather. It is a new experience to walk in a hothouse temperature and humidity; but we found it unexpectedly practicable and really easier than our June walk in Switzerland. We reduced our clothing to a minimum, perspired freely and continuously, ate little, but drank copiously of the weak tea, largely diluted with hot water, and occasionally what they called Champagne Cider, which was sold everywhere, and consisted of little more than a sweetened and fruit-flavoured effervescing water. We found that, when we could correct its sweetness by the juice of the grape-fruit or wild orange, it made a good drink.

At Ikao,[34] a small place of hot springs, crowded on a hill-side alongside a street of steep steps, like Clovelly,[35] with splendid mountain views, we rested two days in a semi-European 'hotel', with matted floors and paper walls, and ever-running common baths, but also with chairs and tables and wash-hand stands and afternoon tea between the usual European meals. Here we lunched and talked with the Irwin family, an interesting type. R. W. Irwin, a direct descendant of Benjamin Franklin, is an American citizen, who has lived for forty years in Japan, was many years Consul for Hawaii, is now evidently well-to-do, has married a Japanese wife who still speaks no word of English, and has a family of seven or eight sons and daughters between sixteen and twenty-eight, the elder ones educated at Princeton and Bryn Mawr Universities, and the strangest mixture, in fact and manner, of American and Japanese. They live normally in Tokyo, but have built themselves a charming house here in Japanese style, in which they live for the summer. They gave us lunch *à la Japonaise* with chopsticks, but served at a long dining table; the wife, an aunt and the youngest daughter of sixteen in Japanese dress, the others in European clothes. There were present also (staying with them) a charming aristocratic Japanese couple about forty, a Mr. Inoue, Ambassador at Berlin for twelve years,[36] and his wife, in Japanese dress, speaking English perfectly, and accustomed to European courts; and also a son, aged twenty-two, of Capt. Brinkley,[37] an ex-University College student, himself a half-caste.

Irwin himself is rather a garrulous old bore, with endless irrelevant anecdotes of America, and incorrect scraps of English politics. He professes to be very pro-Japanese; repeats constantly that their human nature is just like that of other races; but that the common people are more civilised, because more law-abiding than other common people; and that the women especially are hardly ever in any way deliquent (occasional crimes of jealousy excepted). He refuses to admit any corruption, even in parliamentary elections, but allows that the M.P.s are 'corrupted from the top', e.g. by 'gold pills' from the Government in the style of Walpole and Newcastle.[38]

NAGANO 3rd SEPTr 1911

We have reached here in four days from Ikao, walking to Haramachi, 12 miles the first day, starting late as the morning opened wet; staying there in a flourishing village, at a comfortable native inn, where no foreign lady was remembered to have stopped: then catching a humble native diligence which took us for half-a-crown apiece all the twenty-five miles to Kusatsu, but taking nearly nine hours over the hilly journey; spending the night at a semi-European hotel in that high village of hot springs where we did *not* bathe, as the highly-mineralised waters are good for syphilis and leprosy; then starting early with one pack horse and one saddle horse with a man's saddle (which B. strode) for the ascent of Shibu-toge, a pass 7150 feet high, with a long and toilsome ascent and descent of 17½ miles to Shibu, a crowded little village resorted to by [the] Japanese for its hot springs; thence coming on twelve miles in *jinrickshas* and a quarter of an hour in the train to this populous town, where we have introductions to the provincial Governor and to the local banker.

This has given us a splendid panoramic view, on some days of magnificent mountains, on other days of Japanese agriculture. As for the latter, these smiling fields of rice, millet, hemp, mulberry (grown as low bushes for the leaves only), sweet potato, egg-plant, onions, turnips and radishes, and what our guide calls Japanese *macaroni*, are exceedingly picturesque in the sun; without walls or hedges, but divided into small square patches each with a different crop; highly irrigated, manured and hand-cultivated; without a single inch of fallow; in fact, yielding three or four different crops each year; and presenting a picture of century-long patient labour, most successfully applied to yield the largest possible amount of human food. Not an animal is to be seen; and not an inch of pasture. Such horses and cows as exist are kept entirely in their stalls, and fed on the commoner green stuffs of [BW: the mountain side − grass-weeds and the dwarf bamboo.] We gather from our guide that the land is almost entirely owned in small plots, mostly by the cultivators themselves (?) who, however, sometimes rent other patches in addition to their own. The men earn extra money as coolies, whilst their wives attend to the necessary farm work.

These valleys, too, are the scene of the silkworm culture; and in almost every house, one saw the white cocoons being dealt with, the silk often being wound off by a girl, by hand, on primitive spools. Here and there stood a long one-storied spinning-mill, where silk thread was spun by water power. We saw in one house, in Haramachi, the whole industry in a single room; the cocoons, the winding, the transfer to bobbins, the weaving on a primitive hand-loom, and even the dyeing of the cloth, all entirely by the hand-labour of the family. It happened to be the first of the month, when we understood the mills took holiday (the 1st and the 15th being in this way a poor substitute for our Sunday); but as far as we could see, all industry was going on as usual, which our guide ascribed to its being near the end of the season and it being desired to complete as much work as possible! Evidently, in these rural parts at any rate, there is no very strictly observed day of rest, even fortnightly.

In the towns, in the rural villages, and even along the roads in populous districts, the outstanding feature is the endless array of little shops and little artisan workshops, which makes one realise to what an extent Japan is the land of family home industry and petty retailing. In the summer sun, at any rate, this vision of *'petite culture'* and *'petite industrie'*, with its family life, and freedom to leave off at will, appeared very charming − markedly different from the slum 'home work' of English cities.[39] In the absence of any rich or socially superior class, there was everywhere a pleasing social equality, the maids at the inns apparently eating with the innkeeper's family, and being [in a] friendly, humane relationship with [them].[40]

The children, who swarmed everywhere, seemed somewhat neglected − not very efficiently got to school, or well-taught there; the girls suffering in chest development and [lacking] freedom from the perpetual and almost universal burden of a younger child strapped to the back, even from the age of five or so; the babies thus perpetually strapped up, without exercise of limbs, or protection from the sun, or proper sleep; here and there, some with bad sores on the face, etc. (but this is less frequent than might have been expected); and only the boys growing up sturdy and strong, though apparently 'wild' and untaught. This neglect of infantile health and child development in rural Japan is the most serious defect that we have noted so far.

Japan is a land of innumerable temples and shrines and wayside images; but it is difficult to make out whether they mean much to the present generation, even in the country. Moreover, there is a marked absence of priests. Each village has its Shinto temple, usually in a grove of magnificent *cryptomerias*, several hundred years old; but there is usually no priest whatever in attendance or in residence; the temple stands there, open and empty; there are votive offerings and symbols of vows or wishes, and sometimes offerings of part of the harvest, but there is no religious ceremony or observance. At the Buddhist temples, which are far less numerous, there are priests in attendance, usually with their families and their acolytes or apprentices − wholly supported, we gather, from the minute offerings of the faithful who throw small copper coins in an open chest at the entrance. But the services which these priests may be heard chanting before the altar, without anyone at all being present, are unintelligible gibberish to the people, being in some archaic tongue, accompanied by a perpetual strumming on a drum, alternated with occasional strokes of a bell or gong.

The dead are buried, sometimes adjoining a temple, but more often, in a field; and groups of simple gravestones may be seen amidst the rice or millet. We gather that there is often some calling in of the Buddhist priest at death, but with this exception, there seems no priestly intervention in the common person's life.

In the schools, there is apparently no religious instruction, and not even any explanation of Buddhism or Shintoism as a matter of history; reverence for the Emperor, the law, the family, and one's ancestors, are made the sole moral code. On the other hand, the State seems to give some financial support to Shintoism — there *are* Shinto priests attached to the larger temples, and there is even a Shinto College somewhere for their instruction — but we do not feel sure what all this amounts to.

Just beyond Shibu, our guide pointed out a group of several score of houses lying a few hundred yards from the road, as being the village of public prostitutes for this whole neighbourhood. They were confined by the police to this village where they were inspected twice a week by the Government doctors, when any found diseased were at once sent to a special Government hospital — one for each province — and treated, free of charge; the cost being levied upon them in the form of a monthly tax. This village was said to be resorted to chiefly by the peasant cultivators, the coolies, and some of the visitors to the bath-villages; and was therefore not very 'high-class'. We learn that, whilst Europeanised Japanese have now some shame or scruples or doubts, the unsophisticated native regards the satisfaction of this appetite exactly as he does that of other appetites.

We noticed along the rural high road a running newspaper-boy, with his bundle of this morning's Tokyo paper, one or more copies of which he threw down apparently at every house. Our guide said that they were all subscribers, on monthly subscription, at about one sen (farthing) a day. This universal reading of a Tokyo paper is a feature.

5th SEPT^r [1911]

We have now been two days at Nagano, which have been full of interest. On the Sunday on which we arrived, the Governor's office, the banks and the schools were shut; but we sent our cards to the Governor's house by our guide, with a polite message, which produced, on the Monday, telephone messages and a ceremonial visit from two officials, one apparently the head of the Agricultural Department, and the other a sort of 'Assistant Commissioner' in police uniform. They brought apologies from the Governor, who was engaged in inspection business, and enquiries as to what exactly they could do for us. After much general conversation through our guide as interpreter (though they both understood more English than they at first admitted), of which the Assistant Commissioner took copious notes, they arranged to send word what we should do. We got no word until late at night (they had had difficulty in finding an interpreter, as our guide was going for the day with Mrs. and Miss Fairchild, who had come on here to visit the mother of a deceased student-servant of theirs in Boston), when one of them brought word that we should be taken round institutions in the morning, and out by *jinricksha* in the afternoon.

Meanwhile, we had discovered from the balcony of our hotel a cluster of tall houses half a mile away, illuminated at night, which on enquiry proved to be the prostitutes' quarter. So S.W. went off with the guide to investigate it at 8.30 p.m. It proved to be a square, enclosed by a tall wooden fence, guarded by police, with only one entrance, connected with the town by a long lane. In the square were about a score of big houses, with perhaps as many more humble shops, drinking-bars, restaurants, etc. In the ground floor of each of the houses, brilliantly lighted-up, and separated from the street by a bamboo cage, sat from six to ten girls, not particularly gaily-dressed, each with the usual brazier of charcoal and ashes in front, by which to light the pipe she from time to time smoked. Outside each establishment, one or two touts sat or stood, not very importunate.[41]

There were hardly any customers, as business is dull in the summer, it appears, and moreover it was still early. As we looked in at the girls they looked up impassively, but hardly moved or smiled. After walking past all the houses, the guide arranged for admission to one of the houses, for a talk only, for the price of one yen (2/-). This, it seems, is a usual fee here for 'real business'! Entering, we were shown upstairs by a very respectable and indeed nice-looking servant, with a pleasant and even engaging expression. The room was well fitted-up, perfectly clean, open on all sides (as it was a hot summer's night), but with screens that could be quite closed, and with a pile of the usual quilts in an alcove, with which to make the usual Japanese bed. The servant brought tea, and pressed us to buy drinks, which we refused to do; and eventually, produced a large framed set of photographs of the available girls, eight in number, all perfectly dressed and almost undistinguishably beautiful in their own style. S.W. chose the first, and she presently arrived from the ground-floor − not in the least like her portrait, and really repulsive. She poured out tea and lighted our cigarettes, and with some hesitation at first, answered our questions. It is to be noted that the far nicer-looking, respectable servant came in and out all the time, and sat down every now and then and participated in the conversation.

The girl said she was twenty-four; had been here about a year, but had been transferred from a similar quarter at Karuizawa; had been in the business since 19; had taken to it in order to get 220 yen (£22) with which to meet the mortgage on her father's little farm, to save him from ruin; she had no fixed term, but was to serve until the debt was paid off; found that she could pay off hardly anything, and had no prospect of release; the doctor came once a week, and was not at all kind; her tax to the Government for this was 2½ yen (5/-) per month. She said that all the girls here were Japanese, and so, too, were the customers. She never went outside the wall, as this was strictly forbidden by the police. The oldest girl in the establishment was, she supposed, about thirty-two. Asked whether any attempt at rescue had been made by missionaries, she said that the Salvation Army some time ago had distributed bills telling the girls they were free to leave if they liked;[42] but it seems they would have to find some means of livelihood, and still be legally compellable to contribute repayments of their debts, so that this was a failure.

After exhausting all the questions that the vocabularies of the guide and the girl made possible, we gave the girl 50 sen (1/-) for herself, paid 20 sen (5d) for the tea, etc. (total cost, 1 yen 70 sen, or 2/8); and went out. The guide said her story was doubtless true; that practically all the prostitutes were recruited in that sort of way; that the usual custom was agreement, or rather sale, for a fixed term of about seven years; and that it was difficult to say what became of them in the end. It is to be noted that there were families of children about the place, including young girls growing up; and the usual family circles, including children and servants, were to be seen taking their evening meal in the kitchens. As we came away, about 9.30 p.m., men were beginning to arrive in *jinrickshas*, in twos and threes.

It was a gruesome sight. The coarse, weary, apathetic faces of the girls, the crude animalism of the business; the unashamed subjection of these fellow-citizens to the pleasures of the men, even as we subject the horses to our service; the apparently hopeless servitude to which the girls are subjected − all combine to make this feature of Japan very unpleasant; though, of course, the analogous evils of the English system could be painted in as dark a light.

On Tuesday, we were called for by three officials − the head of the Agriculture Department, whom we had seen, a corresponding person in the Education Department, and a young Japanese teacher of English in the local 'middle school', who was to act as interpreter. We were taken first to the largest school — with 1700 boys and girls of all ages, from infants in arms to girls preparing for the normal school (age 15 or so),[43] with some 45 teachers, a few only untrained, at salaries said to be about 300 yen a year (£30); under an intelligent and active headmaster who seemed competent, but was said to get only £72 a year (60 yen per month). The school buildings, all on the ground-floor, consisted of some 37 good class-rooms, with large teachers' common-room, a headmaster's room, and a large hall, with abundant playgrounds. The buildings were quite serviceable, light, airy, clean; but were considered old and inadequate.

We were shown particularly a class of seven or eight deaf mutes, who were writing on [a] blackboard the answers to simple written questions; but who were said to be taught to speak by the visible method (a large mirror was shown us) (one girl did read the alphabet as written on [a] blackboard, and spoke seemingly quite well); and a larger blind class, of mixed ages, who were reading and writing with a sort of 'Braille' system adapted to the Chinese characters; and who played the harmonium and sang to it. It is to be noted that what they were reading were the Government instructions to, and regulations for, the 'amma', or masseurs, to which occupation they are all brought up. There was a full-sized articulated human skeleton, and a large diagram of the nerves and muscles, in the room. There was also a class of a dozen feeble-minded children, selected by the school doctor from among those proving themselves very backward at examinations.

Meanwhile, some thirty or more other classes were at work; but, as there is 10 minutes interval for play after each forty minutes lesson, and as the classes ended apparently at different times, there was a perpetual coming and going of children, a constant sound of play outside the open windows, and a continual stream of children passing along the broad corridors — all giving an impression of life and gaiety and happiness, without the least fear of the masters, or awe of the official and strangely foreign visitors. What struck us was the absence of any unpleasant smell in the class-rooms (in which there were often 60 or 70 children), or from the crowds of children. They were tidy, and not at all in rags. There were no visible sores. But the little girls were narrow-chested and under-sized, as usual; the younger children were often 'pot-bellied', as we had noticed in the country. The boys were much superior in physique to the girls. A group of boys were wrestling, by turns, in the open air, under the superintendence of a master. Each pair of boys struggled violently for several minutes, until one was thrown, amid great clapping of hands by the others — the whole with the most perfect good nature by the combatants, without any loss of temper. The master picked out the boy who was to wrestle with the victor of the last bout.

They were said to play also baseball,[44] and the girls lawn tennis, but we saw no arrangements for this, and it is perhaps confined to middle or high schools.

In the great hall, something like a hundred boys were being drilled by ex-Army men, but this consisted merely of mechanical marching, by twos, to the sound of '*ichi*', '*ni*', (one, two). This seems a common fault of the school drill in schools here. We formed a good impression of this school, on the whole; and of the headmaster, who seemed a competent administrator.

We also saw a 'middle school',[45] which stuck us as poor and pretentious (except three grades of English lesson that we heard, by the 'oral' method). A woman teacher was lecturing, we were told, on 'ethics', which seemed to consist of stories of brave deeds.[46] Both schools had 'mixed' staffs under a male head; both were entirely secular; both were staffed mainly by men, with a few women; in both, the teachers had appallingly low salaries, but struck us as trained and zealous men and women, without distinction.

We were then conducted to the Buddhist orphanage, or 'workhouse' as it was translated, adjacent to the great temple. We were received with great ceremony, as the first foreigners who had ever visited it. It is apparently a small endowed foundation, aided by charitable grants of rice from benevolent people. After our elaborate reception, and the inevitable serving of tea, we were solemnly conducted along a passage. Out of it opened a room, in which there were six or eight little boys, elaborately dressed up, on their knees in a row, elaborately bowing to us. In the next room were half-a-dozen girls, in the same posture. Next, in a room, were three or four feeble-minded youths and men; and there were one or two old women − something like a score in all. And there was nothing else to see! We could not clearly ascertain who managed the institution, or how the inmates were selected. In the entrance lobby were a number of tiny bags of rice, each about as large as a wine bottle, which were the actual gifts of donors.

After *tiffin*[47] at our hotel, we were called for by the officials, and taken out in *jinrickshas* a mile or so into the country, in response to our request to be shown a country gentleman's house. It turned out to be that of a substantial owner of land, who apparently let it all out to small cultivators on old customary rents, paid in kind, and amounting, so he said, to sixteenths of the crop of rice. The tenant bore all the expense of cultivation, irrigation and manuring, and we did not gather that the owner supplied any capital. The house was just like others, clean and bare, with a tiny fragment of yard on each side by way of garden, in which there were a few trees and flowers, including one fine dwarf pine, said to be four hundred years old. The house itself was 120 years old, but [the land] had been in the family for seventeen generations. The owner, a man of middle age, received us courteously and answered our questions, but evidently could not in the least understand our objects. His son, we were told, was at the Government Agricultural College at Sapporo in the northern island. In the room was a large, closed Buddhist shrine, which our officials suggested to our host that we should like to see. But he did not open it, and made some polite evasion. There was not an inch of garden or park land attached to the house, which was closely surrounded on all sides by the buildings of the small cultivators. We gathered that the owner was really a sort of wealthy farming-owner, who had ceased himself to farm, and now let out all his land instead of some of it.

On our way back, we called at the Governor's house, where he received us at the threshold, conducted us to a room furnished in European style, and produced coffee and sweetmeats, and a huge pile of sandwiches. There entered presently his wife, a handsome, intelligent woman, much younger than he (in Japanese dress, as he was). He looked a strong, able man, remarkably like an old Roman senator in his toga.[48] Through the interpreter, he conversed politely, and very sensibly, his wife much interested, and joining in. We interested them at once in the question of the baby-carrying, and the position of women. He was profuse in his courtesies, and spontaneously offered to telephone to Nagaoka and Niigata, whither we were going, to let them know we were coming. [BW: The next day he returned our visit, and stayed some time, chatting pleasantly.]

Next morning, two officials came to escort us to a silk-mill and a reformatory school, six miles out. This proved a long expedition, along bad roads, right into the country. We came to a broken bridge, which the officials thought to have been already repaired; and this involved crossing by boat. (The bridge was a privately owned toll-bridge: and it was on the point of being bought up and freed by the provincial Government. The price, it appears, is usually the capital cost, irrespective of the profits. When I said that the owners might object, he said that public opinion would be so strong that the owners themselves would not object.)

The silk-spinning mill was an old one, 37 years old, employing between four and five hundred people, mostly women. These women entered usually as girls of 10 or 11; were apprenticed (the contract being made with the parent) for a term of years, six months of which they were merely learners, with lessons in school subjects for two hours a day. For the rest of the term, which we think was five years, they were on piece-work, but bound to remain. Afterwards, they were legally free to leave, and might practically do so on marriage, or for family reasons, or to go to some other occupation. But we understood that it was against equity for them (having been taught by one firm) to go to any other firm in the trade; and that it was a criminal offence for any other firm to entice them away, so that any girl going to another firm would run a great risk of prosecution (of the employing firm, and herself, as an accomplice). It was clear, from the repeated assurances that we were given as to the firm making no objection to their going home again on any family misfortune or on marriage, that they were virtually bound, subject to the firm's benevolence.

The hours were from 5 a.m. to 6 a.m. − then half an hour for breakfast − from 6.30 to 12 − then half an hour for dinner − and from 12.30 to 5.30 p.m. = 11½ hours a day, for 7 days a week = 80½ per week. There were supposed to be two full holidays per month, but these were not on fixed days, and were accorded as trade orders permitted. A certain proportion of them were married, either to men about the factory, or others; and these lived at their homes and were paid weekly. The rest lived in houses belonging to the firm, adjacent to the spinning-shed, and were boarded by the firm − thus receiving their board and lodging free, in addition to the piece-work rates. The firm said that this cost them, inclusive, about 15 sen per day per head, or something like 2/1 per week. (But we learnt, otherwise, that 10 or 12 sen, or 1/4 to 1/9 per week, was nearer the mark). We asked how much the ablest woman earned, and were told 60 sen per day (1/3). On our expressing surprise and gratification that it was so much, the firm very frankly said that only ten made as much as that; and that the lowest and youngest made only 6 sen per day (1/½d). We gathered that the common run made about 17 sen (4d) a day, in addition to board and lodging − equal to a wage of about 4/- a week for 80½ hours work.

The living houses were clean, light, airy and not more bare than the ordinary Japanese abodes. Each girl had her own box and basket in the bedroom, and her own tray and bowl, etc., in the dining-room. There was a spacious bath-room, with the usual supply of hot water to a large common bath. There was an (employer's) Friendly Society among them, of which we were given the rules. All the girls subscribed, and out of the funds, gifts were made to any who were married or suffered calamity. The firm contracted with the village doctor to attend to illnesses; and the girls were kept, meanwhile, but any serious case was sent home. The girls who lived in, were paid only every three or six months, but a statement of their earnings each month (or week) was put up for common inspection − it was said, in order to promote emulation. The yarn was done up in nice bundles, and sent to Yokohama for export. There was no weaving done (except for the sake of experimenting with the yarn to test qualities). The cocoons were bought from the peasants all over the district, partly by contractors who undertook to deliver so much at a fixed price, and got it as they could; partly, by two buyers employed by the firm.

So much for the facts as given to us. It was a remarkable scene. After elaborate reception, we were conducted all over the place by the works Manager (of the regular 'mill-manager' type, unaware of the commercial organisation outside). On our return to the outer office, the whole company sat in a circle, the Managing Director (an educated, refined-looking, able man), the works manager, one or two clerks, our two selves, our interpreter, the two Government officials, and [the] local police sergeant and constable in their white suits and swords, who had been summoned to be in attendance to do us honour. The inevitable tea was served, and we spent the best part of an hour, asking questions and cross-examining, being always most courteously and willingly replied to, in the hearing of the whole company.

It remains to be said that the girls looked clean, neat and well-clothed; their hair most carefully done in rather elaborate fashion; and they were healthy and well-grown; they bathed every day. But they looked extremely apathetic and dull — even unhappy; they were absolutely absorbed in their mechanical work (of keeping the threads pieced together), in the most inert and machine-like way; and, although the walking past them of foreigners (and especially a foreign lady) must have been almost a unique experience, they hardly raised their eyes to look at us. Of the animation, light-heartedness and curiosity of the Lancashire factory operative [BW: or of the Japanese village community], there was no trace. We asked what amusements they had, and were told they would occasionally hire a 'lecturer', or a gramophone, to come on one of their bi-mensual holidays, but that this was all. On such days, they were free to go out the whole day, if they chose, on condition that they returned by 6 p.m. The were said to be strictly moral, and at once to report for dismissal any girl who was not so. It was not a pretty vision, this practical bondage to a life of monotonous toil. But it should be noted that it was not altogether new. This mill, and exactly this organisation of labour, was started in 1874; and we read, even before the opening of the country, of girls being virtually sold to the silk industry.[49]

[BW →] Our next visit was to the reformatory school for boys. This was a low, homely, wooden building, with an extensive vegetable garden set down in the midst of the rice fields, with no kind of fence or signs of confinement. The Principal was a kindly old gentleman — with beaming eyes and the most benevolent expression, and he had as his assistants two men and two women who served as teachers and domestics. Two of them, a man and a woman, were enthusiastic Christians — the Principal himself was a Buddhist — [and] one of the women had her old mother living with her. We sat round the improvised table, and drank tea and asked questions — the Principal was obviously an enthusiast, not very learned, and with the Japanese caution in expressing general opinions. He had been entrusted with the task of starting and managing this reformatory, and the police had orders to take any suitable cases of theft or arson on the part of boys straight to this reformatory, and he, the Principal, decided how long it took to reform them.

The parents paid, if they could afford it, a small weekly sum. The boys were given the usual education, and taught the simpler trades — no religious instruction was permitted, as it was a Government institution. When they were reformed, they were sent back to their relations; or apprenticed, if there were no parents, or bad ones. We saw the boys at lessons and also at their meals. They were being treated exactly as if they belonged to the family — and the Principal and the teachers had their meals with them. The eight elder boys slept in one room, opening out of a male assistant's room — the eight younger, in one opening out into the room of the lady and her mother. There was a spare room, for confinement in case of great insubordination, but there was no other punishment. The boys looked thoroughly happy and well — they each had their own gardens and their little bits of personal belongings — they were, in fact, being brought up like the children of well-to-do peasantry, or little shopkeepers. I have never seen such an absence of institutionalism. The Principal, and his wife and children, were living in rooms adjoining those of the boys, and all used the same kitchen and bath and wash-house. The subsidy paid by the Government was £40! A little profit was made by the boys, by selling the vegetables they grew in the market, and they had the product of the vegetable garden to help out the rice. The salaries were probably very small and there were no doubt some subscriptions.

An institution we saw at Niigata revealed a similar spirit — the discharged prisoners' aid society. Here, a man and his wife — a former Judge — obviously of the saint-like type, and very pious Buddhists, lived, with some ten discharged prisoners, in intimate family life. Here again, there was a tiny subsidy from, and kindly co-operation with, the Government, and more substantial support from a philanthropist. Incidentally, here we were told that three years ago the Government had given up the police supervision of discharged prisoners, because it was thought to militate against the future career of the man. The men

here were expected to worship morning and evening before the
Buddhist shrine, and one previous resident, who had been converted
at a Buddhist temple (where he had been taken as a coolie), came over
once a week to preach to the men. There was little book or trade
instruction, and the saint-like Principal seemed quite satisfied if the
inmates got work as coolies. Two male inmates had married two
female inmates and lived in a sort of cabin close by, which, when we
looked in unawares, was a scene of darkness, dirt and nudity. But then,
the home of the coolie, who is not also a small cultivator, is apt to look
squalid to the Western observer. The whole business struck us as a
minute and unscientific, but intensely benevolent effort, to save the
soul and yield a livelihood to a few selected cases of discharged
prisoners.[50]

On our way to Niigata, the capital of Echigo Province,[51] we were
met by the official interpreter of the Governor of Niigata — a well
turned-out and groomed young man, in immaculate European costume
(the Japanese dress extraordinarily well), who both spoke and understood English very imperfectly. He had been [the] English teacher at
the girls' middle school of Niigata. He was very much impressed with
the importance of his task as *cicerone*, and spent many anxious hours at
the telephone, discussing the exact way in which we should spend our
time. He, or his superior, had mapped out every minute of our time in
the province, and certainly the result justified his or their capacity. We
went straight to the office of the Hoden Oil Company,[52] and were
received by the General Manager, in Japanese dress, and the Engineer
in European, who talked excellent English — of the latter, we saw a
good deal, as he came for a talk to our hotel in the evening, and took
us, the next morning, over various establishments. He was an easy-
going, alert little fellow — quick to understand and discuss — a common
little mind of the American business type — the sort of person who
would be checked by shrewdness only in sharp practice.

[SW→] The Hoden Oil Company concern is apparently drooping in
prosperity, owing to the declining yield of its wells, and the
competition (in Japan) of larger concerns, including the great local
enterprise started by the Standard Oil Co. of the U.S. Japan does not
produce enough petroleum for its own consumption, and still imports
from [the] U.S. On this and the following day, we saw (1) the making
of square tin cans out of Welsh tin plates, (2) the refinery, and (3) (at
Niitsu) the oil-wells themselves. The machinery was American, except
a Lancashire boiler, but it struck us as not very efficient, and still using
unnecessary hand labour — no doubt because of the low wages. The
Engineer showed us the wage-sheets, from which it seemed that the
men got from 42 sen (for labourers), up to 60 sen for the mechanics,

per day; while the women got from 25 to 35 yen per day – a sen being one farthing. There was no piece-work, not even where the women were making the cans by nearly automatic machines, each doing one small part of the process. Each can was tested for leakage before being filled, by being immersed in water. There was a marked absence of foremen. The Engineer said that piece-work would lead to scamping and leakage.

We saw also another concern, a paper-mill, making coarse mill-board out of rice-straw, mixed with lime and soda. This was a slackly-managed place, the men and women standing around. The machinery was American and nearly automatic, the labour being wholly unskilled. We were told that the men got 40 sen and the women about 20 sen per day. The limestone was burnt on the spot, by coal fuel. We told our Engineer of R. C. Phillimore's experiment in making the limestone burn itself by intermixing crude low-grade oil – thus using up one of his waste products – and he was quick to see the point, and be interested in it. The soda came from Europe. The rice-straw had formerly been used mainly for manure (and still is), but there was now a great use of imported nitrates and sulphate of ammonia.

At Niitsu, we went to the oil-field, a dismal sight. On the hill-side, a hundred or more rude triangular derricks, each supporting a tube a few inches in diameter, with a slowly moving up-and-down pump, moved by long ropes connecting with a common steam-engine. The whole surface was a mass of mud, ruined vegetation, and waste oil. In the middle of this mess, stood the squalid living rooms of the men, where they were boarded and lodged, at a charge of 12 sen per day, deducted from their wages of about 40 sen per day. The same room served for the day and night shifts, sleeping and eating. The only additional provision was the invariable common bath, and hot water. The men came from distant homes, and it was for this reason that the boarding-house system had been adopted. There were women assisting the men at manual toil, at about 20 sen per day, but not boarded. The whole vision was that of brutal squalor, the employers assuming no sort of responsibility for the life or conduct or recreation of the men. There were about 80 employees there, which was one of many oil-fields in the province. These seem to us the Pittsburg of Japan.[53]

At Niigata, our day consisted of (1) girls' middle school; (2) boys' normal school; (3) discharged prisoners' aid society, already described; (4) ceremonial reception by the Governor; (5) lunch at restaurant by Friendly Society philanthropist, and visit to his office and reading room; (6) afternoon call on wealthy banker at his home; (7) dinner given us by him at Japanese restaurant, with a selection of 'the beauties of Niigata'.

[BW→] We had already seen one girls' middle school,[54] at Nagaoka – but Niigata middle school was supposed to be one of the largest and the best. The first surprise was to find a man as Principal, and the majority of the assistant teachers were also men, women being used merely for sewing, tea ceremony, and for the teaching of the young at classes. The second surprise was to find a boarding department without any kind of permanent lady at the head. The young girl assistants took it in turn, one at a time, to live with the boarders. The Principal was, in both cases, an elderly man, but the assistants were young men, some of them unmarried. The teaching was inferior, with no [SW: individual] laboratory work, and there was the same complete passivity in the students as in other Japanese educational establishments. The only class which seemed, to the rapid observer, intelligent, was the sewing, where the girls were really being taught to make and to mend their clothes. The girls learnt archery [SW: as part of their gymnastics] and were extensively drilled, by an army-looking teacher. In the Nagaoka school, we could not ascertain that the boarding girls were at all supervised out of school hours; but at Niigata, they were supposed to keep a book giving their movements on holidays and recreation hours. Our guide, Nishi, had already told us that these boarding-schools were a scene of a good deal of illicit intercourse, between girls and men, and girls and boys, and we did not doubt his word when we had actually seen their arrangements. It is a strange irony that there should be this lack of supervision over girls, in a country in which women are considered the chattels of men, and when, in the family circle, [they] are given no opportunity of meeting youths and men even as friendly acquaintances. [SW] The class-rooms were good and numerous, and the classes not unduly large.

The boys' normal school[55] was for boys of 14 to 18, training to be teachers – really a sort of secondary school. There was the same abundance of good class-rooms, the same passivity of the students, who were not allowed even to take notes of the perpetual lecturing that went on; the same absence of individual laboratory work. There was absolutely no library; and we could not learn that they did any individual reading, or had any debating society. They had army uniforms and rifles in their rooms; and it appears that their stay (four years) includes military training, and entitles them to be let off with no more than six weeks actual service in the ranks, a practical compromise that looks worth imitating. I asked about drink and sexual immorality, and was told that they undertook on entry to abstain from both; and, that any breach would lead to expulsion. The pupils were mostly admitted free, and there was said to be much competition, so that the Government could pick the best. Others were admitted on a modest payment. A few were said to go on to the higher normal school at Tokyo, but most got appointments immediately on leaving. [BW: There was a primary school in the establishment, and in the classrooms, the students were teaching or listening to lessons being given by the normal school teachers.]

We then went to the official offices of the province, a large European building, with many clerks on the ground floor, where we were received ceremoniously by the Governor in his official apartments. In marked contrast with the Governor of Nagano, he was a stiff, shy aristocrat, in frock-coat, who received us with great dignity and stateliness, spoke a few civil words, listened politely to our civil speeches, and directed the officials − who had obviously prearranged the whole thing − to do all that we desired. This Governor is of royal blood, a cousin of the reigning Emperor, who elected to give up his princely rank to become a mere Count, and to devote himself to official service.[56] He was said to have his wife and family in Tokyo, and to be living in his official residence with a concubine.[57] [BW: This relative is the feudal landlord.]

In the afternoon, we went to the house of a wealthy banker, Mr. Kagimori, a splendid residence overlooking the river, of simple exterior and construction, but with beautiful slides and screens, a harmony in gold and soft browns, with fine pieces of old lacquer and metal work, and ancient *kakemono*.[58] The banker introduced his son (dull), and son's wife, a very pretty ex-pupil of the middle school. They gave us tea and sweets, and the lady played European pieces on the piano. They then and there invited us to dinner in the evening, to show us 'the beauties of Niigata', which we at once accepted.

At 7 p.m., we got to the Japanese restaurant appointed (B. resplendent in crimson *jibbah*[59] and S. in black dinner-jacket and tie), where the company (8 in all) assembled, including the Governor's Secretary, a clever nephew and future partner (who had read our *Problems of Modern Industry*[60] when at Waseda University), the banker, his son, and his son's wife (whom the Governor's Secretary had persuaded to come, to keep B. in countenance), our guide, and our two selves. A purely Japanese dinner was served, with abundant *sake*, and meanwhile, half-a-dozen gaily dressed girls came in, one after another, and sat themselves down casually by the guests, and smoked and talked with them. They were evidently rather glum at the presence of ladies; and, at the kind of conversation, for we discussed banking problems across the room. In the middle of the interminable dinner, they sang and danced at the end of the room, half-a-dozen times, to the music of a drum and kind of zither, or guitar.[61] The dresses and movements were pretty, and the music quaint, though monotonous.

Some much-esteemed and celebrated pieces were given, so we were told. How long the entertainment might have lasted, we know not, but (as we had had a long and tiring day, and had to get up at 4.30 tomorrow for an even greater expedition), by 10 p.m., we excused ourselves, and the party broke up. (We learnt afterwards that this was an entertainment of the first class – the eight *geishas* would cost at Niigata 50 yen, the eight dinners 3 yen each, and that the total, with *sake* and tips, would not come to less than £9; whilst in Tokyo, it might have been £15 or more.)

We were charmed with the banker, a genial elderly man, of sense and humour, who had been in America at the age of sixteen, and who gradually began to find his English again by the time we left. [BW→] At the dinner, he would alternate between *sake*-drinking and confidential chats with the leading *geisha*, and coming across the room and squatting down before Sidney – asking questions, and giving information, and chuckling at Sidney's reasoned objection to some action by the Japanese Government, or some opinion of the economists. He was certainly extraordinarily open-minded and quick to understand – he might have been discussing financial problems with financiers of other nations all his life. And his obvious pride in his pretty daughter-in-law, and devotion to his little grandchild, were good to look at. Altogether, that evening, with its sustained and serious discussions in the forefront, and the brilliant *geishas* dancing in the background, was a very unique experience.

On Sunday 10th [Sept.], we were at the station at 5.30 in the morning. We met the head of the Financial and Industrial Department of the province, and the Secretary-interpreter, to be taken by them to lunch with the greatest landlord in Japan, and to stay with a smaller landlord – the third largest in the province. To this plan, our faithful Nishi had raised some objections, especially if he were to take us – we did not know the rigid etiquette of Japan, which necessitated an immediate present to anyone you stayed with, [and] this would be troublesome, and far more expensive than staying at the hotel. However, he was comforted by the presence of the representatives of the Governor, who, he said, relieved us all of any responsibility. It is noteworthy that, even at this early hour, the clever nephew of the banker, and the Friendly Society philanthropist, came to see us off. We got out at the next station. From there, we took to *jinrickshas*, five coolies trotting our five selves, through pouring rain, across the great rice-plain –through villages and by temples, over little bridges and by field-paths – 12 miles in all, to the residence of Mr. Ichishima. As we approached his house, we noticed the superior charm of the little village – beautifully planted with conifers – very like the drive in an

English park. A coolie on a bicycle darted back when he saw us approaching, so as to prepare the ceremonious reception. A bridge across a moat, and we were within one of the outer courts leading to the house. The two bailiffs of the estate – grave elders in ceremonious Japanese dress – were prostrating themselves at the entrance, and men-servants were running to and fro.

We were ushered into the reception room, and, with many bows, motioned into the European chairs round a European table, which had been placed for our special comfort. The reception room was open on three sides to a beautiful Japanese garden, of water, stone and conifers, and consisted of one large, matted middle room, with three verandas at lower levels, right down to the garden. I have a vision of beautiful sliding screens, alcoves of brown and gold – with here and there a *kakemono* by some famous artist of a branch of a tree, the screen hanging from the ceiling giving an effect of mountain and cloud, all this set in the most beautiful natural wood. It was all very exquisite without being grand. The house seemed to consist of one-storied wooden buildings forming three sides of a square – with a 'go down' or storehouse in the background, where all the valuable possessions of the family were stored, and from which, alas! the European furniture had been brought out for our benefit. Round this European table, on the European chairs, sat ourselves, Nishi, the two Government officials, the two bailiffs, and another official, the Inspector of the provincial schools. With the ease and grace that characterises the educated Japanese gentleman, there was, almost immediately, a lively and intimate conversation – chiefly in the form of question and answer, between Sidney and the bailiffs and the officials – relating to the organisation of agriculture and the management of this great estate.

From this conversation, and also from more private talk with the Government officials, we gathered that our host was the present representative of an ancient family, with some 2,500 tenants, each working from 2½ to 5 acres of land, and also with extensive forests and water rights. The estate was managed by the bailiffs, and these, we understood, were practically selected by the family, and were respon-sible to the family, for the integrity and condition of the estate – the present owner being allowed merely to spend the net income of the estate, after all the necessary expenditure had been incurred. The farmers occupied their land on a customary and hereditary tenure – there were no contracts, and for practical purposes, they could not be disturbed. All rent was paid in rice, and, so far as we could understand, consisted of half the product of the fields, special allowance being made if the remainder were too scanty to support the farmer's family. The usual unit was about 2½ acres, and there was a maximum of 5 acres, beyond which the bailiffs did not permit the land to be monopolised by one family — however large. The landlord had no horses, no cows; and, we gathered, no rice-land in his own occupation — but he had planted an orchard, and in the fruit season, the farmers were invited to come and regale themselves as they chose. There were agricultural shows and agricultural lectures, and the bailiffs' business was to stimulate the improvement of the methods of cultivation, and better the quality of rice or other product.

[SW: We made out that the produce was about £10 per acre gross; of this, the landlord got about £5; but he bore all taxes, national and local, on the land, and these came to about a quarter or a third of *his* receipts. The rent was paid in kind; and the landlord disposed of his share to a dealer, who came round and took it at a price. Ichishima had perhaps 10,000 acres, and a rent-roll of £50,000 a year gross.]

At this point, there was some commotion among the men-servants — and the officials signified to us that our host was approaching. An elderly, aristocratic-looking gentleman, in the Japanese ceremonial costume, with impassive face, drooping eyelids, and extremely modest and humble expression appeared, and, with many bows to every person, and with a shy attempt to shake hands with us, was at last induced by the Government officials, after motionings and bows, to take the head of the table. After some ceremonial greetings, the conversation relapsed into the hands of the bailiffs and the officials. Sidney asked our host whether he had been to Europe — [and] was answered, in dignified tones, that he had not been himself, but had sent many students to Germany. He signified that he had had prepared a Japanese meal for us, and offered Sidney a bath (which Sidney politely refused). Then, he again disappeared into his own apartments. As we were sitting at the table, we saw some of the ladies of the house peeping at us through the trees — but, from first to last, no woman came on the scene. Apparently, our host is constantly travelling to Tokyo and back — ostensibly, on the business of a Member of the Upper House, but really, we were told, in the company of favourite *geishas*. He struck us as a 'dummy', with the fine manners of an ancient aristocrat, and with the morals of an Eastern gentleman — farther West than Japan!

After the most exquisite meal (over which our host presided), served on the mats in purely Japanese style, we were accompanied ceremoniously to the entrance by our host and his bailiffs. We trotted off in our *jinrickshas* for another two hours, across country to the railway station, where we took the train for three hours to the villa of a humbler country gentleman — a Member of the Lower House. This villa stood in a Japanese garden overlooking the plain of rice-fields; the little village, owned by Mr. Takahashi [Koi], nestling round it. It was a modest little Japanese abode, where our host entertained his friends, about a mile away from his own home. Here, we were waited on by two young nephews of our host, and he himself gave instructions as to all the domestic details. He was a simple, kindly gentleman, managing his own estate, and quite as incapable of governing the country as our grander host of the earlier part of the day. He had prepared an elaborate account of all his relations with his 350 tenants, and he told us that he was now devoting himself, almost exclusively, to developing agricultural co-operation, or rather, the agricultural Friendly Society that Sidney will describe presently. After a European meal, on [a] table and with chairs, we all squatted on the ground and wrote axioms and poems, in English and Japanese characters, as mementoes of our visit. The whole of the proceedings were most easy and unembarrassed, largely owing to the gifts of our interpreter, and we intermingled chaff and talk about the customs of England and Japan.

In the morning, we were taken by our host to see the homes of different grades of farmers – which had been carefully prepared to look their best. Each house was divided into two parts – one level with the ground, the other the usual low platform: the kitchen and storehouse, with its mud floor and wooden beams, upon which were piled the boxes of straw-covered stores of rice, with its hollow cooking-hole round which the children were sitting, with its bath and wash-tub: and, on the higher level, the matted living- and sleeping-room, divided by sliding screens, with their family shrine, cupboards, and little family belongings. The shrines had been thrown open for our inspection, and one of these was resplendent in its newness of paint and gilt, the farmer being very prosperous, and having bought a larger and more magnificent one, quite lately, as a visible proof of his prosperity. These farm folk looked kindly, shrewd people, with submissive expressions – they treated their landlord with great reverence, and he, in his turn, bowed extensively, and prostrated himself before the family shrine. One farmer owned the land on his own, and had a cultivator under his control. Outside the gardens, the whole village was assembled to look at us – all smiling and curious, but quite polite.

The impression of this village life, with its ancient customs, and closely knit mutual obligation between members of families, tenant and landlord and fellow inhabitant, with its friendliness, gaiety and social ease, is extremely pleasant. And the new order, whilst it seems to have done little to shake the old, has added to it the primary school, new methods of agriculture, better police and better sanitation. It is from these village communities that the innumerable Buddhist temples draw their funds – the peasants saving up their little profits on the year's

produce, and pouring them out lavishly in pilgrimages and subscriptions to [the] far-off temples of Kyoto, Koyasan, and the Shinto temples
of Ise. But there is also an organisation for more material thrift – of
which the following is a brief description.

[SW→] There is evidently a widespread system of Friendly Society
in Japan, of a curious kind. The philanthropist who entertained us at
Niigata, a man of some means of his own, was the principal official, at a
small salary, of such a Society for Niigata Province, having 45,000
members drawn from all classes, but principally, from the peasant
cultivators and small retailers. Each member paid one sen a day (a
farthing), until he had accumulated a given sum (query, 20 yen = 40/-)
– earning interest, meanwhile, at a low rate. When that sum was
reached (? in about five years) he could either withdraw the sum, with
its interest: or leave it as an ordinary deposit, at a higher rate of
interest. In addition, the Society provided medical attendance in
sickness, loans in need, benevolent gifts in any calamities or losses,
the use of a large system of circulating book boxes, reading rooms and
reference libraries (including English books and '*The Times*') at its
principal centres, and apparently, other useful features (such as lectures
occasionally). When asked how all this was paid for, our philanthropist
explained that it was done, partly by the difference between the
interest given by the bank and that credited to the depositors, partly
by the free services given by the doctors.

On Mr. Takahashi's estate, there was either a branch of this, or else a
similar local society, which seemed to have, in addition, the beginnings
of a co-operative society, by which the members who were peasant
cultivators bought seed, and other necessaries, at wholesale cost price.
This combination of Friendly Society, Loan Society, Co-operative
Society and Benevolent Society, seems long to have been a feature
of Japan, as there is an elaborate description of an analogous
organisation in the *Proceedings of the Asiatic Society of Japan* for January
1894, by one Garrett Droppers, under the name of Hotoku, as having
been established by Ninomiya [Sontoku], a remarkable administrative
reformer and philanthropist (1787–1856);[62] and there seems to be a
monthly magazine describing them since 1892. Whether these societies
are all of the same nature, or of different kinds, we cannot ascertain. It
seems worth while getting a detailed monograph upon them by some
Japanese student.

Note. We learn that (naturally) the rate of fire insurance on the
flimsy Japanese houses and their contents is very high. Our guide said
he had insured his belongings for 1000 yen, £100, at a premium of
between 7 and 8 yen (14/- to 16/-), which contrasts with 1/6 to 2/- in
England.[63]

[BW: The family is still the unit of agricultural Japan, and the head of the family is still both the autocrat, and the minister, of the family party. The eldest son inherits his father's property or occupation. But if he should prove hopelessly unfit, he is removed by the family and the village, and another representative of the family takes his place. The women are subordinate helpmates to the men – they are living on the most free and easy terms with the men, and their expression, though submissive, is happy and easy. In small houses and shops, the wife often looks the better of the two, and quite clearly, takes the lead. There seems, at any rate in the seven months of summer weather, an untiring industry with no appearance of strain. All this makes the contrast of agricultural Japan with urban Japan very ugly.][64]

KYOTO JAPAN 14th SEPT[r] 1911

We have just completed a ten days' tour of extraordinary interest in the provinces of Nagano and Niigata, in the north-west of Japan – already described in detail – during which we were, for ten days, without seeing a single European or American: living entirely in Japanese hotels, among Japanese people; passing our whole days with our excellent interpreter, in the company of Japanese officials, philanthropists, landlords and managers of institutions; seeing schools of various grades, orphanages, Friendly Societies, factories, banks, and the agricultural organisation in two populous provinces (having over three millions of inhabitants), having no foreign population except half-a-dozen missionaries (who were all absent on their long summer holidays), and an isolated American businessman or two, whom we never met. Then, by two all-day railway journeys – taking [in], by the way, the large manufacturing city of Nagoya, with its great feudal castle, and cotton and porcelain factories, and population of 300,000 – to the ancient capital of the country, a city still of 500,000 population, now becoming largely an American tourist resort, with English spoken, and English advertisements on the house fronts.

We have been charmed with the agricultural population and its organisation, including the large amount of petty manufacturing and retailing that goes with it. The extraordinary excellence of the intensive hand-cultivation of the great rice-fields; the simple social democracy; the picturesque family piety of the household shrine and village temple, whether Shinto or Buddhist; the excellence of the provincial officials, and their free and easy intercourse with all classes, from the great landlord or banker down to the peasant; the practical freedom of the villager in his daily life; the patriarchal relationship with

Plate I A photograph inscribed in Beatrice Webb's hand, 'Our Guide – Nishi'. The original is mounted in the second of the three Asian travel diary work-books opposite the opening entry, in Sidney Webb's hand, 'Kyoto Japan 14th Sept[r] 1911'. *Mss Diary*, Volume 30, f.1 (© *The London School of Economics and Political Science*).

the resident landlord, with his customary produce-rents, his recognised obligation to look after the material interests of his peasant tenants, and his free and easy intercourse with them; the perfect order and safety of the whole country-side; and, in spite of incessant work during the summer months, and of a universal hard manual toil for men and women alike, the essential civilisation of the whole people. One could never have believed that a country of peasant-proprietors and small rent-paying tenants, of petty retailers and family handicrafts-men — in short, of home industries and *'la petite culture'* — could present such a pleasing picture. And with it, there goes a centralised Government of remarkable efficiency; with abundant, and apparently quite good, primary schools; a constant and prompt expenditure on keeping up the roads and bridges; some beginnings of medical and sanitary service; good post, telegraph and telephone services; an ever-extending railway and a very efficient police, without sign of oppression or tyranny. On the other hand, there is heavy taxation, direct and indirect, accompanied by an enormous rise in prices; there is very little done for secondary and higher education; there is evidently no desire to teach people to think, and a steady repression of unpopular opinions.

Meanwhile, capitalism is bringing in 'the new industry' on a large scale, without any safeguards. The oil-fields, the paper-mills, the cotton factories, the silk-spinning mills, and, I am told, the coal-fields of the southern part of Japan, are a serious blot on the landscape. The large industrial towns, with their unorganised proletariat, their 'slums', and their lack of municipal amenities, present a far less pleasing spectacle than the agricultural villages. The question is: will Japan learn how to prevent the degradation of the standard of life in time to obviate the growth of a demoralised working-class?

At Nagoya, we went over a cotton-spinning mill, employing 1300 hands, 700 of them living in a boarding establishment of the employ-ers. The girls were said to be taken as young as 12 (by our reckoning, 11); and apparently, much younger. They had to be recruited all over the country, by employment agencies, as few girls would enter from the town itself (a bad sign). The employer complained that they would not stay permanently, but were always leaving after a few years. The work was ring-spinning, on ring-frames made by Platt of Oldham. The cotton was mostly got from India. The yarn was woven at Osaka, etc., mostly for export to China and Korea. The women were said to earn, on an exact average of the preceding month, 30.5 sen per day (= 7½d). They were charged 8 sen per day (2d) for board and lodging, on which the firm purported to spend (including doctor, etc.) 10 sen per day (2½d).

The boarding-house was an absolutely new one (doubtless shown to us for this reason), of the most improved construction. It consisted of a series of blocks enclosed within a wall, having only one entrance, guarded by a permanent gate-keeper. The girls' rooms were large, light, airy and scrupulously clean. They were occupied, ten or twelve in a room of as many mats, practically continuously, by the two shifts. There was a doctor's dispensary, and hospital quarters. An upper floor, near the entrance, was devoted to the parents or other people who might come to visit the girls, and were there put up free of charge. The dining-room, kitchen, and recreation room, were spacious and excellent. Altogether, it was as favourable an example as could be given. The mill worked continuously, day and night, except that it was said to stop for four days a month (Sundays, but not any *fifth* Sundays in a month). The girls worked for twelve hours, day or night, with three intervals of fifteen minutes for rest, during one of which they took a meal, the other two meals, apparently, being outside the twelve hours. Thus, they worked 11¼ hours per day, or 67½ per week, if they really got Sunday off; and 78¾ if they did not. The daily average wage was said to have risen from 16 sen to 30½ sen in the thirteen years that the factory had been established; but whether by improved output, or increased rate of pay, or both, was not clear. The factory was now combined with a dozen others, at Osaka, Tokyo, etc., in a large company or combination (one of two or three such in Japan). It was clear that the girls were practically confined to the premises, and spent their whole life in working, sleeping and eating; and that they were virtually sold to that life by their parents at a tender age (though the employer declared that no money passed on the contract being made).

In Kyoto, we found ourselves tired, and limp in the heat, and bound to spend the first day or so in resting, in the very comfortable Miyako Hotel. Our first expedition proved to be to the Doshisha College, a Christian foundation started 30 or 40 years ago by an enthusiastic Japanese, who got money from American philanthropists.[65] One of the leading professors had been a student of The London School of Economics 9 years ago; and he carried us off. The place now consists of a large boys' school, a smaller girls' school, and a still smaller college, principally in theology, which is aspiring to university rank. We saw most of the girls' school boarding-house (where seventy girls were), at which the 'tea ceremony' was performed for our benefit (etiquette and 'tea ceremony' formed an important part of the girls' curriculum). We thought the 'tea ceremony' a silly business, with its purely arbitrary conventions and elaborate formalities, leading to nothing but a sip of tea. (We were told that the intellectual standard of the girls was low.) On the other hand, there was a competent

American woman as lady superintendent, a nice-looking Japanese matron in charge of the girls' dormitories, and a number of qualified women as teachers, with the male professors coming in for special subjects — altogether, a well-organised staff, in marked contrast with the Government middle schools that we had seen.

The extraordinarily charming simplicity of the Imperial Palace, with its gorgeous contrast in the Shogun's Castle, which reminded us of the Italian Renaissance (a century later than in Europe),[66] will remain in our memories.

We had an interesting visit to the Buddhist College attached to the gorgeous Nishi-Honganji temple.[67] We had a letter of introduction from Viscount Suematsu to the Lord Abbot, an hereditary personage, Count Otani [Kozui], allied by marriage to the Imperial family, a great traveller and archaeologist, said to have vast designs for a universal Asian Buddhist Church. A telephone message to him brought rather an impolite refusal to see us; but the despatch of our introduction, with a formal letter, brought a profuse telephonic apology, and the visit on his behalf of the President of the Buddhist College, and arrangements for a visit to the College and temple. There, we were received in state, and shown over by a series of ecclesiastical professors in ceremonial garb, and an interview with a younger brother and future successor of the Lord Abbot, also a Count Otani. The apartments were most splendidly decorated with the best Japanese (old) paintings we have seen.

The priestly professors looked kindly, educated men, several speaking English and acquainted with Europe; but not men of great ability or distinction. The students (some 300) seemed well taught. The young Count looked a man of piety and simple charm, but not able, or worldly-wise.[68] About the Lord Abbot himself, who was too busy to see us, there seem to be two opinions: he may be an antiquarian scholar, or he may be an ambitious ecclesiastical statesman.[69] As these were reputed to be the ablest and best of the Buddhist priests in Japan, we did not form a high opinion of the chances of a Buddhist revival.

We learnt that they maintained a few schools of their own for boys and girls, unaided by the Government, but that they could make no attempt to influence the mass of government teachers, many of whom were said to be Buddhists, by extraction at any rate.

Another development of Buddhism we saw in the charming and enthusiastic Dr. Kobayashi, one of the leading doctors in Kyoto. We heard of him from our guide as an intellectual Buddhist, and wrote to him opening up acquaintance. He could not come to dinner, but invited us by telephone to come and see him, as it turned out, at his hospital. This proved to be attached to the Toji temple,[70] on the outskirts of the city, the headquarters of the particular Buddhist sect whose holy place at Koyasan we visit next week. The doctor proved to be an eager enthusiast, of the large-eyed, refined, intellectual type of face, with a charming young wife who spoke some English (which he spoke well). He explained that he had had an extensive practice in brain and abdominal surgery, but that he had come to the conclusion that most of the tumours (but not all) were mental in origin, the result of worry and bad thoughts, and that the proper treatment was mental, by 'bromide and religion', as he expressed it.[71] He was an intensely pious Buddhist, and had devoted himself now (he was about forty) to practice at his hospital of some thirty beds, which he had built with the co-operation of the temple and the help of donations. He took in all classes of patients whom he could help, and made no charge, leaving each to put in a common donation-box whatever each chose. Each patient had a separate room, of the flimsy Japanese kind; prayers and religious exercises formed part of the treatment; and rosaries and sacred images were about. At the same time, it was clear that he used all the appliances of medical science, and he said he still operated in extreme cases of cancer, etc; but that he had had great success in getting rid of tumours on which he would once have operated, by merely mental means, and massage by the blind *amma*. He was full of zeal for Buddhism, and stopped to pray before every shrine we passed, in the hospital and outside: but he seemed to have no plans or proposals for Buddhist unity, Buddhist propaganda, spread of Buddhist education or influence, etc. He had heard of Theosophy and Christian Science, and had read some of their books, with sympathy and the characteristic Eastern tolerance of rival manifestations of a common mysticism. (We told him of Edward Carpenter's *Art of Creation*[72] and Bergson's *Creative Evolution*,[73] which he was eager to read.)

He then took us round to the temple itself, where he had arranged to have us shown its treasures, not commonly exhibited. We saw a wonderful collection of ancient paintings and images — notably, a row of five figures in bronze, life-size, each seated on something which looked like a large lotus, supported respectively by an elephant, a hippopotamus, a horse, an ostrich and a swan. Also, a book of ancient pieces of silks, tapestry, embroidery, etc., said to be from 500 to 1000 years old. We then met the Lord Abbot of the Shingon sect, or head priest, who had already been asked by the Governor to arrange for our reception at Koyasan, and who gave us the usual tea and the sweet stuff to take home; a pleasant, but entirely unintellectual man, who looked as if he cared for eating and drinking. Certainly, the doctor's self-sacrificing efforts to advance Buddhism by making it relieve human suffering, will not receive any great assistance from the Buddhist priesthood that we have seen.

We were taken to see the Governor[74] by our zealous professor-friend of the Doshisha College. We had heard tales of this Governor having somewhat unscrupulous dealings with the capitalists (Tramway Co., etc.), which had caused the mayor to resign, and which stood in the way of anyone else becoming mayor. He proved to be a burly, thick-set, jovial sort of ruffian, full of cordial affability, who might well be as he had been described to us. To us, he was friendly enough, though our professor was too poor an interpreter to allow any real intellectual intercourse. He at once agreed to introduce us at Koyasan, and also sent an official with us, to see the local principal weaving-firm, which he wanted us to see. (The prefecture was a very showy new building, only a few years old, exactly like that of a second-rate French town.)

The weaving-firm proved to be one carrying the art to a high pitch. Large designs were being painted, for execution in tapestry for the Hague Peace Tribunal.[75] Beautiful things were in course of weaving on the looms, in most elaborate designs, involving great skill in the weaver. We could get no information of value as to organisation or wages; it was all piece-work: apprentices were taken young and trained, finding themselves virtually bound for life to the firm, which had a monopoly position. We were told that the best men earned 1½ yen per day, and the general run, 70 sen per day (doubtless far higher than the truth). The women got the same piece-work *rates* as the men. Our impression was that the twenty or thirty young weavers in the factory were mainly apprentices; and that the bulk of the work was given out to be done in the operatives' own homes. A whole district in Kyoto seems devoted to this hand-loom silk-weaving.[76]

We also saw the Acting-Mayor and the Assistant-Mayor at the city offices. We gather that the Mayor in all the great cities is a salaried official, much like the German *burgomaster* in position and status. In the largest cities, the salary is 5000 to 10,000 yen a year. He is elected for four years, and often re-elected. The City Council submits three names to the Government, and the Government appoints one of them — usually, we are told, the one to whom the council has given the largest number of votes. If the Council cannot find an approved candidate within a given time, the Government itself appoints. The Mayors were said to come principally from the bureaucratic class (one had been, at one time, Minister for Education in the Cabinet, but they were not often politicians). The late Mayor of Kyoto had resigned — some said on account of differences with the Governor, some said because of the troublesome conduct of the Town Council, and some again said the main reason had really been his own ill health.

We gathered that the city had to get express Government sanction for loans. It was said to be free to govern as it chose, and its maintenance budget needed no Government sanction, so long as the expenditure necessitated only taxation below a fixed limit. When this limit was passed, the budget needed Government sanction. We elicited that this limit *had* been passed in Kyoto and nearly all large cities; so that, one way or another, there was very full Government control, and little effective autonomy. Kyoto had just raised a loan of forty-five million francs *in Paris*, for tramway extensions, canalisation for water and power, etc., which the city was keeping in its own hands, though an existing tramway company had an unexpired concession, and was not yet bought out. The taxation seemed to take the form — as we gathered, exclusively — of *'centimes additionnels'* to the three Government taxes on land, on business enterprises, and on income. Asked how it was settled *where* a rich capitalist *rentier* was taxed for income, they said where he had his real domicile; and they admitted that there was undue concentration of great incomes in Tokyo, to the loss of other places. The Council is elected for four years: it meets only occasionally; it appoints an executive of about nine members (Aldermen), with whom the Mayor, and his two paid assistants, sit.

We saw a good deal of the Government University, which has, in all its faculties, over 1300 students, under a paid President (£500 a year), Baron Kikuchi,[77] a Cambridge wrangler,[78] sometime professor, then Minister of Education, now administering this University — a man of the type exactly of Peterson of McGill[79] or Rucker of London[80] — well-acquainted with European and American developments, 'official', and conservative in tendency. The University library has lately been dispersed among a splendid range of forty or fifty rooms, for professors and their students, so that each subject was really accessible. It was characteristic that a score of our books and pamphlets, great and small, were produced for us to inscribe our names in. He gave us a Japanese dinner, to meet a dozen professors and suchlike, in the house of a local millionaire (one Murai, now a banker in Tokyo, once a small tobacco shopkeeper in Kyoto, who has built himself a villa here, in the most extravagant style, in the worst possible European taste, which he seldom inhabits, and apparently lends to the University and others for such entertainment purposes).[81] The professors are Government officials, paid, apparently, only £200 a year about [and] evidently much in subjection. One who spoke against the family had been severely dealt with, but this was said to be the only case, and Baron Kikuchi claimed that they had *'lehrfreiheit'*[82] within the University, though they must not engage in politics outside. But evidently, they feel great difficulty in doing anything that the Government dislikes. Japanese history, for instance, cannot be frankly and scientifically dealt with, especially as regards the earliest times, because the current myths as to the divine descent of the Emperor must not be disturbed.

The ablest of the professors in the range of economics, law, etc., came separately to see us (Toda), an attractive and well-informed young man of thirty or so, who had studied in Germany, and spoke German fluently, besides reading English. He said the professors might be described as mostly '*katheder-socialisten*'[83] in opinion; that social problems were much under discussion; that the gravest of all was that seen by Malthus; that Japan could not increase its supply of food, and was pressing hard on the production, this causing a continuous serious rise in [the] price of rice; that it was difficult to import food, as other rice did not suit the Japanese taste, and perhaps stomach; that any neo-Malthusian practices would be violently against Japanese ideas; that this made the industrialisation of Japan an inevitable and patriotic duty.[84] He confirmed our impression as to the evils of the factory system for girls and women; and spoke in grave terms of the bad result on them, physically, in causing phthisis, etc., and morally, in spoiling character, when they returned to their country homes (as they all did) in order to marry. But the difficulty was that the factories could get no local labour, and they were able to show that, in no other way could they carry on the industries indispensable for Japanese progress. He saw no other remedy but steady work for improved factory legislation, against which the capitalist forces were strong, and had influential official support. He said, however, that what the factories did for the girls, in the way of wholesale provision of food, etc., and personal arrangements of different sorts, amounted to a quite substantial addition to the nominal wages. He said that there was a tendency for the customary relations between landlord and peasant to be replaced by money contracts and money rents; and for the peasant owner to lose his land, which was bought up by the new capitalists. (But we could not make out whether this was more than apprehension.) He said there was *no* tendency visible towards any agriculture on a large scale.

We had to lunch, Mr. and Mrs. Phelps, of the American missionary type, who have been here for nine years as secretary for the Y.M.C.A., started from America but now completely in Japanese hands, and under control of the influential Japanese: as we gather, to no small extent, even governmental. They confirmed our impressions as to the evils of the factory system; and added strong condemnation of the smaller factories and workshops where boys and girls were boarded and lodged in promiscuity, with very grave results on character, and the production of great numbers of illegitimate babies – the local maternity hospital being said to deal with hundreds of such cases. Slum life in the great cities was said to be very bad and degrading. The Y.M.C.A. is apparently run mainly as a club for young men, with billiards, evening classes in English and other useful subjects, reading rooms, lectures, etc., and it naturally attracts hundreds of clerks, etc., some of whom get converted to Christianity in the process.[85]

There seems an opening for a Christianity of a sort which should go in for social reform on an ethical basis, dropping its literal belief in impossible happenings, with an attitude of tolerance towards Shintoism and Buddhism as being only other manifestations of the same mysticism. But whether any Christian, Protestant or Catholic, can rise to this height of comprehensiveness, is more than doubtful. The missionaries of whom we have heard, or whom we have seen, cannot forgo the insistence on the disuse and destruction of the family shrine – they can find no useful significance in what they condemn as 'the worship' of ancestors, though in what way this amounts to more than a quite useful respect and reverence for the past generations, for the family, for the race, and for those larger expediencies which are embodied in social custom, we could not discover.

We went out to another suburb, to a great silk-spinning mill, said to have ideal conditions on Japanese lines.[86] This is one of a score of mills in Tokyo, Osaka and elsewhere, owned by one great company, with nearly two millions sterling capital, and some 15,000 operatives in all. It spun both cotton and silk, and also wove cotton. In this particular mill, which did only silk-spinning, there were some 1300 operatives, of whom some 800 were female, and of these, over 700 were boarded and lodged. The firm also provided separate houses and flats for a large number of its married workmen. The Manager, who had been twenty years in the service, was evidently a man of sincere philanthropy, who was devoted to the well-being of his operatives, on the necessary capitalist lines. The factory was full of excellent machinery, imported from England and Germany; run by steam made by coal fuel. The machines were fenced, and the operatives in the dusty processes wore guards over mouth and nostrils. We noticed that the Assistant Managers, Engineers, etc., were often graduates of Kyoto University, or high technical schools.

The 900 female operatives were nearly all under twenty, some as young as twelve or thirteen. They were engaged by contract for three years, apparently at any age that they could be got, entirely from the country. For the first three months, they had half-time in school subjects (perhaps as a way of breaking them in to the twelve-hour day). There was here no night-work, as the silk-spinning was said to suffer in quality if done at night. The twelve-hour day had three breaks for rest, two of a quarter of an hour each, and it was mentioned with pride, that, at the middle break of half an hour, the machinery actually stopped (unlike other mills). The work was all paid by the piece, but there appeared to be a good deal of collective piece-work by groups. The earnings for each day were placed on a card attached to each machine, showing the deductions for bad work. The very best girls made as much as 60 sen per day (1/3), and the average was about 28 sen (7d). The girls were said to be allowed, quite freely, to terminate their service, if they wanted to go home for any family reason, and it was clear that they did not stay much after its close. (We saw from the magazine that the firm publishes for all its 15,000 operatives, that it recently made a distribution of medals for long service; and ten women only were found to gain the award for ten years service, and only a few hundred the smaller award for five years service, out of this enormous staff.)

The girls' living-rooms were certainly excellent in every respect, with large looking-glasses, extensive baths, clean and decent sanitary arrangements. The firm ground its own rice (as the only way to check adulteration), and supplied it to the outdoor operatives at wholesale cost price. It also conducted a store for the girls' little toilet necessaries, etc., and an extensive shop for [the] supply of groceries, etc., to the outdoor operatives, run so as just to cover cost. The girls paid 8 sen a day (2d) for their board, etc., which cost the firm 12 sen (3d). There was a nice little hospital and dispensary, and excellent rooms for the families to visit the girls and stay (some *were* staying there). The married men's houses were built in blocks, two stories high, Japanese-style, open back and front. For a dwelling of two small rooms, including water and electric light free, the rent was 1½ yen (3/-) *per month*, which is certainly very cheap. The men were said also to be engaged in a three-year contract, perhaps to prevent strikes.

The dark side of this philanthropically-run mill was (1) the twelve-hour day, less one hour for rest and meal, with only two days in each month as holiday; (2) the virtual bondage of the young girls for three years, away from their families; (3) the lack of superior women superintendence — there was, over these 700, only a young woman of 25, an ex-teacher of peasant class — Cadbury or Rowntree[87] would have had a lady of 40, of character and experience, at a high salary, with two or three assistants; (4) the 'gassing-room', where young girls were working at a temperature of 100°, amid innumerable gas flames giving off sulphurous fumes — they were said to be there continuously.

(At Kyoto, we say farewell to Mrs. and Miss Fairchild, whom we found here, and who stay on here, before visiting a son who is an Assistant Attorney-General in Manila.)

[OSAKA]

Our two days at Osaka (the Manchester of Japan,[88] with a population exceeding a million and a quarter, and increasing at the rate of 15,000 a year) were devoted chiefly to factories, slums and municipal institutions. This flourishing industrial city, with its 5000 factories, its teeming population in crowded, narrow streets, its forest of smoking chimneys, its numerous great stone buildings in 'foreign' style, and, unfortunately, its paupers and its slums, represents the 'new industrialism' of Japan in its most extreme form. It is remarkable for its energetic and 'progressive' municipal government, which has constructed great harbour works, runs municipal trams and ferry boats, gets a considerable revenue from the gas and electric-light concessions, has an extensive main drainage system and water supply, a daily collection of house refuse, municipal cemeteries and crematoria, and extensive secondary and technical educational institutions.

Arriving in the evening, we were whirled in *jinrickshas* through miles of crowded, narrow streets, apparently escaping collisions by the narrowest shaves — including one long street[89] of lighted shops, about as wide as the Burlington Arcade, over a mile long, with two-storied houses, often joined by awnings, with every conceivable article of dress and food and literary and scientific and domestic need, wholesale, retail, and for export — a curious combination of Regent Street and Cheapside and Wood Street and the Middle Row of Covent Garden with a dash of the New Cut, but always coming back to the recollection of Burlington Arcade with the roof off; or a greatly prolonged 'Merceria' of Venice — without horses or other vehicles than *jinrickshas*, bicycles and hand-carts, and with a constant throng of foot-passengers, of every age and class and both sexes. This struck us as one of the great streets of the world, a brilliantly-lighted narrow thread of busy life through the prevailing gloom of night in a Japanese city.

In the morning, S.W. went off with the Secretary to the municipality, an alert ex-student of The London School of Economics, to see one of the largest cotton factories (doing both spinning and weaving). This did not differ much from those seen elsewhere — the same very extensive premises, boilers, ring-frames and looms from Lancashire, all apparently in high perfection; the same day-and-night running, with two shifts; the same twelve-hour day, with two breaks (of fifteen minutes) for rest; and one (of thirty minutes) for dinner. The machinery was said actually to be stopped for the middle break. There were four holidays a month allowed. There were the same dull, apathetic and almost brutalised operatives, the men in the blowing-room, full of cotton dust, working nearly naked for 50 sen (1/- per day), the female operatives said to earn, at piece-work on an average of the whole, 35 sen (83¾d) per day. There was the same arrangement for recruiting labour all over Japan, for terms of three years, and the same complaint that they would not continue in the service, or even, very often, complete their term. Half-a-dozen new hands were just arriving, with their '*kori*' (baskets); girls and women, of any age from 11 to 25, who were put to learn for three months at 15 sen a day, with some provision for elementary school instruction. Very few boys seemed to be employed; and we gathered that most of the men were taken on as adults, having spent their youth in other occupations. (The firm had once had mule-spinning, but had discarded it for the ring-frame, probably because of the difficulty of getting skilled men spinners.)

The boarding-houses were crowded, dilapidated, untidy, and dirtier than those we saw at Nagoya and Kyoto (which were evidently new and 'model' places). At 10.30 a.m., many of the night-shift girls and women were up and about, playing, talking, cooking food, etc., whilst others were more or less asleep in their midst. We were told there were no hours for quiet or sleep, all being left optional, an arrangement that seems calculated to produce great discomfort and loss of sleep. The 'mother' whom we saw was the same sort of ex-peasant woman, once an elementary teacher of some kind, entirely subordinate to the male officials, and quite inadequate as 'lady superintendent' of hundreds of women and girls. The operatives looked depressed and even squalid. They were charged 9 sen a day for their board and lodging (2¼d), and the firm professed to lose on this, when the dispensary and doctor, the occasional gramophone and lecture entertainment, etc., was included.

The Managing Director deplored the difficulty of getting enough labour, and sufficiently-skilled labour, and expatiated on how much was done for the girls, without success, in inducing them to stay. Even in a city of 1¼ millions, girls could not be got to come to the mill, as a rule. One wonders why it does not occur to these capitalists that it might pay them better to make a decent life for their operatives, transform their two shifts into three, multiply the holidays, and recover something like the freedom under supervision of the family group. There were, a quarter of a mile off, in a squalid new suburb, some crowded blocks of two-storied houses for the married operatives, swarming with uncared-for children, one water-tap stand-pipe for ten families. The firm let these four-roomed dwellings for 2.10 yen (2/2) per month, if the man alone worked for them; *running down to no rent at all*, if all the family, or four or five members, worked in the mill. The commercial rent for such dwellings in [the] outskirts of Osaka was said to be 8 yen a month (16/-).

In the late afternoon, just before the sudden oncoming of night, we went 'slumming'. We had asked to be shown the very poorest quarters; and, after much telephoning between municipality and police stations, we three (S.W., B.W., and guide), escorted by the Municipal Secretary and the principal 'charity' (?) official, were taken by two police officers in uniform with gilt swords (looking like a Naval Captain and Lieutenant), in procession of seven *jinrickshas*, through miles of dimly-lit, narrow lanes, descending here and there to penetrate on foot into back premises in narrow alleys, unpaved and filthy. We entered dark rooms in which families of seven or eight resided, for which they paid 8½ sen rent *per day* – said to be collected each day by the house owner. A tiny room, a two-mat room, six or eight feet square, occupied by a *jinricksha* man and his wife only, cost only 6½ sen a day (1½d). The husbands were described as labourers, and were said to earn 40 sen or 50 sen a day. One woman, found at home-work, was plaiting straw sandals at 3 sen (¾d) a pair. These dwellings, with their dirt and garbage, and foul gutters, evidently full of fleas, dark and destitute of all conveniences, struck us as being as bad as anything in London. On the other hand, there was far less offensive smell than in a London slum, probably because there were fewer piles of dirty rags, and generally less filthy furniture, as well as cleaner bodies.

One such house had a bath (of the wooden tub kind), big enough to squat in up to the neck, [and] with [a] place for fire underneath, *outside* the front door, on the roadway. There was a bath-house, not far off, where a hot bath could be got for 2 sen (½d). And, owing to the absence of brick walls and glass windows, there was constant ventilation; however, they were much *darker* than a London slum. The worst feature was the neglected state of the children. Education is not compulsory until six, and there is hardly any provision for admitting younger children – so that, until six at least, they are in the gutter. This means that there are in school hours, twice as many children to be seen in such a slum as in London. We learnt (and verified it by the public statistics) that nearly 4000 children were exempted by the police from school attendance (between 6 and 12), on account of 'poverty'. These children went out to work, at match-box-making or packing, or some similar occupation, earning 6 or 8 sen a day. We find that, whilst a good labourer can earn 85 sen or 1 yen a day, and can manage to maintain a family even at the high price of rice, a weak or inferior labourer, or one who is ill, may only get 40 or 50 sen; and this is not enough to buy rice (at 27 sen per *koku*)[90] for more than three persons, apart from rent, clothing, etc. The children of 6 or 7 are said to eat as much rice as an adult. There was a marked absence of drunkenness; there were no public-house bars; there was no disorderly conduct. But the people looked much weaker than those of an English slum. The children had many sores, bad eyes, and other signs of neglect. The adults were often suffering from want of sufficient food. Altogether, it was a vision of extreme destitution. The question is, how much is there of it in Osaka?

We were able, next day, to cross-examine on the subject the Secretary to the municipality and the chief officer for charities. They explained that, partly by charitable donations, partly through the collections of a local newspaper, and partly by grant from municipal funds, arrangements had lately been made by which, whenever any case of starvation was found by the police or others, a grant of rice for the family was at once made by the ward office (municipal), to be distributed through the police (national). To their surprise, it had not come to much, as people were ashamed to apply;[91] and the expenditure had only been in the order of 50 yen (£5) per day, representing some 500 families fed (at a sen each). They were now on the point of organising a department of poor relief, comprising institutions for (a) foundlings, (b) orphan children, (c) infirm persons, (d) destitute aged, and (e) sick persons – in short, the general mixed workhouse and relief administration of the English Poor Law, including a labour exchange for the able-bodied! We explained how bad this was, and how we were struggling in England to escape from a mere general relief of destitution as such, in favour of specialised dealings, class by class, with the very beginnings of evil, in order to prevent destitution from settling in. We shall send them the *Minority Report* and *The Prevention of Destitution!*[92] It is interesting to find Osaka in this respect, as in its factory conditions, at much the same point as Manchester a hundred years ago. Will Japan be able to avoid making all the same mistakes that England made?

The Mayor gave us lunch – an able business administrator, formerly a railway official, chosen for this important municipal post nominally by the Municipal Council, but largely, we are told, on the suggestion of the Government. We also saw the Governor, who had only just reached here from Nagasaki, whence he had been promoted.[93] He spoke English fluently, and proved to be an old friend of Frederic Harrison,[94] E. H. Pember, K.C.,[95] and that generation, whose 'enlightened' liberal individualism he evidently shared. His wife was a Japanese-dressed lady of charm and refinement, with slight knowledge of English.

A charitable institution for the relief of soldiers' widows and children that we visited, turned out to be a place where between 40 and 60 women were maintained and taught rough tailoring (making of uniforms). They were paid 10 sen per day, but charged 8 sen for their board. When instructed, they were said to find situations readily, the skilled workwomen getting about 50 sen (1/-) per day – the mere 'finisher' getting only 10 or 20 sen. (But it appeared that the trade is differently organised from with us, there being four kinds of workers, for machinery, pressing, etc., and the actual 'finisher' being the most skilled and best paid.)

Cross-examination of the Secretary of the municipal Education Dep^t. revealed a number of unexpected facts, viz., (1) that there is no effective compulsion to attend school, as there is no power to compel or to punish negligent parents; (2) that getting the children to school depended on the police exclusively, only those known to the police coming into view; (3) that births are registered where the family happens to have its registered domicile, not where they take place, and that a family may have moved for years before [sic] or without changing its registered domicile: e.g., our guide's parents lived in Osaka, and his domicile is registered there still, and his child's birth was reported there. But for years he has lived at Kyoto, and his child of five, who will soon be liable to attend school, will not be found or searched for at Osaka, and may easily not be known to the police at Kyoto; (4) that, accordingly, there can be no assurance that all children are got on the school-rolls, and this may explain the fact that Osaka has fewer than eight per cent of its population in school, whereas Manchester (with perhaps fifty per cent longer effective attendance) has probably sixteen per cent; (5) that when a child is enrolled, but remains absent for a whole week, an official is said to urge attendance, but nothing more can be done. There is no child census, and no school attendance officer, and no statistics of percentage average attendance to school roll.

The above facts probably help to explain why the published birth-rate of Osaka is only 20 per 1000, actually less than the death-rate. Probably one third of the births, in this newly enlarged city of immigrants from the country, are registered in the country, at the parents' old domicile, if registered at all!

Certified teachers, graduating from normal school, begin at (males) 20 yen a month (£24 a year) (females) 16 yen a month (£19 a year), plus 3 yen a month for residence and 1 yen for clothes. (Tramway conductors get 14 yen a month.) On the other hand, artisans get 1 yen a day, and *jinricksha* men are said to average as much! We were told that the lower salary of the teacher was made up by the public esteem in which he was held!

[BW→] OCT^r 1st [1911]

We have not spent our time exclusively in visiting slums, factories and universities, and in getting statistics of wages and prices! Just as we had a glimpse — but an illuminating glimpse — of the village community of Japan, so we have had a passing vision of the religious life of Japan. In our account of the villages, we noted the family shrine in the home, the village temple in its grove of *cryptomerias*. Usually, the temple is deserted, and the priest, if he exists at all, seems to live wholly remote from the life of the village. If the religious feeling of the Japanese peasant depended on the village temple and the village priest, there would seem to be little of it. How far worship at the family shrine is a living thing in the mass of families, we do not know. But one living religious institution is the pilgrimage to the famous temples and holy places of Japan. And the institution has enormously extended its sphere by the introduction of railways — so that, where hundreds used to wander on foot, now thousands crowd into the third-class carriage, and are carried to and from the holy place of the ancient religions of Shintoism and Buddhism.

When we were at Kyoto, we saw some of these pilgrims, and we heard of the enormous concourse — hundreds of thousands — of pilgrims who had streamed in to the Honganji festival in the spring — contributing largely to the funds of the temple of the western sect — and of the million yen that had been subscribed to the rebuilding of the great temple of the eastern sect.[96] And at [the] Kyoto temples, we had noticed the humblest-looking peasants kneeling inside the rails, whilst the Buddhist priest beat the gong and intoned the *sutras* — a privilege accorded only to those who have contributed £5 or upwards. Quite clearly, if long journeys, and contributions large relatively to income, mean religious feeling, then the Japanese peasant cultivators and little artisans are inspired by religion. Perhaps the unpleasant side of this manifestation is the intense desire shown by the faithful that their names and gifts should be recorded, so that gods and men may give them their due reward, in heavenly appreciation and in human approval. Our guide Nishi declares that the motives are superstitious and not religious — that they are asking for material benefits in this life and not for spiritual communion with the higher life of Buddha in eternity.

But he suggested that we should visit the 'old Japan' of Shintoism and monastic Buddhism — Ise and Koyasan. This visit proved to be of extraordinary interest, and would [have] been of far greater interest, if Nishi had been with us. But alas! our little friend had fallen down his

own stairs (perhaps because he had become accustomed to the rail of
European fashion), and was on his back, incapable. So we started with
another guide – the ordinary commercial article – a common little man,
who could not interpret because he could not understand more than
the daily necessities of life, and who, through over-eating and over-
drinking, puffed and panted uphill, so that we had, in these long walks,
to be perpetually waiting for him. That had its advantages, because it
delivered us from his somewhat jarring presence. And, with all Nishi's
excellences, I am not sure that for a pilgrimage to holy places, he is the
most sympathetic of companions. He is a determined secularist, and
any sympathy he has for Buddhism is because he intensely dislikes
Christianity and its missionaries.

First, we journeyed to Ise – the home of the most ancient Shinto
shrines – a lovely country of sea islands, rocky shore, with a belt of
rice-fields encircling the great primeval groves of *cryptomerias* – these
spreading upwards to a range of almost uninhabited mountains. To
these shrines come literally millions of pilgrims every year, and the
picturesque gabled town of Yamada is almost exclusively made up of
streets and houses and shops for pilgrims. But the Japanese Government has laid a heavy iron hand on these great relics of antiquity – a
hand that has been meant as the hand of protection, offering them
Government support and approval, but which has certainly made the
place look to be dead and barren of religious feeling. As Shintoism,
with its cult of the ancestor, and its adaptation to the cult of the
Emperor and the Emperor's family, suited the political exigencies of
Japan better than the cosmic mysticism of the Buddhist religion and the
foreign tutelage of Christianity, Shintoism has been, to some extent,
'established'.[97] The Government maintains its most famous shrines, and
provides for the education and maintenance of its ceremonial priests. It
has even issued, just recently, an order to all Government schools to
take the pupils every week to worship at the local Shinto shrine! What
this Government patronage has meant at Ise, is that the great groves of
forest trees, and all the approaches to them, have assumed the
appearance of a meticulously-kept national park[98] – with just a flavour
of a barracks or a police office – trophy guns, and white-uniformed
policemen being dotted here and there, as the outward sign that the
spirits of the ancestors of the Emperor, and those of his subjects, are to
watch over the modern imperialism of Japan, in return for the forcible
protection of their shrines. This official garb, imposed on Ise by the
Government of today, is possibly intensified by the old custom of
rebuilding every twenty years, from the most accurate specifications
(handed down by past ages) of the existing building, these ancient
structures – a custom that preserves the ancient form absolutely intact,

but which gives an outward appearance of extreme newness to the actual substance of the shrines.

But, in spite of the trophy guns and of the uniformed policemen in their little police boxes, in spite of the new wood and gilt of the buildings, the Shinto shrines of Ise, with their severely simple forms, in their great groves of *cryptomerias*, through which rush mountain streams with the visions of sea or mountains encircling and enclosing them, are extraordinarily impressive. And the peasant pilgrims, with their naïve expression of devotion — the ceremonial washing in the stream or fountain, the prostration and clapping of hands, the seriousness and sincerity of their expressions, the perpetual lavishing of small coins — all seem to prove the presence of reverence and consciousness of obligation, a true worship of a spirit greater than themselves.

Early in the morning, we sped to the most distant of the Ise shrines, and from thence, walked up Asama-yama to the summit, crowned by a Buddhist temple, a temple which seemed to grow in and out of the tree, stone and water — overlooking, on the one side, the beautiful bay of Ise, [and] on the other, a wide expanse of wooded mountains. Very delightful was this ten-mile walk back, by Toi and the holy rocks, to Yamada.

Two days seeing the sights of Nara and its neighbourhood, and then, a pilgrimage to the great mountain monastery, Koyasan.[99] Exhausting, but interesting, was the long pull up the mountain side, by innumerable tea-houses and tiny shrines, through the great forest and then on to the cup-like table-land, 4000 feet above the sea, in which sixteen temples and their dependencies are situated. Though it was out of the season of peasant pilgrimages, there were groups of pilgrims, some clothed in the ceremonial white, others in sombre or gay attire, old and young — all in a subdued holiday humour — friendly and laughing, but never boisterous or vulgar. All the pilgrims, whether rich or poor, are taken in by the temples, where they are provided with apartments and vegetarian fare, suited to their rank. They pay, according to their ability, a 'contribution' towards the upkeep of the temple, in return for hospitality.

We had an introduction from the Lord Abbot of the Shingon sect to the principal temple — Shojo-Shin-in.[100] Foot-sore and dirty, we were ushered into a set of exquisite rooms looking on to the temple garden, by a young priest. In a few minutes, the head priest, in purple and gold, came to receive us. He was a sullen and suspicious-looking mortal, whose words were hospitable, but whose looks were by no means so — but here, of course, we suffered from the stupidity and commonness of our interpreter. After this head priest had escorted us over the more public parts of the temple, and showed us some of the rare paintings and screens, he suddenly disappeared, leaving us in charge of the young priest and two acolytes. The young priest was pleasant, talked a little English, but he looked somewhat weakly, and evidently had no particular intelligence. As we sat round the European table that had been provided for our meals, discussing the programme for tomorrow, there appeared, from out of one of the innumerable sliding screens, a hairy little man, with great wondering eyes and eager manner, in academic dress, talking broken English with more speed than lucidity. The young priest introduced him as Professor Abbé, the lecturer on Buddhist history in the college for Buddhist priests at Koyasan.

For the next twenty-four hours, this little man was always about us. He was overflowing with enthusiasm for the 'New Buddhism', which he explained was indistinguishable from the 'New Christianity'. He belonged to the same large-eyed type as the Buddhist medical man — and had the same eager, simple mysticism — intensely emotional, but with little capacity for scholarship or intellectual criticism. He brought us various volumes of rather shoddy stuff, written by quasi-Christian missionaries, to prove that the great Buddhist saint — Kobo Daishi — (who had founded the monastery) had associated with Christian missionaries in China. He himself gesticulated his faith in the great truths underlying all religions equally. For practical purposes, he preached the same modernist doctrine as Sir [SW: Oliver] Lodge,[101] Father Tyrrell,[102] Dr. R. J. Campbell[103] or Edward Carpenter, but he had neither the powerful personality of some of these preachers, nor the subtle and scholarly thought of the three of them, who are really original thinkers. If his purpose was original to himself, his method was the method of the illiterate, nonconformist minister. He had a kindly contempt for the self-absorption and aloofness and narrow-mindedness of the monks of Koyasan, and deplored the lack of character and intellect in the Buddhist priests generally throughout the country.

As we wandered through the temples and the great [SW: cemetery] of Koyasan, as we lay on the mats of our beautiful room — open on three sides to the temple garden and the forest trees — we wondered whether Buddhism had any future in Japan, and if not, whether Christianity can take its place?

Quite clearly, these pilgrimages, combining as they do the holiday pleasures and the religious emotions of the bulk of the Japanese working-class of small cultivators and artisans, are not likely to be given up. Will the holiday element gradually kill the religious element? Today you see touching scenes of whole families — grandparents, parents and children — in honest, homely worship before the Shinto shrine or the Buddhist temple. Very beautiful is the expression on some of the faces, of genuine piety, of love, of awe — even in quite young faces. But these faces are nearly always the faces of humble folk. At the popular shrine of [SW: Nara], parties of young clerks in European dress, with perhaps one or two *geishas* and tea-house attendants, will come up with jaunting air — the young men will lift their hats and nod perfunctorily, the girls will giggle and clap their hands and sometimes throw a tiny coin; and then, they will all turn away, obviously taking these temples as a succession of tea-houses.

Will this attitude become gradually the rule, and the other, the exception? And if all the old reverence and sense of domestic and social obligation, which have been associated for centuries with Shinto shrines and Buddhist temples, falls away, is it possible for Christianity to fill the gap? Certainly not the Christianity of Christendom — Catholic or Protestant. If the [SW: rationalisation] of the modern Japanese educated world becomes the attitude of the whole Japanese people, then the myths of Christianity will appear as childishly ludicrous as the myths of Buddhism. And, if all supernaturalism becomes an absurdity, will any new philosophy other than agnosticism or materialism rise to give noble purpose to the life of the individual or the race? Is there any kernel of truth embedded in the somewhat shoddy intellectual eclecticism, but quite genuine emotion and faith in the development of a higher nature in man, of the little Buddhist professor and the enthusiastic Buddhist surgeon?

We rose at the first break of dawn, and, after a splash of water over face and hands, and the donning of some outer garments, we attended 'matins' in the long, low, highly-decorated hall that serves as the chapel of the temple. There were some ten priests — mostly young, so far as we could distinguish their faces in the twilight — kneeling in Japanese-style, all in vestments, and some of them with the scroll of the scriptures. The head priest, in purple and gold, came in a few minutes after 5.30 a.m., and, after various prostrations, seated himself in the low seat before the altar. Then began the monotonous intoning of the 'sutras' — an ugly, nasal chant. To the uninitiated, it seemed like a perpetual repetition of various words or phrases — not always the same words and phrases, [but] simultaneously by all the priests — with occasional intervention by the head priest, either in monologue chant, or by the beating of some instrument — these instrumental sounds being sometimes executed by the priests on either side of him. There was no beauty in the service, nor did the priests seem to be doing more than an *exercise* — mechanically repeated, day by day. The hall, with its beautiful [SW: proportions] and sober but rich ornamentation, gave the scene a weird picturesqueness; but, to the outsider, at any rate, the atmosphere was not devotional.

We have had the same impression of mechanical sounds and movements of an almost terrifying ugliness, executed by dull-looking men, some of them of a very low, sensual type, at all the services of Buddhist temples that we have attended. There may be holy men among the Buddhist priests – there certainly are men of scholarship in the learning of the *sutras* – but these priests do not appear as the leaders of Buddhism. On the other hand, there is certainly a general impression that the majority of priests are not in any way above the average in morality, and are decidedly below the average in practical energy and active intelligence, whilst some, undoubtedly, take advantage of their idleness and the revenues of their temples to live a life of gross dissipation. There are a few women who live the conventual celibate life, in old foundations, presided over in some cases by a lady of the imperial family; but they have no influence and do no practical work – they are simply female priests, whose duty is to attend on the temple, and execute its archaic rites.

'Educated Japanese people think that the race could do without any religion', summed up an able and accomplished official, after a discussion on secular education. This undoubtedly represents the present opinion of the Japanese ruling class, though there are signs of uneasiness at the upgrowth of the hooligan of the big city, and the breaking down of the spirit of unquestioning loyalty to the Emperor. Hence, the rather absurd and insincere order, to all Government teachers, to take their pupils to worship at the shrine of the 'local god'! As the great majority of teachers are secularists, and those who are not are frequently Christians, the order is not likely to be obeyed – at any rate, in the right spirit.

[SW→] MIYAJIMA[104] 16th OCTOBER 1911

Our eleven days in Tokyo (1–12 Oct.) were one perpetual round of receptions and entertainments, almost entirely Japanese, which left us without time, or energy,[105] for writing. A quiet morning at this seaside temple may enable some notes to be set down.

We were entertained by four universities, each demanding a morning's inspection of laboratories and professors, and an elaborate lunch, with speeches and (in three cases) a lecture. The Imperial University (as at Kyoto) was afraid to ask us to speak, but was otherwise most polite. It struck us as suffering somewhat from arbitrary Government control, the President a man of no personality, the professors not men of distinction (with some exceptions), and the few foreign professors (except one German) the usual very third-rate

English and Americans, now retained for languages only. The German, whom we met again later, was an able young man, who taught economic history. There was a large library, enriched by the purchase *en bloc* of several libraries of German professors, and that of Max Muller.[106] It had, of course, a large collection of Japanese books, but it was paying no attention at all to the ephemeral pamphlet and election literature, and it struck us generally as run without intelligence. The lunch was an elaborate affair, in the University's own refectory with the professors, which was part of the old *daimyo*[107] palace. Some fifty professors were present, and pleasant little speeches were made.

Waseda University, a private foundation of Count Okuma's, struck us as much more alive; full of able young Japanese as professors, most of whom had been in Europe and America, and all of them, eagerly 'progressive' in tone. Okuma himself, who gave us lunch, now Hon. President, is a 'grand old man',[108] a courtly old gentleman of seventy, living in a pleasant house and European garden just at the University gates, speaking no English, but eager to entertain all foreigners. His adopted son, who married his daughter, [is] an accomplished and polished gentleman, with European 'finish' on him, [and is] himself teaching English composition in the University (which has, as part of it, a great primary school, a middle school, a commercial school and so on). It has translated and published a lot of books, it had all sorts of societies among its students, it sends a baseball team to America, and generally, is full of 'go'. Among its professors is Abe Isoo, whom we saw something of, and who does not fear to publicly avow himself a socialist.[109] We are inclined to think that Japanese higher education and thought owes much to the freedom of Waseda and other private foundations, with which the Government apparently cannot interfere. (Their income is derived largely from the fees of their very numerous students, and partly from the donations of rich men.) Because it is not only in economics and politics that the Government closely watches the teaching of its professors: even in ancient Japanese history, it is not allowed to question the divine ancestry of the Emperor. And when it was found that a school book had used a term (*brocade*) of the standard of one of the old rival chieftains, which implied that he was actually Emperor, there was a great fuss, and everyone concerned got into trouble. Keio, the third University, also a private foundation, seemed to us to have lost the impulse of its founder (Fukuzawa), one of the inspirers of 'young Japan', a voluminous writer and instructor, who became rich as a newspaper proprietor.[110] It was said to be now resorted to by well-to-do youths who had an expensive standard of living, and who mostly entered their fathers' businesses. There, too, as at Waseda, S.W. lectured to the economic and political students. We

were entertained at lunch in a neighbouring restaurant, where we met a
dozen of the professors, and eight or ten past students of The London
School of Economics. Keio, too, had its primary and middle schools,
resorted to chiefly by the well-off Japanese.

The fourth 'university' was that for women, also a private foundation, built up by the lifelong energy of its President (Naruse) and Dean
(Aso Shozo), with the aid of rich men (including Baron Shibusawa) who
saw the need for women's education.[111] It cannot be deemed of
university rank, and consists really of a great girls' school, from
kindergarten to high school grades, from five to twenty years of
age. Altogether, there seemed to be two or three thousand pupils.
Several hundred were boarders, and the institution, in marked contrast
with the Government middle schools, paid great attention to their
supervision, having responsible women at the head of each hostel (two
of them English women, one an American, and so on). But the men
President and Dean were supreme, and were said to control and
interfere with even minute domestic details. As the institution has to
suit the demands of the rich Japanese families, etiquette and 'tea
ceremony' occupy a large place in the curriculum.

Among other professors, we had to dinner two leading Buddhists,
one (Takakusu) Prof. of Buddhism at the Imperial University,[112] the
other (Inoue)[113] also there, with some similar chair. They were gentle,
courteous, cultivated men; conversant with English books, and past
residents at Oxford. They were both desirous of seeing a Buddhist
revival, but were taking no steps to evoke it, and deplored the lack of
any great personality. We did not gather that the Buddhist priests and
temples did anything with their time and wealth for the benefit of the ·
people. Beyond a few seminaries to prepare for the priesthood, and a
few middle schools which seemed to be recruiting grounds for these
seminaries, they ran no schools, not even Sunday schools. Takakusu
had published a book of fifty-two lessons for Sunday schools, but had
failed to get more than a handful started. They ran no hospitals
(except Dr. Kobayashi's own venture at Toji, Kyoto, already
described); and practically no orphanages or other good works.
These gentle-natured professors admitted all this, and also, that the
priests exercised very little, if any, influence on conduct, with which
they concerned themselves only to the smallest extent. The professors
were interested in the 'Higher Buddhism' and 'Higher Christianity'[114]
speculations, which they were reading and following with open mind;
[but] it seemed to us an uncritical desire to get support for Buddhism
anywhere.

Of socialists, we saw one Katayama, who wrote to us: a journalist,
who had been in America, and who told us that he had been personally

acquainted with nine out of the twelve who were executed. The police had rigorously examined him during four whole days, producing marked extracts from every scrap he had published, but could find no evidence against him. He was an earnest man, not embittered, realising how slow progress must be, and gallantly keeping on, to the extent of his very limited opportunities, under close police surveillance.[115] We saw also Prof. Abe Isoo, of Waseda University, who openly avows himself a socialist, but as he is frankly a man of peace, he has not been interfered with. Also a Dr. Kato, a philanthropic physician in large practice, friend of Abe. We gather, from what we learn, that the real instigator and leader of the dynamite plot was the woman, the so-called wife of Dr. Kotoku, who, finding that phthisis gave her only two or three years to live, determined to make a big effort before she died. She seems to have been rather a crazy anarchist, but of personal influence.[116] She won over various adherents, including an iron-worker who made clumsy bombs, which were to be hurled in succession at the Emperor and the leading statesmen as they passed by at some official function. What is in doubt, is how far (a) *all* the score or so who were condemned were even aware of the plot, and (b) Kotoku himself, with whom she was living, knew or acquiesced in it. It seems clear that she, and a number of the others, were guilty of a design, and of taking overt acts, and thus of high treason by our law, involving [the] death penalty. Perhaps the Japanese Government were too eager to include in the net a number of those whose agitation they feared: perhaps, too, they sentenced too many to death; but it does not seem that they were formally in the wrong. The secrecy and expedition of the proceedings, though contrary to our ideas, do not seem to have been actually against the law or the constitution: and they were apparently thought to be justified by the importance of preventing the people at large becoming aware that such a crime was possible or conceivable. It is, by the way, not known who was the informer. He is believed to have been a certain one of the twelve who were executed! The Government thought it safer to silence even him!

[BW→] We dined with the Mitsuis[117] – the Rothschilds of Japan – at the Mitsui Club, a house of entertainment used by all the members of the firm to meet in and receive friends. This function was curiously 'of the type' of the cosmopolitan financier. When we arrived, a few minutes after seven o'clock, we found a whole bevy of Mitsuis – the Baron, a youngish, effete-looking sort of person,[118] and various other middle-aged or elderly men – all looking the hereditary plutocrats to perfection, with good manners, but without much brains. Standing out from these were 2 or 3 able outsiders – 'partners' who had been called in to do the hard work – [SW: Masuda][119] and [SW: Komuro] are the

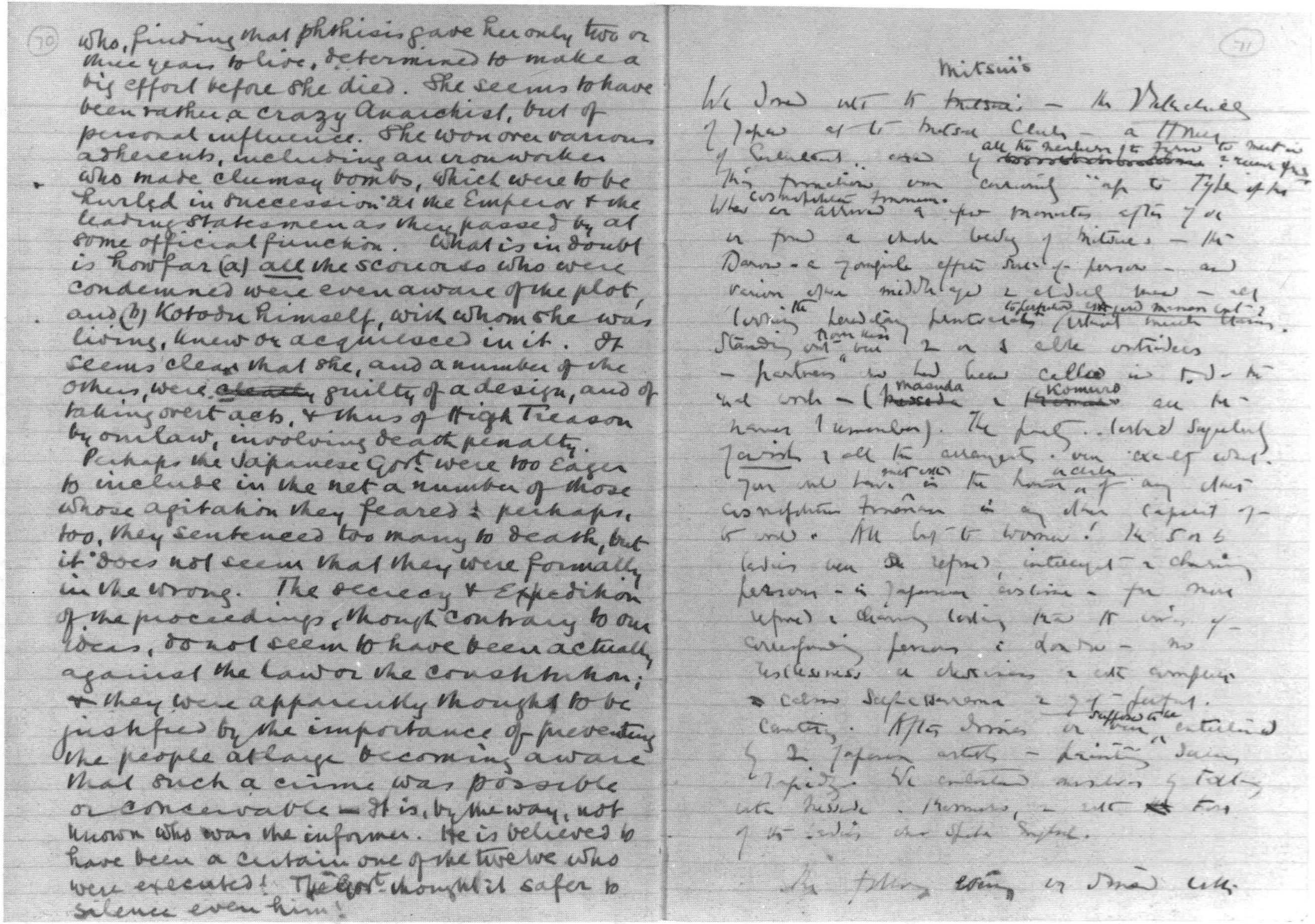

Plate II Holograph diary entry illustrating the Webbs' practice of joint composition. The folio on the left is in Sidney's hand, the continuation on the right in Beatrice's, overwritten in several places by Sidney. *Mss Diary*, Volume 30, ff. 70–1

(© *The London School of Economics and Political Science*)

names I remember. The party looked singularly *Jewish*, and all the arrangements were exactly what you would have met with in the house or Club of any other cosmopolitan financiers, in any other capital of the world.[120] All but the women! The five or six ladies were refined, intelligent and charming persons, in Japanese costume – far more refined and charming-looking than the wives of corresponding persons in London – no restlessness or dressiness; with an air of calm self-assurance, and the quiet friendliness of perfect courtesy. After dinner, we were [SW: supposed to be] entertained by two Japanese artists – painting screens rapidly. We entertained ourselves by talking with Masuda and Komuro, and with those of the ladies who spoke English.

The following evening, we dined with Mr. [SW: Soyeda] – the President of the Industrial Bank – an accomplished and eloquent person – a Cambridge wrangler versed in European culture and politics.[121] At the dinner, we met the fascinating Count [SW: Hayashi], formerly Ambassador in England, and now, a member of the Japanese Cabinet[122] – a sort of Japanese Arthur Balfour,[123] with a detached philosophical mind and delightful manners. After the usual European dinner, we adjourned to the Japanese reception-room and listened to four famous Japanese 'singers' *performing ballads* – I will not say singing, because apparently, the Japanese are incapable of music – a curiously monotonous recitation by two men accompanied by the clanging of the Japanese guitar by two other men – interesting, but hardly entertaining to those who could not understand the words.

We were taken by the indefatigable Baron [SW: Shibusawa] to the new Imperial Theatre – one of his innumerable enterprises – where women, for the first time in Japan, are performing women's parts. The play was a modern one, turning on the conflict of jealousy and filial piety – and was well-acted. We would have preferred to go to an old Japanese play, in Japanese style, but the Baron was determined to show us something that was up to date, and that he had started. The Baron is certainly an extraordinary man – not merely the promoter and active director of many industrial and commercial enterprises [SW: including gold mines in Korea], but the founder and patron of numberless philanthropic enterprises, like the municipal poor house, the women's university, and the new theatre – and the ardent helper of Prince Katsura in his new 'charity organisation' society. He also seems to entertain every distinguished foreigner or company of foreigners visiting Japan.

But we were weary of Tokyo, and we were glad to get away. The city is an ugly wilderness of streets, mostly narrow, of mean shops and low houses, and the life that appears on the surface is without system or artistic charm. 'Society' here is like society anywhere else, and one loses all sense of old Japan: without seeming to be in close touch with the new problems. Also, one runs across Europeans who are always 'crabbing' Japan, and one feels oneself in an atmosphere of hostility. If our visit to Japan had consisted of days spent in the European hotels of Tokyo, Yokohama, Kyoto, and Kobe, we should have been as disappointed with Japan as many other English and Americans, who come away with tales about the 'bad butter' and 'lukewarm tea'. As it is, the only unpleasant impression of Japan itself — and perhaps unpleasant is too mild a word — was that of a visit to the famous [SW: Yoshiwara] — the public quarter of Tokyo.[124] A description of these streets of caged women is to be found in every guide-book. The impression was hideous — a sort of horrible nightmare — a Zoological Garden of Human Beasts being visited by human beasts. Some of the girls were sitting in sullen silence and misery, others were coarsely giggling and noisily soliciting the passers-by. The two men keeping guard on either side of each cage of girls, were of the lowest type of procurer and prostitute's bully. And alas! the majority of those who came to look, and most of whom came to stay, were students, some quite young boys, drawn there by the notoriety of the 'show'. To think that this public quarter was established in Japan [SW: in 1872] on the advice of a Surgeon-General of the British Army! Oh! ye foreigners in Japan, hide your faces in shame!

We lunched with [SW: Robert] Young, of the *Japan Chronicle*,[125] on our way through Kobe. He is, perhaps, the centre of the European hostile criticism of the Japanese Government and the Japanese people. A bitter secularist radical of the extreme individualist type [SW: friend of Bradlaugh,[126] Moncure Conway,[127] J. M. Robertson[128] (cousin of Andrew Young,[129] the pious nonconformist valuer to the L.C.C.)], he can see no good in the Japanese race! If you say they are kindly and courteous, he retorts that is 'mere servility' — the product of the feudal system, or he tells you stories of the naughty words which the children shout in the streets when a European woman goes past. If you remark on their courage and loyalty, he tells you that it is merely ignorance and 'superstition'. The Government is wholly corrupt and the people without spirit. Curiously enough, the only institutions which he was induced to defend from [SW: our criticism] were the factory boarding-house and the public quarter! We parted in a state of veiled hostility between him and us. My only consolation was that he looked quite unhappy in his chronic depreciation of the people among whom he lives, and in whose country he had made his livelihood — an unhappiness which satisfied one's sense of fitness.

SEOUL OCTOBER 19th [1911]

On the shores of the Inland Sea, our last impression of Japan was one of extraordinary grace and beauty — of untiring industry, of sensitiveness and open-mindedness. And there is something pathetic in the impression one gathers of the stress and strain through which the whole Japanese race is now passing. In physical form and constitution, and in their mentality, they seem too slight and frail for the terrific task of taking their part among the great governing races of the world — alone among coloured races — and subject to the hostile criticism of the western peoples. For Japan not only possesses her own country completely, but she is entering into the arduous heritage of a race of colonisers and conquerers. To watch her in this capacity, we find ourselves in Korea, on our way to Mukden. And whilst we travel, we hear the rumblings of the revolution in China, which may mean the break-up of the Chinese Empire, and more work for gallant little Japan.

OCTOBER 25th [1911]

There is perhaps one characteristic of the Japanese race that we have not emphasized sufficiently, because it is not so much a definite quality, as the whole atmosphere of their lives — and that is their capacity for reverence. Children reverence their parents, women reverence men, students reverence their teachers, soldiers reverence their officers, and the layman reverences the official, and the whole race reverences, and even worships, the Emperor. The only persons who seemed to inspire no reverence as such, are women and priests! The woman may be a mother and be reverenced as a parent, the priest may be a teacher and be reverenced as a teacher; but there is, in Japan, no such feeling as the chivalrous reverence for the woman of the Christian gentleman, or the fervent reverence of the priest among Roman Catholic peoples. But, in spite of this, reverence, and a sense of the personal obligations towards the revered person, plays a far greater part in the life of the whole population than in any other part of the world.

It is perhaps a result of this atmosphere of reverence that the Japanese are an intellectually modest race — are always in the attitude of learners. When one thinks of the conceit of the ordinary Englishman, still more of the childish vanity of the American, the modesty and anxiety to improve themselves of the Japanese is very remarkable. With their growing success and prominence, will they lose this quality?

The most unpleasant quality of the Japanese race is one which we had little opportunity to observe directly, but which we heard of from every European resident – their shiftiness, and untrustworthiness, in all pecuniary transactions. Apparently, it is impossible to trust them to fulfil their contracts, and they are always ready to shave off quality and increase price.[130] As for the perpetual accusation of corruption in statesmen and officials, it may or may not be true, to a small or great extent. But there seems to be none of the fruits of corruption as in Russia or America. The goods supplied to the Government, and the work done by the Government, are always good and efficient; and it is difficult to believe that this would be the case, if persons in high positions habitually took bribes. Anyway, as our friend the Norwegian contractor unconsciously testified, those in authority will 'not take bribes from foreigners'! So far as we ourselves are concerned, as mere tourists, we have found the Japanese exceptionally honest – one leaves money and jewellery and odds and ends of clothing about, in a room which cannot be locked, and nothing is ever taken. In fact, a paper yen (2/-), that had been accidently dropped with waste-paper, was returned to me by the boy who swept out the room.

The stories of the incapacity and corruption of Parliament seem to be even more universal, and [the] Japanese themselves are ready to admit the failure of parliamentary institutions [in their present constitution]. One able official told us that parliamentary or party government would be impossible so long as *revenge* was considered an honourable motive, because, without some respect and consideration for opponents, party government was impossible! But he explained that, unless the Government was prepared to prohibit all the literature of old Japan, revenge would still be accepted by public opinion as a legitimate feeling. This seems almost fantastic to us. But the kind of crime that exists in Japan seems to bear out this characterization. The same official, and others too, were strong in their apprehension that Japan was producing an educated proletariat, and that it would be impossible to find occupations for the 100,000 of simultaneous university undergraduates.[131] Possibly it is this thought that impels the statesmen of Japan to extend their dominion beyond the sea – certainly, China could absorb countless active, open-eyed, self-controlled little Japanese men as its ruling class in government and industry – at least, so one thinks before one goes to China!

Notes

1. *Passfield Papers*, VII, 2 (XV), A-F. This 'Introduction' reproduces the matter on six folio sheets headed '*Our Partnership*, Volume III, Chapter 1'. Other materials in the same box clearly show it to be part of an introduction to 'Chapter 1, Japan' of '*Our Partnership*, Volume III, *The Far East*', with a similar format envisaged for 'Chapter II, China', and so forth, but never completed. These materials also include a draft 'Preface' for the projected *The Far East* volume. It reads: 'I intended to include the following pages as the last chapter of Volume II of *Our Partnership*, 1899–1911, exactly as I ended Volume I by the chapter entitled 'Round the Anglo-Saxon World'. But when I came to dive into the mass of disjointed observations and casual reflections about Japan and China, Malaya and Burma, and finally our four months in India, I realised that it differed, alike in aim and achievement, from the diaries of our travels [through the USA] and Australia in 1898. Our first journey round the world was in a very real sense part and parcel of our specialised research into particular social institutions. For, in spite of differences in magnitude of territory, in climate, in natural resources, and in an admixture of races, the political and economic structure and social habits of the U.S.A. [New Zealand] and Australia were varieties of the British species; expressed in the same language and embedded in the same cultural traditions. All alike, whether situated in Europe, America or Australasia, were in fact firmly rooted in that trilogy – the Christian religion, capitalist profit-making and political democracy – which constitutes what is called Western civilisation. Hence we could pick out the municipal government of the U.S.A., labour legislation in New Zealand, or the working of the party system in Australia for detailed study and description, with the assurance that any such entries in our diary were of some sociological value.

   Utterly different in content are the MS diaries of our Far Eastern tour. Here I am confronted with some 150,000 words of mere touristic observations of coloured peoples speaking unknown languages, inspired by strange mythologies, practising unfamiliar rites; belonging in fact to ancient civilisations outside our ken. It is useless to attempt to select particular entries for publication as they are all, from the scientific standpoint, equally useless. On the other hand, this year's sojourn in strange worlds acted as a powerful ferment, altering and enlarging our conception of the human race, its past, its present and its future. Speaking for myself, I was never again quite the same person after this exciting journey. Our diaries were in fact predominantly autobiographical. This purely personal aspect cannot be expressed by a limited selection from the entries. It can only be inferred from our experience [of the Far East] taken in [its] entirety. So I decided to make them into a separate volume with introductory paragraphs and explanatory notes, derived from unnoted recollections, or from the reading of contemporary books and newspapers.

   [To] this statement I must add that the first five weeks of our tour – our passage through Canada, a British Dominion with which I had been, as a girl, intimately connected through my father's presidency of the Grand Trunk Railway – has been omitted [from this volume] and added as an appendix to our chapter on 'Round the Anglo-Saxon World'.'

2. Near the close of Lord Salisbury's third Ministry, in January 1902, Britain and Japan had concluded a five-year Anglo-Japanese Alliance, providing for the independence of China and Korea and the recognition of Japan's 'special interests' in Korea. In the event of a war involving either party with a third party, its ally was to remain neutral; but if another power became involved, the allied power was bound to join the conflict. Neither party was to enter into separate agreements with another power (Russia) without consulting the other. Arthur Balfour became Prime Minister in July 1902 and held office until December 1905. In August of 1905, his Government had negotiated a modified renewal of the Alliance for ten years. See also Korea, page 113, Note 1.

3. At the foot of the page is the entry 'Letters From the Far East by Sir Charles Eliot, K.C.M.G. (1907), pp. 2, 6, 20–21, 27.'

4. The Canadian Pacific Railway's trans-Pacific passenger steamship service (no longer in operation) would have been the obvious alternative for tourists departing from the West Coast of Canada bound for Japan in 1911.

5. The Webbs had been entertained by Mrs Fairchild and her daughter Sally, socially prominent Bostonians of the day, on the United States leg of their first world tour in 1898.

6. 'The guide Nishi turns out to be invaluable', Beatrice wrote home to Kate Courtney on 22 August 1911. 'He is really an extraordinary combination of a first-rate valet & courier & the agreeable, cultivated companion. He is bitterly against the Government on account of its taxation & military regime & is rather a severe critic of the corruption of the Parliament. If he is a Police Detective commissioned to look after us, he is really extraordinarily astute!' In a letter to Mary Playne dated 15 September 1911, she is effusive in her praise of 'our dear little guide – Nishi – who is fast becoming an intimate personal friend as well as a devoted attendant'. The original plan called for Nishi to remain with the Webbs throughout their stay in Japan and Korea, accompanying them as far as Peking. But Beatrice notes in a letter to her sister Kate, dated Tokyo, 9 October 1911, that 'we shall miss our invaluable guide when he leaves us at P'yongyang. He refused to come with us to Peking, as he said he would be little or no use, as the Chinese are very hostile now to the Japanese, whom they suspect of wanting to annex Manchuria!' As events transpired, Nishi left the Webbs at Mukden.

7. The Peers' School, or Gakushu-in, founded in 1877 with separate boys' and girls' departments, was subsidised by the Imperial Household Department and intended for the education of children of the peerage, a restriction eventually relaxed. Graduates of the high school course were admitted without examination to the Imperial Universities.

8. 'By the way,' added Beatrice, 'a woman of 50 is very old, "about to die", & when I tell anyone I am 53, they either think I am joking or look at me as a physical monstrosity!' Beatrice Webb to Mary Playne, 30 August 1911.

9. Suematsu Kencho (1855–1920), an accomplished literary man as well as politician of the Meiji Cabinets of Prince Ito Hirobumi (1841–1909). Suematsu, whose wife was a daughter of Ito, produced the first English translation of Lady Murasaki Shikibu's Tale of Genji.

10. David Lloyd George (1863–1945). As British Chancellor of the Exchequer in 1909, his radical 'the People's Budget' had been rejected by the

Conservative-dominated House of Lords, precipitating a general election in January 1910. A resounding Liberal victory saw the Budget's passage, and in the following year, the establishment of Lloyd George's contributory scheme of health and unemployment insurance in Great Britain.

11. Otani Kozui (1876–1948). 24th Chief Abbot of the Nishi-Honganji temple at Kyoto, one of the head temples of the Shinshu sect of Japanese Buddhism.

12. William Archer (1856–1924). Theatre critic and journalist, and a London acquaintance of the Webbs.

13. George Etsujiro Uehara (b. 1877). *The Political Development of Japan, 1867–1909* (London, 1910) was Uehara's LSE Ph.D., and was published in a series edited by W. A. S. Hewins, an early Director of The London School of Economics. In light of Sidney's observation that he 'thinks of going into Parliament', it is worth noting that Uehara not only did so but was to prove, in tumultuous times, a remarkably intrepid politician. First elected to the Diet in 1917, he was re-elected a dozen times and survived down into the post-Second World War period, representing the Japanese Diet upon Japan's admission to membership in the United Nations.

14. The clan oligarchs, or *hambatsu*, who had brought about the Meiji Restoration, were the effective rulers of Japan. As a consequence, the establishment of a party system based on the principle of an executive responsible to the majority in the national legislature had been thwarted. In the years 1885 to 1918, the choice of every Prime Minister except two alternated between the Choshu and Satsuma clans.

15. Eclectic borrowing from overseas railway engineering had resulted in the proliferation of gauges on the Japanese railway system — 6', 4'8½'', a metre, 3', and even 2' in the mountains. As Japan modernised, there was pressure to adopt a standard usage, and on 31 July 1911, the Diet had approved a Government scheme involving the creation of a wide-gauge line stretching from Shimbashi and Tokyo Central Station to Hiroshima and Shimonoseki. But it was not merely a question of modernisation: Katsura's scheme of adopting a broad gauge (compatible with that of Manchuria) was viewed with suspicion by political moderates, who saw behind it pressure from the military. There had been a conspicuous expansion of national armaments following Japan's defeat of Russia in the 1904–5 Russo–Japanese War. Japan's standing army had increased from 150 000 to over 250 000 and, with conscription, the available force in the event of war was increased from 600 000 to some 2 000 000. Naval tonnage had grown threefold, with ambitious plans for further growth. The incoming Saionji Cabinet was to recommend an expenditure of some 90 million yen for military expansion and adjustment programmes. It was a feature of the politics of the day that the pro-military oligarchs of the *genro*, or elder statesmen, chief amongst them General Yamagata, struggled to out-manoeuvre an unwilling House of Representatives, aiming to effect these military expansion programmes without forfeiting any of their executive control.

16. Kato Takaaki (1860–1926), a key figure in the diplomatic negotiations leading to the Anglo-Japanese Alliance in the early years of the century. Four times Japan's Foreign Minister and, late in life, Prime Minister, the Webbs had met him, as Beatrice's draft 'Introduction' to the Japan matter indicates, when he was Japanese Ambassador in London.

17. 'They are all civil servants & have to be careful not to incur the reproach of "dangerous thoughts"', Beatrice wrote to Kate Courtney of their professorial acquaintances in Tokyo. 'But certainly in their talks with us they were quite free & easy in their criticism of the Government & the *status quo*. Nearly all the professors of Political Economy in Japan are "Socialists of the Chair".' 18 September 1911.

18. Kotoku Shusui (1871–1911), journalist and socialist activist with anarchist leanings, had been arrested along with a number of other socialists in a police swoop the previous year, on suspicion of involvement in a thwarted plot to assassinate the Emperor Meiji. He was convicted and sentenced to death, along with eleven others, and executed in 1911. See also Notes 22 and 116 below.

19. Kuwata Kumazo (1868–1932), as Sidney notes, had assisted the Ministry of Agriculture and Commerce at the turn of the century in compiling a report on labour on which the Factory Act of 1911 was based. A Member of the House of Peers from 1904 and a staunch supporter of labour, Kuwata eventually became Dean of the Faculty of Economics at Chuo University.

20. Komura Jutaro (1855–1911), was Foreign Minister in the Katsura Cabinets of 1901 and 1908 and an advocate of Japan's overseas expansion. His 'indisposition' at the time of the Webbs' visit was genuine: he was to expire before the year was out.

21. Ishii Kikujiro (1866–1945). Diplomatist, later Ambassador to France, Member of the Imperial Privy Council and Special Envoy in 1937 to the United States. Author of *Gaiko Yoroku*, a shortened version of which was published by Johns Hopkins University Press in 1937, translated and edited by William R. Langdon as *Diplomatic Commentaries by Viscount Kikujiro Ishii*.

22. Katsura Taro (1847–1913). Army leader and prominent statesman of the Meiji and Taisho periods, who had overseen the formal annexation of Korea in 1910, and whose steps to suppress the socialist movement in the same year had been highlighted by the so-called 'lese-majesty affair': see Note 18 above. The Webbs left Tokyo on 24 August and the following day, Katsura resigned the Premiership, to be replaced by arch-rival Saionji Kimmochi (see Note 34 below) – but he was to re-emerge out of the obscure workings of the prevailing system, backed by the *genro*, to form a new Cabinet in December, 1912.

23. An Imperial Rescript on Charity, issued on 11 February 1911, had 'ordered a sum of money belonging to Our Household to be set aside and to use it as a fund for the relief of Our helpless people'. With the Emperor's gift of 1.5 million yen as its original endowment, Katsura had formed the *Saiseikai*, or Imperial Charity Organisation, aimed at establishing free hospitals in Japan's major cities, and the distribution of medical care vouchers exchangeable for the services of individual medical practitioners in rural areas.

24. Although small government subsidies for social welfare had been instituted in 1909, the responsibility for poor relief was in fact turned back to local governments in 1912.

25. 'Prince Katsura talked of "civilisation" as a disagreeable medicine which the country had to take, & was willing to acquiesce in anything it entailed.' Beatrice Webb to Mary Playne, 30 August 1911.

26. Shibusawa Eiichi (1840–1931). A leading entrepreneur of the Meiji period, associated with more than 300 business enterprises in his lifetime. Though at home in the cut-and-thrust of the commercial world, he was said to have been deeply influenced by Christian notions of charity and philanthropy, while remaining convinced of the continued relevance of traditional Confucian moral precepts in an increasingly secular age.

27. Sir Charles Tennant (1823–1906). A wealthy British industrialist, Liberal MP, art patron and social acquaintance of the Webbs.

28. Tanaka Hozumi (1876–1944). Journalist and educator, who would become, in 1931, President of Tokyo's Waseda University, from which he had graduated in 1896.

29. Iwasaki Yataro (1834–1885), business magnate, founder, with his brother, of the Mitsubishi *zaibatsu*, or business combine.

30. Presumably the references here are to John Stuart Mill's classic *Principles of Political Economy* (1848; 7th edn, 1871); Alfred Marshall's neo-classical *magnum opus*, *Principles of Economics* (1890); and the American applied economics theorist Frank W. Taussig's *Principles of Economics* (1911).

31. This 'junior at the British Embassy' was to become Sir George Sansom (1883–1965), and to enjoy a long and distinguished career as a British diplomatist and scholar. He achieved a wide reputation among Western students of Japan in his mature years, as the cultivated author of *Japan, A Short Cultural History* (London and New York, 1936) and of a monumental three-volume study, *A History of Japan*, published by Stanford University Press as recently as 1958–63.

32. An Oxford don, President of the Oxford Fabian Society, and author of Fabian Tract 72, *The Moral Aspects of Socialism* (1896).

33. [Ikaho]. In the course of their 'mountain walk', the Webbs passed through what is today Nikko National Park and Joshin'etsu Kogen National Park.

34. Pinned to the original diary at this point is an 'Advertisement', a newspaper galley-proof written in Japanese, bearing the pencilled notation, in Sidney's hand: ' "Extra Special Announcement", formation of New Ministry, sold at Ikao for 1 sen (a farthing). 30/8/11'. *Mss Diary*, Volume 29.f.100A.

35. A picturesque Devon fishing village and sea-side resort situated on a steep hill-side overlooking Bideford Bay on the Bristol Channel.

36. Inoue Katsunosuke (1860–1929). Diplomatist and Privy Counsellor, Minister to Germany and Belgium and Ambassador to Great Britain. Created Marquis in 1915.

37. Francis Brinkley (1841–1912). A resident of Japan since 1867 and one-time commander of the British artillery troops garrisoned there, Brinkley had taken over management of the *Japan Mail* in 1881, and was later Tokyo Correspondent of *The Times*.

38. The allusion is to the political corruption of the Hanoverian era in England, notoriously illustrated in the 'South Sea Bubble' of 1720. Sir Robert Walpole is popularly known as England's first Prime Minister, although, since the modern system of political parties and responsible cabinet government had not yet come into existence, he never had the title. But he effectively *was* 'Prime Minister' from 1721–42, after which ascendancy amongst the Whig factions that dominated Parliament passed to Henry Pelham and his brother, the Duke of Newcastle. The atmosphere of

Hanoverian politics, and the reason perhaps that Sidney Webb thought they provided an apt comparison with the Japanese political life of the early years of the present century, is illustrated in the memorable words of Sir Robert Walpole's son Horace: 'It is true that [Henry Pelham] chiefly maintained his influence in Parliament by an elaborate system of corruption; but . . . he "would never have wet his finger [in corruption] if Sir Robert Walpole had not dipped up to the elbow"; but as he did dip, and as Mr. Pelham was persuaded that it was as necessary for him to be Minister as it was for Sir Robert Walpole, he plunged in deep.' *Memoirs of the Reign of George II*, vol. I, pp. 234–5, cited in *Dictionary of National Biography* (edited by Leslie Stephen and Sidney Lee) (London, 1917) vol. XV, p. 691. Compare this with Walter McLaren's views of the Japanese situation near the time of the Webbs' visit, in his *A Political History of Japan During the Meiji Era, 1867–1912* (London, 1916) p. 371: 'Bribery is a national institution . . . There apparently is no ethical question involved, no moral degradation . . . and to consider the giving or receiving of a mere bribe as immoral is to think in terms worthy of a pettifogging attorney.'

39. 'Here, at any rate, is the proprietary state, with the family group as the economic unit, which Mr. Hilaire Belloc finds so attractive. And certainly, nowhere is this society more alluring than in rural Japan.' See Appendix to this volume, page 361.

40. But the Webbs saw clearly, as the very next paragraph suggests, that there was another side to this ostensibly idyllic *gemeinschaft* scene. 'The village life & the people one meets on the way are so entertaining & picturesque that one never seems to tire of wandering on,' Beatrice was to reflect, adding: 'I doubt whether one could stand it for long – the Japanese certainly age quickly. The village children, too, tho they are happy little persons, seem to suffer from "pot-bellies", blindness, & have a somewhat neglected look. The peasants are a docile, patient beast of burden people, of a distinctly lower type than the officials & governing class.' Letter to Mary Playne, 30 August 1911.

41. Prostitution, or *baishun*, had for many centuries been a highly institutiona lised feature of Japanese culture, and indeed, especially in the Edo period (1600–1868), was closely associated with a *genre* of literary and artistic work known as *Uriyo-e*. In the Meiji era, as under the former shogunates, the Government continued to license and supervise brothels, so that, at the time of the Webbs' visit to Japan, there were hundreds of licensed brothel districts similar to those they encountered at Shibu and Nagoya, and perhaps 500 000 prostitutes. Influenced by Western humanitarian ideas, Japanese reformers concerned over the *de facto* sale of young girls into prostitution had managed, as early as 1872, to secure the passage of measures designed to free women from unreasonable indenture contracts – although, as the Webbs discovered, these had not been especially effective. But in 1920, the Home Ministry was to ban the prostitution of girls under the age of eighteen. Meanwhile, the introduction into Japan of Western-style bars and cafés encouraged unlicensed prostitution, beyond the reach of the required medical inspections aimed at stopping diseased licensed prostitutes from working, a system itself far from perfect. In a 1920 survey, 22 per cent of men reporting for military service were found to suffer from

some form of venereal disease, and most cited contact with prostitutes as the cause. It was not until 1956, with the passage of the Prostitution Prevention Law, that prostitution was eventually declared illegal in Japan. See also Note 124 below.

42. The Salvation Army (*Kyuseigun*) was first organised in Japan under Colonel Edward Wright in 1895, some thirty years after its foundation by Major Booth in London. In 1900, it had launched a drive against prostitution.

43. This would have been a combined ordinary and higher elementary school, the first comprising a six-year compulsory course for 6 to 14-year-olds, the second an optional further course of two or three years.

44. Baseball was first played in Japan as early as 1873, when it was introduced at Kaisei Gakko (now Tokyo University) by an American, Horace Wilson. In the period 1890–1902, a Tokyo high school team played and often defeated a team made up of Americans resident at Yokohama. The game was already on the way to becoming, as it is today, Japan's most popular team sport.

45. A school for boys involving a five-year course beyond the six years of ordinary elementary school. The typical entrant planned to continue on to university on completion of the course of studies, but graduates were also deemed qualified to become clerks in government service without having to undergo a civil service examination.

46. In the Japanese educational arrangements of the day, 'ethics' or morals was taught two hours a week in elementary schools, one hour a week in middle schools, and one hour a week in the third year of the high school course. By the age of ten, children were expected to have committed to memory the Imperial Rescript on Education of 30 October 1890, which was generally regarded as a succinct embodiment of Japanese moral aspirations. Aiming to instruct by edifying example, 'ethics' text-books emphasized the lives of famous men and women.

47. An Anglo-Indian term for a light meal or lunch.

48. S. Shiba.

49. Practically nothing had as yet been done by the state for the protection of workers, and Western-style trade unions, though attempts had been made to introduce them as early as 1897, were virtually non-existent in Japan. What the Webbs discovered first-hand at Nagano, the leading silk centre in Japan, and had further corroborated in their inspection of mills at Nagoya, Kyoto and Osaka, was that female labour, including the employment of young girls, constituted a main part of the factory economy of newly-industrialised Japan. Inquiries carried out by the Department of Agriculture and Commerce in 1909 showed that, in some 10 502 factories employing at least 10 operatives, male labour accounted for 37 per cent and female for 73 per cent of the total work force. Some 23 per cent of workers in the spinning-industry were child operatives under the age of 16, and of those under 14 years of age, 77 per cent were girls.

50. As of September 1910, there were some 71 such homes throughout Japan, aimed at the rehabilitation of ex-convicts and 'depraved children' — the original impetus deriving from the granting of a general amnesty on the occasion of the death of the Empress Dowager in 1896, when the Government first undertook to subsidise such work. With revisions to

Japan's Criminal Code in 1900, the Home Office had further encouraged the growth of reformatories.

51. A former province in northern Honshu, now Niigata Prefecture.

52. Headquartered at Nagaoka and Niigata, Hoden Petroleum Co., founded in 1893, was one of the leading Japanese oil companies of the day.

53. The description parallels that of a popular touristic guide-book of the day, T. Philip Terry's *Terry's Guide to the Japanese Empire, Including Korea and Formosa* (London: Constable, 1920) (1st publ. 1914), which says of Niigata and environs: 'The numerous oil-wells and tall pumps on the hill-sides remind one of a Pennsylvania town.' The imagery is especially apt since there had been considerable American technical assistance in the development of Japan's fledgling petrochemical industry, beginning in the 1880s. But the product of these oil-fields was never to be sufficient for Japan's domestic needs: in 1911, as the Webbs note, the Japanese were reliant on imported oil, and have remained so.

54. What the Webbs had seen at Nagaoka, and now at Niigata, was either a girls' higher elementary school or a girls' high school (in each of which 'Housekeeping' and 'Sewing' were taught), inasmuch as, strictly-speaking, the 'middle school' was an institution for boys only.

55. The curriculum of the Japanese normal school, as the Webbs indicate, was designed to prepare entrants to become future teachers. There were normal and higher normal schools for both boys and girls.

56. Count Kiyosu Iyenori (b. 1862 at Kyoto), twelfth son of the late Prince Fushimi Kiniiye.

57. In the original, in Sidney's hand, but deleted: 'We heard from our excellent hotel at Nagano afterwards that he always stayed there on his way to & from Tokyo, & that he was always accompanied at the hotel by what was euphemistically called a *geisha* girl!' *Mss Diary*, Volume 29.f.149.

58. A calligraphic or pictorial scroll, hung vertically.

59. A long cloth Muslim coat, variant of the Arabic *jubbah*.

60. London (1898), the third of a trio of related works published by the Webbs in the 1890s that had established their credentials as 'brain-workers', including *The History of Trade Unionism* (London, 1894) and (in two volumes) *Industrial Democracy* (London, 1892).

61. The *koto*, a thirteen-stringed, plucked zither. About six feet in length, it is modelled on the Chinese *cheng* and dates from the Nara period (710–794).

62. Garrett Droppers, 'A Japanese Credit Association and Its Founder', *Transactions of the Asiatic Society of Japan*, vol. XXII, (Yokohama, 1894) pp. 69–102 — presumably the materials loaned to the Webbs by George Sansom of the British Embassy, Tokyo, noted in an earlier diary entry. The 'Hotokukai', or Ninomiya Society, had been actively promoted by the Japanese Government from 1906, as an agency of secularisation and modernisation.

63. In August 1907, 12 390 houses were burned down at Hakodate, and in Osaka in July of 1909, some 11 368 houses. The insurers of these properties were required to pay out millions of yen to their policy-holders. The five leading Tokyo-based insurance companies responded by raising their rates sharply. Agreeing in future to set common rates, they in effect limited any further competitive pressure to reduce them.

64. This is the final entry in the first of the three original diary books containing the Webbs' account of their 1911–12 world tour. *Mss Diary*, Volume 29.f.163. The second work-book opens with the entry in Sidney's hand 'Kyoto Japan 14^[th] Sept^[r] 1911', opposite which is mounted the photograph of 'Our Guide – Nishi' identified in Beatrice's hand. *Mss Diary*, Volume 30.f.1.

65. Literally, 'one purpose institution', Doshisha was founded at Kyoto in 1875 by Joseph Niijima, in collaboration with Jerome D. Davis, an American Congregational Church missionary (now United Church of Christ). A full-fledged University since 1920, Doshisha today maintains close ties with America's Amherst College.

66. Kyoto was the residence of the Japanese imperial family for eleven centuries, and Japan's capital prior to the Meiji Restoration. Devastated by the Onin no Ran War (1467–77), the historic city had been magnificently rebuilt, beginning in the late sixteenth century, by the fabled warrior Toyotomi Hideyoshi (1536–98), the Napoleon of mediaeval Japan. The Shogun's, or Nijo Castle – recalling to the Webbs the assured architectural achievement of the Italian Renaissance of the fourteenth to the sixteenth centuries—was begun in 1569. It is famous for its squeaking floor-boards, which are said to chirp like nightingales to warn against silent attack. The slightly later Imperial Palace dates from the early seventeenth century.

67. The Kyoto head temple, noted for its architectural monuments and artistic masterpieces, of the Jodo Shinshu Honganji branch of the Buddhist True Pure Land sect, the so-called 'western' sect.

68. This would have been Otani Sonyu (1886–1939), who became Chief Abbot in succession to his older brother, and a Member of the Japanese House of Peers, when the Tanaka Cabinet was organised in 1927. He later relinquished the priesthood to assume the Presidency of the North China Development Company, a move calling into question perhaps the Webbs' impression that he was not 'worldly-wise'.

69. Kozui Otani's reputation was chiefly based on his having led a party of Buddhist researchers in the early years of the century from Europe to Central Asia, India and China, in order to explore the vestiges of ancient Buddhist culture and to collect *sutras* and other valuable Buddhist materials. He eventually stepped down as Chief Abbot under something of a cloud, the consequence of financial mismanagement in his sect.

70. A monastery temple, founded in 796 and located in the Minami Ward, Kyoto, the head temple of the Toji branch of the Shingon or Shingon-shu sect of Mahayana Buddhism. The original buildings have not survived, but some of the existing complex dates from the late sixteenth century. Mahayana is one of the two great schools of Buddhism, formerly prevalent in China and Tibet as well as Japan. It is characterised by eclecticism and a general belief in a common search for salvation sometimes thought to be attainable by faith alone. The other, earlier form of Buddhism, Hinayana, which is still prevalent in Ceylon, Burma, Thailand and Cambodia, emphasises personal salvation through one's own efforts.

71. 'He practised three grades of treatment,' Beatrice wrote to Mildred Bulkley on 30 September 1911, '(1) "mind cure", (2) "mind cure plus medicine", (3) "mind cure plus surgery" . . . some cases needed medicine and a *very few*

needed an operation . . . He had read all the Christian Science books and looked forward to one universal religion based on a mystical appreciation of the Supreme Power of Spiritual Communion and the gradual emancipation of the human spirit from the body of the beast, both in the individual and the race . . . of the simple, childlike type of mystic, except that the medical man was reported to be a really fine surgeon. Even the unbelieving Nishi, our clever guide, admitted that.'

72. Edward Carpenter (1844–1929), socialist iconoclast, author in rebellion against Victorian convention and respectability, sandal-maker. His *Art of Creation* (1904), Carpenter's thoughts on art, was a variation on a theme running throughout his extensive publications: the attempt to analyse and interpret an ineluctable emotional state he believed to be the driving force of his own intellectual development, and a crucial element of the human understanding.

73. Henri Bergson (1859–1941), the French philosopher, was something of a cult figure in the years prior to the First World War, and his lectures at the Collège de France drew large crowds. The English translation of a 1904 book, his *Creative Evolution* (1911), extended the insights of a still earlier work of 1889 translated as *Time and Free Will* (1910), in rejecting the prevailing mechanistic, passive account of the phenomenon of evolution. It is characteristic of Bergson's general system of ideas that the 'real world' is seen as one of continuous becoming or process, informed by living energy, the *élan vital*. Contrasting 'duration', the mechanised clock time of scientific thought, with 'time' as an amorphous Heraclitian flux, he insisted that it is not the task of science to reveal the true structure of the world, but instead, to provide blueprints for the imposition of human will on a wholly fluid and continuous nature. He was awarded the Nobel Prize for Literature in 1928.

74. Omori Sho-ichi (b. 1856), Governor of Kyoto from 1903, and previously Governor of Nagasaki and Hyogo.

75. Construction of the Peace Palace had begun in 1907 but was not completed until 1913. It was to be the seat of the International Court of Justice and the Permanent Court of Arbitration, created in consequence of two international conferences held at The Hague, Netherlands, in 1899 and 1907.

76. Nishijin, Kyoto.

77. Kikuchi Dairoku (1855–1917), created Baron 1901. Professor of Physics and Mathematics and President of Tokyo University, and subsequently, President of the Peers' School and of Kyoto University.

78. A student placed in the first class of the Mathematics Tripos at Cambridge University.

79. Sir William Peterson (1856–1921). Scots-born classical scholar and university administrator. Appointed President of McGill University in 1905, the Webbs had met Peterson on the Canadian leg of the 1911–12 world tour.

80. Sir Arthur Rucker (1848–1915), Professor of Physics at the Royal College of Science, South Kensington (now Imperial College), and from 1902, Principal, University of London.

81. Murai Kichibe (1864–1926). Born in Kyoto, Murai travelled to America in the early 1890s to study methods of tobacco-blending, and on his return introduced Japan's first home-made cigarettes, known as *Asahi*. He

eventually merged his concern with an American firm to create Murai Bros.;
the takeover of the tobacco industry as a Government monopoly in 1904
led him to broaden his financial interests by founding the Murai Bank.

82. Freedom of expression in their teaching duties.

83. Socialists of the chair or lectern. See Note 17 above.

84. Thomas Malthus (1766–1834), in his *Essay on the Principle of Population as it Affects the Future Improvement of Society* (1798), had famously expounded the principle that, since population increases in a geometrical ratio while subsistence does so only in a mathematical ratio, population is inevitably and necessarily limited by the 'checks' of vice and misery. The same conclusion was less bleakly stated in the largely re-written second edition of 1803, where Malthus makes more of the case for prudential intervention, and less of what, in the earlier edition, had appeared to be insuperable obstacles to all social improvement. At the time of the Webbs' visit to Japan, a steadily rising birth rate was nearing its peak: whereas the 1872 Meiji enumeration had given Japan's population at 33 111 000, the 1920 census would show a total of 56 963 000 (close to half its present total). Birth control measures of a 'neo-Malthusian' sort had made little headway, and abortion was strictly illegal; it was not until the early 1950s that liberalised access to induced abortion was legally condoned in Japan. The somewhat sanguine 'patriotic' assumption alluded to here, drawn from classical economic reasoning, was that industrialisation and urbanisation must cause both the birth and death rates to fall.

85. Introduced at Tokyo from America in 1881, the YMCA had spread rapidly so that, by 1911, there were some 72 associations in Japan with over 4000 members, including many middle school and university students, as well as professional and business men. But it was the YMCA's educational and social activities, more than its religious aims, which appealed to the Japanese philanthropists who contributed money to build its new hostels. They condoned the YMCA as another desirable Western borrowing in the cause of the modernisation of Japan.

86. The reference is probably to the Osaka Goda mill.

87. The cocoa and chocolate manufacturers George Cadbury (1839–1922) and Joseph Rowntree (1836–1925), were leading business men in Victorian England. Cadbury's factory at Bournville, near Birmingham, with its attractive adjacent housing for workers, was regarded as a model of enlightened industrial practices. For his part, Rowntree had introduced reasonable hours and adequate wages, consulted workers about working conditions, provided widows' pensions and, in 1891, brought social workers into his factory.

88. The allusion is to Osaka's importance as Japan's leading manufacturing and industrial centre: but the city was perhaps better known as 'the Venice of Japan' on account of its elaborate system of canals and waterways. The city the Webbs saw in 1911 was almost totally destroyed in the Second World War, and subsequently rebuilt.

89. This must have been Shinsaibashi-suji.

90. A traditional Japanese unit of dry measure equivalent to 5.12 bushels.

91. In *The Monthly Report of the Tokyo Municipal Poor Asylum*, close to the time of the Webbs' visit, there appeared the results of an investigation into the

causes of poverty based on the cases of 3224 Tokyo men all over forty-one years of age in the period 1902–09, and its findings are not irrelevant to the Webbs' point about poverty in Osaka. Although the single largest number of cases (461) was entered under 'chronic illness or hereditary illness', this was followed by 'confirmed wanderers' (392), 'intemperance' (324), 'prodigality' (277), 'tired of occupation' (237), 'imprudent sexual relations' (201), and so on. Even a cursory glance at these suggest that, in Japanese eyes, amongst the primary 'causes' of poverty was weak moral character.

92. Beatrice Webb, *The Minority Report in Its Relation to Public Health and the Medical Profession* (London, 1910), the fruit of Beatrice's dissenting membership on the Poor Law Commission of 1905–09; and Sidney and Beatrice Webb, *The Prevention of Destitution* (London, 1911) which attempts to set out in more positive terms the wide-ranging proposals of the Minority Report itself. The Webbs had urged (as had the Majority Report) the abolition in Great Britain of the general workhouse which was a feature of the nineteenth century Poor Law, and the transfer of the administration of relief to local authorities. Their characteristic view, that so far from poverty being the fault of individuals, it was 'a disease of society itself', would come to be regarded as an important contribution to the eventual emergence of the welfare state.

93. Inuzuka Katsutaro (b. Tokyo 1868). He had been in America and Europe in 1895 to inspect railway affairs, and again in 1910, and had served briefly as Governor of Nagasaki from September 1910, before taking up his position at Osaka.

94. Frederic Harrison (1831–1923). Author and leading British positivist.

95. E. H. Pember (1833–1911). Intellectual lawyer and prominent figure in the social and literary life of London.

96. Kyoto's Higashi-Honganji temple, home of the Otani Shinshu or 'eastern' sect. Periodically destroyed by fire, Higashi-Honganji had fewer treasured artifacts than Nishi-Honganji, but the recently rebuilt temple at the time of the Webbs' visit to Kyoto was none the less an impressive structure in its own right, ranking amongst the world's largest wooden buildings.

97. In an earlier diary entry, during their mountain walk to Nagano, the Webbs had noted that 'the State seems to give some financial support to Shintoism ... but we do not feel sure what all this amounts to'. By the time they reached Ise, they had come to realise that, in Meiji Japan, State Shinto (Kakko Shinto), with its complete separation in principle of Japan's indigenous religion of Shinto from Buddhism, had meant in consequence the effective downgrading of Buddhism. This special status of State Shinto had gained institutional recognition in 1900, when it was placed under the jurisdiction of a new Bureau of Shrines in the Home Ministry, with Buddhism, the independent Shinto sects, and Christianity, relegated to the supervision of a lesser Bureau of Religion. And while the educational curriculum of the day was self-consciously devoid of traditional religious instruction, the Ministry of Education, shortly before the Webbs' arrival in Japan in 1911, had ordered schools to take their pupils to local Shinto shrines on festival days, to pay homage to the shrine deities. Shrines were 'ranked', with the highest rank accorded to the grand shrine of Ise – and amulets from Ise were to be found on the little Shinto altar of households

throughout Japan. State Shinto was abolished following the Second World War. No doubt, in imperial Japan's immediately preceding decades, its ancient ideal of *saisei itchi*, or the unity of religious ritual and government administration, had come to circumfuse the prevailing atmosphere of nationalism and militarism.

98. Today the area is, in fact, Ise-Shima National Park.

99. Shingon Buddhism was introduced into Japan by Kukai, scholar, artist and calligrapher, posthumously known as Kobo Daishi, the Great Master Kobo (774–835), who had studied Shingon – literally, 'true word', a sacred spell or mantra – during a two-year stay in China. The special significance of Koyasan is that, in 816, Kukai was granted an imperial concession on Mount Koya, where he built the Kongobuji, the first exclusively Shingon temple in Japan, later the head temple of the Koyasan Shingon sect. There are, in all, some 110 temples and monasteries at Koyasan.

100. But strictly, Kongobuji is the 'principal temple' at Koyasan.

101. Sir Oliver Lodge (1850–1940). Physicist, first President of Birmingham University, and a pioneering researcher in psychic phenomena.

102. George Tyrell (1861–1909). Modernist English Jesuit priest, whose attacks on conservative Catholicism, reaching a large audience, led to his eventual excommunication.

103. English proponent of the 'new theology', whose *The New Theology* (London, 1907) urged a radically simplified and liberal Christianity, emphasising the nearness rather than the transcendence of God – a project later echoed in John A. T. Robinson's *Honest to God* (London, 1963).

104. [Hsuku-shima]. Sacred island in Hiroshima Prefecture, 6 miles south-west of Hiroshima, where the Webbs spent two nights before departure by sea for Korea.

105. 'We were completely exhausted by the 11 days' entertainments at Tokyo,' Beatrice wrote to Clifford Sharp, 'and collapsed with bad colds in the head.' 18 October 1911.

106. Max Muller (1823–1900). Enormously productive and influential Oxford philologist and orientalist, whose large library was acquired by Tokyo University in 1901.

107. A feudal vassal or nobleman.

108. Okuma Shigenobu (1838–1922). Meiji-era statesman, who narrowly survived an assassination attempt in which he lost a leg. Founder of the Tokyo Semmon Gakko, predecessor of Waseda University.

109. But when the Webbs met Abe Isoo (1865–1949), socialist educator and politician, shortly after the trial and execution of Kotoku Shusui and his fellow revolutionary co-conspirators, he had temporarily given up his party political activities, and become popular as manager of the baseball club of Waseda University. Appointed director of the Japan Fabian Society in 1924, he was to re-emerge in the House of Representatives in 1927, and become a leader of the Shakai Taishuto (Social Mass Party) prior to the Second World War.

110. Fukuzawa Yukichi (1835–1901), founder of the Keio Gijuku, later Keio University. Taught himself Dutch (and in his early twenties ran his own Dutch-language school in downtown Edo, as Tokyo was then known), as well as English. A champion of English utilitarianism and individualism, he

was an extremely successful populariser of Western learning, his *Western Affairs* selling 250 000 copies in 1866–69, and his *Encouragement of Learning*, an even more impressive 700 000 in the period 1872–76. In 1862 he had established the newspaper *Jiji Shimpo*, here alluded to by the Webbs.

111. Naruse Jinzo (1858–1919), a convert to Christianity, was the founder of the Baika Girls' School in Osaka, 1888, and, with Aso Shozo, of the Nihon Women's College, which opened in Mejiro, Tokyo in 1901. Known today as the Japan Women's University, it attained university status in 1948.

112. Takakusu Junjiro (1866–1945). An Oxford student of Max Muller, his crowning achievement in a career full of honours was the collaborative editing and publishing, with Watanabe Kaikyoku, of the *Taisho shinshu daizoko*, a hundred-volume edition of the Tripitaka, a basic source for the study of Buddhism.

113. The reference is presumably to Inoue Enryo (1858–1919), whose *métier* was the application of Western philosophical insights to the systematic analysis of Buddhist thought.

114. As with earlier references to 'New Buddhism' and 'New Christianity', the allusion is to a body of religious learning, originating in Germany but pioneered in England, beginning in the early 1880s, by W. R. Smith and others. It emphasized the study of the historical circumstances surrounding the composition of seminal biblical texts in the belief that a more intellectually creditable account of the theological impulse would address the pervasive sense of a spiritual void left by the collapse of the institutional churches and the relentless materialism of the modern world. A similar aim, it appeared to the Webbs, informed the 'Higher' or 'New' Buddhism they had encountered in Japan. See too the 'New Hinduism' matter in the India portion of the diary.

115. Katayama Sen (1859–1933). Educated at Yale University, co-founder (with Abe Isoo, and others) of the Shakai Minshuto (Social Democratic Party), outlawed from the day it was founded in 1901. Attending the Second International in Amsterdam in 1904 as representative from Japan, Katayama had shaken hands with the Russian delegate, George Plekhanov, in a dramatic gesture of protest against the Russo-Japanese War. An early associate of Kotoku Shusui, he opposed the latter's call for direct action, advocating instead the route of parliamentary reform. After Kotoku's execution, he acted as a leader of the Tokyo street-car strike. He would return to America in 1914, and then, to the Soviet Union in 1921, where he was appointed to the permanent executive committee of the Comintern, and a leader in the international communist movement. Katayama died in Moscow in 1933, and is buried in the Kremlin.

116. Suga Kanno (1881–1911), journalist and anarchist. Fleeing confinement in an arranged marriage to work for a socialist newspaper, she had begun living with the leftist Kanson Arahata in 1906. Both were arrested and imprisoned for their role in street demonstrations in 1908, but she took up on her release with Kotoku, Kanson remaining in prison. For a time, she became Kotoku's common-law wife, but eventually left him, thinking him too moderate politically. Both were amongst the two dozen arrested and brought to trial for high treason in 1910, and both were among the twelve subsequently hanged.

117. The wealthiest merchant house of pre-Meiji Japan, the largest *zaibatsu* of the pre-Second World War era, and a major enterprise grouping or *keiretsu* of the post-war period. A vast conglomerate based on banking, trade and mining subsidiaries.

118. Mitsui Hachirojiro, President of Mitsui's trading department, the Bussan Kaisha, who had just been created Baron earlier in the year.

119. Masuda Takashi (1848–1938).

120. The notion that the Japanese might be of Semitic stock was one fairly widely entertained in England, initially encouraged perhaps by the reissue in the mid-nineteenth century, in abridgements and anthologies, of an English translation of Engelbert Kaempfer's comprehensively-entitled *The History of Japan, Giving an Account of the Ancient and Present State and Government of that Empire: of its Temples, Palaces, Castles and Other Buildings; of its Metals, Minerals, Trees, Plants, Animals, Birds and Fishes; of the Chronology and Succession of the Emperors, Ecclesiastical and Secular; of the Original Descent, Religions, Customs, and Manufactures of the Natives, and of their Trade and Commerce with the Dutch and Chinese, Together with a Description of the Kingdom of Siam* (1727). Kaempfer's book had pioneered the proposition that the Japanese were probably descendants of the lost Babylonian tribe of Israel. Could not this serve to explain the markedly different aptitudes of the Japanese and Chinese in respect of organisation and money-making?

121. Industrial Bank of Japan Ltd. [Nihon Kogyo Ginko]. A private bank founded in 1902, specialising in long-term credit to industrial enterprises. Head-quartered in Tokyo, Industrial Bank is today the largest of three such credit banks in Japan. Soyeda Juichi (b. 1863), educated at Cambridge and Heidelberg, retired as President of the Bank in 1912, and in 1915 became Governor of the Imperial Government Railway.

122. Hayashi Tadasu (1850–1913). As Minister to Britain from 1900, he worked to bring about the Anglo-Japanese Alliance of 1902. He was Foreign Minister in the 1906 Saionji Kimmochi Cabinet, and in the second, of 1911, when the Webbs met him, the very recently-appointed Minister of Communications.

123. Arthur Balfour (1848–1930). English philosopher and Conservative Prime Minister, 1902–05, author of works of philosophy and metaphysics widely noted in his day, and a personal friend of the Webbs.

124. Now part of the Senzoku district, Taito ward, Tokyo. From the seventeenth century until the 1950s, Yoshiwara was the location of the most famous of the Government-regulated centres for prostitution – the so-called *yukoku* ('play quarters') or *iromachi* ('love towns') – throughout Japan. In its hey-day, the quarter housed between two and three thousand prostitutes in some 200 establishments. In 1916, the practice alluded to by the Webbs of exhibiting the women 'in cages', or behind bars, was ended. And, with the eventual passage in 1956 of the Prostitution Prevention Act, prostitution was declared illegal and the licensed quarters were abolished.

125. The *Japan Chronicle*, of which Robert Young was proprietor and editor, was one of some eight English-language papers, mostly British, published in Japan and Korea at the time.

126. Charles Bradlaugh (1833–91). Free-thought advocate and radical politician.

127. Dr Moncure Conway (1832–1907). Author and Unitarian minister.

128. J. M. Robertson (1856–1933). Free-thought author and Liberal MP.

129. Andrew Young (b. 1858). Socialist schoolmaster and Labour MP, 1923–4.

130. 'In feudal times merchants and labourers were classed in the lowest rank of the social hierarchy, and as they were treated with little respect they responded by deserving such treatment. With few exceptions, commercial morality was little heeded, and a very slight sense of obligation troubled their conscience . . . This must all be entirely changed now. When such merchants undertook to transact business with foreign merchants whom they could not help looking down upon as barbarians, because they had been so taught, many undesirable things crept into business. Unpunctuality, foisting of inferior goods, unreasonable charges, and other evils were perpetrated with[out] the least possible concern. No doubt we are greatly improving in this direction, and commercial morality is much better understood now than in the old days, but I cannot altogether attribute it to jealousy on the part of foreign merchants against the great development of Japanese trade when they raise their voice against the low state of commercial morality in Japan.' From 'Prof. Ukita's magazine article recently published in Tokyo', cited in Y. Takenob and K. Kawakami (eds), *The Japan Year Book, 1911* (Tokyo [n.d.]) pp. 636–7.

131. 'Tens of thousands of young men who are turned out by higher institutions every year with diplomas find themselves in [a] sad predicament, and it is to be feared that the sentiments of discontent or even despair which these unemployed youths of education naturally experience may in time develop into some alarming socialistic troubles.' Y. Takenob and K. Kawakami (eds), *The Japan Year Book, 1912* (Tokyo [n.d.]) p. 264.

2

Korea[1]

We conclude today an interesting six days in Korea, beginning with a fearful night's passage from Moji to Fusan, when the daily steamer could not start at all for seven or eight hours, and then was tossed about for twelve hours, we lying sick in our cabin. We then had an uncomfortable night in an inferior hotel, the best that Fusan could afford; a long day's railway to Seoul, the capital; two days there; seven hours rail to this place, the ancient capital, where we have spent an interesting twenty-four hours; and then seven hours more rail to the Manchurian frontier (Yalu River). Through the introductions of the Japanese Government, and the Mitsui firm, we have been most elaborately entertained; met at each railway station by a bevy of officials; furnished with a free pass on the railway; taken round Seoul in one of the Governor's state carriages; and escorted about this place by officials. Certainly, the Japanese–Korean administration has spared no pains to show us hospitality, and perhaps secure our good opinion.

The Koreans strike us as a degraded and disagreeable people; apparently without religion, or, at any rate, without temples and religious observances, and seemingly without a priesthood (beyond some Buddhist priests here and there, mainly incomers from Japan, and beyond a great array of Christian missionaries, who claim only three or four per cent of the population as their converts).[2] They are a people of small cultivators (some owners and others tenants), growing rice, barley, rye and radishes, in patches amid a waste of bare hills and untilled grass slopes, from which all trees have been cut down improvidently for fuel, having more cattle and pigs than the Japanese, but living in dirty hovels of mud and thatch, wholly illiterate and uncivilised. Though Seoul, the capital, has 200,000 people, and this place has over 30,000, with Fusan, Chemulpo,[3] Gensan and other busy shipping ports in addition, the overseas commerce, the banking and all the principal trading, is in the hands of foreigners (mainly Japanese, with some Chinese). We could hear of only one Korean merchant doing overseas business (he shipped cattle from Gensan to Vladivostock); and our impression is that the very tiny proportion of Koreans

105

of other than the peasant and small retailer classes, were all in the Government service, to enter which is the desire of every Korean boy who learns to read. (There are a handful of Korean doctors and lawyers, but nearly all these professional men are Japanese.) There *are* a few wealthy Koreans, apparently owners of land, having some scores of small tenants; but one sees absolutely no Korean house above the mud hut level; and where these wealthy Koreans live, we could not discover. Our impression is that numerous Korean pensioners of the Japanese administration (ex-Ministers, etc.) and the small number of landowners above the peasant class, live entirely in Seoul, and are really now merged in the official class, the Japanese Government wisely appointing them to posts, even when supporting them and really controlling them by Japanese 'understudies' and Secretaries.

The curious thing is that this nation of dirty, illiterate, uncivilised peasants,[4] had once a refined literature, art and manufactures; it was, in fact, from them that Japan is supposed to have derived its civilisation a thousand years ago. In some of the picturesque barbaric buildings within the vast enclosure of the principal palace at Seoul, the Japanese Government has established a beautifully arranged museum of choice specimens of pottery, metal work and pictures, executed in Korea between 900 and 1400 A.D., and discovered for the most part in tombs and palace ruins of this very (Heijo) district. This collection, far exceeding in beauty of design and execution anything in London or Boston or Japan – though small – shows not only astonishing skill in handicraft, but also a refined beauty of design, a feeling for both form and colour, and an 'unbarbaric' taste, which is truly remarkable.[5] Now, no Korean can do anything but till the soil (very imperfectly), and make the roughest kind of thatch and straw matting, the rudest earthenware jars, and the simplest and coarsest textiles.

We could learn no cause for this national degeneration, except the insidious effect of several centuries of continuously arbitrary and uncertain taxation. The Korean officials apparently carried to an extreme the Oriental system of 'squeeze'. Whenever anyone showed any superiority in wealth, or comfort in living, he was remorselessly 'squeezed'. The result was that no one dared to strive to rise above the mud hut level. Apparently, the Court, and the provincial officials (who in Korea seem to have been the only noble class), themselves degenerated into barbarism, and the skilled handicraftsmen died out. Largely owing to its geographical situation, Korea was able to maintain seclusion from the world until a generation ago. It is a striking example of the result of governmental oppression, and ignorance of the elements of taxation policy; and also, of how a whole nation may take a wrong turn, and steadily decline in civilisation with accelerating speed, until nothing is left but barbarism. At the same time, we must not assume that the ten millions of Koreans were themselves ever civilised. It may be that there existed among them a small upper class, able to appreciate art and literature, with a still smaller class of skilled handicraftsmen to minister to these, amid a nation of barbarous peasants and petty retailers – the latter mass alone surviving, at a practically unchanged level.

The Japanese have been here for about fifteen years; first, since the Japan–Chinese [*sic*] War, merely as influential advisers of the Korean Emperor, who became their vassal instead of China's; then, since the Russo–Japanese War, as exercising (since 1905) a definite 'Protectorate', somewhat on the model of our English dealings with the Indian Native Princes and the Khedive of Egypt; and finally, since August of last year (1910), frankly as rulers, the country being annexed to Japan. From the first, they seem to have set themselves, with amazing energy, resourcefulness and persistency, to 'civilise' the country; and it was their failure to secure this end through the corrupt, effete, suspicious and perpetually-intriguing Court, and its entourage of concession-hunters, fortune-tellers, plots and counterplots, with successive assassinations of Queens, Japanese statesmen like Prince Ito,[6] and Korean Ministers [that led to annexation]. Since the annexation, Japan is spending two or three million sterling annually (in spite of its own great needs and heavy taxation) on improvements in Korea; and even the most optimistic officials do not expect to make the administration self-supporting for ten or twenty years.

It is, to our thinking, a magnificent example of far-sighted energy: it may be deemed national ambition, and it is denounced by some Europeans as 'imperialism'; but, even if it be assumed that nations and statesmen cannot be altruistic, it is something of which Japan has every reason to be proud. Last year, travel was unsafe even on the main railway line; Japanese officials were frequently assassinated; the post could, in some places, be carried only under armed escort, and bands of robbers were still at large. Now, law and order reigns supreme.

Late as it was when we reached the Seoul hotel (the only European hotel), we were waited on by an official in gold-laced uniform – all the civil servants, like the army and police, the rural *gendarmerie* and the postmen, are in uniform, to impress the populace – who undertook [to escort us during] our whole two days, during which we went about in the Governor-General's carriage and pair – seemingly the only carriage in the town – with coachmen and groom in gold-laced uniform. We went first to a trade training-school, in which a couple of hundred Korean boys were boarded and taught carpentering, brickwork, hand-loom-weaving, pottery, blacksmithing, etc., the whole in the most practical way, calculated to turn them out competent artisans. We then went to the palace, with its degenerate barbaric splendour of gaily-painted roofs and ceilings, with furniture renewed in the commonplace 'European' style of Paris and the Tottenham Court Road: then, to an excellent winding road through the English park-like grounds, constructed by Prince Ito in a vain attempt to induce the Emperor and his suite to take some exercise, even if only 'carriage exercise'; then, to the exquisite museum already referred to. The next day's programme included a curious manufactory of artistic crafts – stonework, textiles, metal-work, pottery, etc., all in one compound; the whole, apparently, run as a subsidised commercial venture to employ the trained Koreans (who were said to make three yen (2/-) per day); and [to] start a trade in artistic products. We also went to the boys' normal school, [BW→] where some hundred Koreans were being taught by Japanese teachers. The singing class was pathetically amusing – the Japanese teacher had not much notion of music, but the unfortunate Korean boy whom we listened to was failing, after obvious effort, to get within measurable distance of a tuneful sound – one official told us that the vocal cords of the Koreans were very undeveloped – [whatever] that [may] mean physiologically. The girls' higher elementary school had gone off for an excursion, and our official was not able to find a primary school – there seem, in fact, to be very few of the Korean children actually at school (though the Government have every intention of establishing a complete system of national education). At present, we gather that the missionaries are doing most of the [common] schooling that is actually accomplished.

Our lunch with the Governor-General was a ceremonial affair – a bevy of high military, naval, and civil officers in uniform to meet us. The Governor was an accomplished Japanese[7] – speaking French with a Parisian accent, and keen to make a notable success of Korea on materialist and secularist lines. Unwittingly, I got into a heated [discussion], through the English Consul, on the question of the persecution of Buddhism by the old Korean administration of hundreds of years ago, and the consequent absence of any kind of religion in Korea. 'Priests were always corrupt and oppressive', was the Governor-General's attitude, and 'Religion was wholly unnecessary'. Three or four ladies, the wives of the high officials, were present, and entertained us with the grace and charm characteristic of the Japanese lady of high degree.

In the [evening we] dined with the representative of the Mitsui firm – Mr. Assano, at his little Japanese home. His wife was in Tokyo, and we were entertained and served by three *geishas* in sober costume, whom one would have taken for very superior servants, or for members of the family, except that their attentions were carried out with professional skill. The party consisted of our host, Dr. Hashida (the official who accompanied us throughout, and of whom more presently), and the Private Secretary of the Governor-General. All three men talked English fluently, and were highly intellectual. The dinner was served in Japanese style, which, with its easy posture of squatting or lying on cushions, the length of time it takes, and the constant imbibing of hot *sake*, certainly promotes [intimacy] and pleasant conversation. We talked far more freely with these men than we should have done with Englishmen under similar circumstances – discussed the administrative problems of Korea compared to India – the relation between the governing and the governed [race] – Japanese institutions, and even the pros and cons of the 'public quarter'. They told us that they were not intimate with any Koreans – that difference in habits and cultivation [prevented] any real intimacy – they were evidently [sceptical] about the possibility of [fusion]. When first the Japanese came to [Korea], there had been a little intermarrying in lonely places; but now, the Japanese women were arriving, and the Japanese home and the Japanese settlement were becoming self-sufficient, the Japanese always preferring to employ Japanese, because of their cleanliness. The fact that [the] Japanese were a particularly cleanly race, and the Korean an [outrageously dirty] one, was the biggest barrier to any kind of intercourse.

One word about the official who [was deputed] to look after us – Dr. [SW: Hashida Seigi]. He was a sort of 'Foreign Secretary' for the Governor-General, and wrote the English Reports of Korean administration which are issued [every year]. He was an unattractive personality – of the [wily] type – fat, excessively deferential and 'all things to all men' in conversation. But he was a remarkable example of the extraordinary intelligence and open-mindedness and assiduous industry of the Japanese official. He had graduated at Columbia, having preferred to go there [than] to Harvard, because he learnt on arrival in America that the [Economics] and [P]olitical [S]cience were better at Columbia. He had visited England and America, and he was [well] versed in the writings on economics and public administration in all countries. He was quite frank with us – said that the Japanese official was at present too ambitious to produce 'paper results' in order to get promotion. He had accurate and full information on every subject of Korean administration, and was very [insistent] that we should [carry] away with [us] the Japanese version of the annexation. He had [written] a treatise [SW: on the international position of Japan (Columbia University series) and has another MS. on Japan as a colonising power, which we may get published for him in London]. But he was as inquisitive as he was informing, and cross-examined Sidney on all sorts of administrative points. And, in spite of very considerable attainments, he was not conceited, either for himself or his race — was always on the look-out for [defects] which could be remedied. We parted as quite intimate acquaintances. I am inclined to think the Japanese world will hear more of Dr. Hashida.[8]

We had a day at [SW: P'yongyang (Heijo)] — an old capital of Korea and now the [second] largest town. Here again, we were met at the station by uniformed officials, who drove us off to the prison, which [Sidney] inspected — I was only allowed to see the women's quarter, so I will let S.W. describe it.

[SW→] The prison was surrounded by a high wooden palisade, within which were a series of well-built wooden buildings, containing about 900 men and women — far above its intended number. The cells seemed ingeniously built for ventilation in the hot summer, but the means of warming in the cold winter seemed defective. But the great defect was the overcrowding. Usually, eight or twelve prisoners slept in each narrow cell; and, owing to insufficient workshop space, a third of the inmates had to remain confined in their cells all day as well as all night, being taken out only for exercise. At the time of our visit, there seemed hundreds thus shut up in the early afternoon, sometimes as thick as they could sit. The first cell that was opened for us (a tiny one) contained only 2 prisoners, evidently Europeans; and I was shocked by one of them starting up and saying, in good English, 'I want to make a statement'. He was, of course, ordered back, and told to make it afterwards. On enquiry, I was told the two were put together, and apart from the Koreans, at their own request; and that they were a German and a Greek, condemned for obtaining money by trick [sic] (apparently, 'ringing the changes').[9] I took several opportunities to press on the officials, high and low, that Europeans must be put into a separate prison, and I was assured that this would be done (and was done in Japan).

The men at work were doing simple manual tasks, involving little technical education, and were plainly being used only to make part of their cost. The head of the prison was a somewhat coarse and brutal-looking man, of the promoted warder type; and the warders were inferior in humanity (so far as appearances went) to those in the Tokyo prison (as was natural). I was taken to the execution place, hanging by the long-drop, quite well devised. They had had eleven or twelve executions in the past six months, all for aggravated murder cases. Altogether, it represented only a low grade of prison administration, but clean and sanitary with a good hospital, and without solitary confinement; and all the officials professed eagerness for improvement.

There was a Buddhist chaplain, an inferior sort of man speaking a little English, who gave his lectures on secular subjects, for mental improvement, to the men in daily batches of two hundred, so that all got it once a week; but no religious services, and only very perfunctory personal interviews.

[BW→] The following morning, we sallied out with the official who calls himself an 'interpreter', but who cannot understand English, though he [speaks] some words fluently — and with Nishi to help us out. [The official] had thought out a delightful excursion — by Koruma to the [old] gate, then a two or three mile walk by the old town, round the ramparts to a Government experimental farm; and back by boat down the river. The sunshine was brilliant, with a cold wind, and the russet-coloured hills and [rocks], the wide expanse of brown plain, the broad stretches of river — even the closely-packed mud and thatch dwellings, dominated by the barbarous [but picturesque] ornamentation of the old gates of decayed [palaces] — formed themselves into a landscape of unique interest and some beauty. The white-[clothed] Koreans add to the picturesqueness of the scenery, when you view them from afar. Looked at near at hand, [crouching] in their [huts], or lounging in the street, they are the most [unsavoury mortals]. Their clothing, from their absurd little black hats to their equally absurd baggy trousers, is the most perfect example of the hideousness of unfitness. The women's clothes are even more [absurd] — yards of stuff gathered into long skirts, sometimes trailing on the ground, with tiny little upper girdles, so short-waisted, that the breasts are always appearing between the upper and nether clothing.[10] The hair of both sexes is [dirty] and unkempt, and the expression unintelligent and sulky. (In Seoul, the women of the more well-to-do class half hide their faces with a wrap, which looks like a coat with sleeves hanging down.) Apparently, the explanation of the silly little black hat and the dirty white garments is that both are ceremonial mourning, and that the Koreans were [required] to be so frequently in mourning, either for the imperial family or their own, that it was less trouble to take to the ceremonial dress for everyday wear![11] That is very characteristic of the hopeless conditions of [slovenliness] into which the whole race has drifted.

Will the Japanese really succeed in civilising the Koreans? Or will they merely colonise Korea, and keep the old inhabitants as a [race] of [hewers] of wood and [drawers] of water? Both the good intention and the intelligence of Japan will be tested by the event.

On [crossing] over the Yalu River into Manchuria, we ran across the British Ambassador, Sir Claude Macdonald,[12] who was journeying in state through Manchuria and Korea, as the guest of the [SW: S.M. Ry]

(Japanese) administration.[13] Our relation to the British Embassy has been somewhat peculiar. We had made friends with Mr. Sansom, the Private Secretary, on first arrival in Tokyo, and he dined with us on our second visit to Tokyo. Although we had brought introductions, both official and personal, to the Macdonalds and to two of the attachés, they had not managed to see us. When we did meet at Antung, they were extremely desirous to be civil, and they were, I think, [conscious] that they had not 'played up' sufficiently. Sir Claude is of the ordinary type of pleasant and personally attractive Army officer; the wife and daughter, the unattractive, conventional society Englishwomen. We had some talk with Sansom, who was in attendance on the Ambassador. When we remarked to Sansom how interesting we had found Dr. Hashida – he [said] that, though he had known him for some time, he had never discussed anything with him. He rather bitterly added that the Japanese official always treated the officials of the British Embassy as hidebound persons, who were either incapable of, or indifferent to, intellectual considerations. But certainly, Sansom's manner to Dr. Hashida was singularly abrupt and discouraging – he almost ordered him about. We have gained immensely, I think, by honestly attempting to carry out the Japanese etiquette of politeness as a preliminary to intimacy. Once or twice, officials have remarked, with both pleasure and amusement, on the perfection of Sidney's elaborate bowings and polite ceremonial speeches. They have seen that we genuinely respected their conventions, and that it has only been through ignorance if we offended. But the majority of Englishmen in Japan seem to think that the Japanese must conform to *their* conventions, and that it is absurd to expect Englishmen to do otherwise than they would at home. Robert Young actually gave as a reason why there was no intercourse between the Japanese and the Europeans at Kobe, that when Europeans visited Japanese houses, they were expected to take off their shoes, and that this was an intolerable nuisance. The less well-off Japanese could not afford to have a European room, and so, feeling that the European was bored by their customs, ceased to ask the Europeans to come to their private houses. When one thinks of the remarkable way in which the Japanese conform to all our manners and customs when they come to England, and how those who can afford to do so always try to entertain you, even in Japan, in European style, unless they know you prefer the Japanese style, one feels rather ashamed of the pretensions of one's fellow countrymen.

Notes

1. Or Chosen, as the Japanese called Korea when it was their colony from 1910 until 1945. Before the closing decades of the nineteenth century, Korea had been virtually a vassal of China, without any diplomatic relations whatever with other nations. But in 1876 the expansive Japanese had forced a commercial treaty on the Koreans recognising them, *inter alia*, as an independent people with the same sovereign rights as Japan. Fearing the implications of this but too weak to challenge the Japanese directly, the Chinese had responded by encouraging the Koreans to conclude treaties with various Western powers as a means of diluting Japanese influence – and in the course of the 1880s Korea did sign treaties aimed at encouraging commercial intercourse with the United States, Germany, Great Britain, Italy, Russia and France. Many Koreans were alarmed at the speed of change. Anti-foreign feeling ran high; and continued conflict between pro-modernisation and conservative factions led to an open revolt triggered by the conservative *Tonghak*, or 'Society of Eastern Learning'. The Korean government of the day appealed to the Chinese for help. The Japanese responded by seizing the Korean Queen and appointing a Regent in her stead. When a British ship carrying Chinese troops to Korea in July of 1894 was intercepted and sunk by the Japanese, the Regent declared war on China, triggering declarations of war in turn by China and Japan on each other. In the 1894-95 Sino-Japanese War that ensued, the Japanese, equipped with modern weaponry, were easy victors over a Manchu dynasty in chronic decline; and in the Treaty of Shimonoseki ending the War, they imposed humiliating terms on the defeated Chinese. In addition to agreeing to pay a large indemnity to Japan and to open up further ports to foreign commerce, China was required to recognise the 'independence' of Korea and to cede to Japan the island of Formosa, the Pescadores Islands and the Liaotung Peninsula. But within a week of the signing of the Treaty, Russia (viewing Japanese claims to Liaotung as threatening to its own sphere of influence), joined by Germany and France, intervened to oblige Japan to return the Liaotung Peninsula to China in consideration of a further large indemnity to be paid to the victors. Once this was achieved, a secret treaty between Russia and China, concluded at the Moscow Coronation of Nicholas II less than two months later, was to grant Russia, in return for a defensive alliance, the right to build and operate the Chinese Eastern Railway across northern Manchuria. The precedent signalled a so-called 'scramble for concessions' in which the great European powers extracted (or extorted) one-sided leases and trading rights from the hapless Chinese, including a further 25-year Russian lease of the southern part of the Liaotung Peninsula, with the right to construct a second railway, the Southern Manchuria Railway (see Note 13 below). As earlier in Korea, anti-foreign resentment in China, culminating in the 1900 Boxer Rebellion, led Russia to strengthen further its military presence in Manchuria. Meanwhile, in Korea, the murder of Queen Min (in which the Japanese Resident, Miura Goro, was implicated) only four months after the signing of the 1895 Treaty of Shimonoseki ended the Sino-Japanese War, dramatically under-scored Japan's determination to dominate and reorganise the Korean government. Fearful for his own life, the Korean King sought refuge in the

Russian Legation, remaining there until 1897, by which time it was clear that Russia had displaced China as Japan's principal rival for control of Korea. Continued friction between the two, exacerbated by Japan's lingering resentment at Russia's success in thwarting her ambitions in the Liaotung Peninsula, was to result in the severance by Japan of diplomatic relations with Russia — followed almost immediately by a Japanese attack on Port Arthur (Ryojun) which bottled up the Russian fleet and provoked the Russo-Japanese War of 1904-05. A Japanese treaty with Korea, in return for guarantees of integrity, rendered Korea a *de facto* Japanese protectorate, while in the war itself, the Japanese defeated the Russians in key land engagements at the Yalu River, Liaoyang, and, following the surrender of Port Arthur, at Mukden. To these the Japanese added a decisive sea victory in the Straits of Tsushima, when Russia's European fleet of some three dozen vessels, sent to achieve the relief of Port Arthur, was annihilated by Admiral Togo on 27–28 May 1905, entering the history books as the first major military engagement in which an Asian power had defeated a European power. The Treaty of Portsmouth at the War's end required the Russians to surrender the Liaotung Peninsula to the Japanese, to cede to her the southern half of Sakhalin, and to evacuate Manchuria. The Treaty also recognised Japan's special position in Korea, as had the Anglo-Japanese Alliance of 1902, and stipulated that the sovereignty of Korea should not henceforth be mentioned in any international treaty. Even before the signing of the peace treaty, Japanese diplomatic representa-tions in the United States, England, France, Germany and Austria had been elevated to the status of embassies; and Japan's demonstration of naval prowess had encouraged a ten-year renewal of the 1902 Anglo-Japanese alliance. Late in 1905, the Japanese secured by treaty with Korea the outright control of her foreign relations, while in a separate treaty China confirmed the terms of the Portsmouth Treaty. Two years later, the Korean Emperor abdicated in favour of his son, and Korea became a Japanese protectorate with complete control of governmental affairs in the hands of a Japanese Resident-General. Japan formally annexed Korea on 22 August 1910.

2. Indigenous forms of shamanism and animism had flourished in Korea long before the introduction of Buddhism, Confucianism and Taoism. When these more advanced religions did eventually arrive from continental Asia, the tendency was for them to be adapted to the older forms of belief. The resulting religious syncretism has profoundly coloured Korean attitudes to spiritual matters. As the government-sponsored *A Handbook of Korea*, 5th edn (Korea: Seoul, 1983) notes: 'In his religion as in much else, a Korean tends to be pragmatic. He will try anything once, and his criterion for evaluating a system of belief or a course of action is whether it works for him in a pinch.' (p. 193)

3. Jinsen, now Inch'on.

4. Lest the Webbs appear uniquely prejudiced in rendering this and like judgements to follow, note the following passage from T. Philip Terry, *Terry's Guide to the Japanese Empire, Including Korea and Formosa* (see this volume, Ch. 1, Note 53): 'In many respects the Korean is *sui generis*. Frugal in the use of water (to which he has a determined hostility), fond of a frowsy smell, economical of the truth, as avid of "fire-water" as the red man of the American plains, and with light prehensile fingers that readily assimilate the detachable impedimenta of the "foreign devil", he suspects the wide world

and possesses to a sordid degree the Oriental vices of duplicity, cunning and general untrustworthiness. He steals freely when the opportunity offers, and his capacious sleeves and balloon-like trousers make ideal places of concealment for one's cherished belongings. The spawn of a low order of civilisation, he is untidy and swinish in his habits, and apathetic in the face of work – for which he has a fervid distaste. He is a born dawdler, gambler and brawler; and, like the Chinaman, he has, in his fathomless conceit and besotted ignorance, a sturdy and unshakable faith in his own impeccability and the flagrant worthlessness of everything foreign. He is lethargic, purposeless, devoid of thrift or ambition, and he dwells contentedly amidst incredible dirt and discomfort.' (p. 719)

5. The collection, begun by the Japanese, has grown to over 90 000 items, and is located at Seoul's *Kyongbokgung*, the so-called North Palace, a complex of buildings periodically rebuilt on the same site since 1395. Since 1972, the collection has been housed in a new National Museum Building on the palace grounds. On display are artifacts found in excavations of the Nangang and Three Kingdoms periods, including Buddhist images, gold crowns and gold slippers, royal ornaments used by the kings and queens of Silla, as well as porcelain of the Konyo dynasty, lacquer inlaid with mother of pearl, and ornamented paintings of the Yi dynasty.

6. Ito Hirobumi (1814–1909). Ito had been the first Meiji-era Prime Minister of Japan, under the Cabinet system introduced in 1881. He formed three subsequent Cabinets. A leader of the more moderate exponents of Japanese hegemony over Korea following the Russo-Japanese war, he was appointed Resident-General of Korea in 1905. He was shot to death on 26 October 1909 by a young Korean nationalist, An Chung-gun, while on a visit to meet a Russian official at Harbin, Manchuria.

7. General Count Terauchi Masatake (b. 1852), had been War Minister in the Katsura Governments of 1901 and 1908, resigning to take up the position of Governor-General of Chosen in 1911.

8. Beatrice's enthusiasm notwithstanding, there is no entry for Dr Hashida, who oversaw production of the *Annual Report on Reforms and Progress in Korea*, published at Seoul by the Government General of Chosen, in the standard Japanese biographical dictionaries.

9. A slang expression signifying the substitution of bad money for good.

10. Cf. T. Philip Terry, *Terry's Guide*: 'One pities [Korean women] for the style of dress evidently forced upon them. As the feminine waistline is supposed to be at the arm-pits, and as tight swathing of the bust does not permit the mothers to respond readily to baby's hungry and imperious clamour, the twin maternal founts are worn, as it were, on the outside. Thus the firm buds of youth and the flapping rags of age are displayed to the world – exposing to all Korea what antipodal women strive to conceal. The bulging trousers of the women are the acme of unpicturesqueness, and they render them devoid of all grace and charm ... The present humane government is striving to ameliorate the condition of Korean women, and the closer observation by them of Western ways and manners, aided by the uplifting work of the missionaries, is having a beneficent effect.' (p. 724)

11. Until near the end of the Yi dynasty, the characteristic white Korean attire alluded to in this passage had been worn exclusively by the *yangban* or

gentry, but had since been more generally adopted. As for the 'silly little black hat', an adult Korean male was traditionally expected to have two hats, a black, wide-rimmed spherical hat, or *t'angon*, and a bamboo reed hat, or *kat*, which fitted over the black hat for formal indoor wear.

12. Sir Claude Macdonald (1852–1915). A career soldier and British Minister at Peking during the Boxer Rebellion, who served from 1900 to 1912 as Britain's first Ambassador to Japan.

13. Russia, having already built the Chinese Eastern Railway across Manchuria to Vladivostok under lease from China, had in 1902 completed a second line under similar arrangements, the South Manchuria Railway. But under the Treaty of Portsmouth ending the Russo-Japanese War, Russia's transfer to Japan of her rights and leases on the Liaotung Peninsula included the South Manchuria Railway – and Japan's new jurisdiction included not only the land immediately alongside the Railway but many cities and settlements as well, denying China the exercise of its sovereign power within an extensive Japanese zone. The acquisition of the Railway would thus enable the Japanese to penetrate Manchuria and in due course, to extend further their imperial ambitions in East Asia, an eventually already intimated in the opening Mukden entry of the China portion of the diary.

3
China

A long and tiring two days in the tiny little ramshackle service train, over the mountains and plains of South Manchuria, has brought us to Mukden. For the first day, we travelled in the company of the Inspecting Officer of the soldiers stationed along the line. It was interesting to watch, at each station, two private soldiers come to the door of the compartment, present arms, and then make a short, concise statement of everything that had happened. Our invaluable Nishi interpreted the statement to us. These extraordinary rank and file [soldiers] showed the typical reverence for the superior officer, and the intelligence and good judgement of the Japanese lower class, both in their attitude and in their words. It was a curious sensation, travelling under armed escort, along a line guarded by troops – all in times of peace. The Chinese coolies working on the line were tall and rather good-looking, with pleasant, intelligent faces. But some of them looking awful blackguards – most of them with a sly and shifty expression – without any consciousness of responsibility. We hear that they are terrible thieves and the line having to be guarded against their pilfering instincts. But up to now, we have only heard the Japanese side of the question.

MUKDEN OCTOBER 25–28th [1911]

The very evening we arrived here we were waited on by a young Chinese gentleman, speaking excellent English, who came at the request of our friend, Mr. Shen (an old student of The [London] School of Economics,[1] and now a Secretary of the Board of Foreign Affairs at Peking), to see what he could do for us. With quiet courtesy, he signified, when we told him that we had an introduction to the Japanese Consul and the Mitsui representative, that we were now in China and that these gentlemen would not be able to show us Mukden. We at once signified that we were aware that the Japanese Consul was here no more than the English Consul, but that unfortunately, not

117

thinking that we should be in Mukden, we had omitted to procure an introduction to the Viceroy. He at once offered to arrange for us, during our stay. So for three days, we have been exclusively in the hands of the Chinese officials. After the first day, we found that, though the officials were very courteous to Nishi, they evidently preferred to have us alone — one of the younger men even remarking in his presence as making it impossible to speak frankly — 'The Japanese are our most dangerous neighbours' — so Nishi now stays at home, and we sally out with the Chinese officials.[2] Unlike the Japanese, they are always in native costume.

The officials, of whom there seem an abundance in all the departments of Government, are, of course, immeasurably inferior to the Japanese officials — a self-indulgent, indolent-looking lot, who seem to be perpetually smoking and drinking tea, and who are only too ready to leave their offices at any excuse. Some of them speak excellent English, and have quiet, dignified manners, but with the exception of the young Private Secretary and another young official, they are repulsive, dirty, disingenuous, and coarse-looking and sensual. Also, there is a general appearance of inefficiency and drift. The old Viceroy is a kindly and dignified-looking old aristocrat,[3] but all his words are ceremonial, and he is surrounded by a lot of sloppy personages, who do not seem to have any particular function. Judged by the Government of Manchuria, the Chinese administration seems that of an uncivilised race, and it makes one feel how essentially Western in its standards is the Government of Japan.

At the gorgeous but barbarous tombs of the Manchus, we were met by half-a-dozen officials, and one soldier as escort, who had jolted over the plain in the slow Chinese wagons to do us honour. The younger official talked English, but neither he nor the others knew anything about their great antiquities. The day was brilliant and the stately but empty mansions of the dead Emperor — the first of the Manchus — looked barbarously beautiful, with the golden-hued, tiled roof standing out against the deep blue sky, and harmonising with the autumn tints of the forest trees.[4] There was no sign of religious observance or religious feeling — all the labour and art were devoted to the glorification of the ancestor of the living man. To and from these tombs of the great, we pottered over the graves of innumerable unnamed inhabitants — some mounds were already ploughed up, others were standing in marsh and water — none were respected. It is not the spirit of the ancestor that is revered: it is the power of the inheritor of the ancestor.

We were received ceremoniously by the old Viceroy — offered tea, wine and cigarettes, and most kindly and courteously treated. He held

Sidney's hand on parting, and effusively assured him of his gratitude for the kindness we had shown to the Chinese students in London! The old man looked weary – he had the expression of old-world meditation on the vanity of all things – an abstraction from the practical and executive side of life – so different from the business-like officials and matter-of-fact conversation of the Japanese governor or statesman.

During our stay here, we have met the old veteran British Consul of Yokohama – Mr. [Carey] Hall,[5] for forty years in Japan, and the young Consul-General of Manchuria – Mr. Willis, a pleasant and shrewd Cambridge man, who has been some [SW: eighteen] years in the East in the consular service.[6] Both dislike the Japanese and speak well of the Chinese. Hall, who is a kindly and boresome old gentleman, a fanatical Comtist,[7] could not tell us clearly what was wrong with the Japanese, except that they were, in their legislation and administration, unjust to the foreign resident. When we cross-examined him, he could only cite the tariffs and the partial administration of the customs, and the way in which all the town improvements of Yokohama had been laid out to depreciate the property of foreign settlement! He said that, though the Judges were just, the procedure of the courts was unjust to the foreigners. Moreover, this hostility to the foreigner and determination to squeeze him out of the Japanese business world, was done in a cunning, underhand way. On the other hand, though he asserted that Parliament was corrupt, he said that, as far as he knew, the Government was financially as pure as in England, and that there was little or no corruption in the giving of contracts. 'They are a cruel race!': for had they not murdered the Queen of Korea? He also had a story that Prince Katsura had sent Prince Ito to Korea knowing that he would be murdered by the Koreans in order to get rid of him! His only ground for liking the Chinese and believing in their future, was that they were followers of Confucius – and Confucius had anticipated some of the infallible doctrines of Auguste Comte. Confucius was a 'scientific moralist', free from all superstitious mysticism; and upon so firm a basis a great people would arise. When I somewhat flippantly suggested that there had already been plenty of time for this event to come to pass, he lost himself in some long-worded explanation of their past failures, the gist of which has passed out of my mind.

Willis was much less demonstrative in his bias. He even admitted the superiority of the Japanese. The Japanese administration of the S.M. Railway, and of Japanese industry in Manchuria, was a monument of real efficiency – he doubted whether any European race could have done so well. But, their method of sending bevies of prostitutes in advance, to get hold of the men of the place, was only one illustration of their unrighteous cunning![8] [And] though he asserted that the

Chinese were an abler and better race, he declared that, after ten years in China, he had become hopeless as to the future of the empire. There was no hope in the present revolution – the only hope was in the Manchu dynasty and its centralised Government. No new Government could keep the great carcass intact – and if it once broke up into fragments, the other [P]owers would either intervene to re-establish the old order, or divide the whole place up. Mrs. Willis, a pleasant but commonplace woman – was more outspoken in her preferences. The Chinese were excellent servants – and all the Chinese coolies understood the respect that was due to the wife of the White Man in command. But the Japanese clerk in the hotel had actually dared to finish the job he had in hand, before taking her card to a visitor in the hotel! In fact, to sum up her objection, the Japanese did not know their place as an inferior race. There was no such pretension among the docile and obedient Chinaman.

[SW→] Our three days at Mukden were spent in a series of drives in the primitive 'droshky'[9] costing 8/- a day, drawn by a miserable horse and driven by a Chinese driver, speaking no word of English, whose neatly-plaited pigtail ending in blue cords was surmounted by a fur cap of Russian type. In going to and from the comfortable S.M. Railway Hotel, the Chinese Bureau of Foreign Affairs, the Palace and the nine separate Chinese Government institutions that we visited, we seemed to traverse every street, and to penetrate into every part of the crowded, walled city, where 200,000 Chinese herd in one-storied tiled houses of indescribable dirt and disorder. Up and down the densely-crowded lanes we drove, through masses of men (and few women) in all shades of blue clothes; rude teams of two, three or four horses, asses or oxen drawing country produce, wood, charcoal and building material; Chinese carts and *rickshas* and now and then a primitive 'glass-coach' (as the English called it 200 years ago)[10] containing some Chinese official, with pigtailed servant standing on the seat behind, and outriding horsemen preceding and following.

But Mukden, even Chinese Mukden, had felt the stimulus of Japanese competition, and had been for the past 5 or 7 years trying to adopt Western improvements – there was a decrepit horse tramway run by a Chinese-Japanese Company, which bought up and transplanted the horsecarts that Tokyo discarded six years ago; there were two steam-rollers at work on the crowded lane leading to the main gate of the town, making a real macadam road; there were Chinese policemen in elaborate uniform with swords every fifty yards, to keep order in the crowd and regulate the dense traffic; there were perpetual marches to and fro of companies of Chinese soldiers, got up in European army style, but still looking most unwarlike; and there were the nine new

Government institutions over which we were conducted by one or other official of the 'Bureau of Foreign Affairs'.

We had asked this 'Bureau' and the Viceroy, besides the inevitable palace[11] and tomb which every tourist sees, to let us see 'institutions'. It took some trouble to convince them what we meant, but when they did understand, they did the job thoroughly! In a day and a half we were taken to no fewer than 9 institutions; a girls' school for training teachers; an elementary school for young children; a boys' normal school for turning out men teachers; a 'college' for young men; a technical school; a sort of industrial training-school for poor boys; a domestic arts training-school for women; and two remarkable new prisons, one for minor offenders, the other for long sentence convicts. Not one of these existed five years ago!

The schools were primitive, and almost farcical in their inefficiency. The girls' school, which seemed to include girls of all ages, including some already adult, had a nice-looking Chinese woman as matron, under a man Principal. The teachers were all Chinese girls in native costume, who seemed inefficient [*sic*] enough. But it is to their credit that they are putting their girls under women teachers, and not (like Japan) under men. Only a few classes were at work, and we could not form any idea of the curriculum.

We then went to what was shown to us as an elementary school, presumably the only one in Mukden's 200,000 inhabitants. It was elementary enough – indeed, mere kindergarten exercises were elaborately performed by over 100 children said to be from six to ten years old, boys and girls only distinguishable by the latter wearing earrings. The kindergarten tunes were those adopted from England or America that we had heard in Japan: and there was present one Japanese woman teacher in her own costume, by whom the others had apparently been taught. These others were three Chinese women (two with Manchu head-dress, and one without), who had the typical kindly expression of the infant mistress – a promising beginning of the professional woman teacher-class. The school was for the middle class, and we gathered that there were no schools for the 25,000 children of the 'coolies' and labouring class. We were kept so long looking at the infantile kindergarten exercises – done by boys and girls who were, some of them, just on ten years old – that when we got to the boys' normal school, it was empty. We saw the buildings which, like all those of institutional Mukden, were in European style, not badly built, but flimsy, and still under construction or repair. (In all these institutions, building work of one sort or another was going on.)

Next day, S.W. went alone to the 'college', which turned out to be a residential institution in which boys (and adults of as much as 30) were taught literary subjects. (Chinese classics and Chinese history and elementary geometry were all that were actually seen, but English was taught, and also German!) The students were said to remain for ten years (but the place was only opened about four years ago). They paid, for board, residence and education, about 8/- a month only: and even at this price, half were Government scholars paying nothing. They were trying to get out a Cambridge graduate to teach English. The students were said to be going to become 'officials' — perhaps 'clerks' was meant. The teaching seemed poor, the teachers mechanical and untrained, and the chemical laboratory was of the most elementary kind, without provision for individual work. There was no library.

The technical school, apparently for boys and men of 15 to 30, was somewhat better: it had, in its laboratory, benches for individual work; there was an able but unfortunately 'pert' young Chinese in European dress who taught English (he had been six years at Manchester Grammar School and Owens College); and there seemed more reality in the teaching. Most of the students were said to be likely to become teachers. They were certainly not likely to become chemists, or Engineers! They paid 10/- per month, including board, lodging and education. They slept 30 or 40 together in long dormitories, with a raised platform, heated by flues underneath in the same style as in Korea, on each side some three feet high, divided into separate places by partitions a foot high, in each of which was a rude mattress and coverlet. They washed in common in an adjoining room, having open-cupboard pigeon-holes on each side, in which were kept each man's primitive toilet requisites. There was said to be a common bath-room somewhere close by. The herding together of several hundred young men of different ages in this way, for years together, appears open to grave objection. Altogether, these five educational institutions, well-intentioned as they were, and promising as they may be for China as a beginning, were amazingly imperfect; and showed markedly less capacity for adaptation than the Japanese institutions.

The next place was more indigenous and peculiar. It was a sort of industrial or trade training-school for poor boys. Some 300 boys and youths from 15 to 25 were at work in a range of workshops, actually making things — carpentry, cabinet-making, boot-making, smith's work, spinning, hand-loom weaving, and sword-making. There was said to be some literary instruction in the evening. It was particularly stated that the boys had committed no offence, so it was not a reformatory school in our sense. They were said to be admitted free, on account of poverty, to be maintained whilst under instruction, to be not allowed to go out, and to be expelled for grave misconduct. It was not an orphanage or foundling hospital, because the boys were said to have parents in Mukden, who visited them from time to time. Apparently it was a system of state apprenticeship, an institution for training up a race of skilled artisans; and for that it does not seem ill-contrived, though costly. But there seems to be a steady sale for their products; and as the cost of bare living is small, the net cost may not be great. Such as it is, it is defrayed by the Manchurian Government.

In the afternoon, we were taken to a school of domestic arts for women — aged from 15 to 40. Some were being taught to read and write. But the bulk of them were at work at different kinds of needle crafts — embroidery, brocade (hand-machine), crochet, knitting, dress-making, etc., together with painting or rather illumination, and hand-loom weaving. Apparently an attempt to supply education to women! The matron in charge was a kindly-looking Chinese woman with small feet, who toddled from room to room with us.

But the greatest surprise was the couple of prisons with which we concluded our programme. Our idea of Chinese prisons was that of noisome dungeons, with cruel and avaricious gaolers, who perpetuated all sorts of torture, and left the unhappy prisoners to feed themselves or die of hunger. Imagine our surprise to find two new prisons built on modern European patterns, clean and sanitary, with the most humane arrangements.

The first prison was what used in England to be called a house of correction, for relatively minor offenders. But it apparently took in those sentenced to anything up to five years imprisonment, and had some 300 inmates, all males. These were all busily at work in a dozen light and airy workshops, at as many different trades — boot-making, carpentering, blacksmithing, printing, tailoring, hand-loom weaving and even sword-making! The products were sold to the Government as to other buyers; and the Director told us that he could now get no money from the Government for extensions or improvements, because he had been able to report that the prison completely covered its maintenance expenses! The men were lightly chained at the waist and ankles, but they came and went freely, going to relieve nature as they chose, and there seemed to be little formality or restraint. There were armed police or warders in uniform standing about; but there was no martial discipline. The Director (in civil Chinese dress) was evidently a philanthropic enthusiast, who had thought out for himself this plan of prison administration, without having been to any other country, though he had studied a model prison at Tientsin — explaining to us, with natural pride, that the Tientsin prison officers had since come to study his prison. The two defects that we noticed were that the sleeping cells (built as one-storey rows of cells radiating from a centre, exactly after Bentham's model)[12] were occupied each by half-a-dozen

prisoners; and that there was no effective separation of young
offenders from old. We put these criticisms to the Director, who said
that he had been convinced by experience on both these points, and
only wished he could extend the accommodation to enable what he
had fully recognised as defects to be remedied.

The second prison was for long sentence men, apparently from 5
years upwards; and it contained some 700 men and 30 women. Here,
too, the Director was in civilian (Chinese) dress, though all the warders
were in the gorgeous police uniform and fully armed. He, too, was of
the philanthropic enthusiast type, but more doctrinaire and opinionated. He had travelled and seen prisons in Europe and America, and
apparently knew all that there was to know on the subject. This prison
was larger than the house of correction, and more complicated in
structure. There was the same crowding together of half-a-dozen
prisoners in a cell – even in the afternoon, half-a-dozen were idle in
a cell, it being explained that they were put there for safety when their
job was done. There was the same mixture of young and old. But there
was also the same extraordinary extent and variety of productive
work, in the same sort of light and airy workshops; including even
spinning and weaving by steam-power, lithographic printing (of
illustrations for a school book), and, most extraordinary of all, the
printing and machining of the Mukden daily (Chinese) newspaper: the
issue for 'tomorrow' was actually being machined off when we were
there. We asked about punishments in both places, and were told that
these consisted only of putting on short rations and confinement in [a]
dark cell (the maximum being five days in one, and seven days in the
other prison). The ration (of *kaoliang*,[13] apparently) was served out in a
sort of quart measure, which was the full quantum. For slight offences,
one disk of wood an inch thick was put in this measure, thus reducing
the space for food. A second, third and fourth disk could be added; so
as to reduce the food to a bare minimum.

Curiously enough, it was in the long sentence prison that half the
men were working unchained, we could not ascertain why.

All these institutions of mushroom growth, sprung up within a few
years, extraordinarily 'uneven' in their development, without system or
co-ordination, dependent on the accident of particular personal whims
or enthusiasms, plainly quite without popular support or real root, and
therefore quite unstable – represent, it seems, the best hope that China
affords. We do not yet see much ground for hope in a New China, or
for belief in a possible regeneration of the race.

Leaving Mukden, we sped for 24 hours to Peking – across wide
stretches of plain, only partly cultivated (for *kaoliang*, apparently) –
partly almost desert and devastated by periodical floods which

transform the trickling streams into torrents half a mile wide, against which the railway has to construct elaborate embankments and training-walls. The villages seemed sparse, in style like those of Korea, each family living in a quadrangular compound, one side being a row of one-storied rooms with a curious 'barrel' roof of mud, the other sides forming stables for cows, etc., or more rooms, probably for sons' families, etc. Occasional flocks of sheep; more commonly, black pigs routing about for a living, indiscriminately. We saw no temples and very few little shrines. But everywhere the eye was caught by the little mounds which represent graves – the unmarked, neglected graves of the unnamed dead. The plain is almost bare of trees, which have been improvidently cut for fuel; and it is bordered by jagged chains of bare, rocky mountains. Altogether a most uninviting landscape.

Toward Peking, the aspect becomes more civilised. There has been much planting of trees. There are fruit orchards, and presently, endless market-gardens. Then our attention is caught by trains crowded with Chinese, who not only fill every carriage, but are even riding on the buffers. The Chinese, we are told, are fleeing from Peking, in fear lest the Manchus should revenge on them the successes (and perhaps the atrocities) of the Revolutionaries who are holding Hankow, and so much of the South. What shall we find at Peking?

PEKING 29th OCTOBER 1911

'Peking is as quiet as London,' had said one consular person who had just left it. We saw nothing unusual in the crowded, noisy, dirty streets of the Chinese City, where we walked this afternoon, under the guidance of the only Fabian in Peking (a mild Irish youth, son of a clergyman, who is an instructor to the Chinese candidates for the Imperial Maritime Customs service).[14] 'Nothing is going to happen,' said to us the French banker whom we called on. But the Japanese Minister, whom we saw in the afternoon, said that the Chinese were so 'panicky', that it would not be safe for us to go to the Nankow Pass, and that (whilst the Legation Quarter[15] was safe enough) there might well be outbursts of riot, etc. Long strings of dromedaries, heavily laden with miscellaneous goods, the nose of each attached by a cord to the preceding animal, the one driver of the whole procession walking by the leader – form, to us, an unexpected sight. They are caravans to and from Mongolia, through the Nankow Pass, carrying tea and petroleum from Peking, and bringing in produce and skins. We left Mukden already under ice; but Peking is still hot.

1st NOVEMBER [1911]

After three days of Peking (crowded with lunches and dinner with the cosmopolitan foreign set, and interviews with Chinese ex-students of The London School of Economics and some other officials to whom we have been introduced), we jot down a few impressions.

Certainly, it is a most exciting moment to come to Peking; or rather it would be if one had any confidence that anything new would really come about in this unchanging country. We live from hour to hour without knowing whether the Revolutionists will defeat the Imperial troops and seize the rest of the country; or whether the Imperial troops will defeat the Revolutionaries and end the rebellion. And the uncertainty is that, whether one or the other event happens, there may be a massacre in Peking itself – either an uprising against the Manchus, in which an attempt will be made to kill as many of them as possible, or an outburst of wild revenge by the Manchu troops against the Chinese – or, again, merely an angry 'hunger riot' among the many tens of thousands of *ricksha* men and coolies if their miserable subsistence is somehow interrupted. How real is either of these dangers we cannot judge. The Legation seem to be very quietly taking a few precautions (we hear a little of such in respect of Japanese subjects, and of the Roman Catholics, and the American Legation has served out arms to some American missionaries to enable them to protect themselves. But the British Legation is wholly absorbed in the wedding of the Ambassador's daughter which takes place today, and has simply refused to attend to some anxious British residents' enquiries and appeals). We are assured that foreigners will not be molested. But on the other hand, the Chinese are full of rumours. For the past week, each night in succession has been named as that on which the rising has been quite definitely fixed to take place. Something like a hundred thousand people have actually fled out of Peking. Everywhere we go, we find the most absurd panic. Every available room in this and the only other foreign hotel has been taken by the wives and daughters and young sons of Manchu and Chinese of high official position or rank, in the belief that they would be safe in the foreigners' hotels. The other morning there trooped into the breakfast-room two Chinese ladies and eight or ten children – we were told the families of the principal officers of the Bureau of Foreign Affairs. The families of Prince Ch'ing,[16] the Prime Minister who has just been dismissed, and of Na-tung his Assistant,[17] are said to be also here. We hear of the 'boys' of our European families begging that their wives and children may be taken in for protection. One of Bishop Scott's[18] women servants has seriously prepared two dresses to flee in, if the massacre occurs, one in which to pass as a Manchu and the other in which to pass as a Chinese, according to which may turn out to be the massacring party! (This is authentic.)

The University, and all the schools, even down to the foreign kindergartens for the rich, are depleted, three-quarters of the pupils having fled away. We saw the university professors addressing classes of five and seven, and so on. At the instruction college of the I.M. Customs,[19] where the same depletion has occurred (though leave to go had been actually refused), we were being shown over the half-deserted premises by the Director (Brewitt Taylor),[20] who threw open the door of one of the dormitories. We there found a pale and trembling youth, with a half-packed portmanteau. 'Are you packing or unpacking?' asked the Director. It appeared that the youth was preparing to flee, and when asked why, he could only stammer that he was afraid. 'Silly boy,' said the Director, and let him go.

It is not a propitious moment to try to see the Chinese. Lord Li (Vice-President of the Board of Communication),[21] the son of Li Hung-chang,[22] is hiding in M. Cazenave's compound (a French banker);[23] and has naturally not responded to the letter we sent on. Our friend G. K. Shen, who is a Secretary of the Bureau of Foreign Affairs, who had so effectually befriended us at Mukden, and who had written so warmly promising us help at Peking, made no sign for three days. At last we sought out his house in the far recesses of the Tartar City.[24] After much hammering at the closed outer door, he made his appearance. The house had been cleared of all its contents, which he had shipped off, with all his family, actually to Shanghai; apparently on a sudden resolve between 21st October, when he wrote to us at Mukden, and 26th October. He had just returned from Tientsin, to which he had conducted them, and where he placed them on board a British ship. Naturally, he was agitated. But he was most friendly, gave us tickets for the National Assembly or Senate, spent an hour talking with us at the hotel, and has invited us to lunch next Sunday at the Summer Palace, where he seems to be on duty.

The tension was a little relieved on Tuesday, 31st Oct., by the news of the re-capture of Hankow by the Imperialists, a success more dramatic than strategically important, but one which was made the most of in Peking, and doubtless elsewhere — and by the issue of an extraordinary Imperial Edict, in which the Emperor (or Regent)[25] confessed he had been all in the wrong, dismissed and censured the existing Prime Minister and other Ministers, promised 'Responsible Government' for the future, and amnestied all offenders.[26] The terms of self-abasement and contrition in which this document was couched were extraordinary. This Edict seemed to make the officials whom we saw quite confident that all would now be well; that the Revolutionaries would lay down their arms, and that the promises of reform would be kept.

We happened to be lunching with Dr. Morrison, the celebrated '*Times*' Correspondent here,[27] with whom were Lord ffrench (agent of English railway contractor and banking interests here),[28] the Willard Straights (he representing American banking interests, Pierpont Morgan, etc.),[29] and the representative of the *New York Tribune* (Patchin).[30] There came also Dr. W. W. Yen, a cultivated Chinese official in high position, described to us as the habitual 'go-between' the Court and the Legations.[31] He adumbrated, as possible Prime Ministers, either Hsu Shih-ch'ang[32] or Na-tung, these having been the Assistants of Prince Ch'ing. It was interesting to see Morrison, ffrench, Straight and Patchin say with one accord that this would not do; that if so, it was 'all up with the Manchus'; that it would create the worst possible impression in Europe; that the Revolutionaries would continue to have the sympathies of the world, and so on. 'Why not make Yuan Shih-k'ai Prime Minister?' they said. Now, Yuan Shih-k'ai[33] seems to have been the man whom the popular voice called to be put in command of the Army, with power to treat with the Revolutionaries. Unknown to Peking, he had (Dr. W. W. Yen now told us) been given this appointment and sent to the South on the preceding Saturday. It may be that he had been given this appointment as a concession to public opinion, with a view to removing him from the chance of [the] Prime Ministership. Dr. Yen of course said nothing. Next day, we find that it is *Yuan Shih-k'ai* who, to everybody's surprise and relief, is appointed Prime Minister, in spite of his absence. We could not help wondering whether we had not perhaps been 'assisting' at his real appointment!

Next day we were dining with the Willard Straights, when a new Edict arrived which appointed Prince Ch'ing and others to the Privy Council — this seemed a retrograde step, as if the Manchu oligarchy intended to set up the Privy Council as an obstacle to Yuan Shih-k'ai as Prime Minister, and to the National Assembly.

In reality we know nothing, and I don't believe anyone in Peking knows anything, about the real position throughout China. There is the very minimum of news, either from the seat of war or from the other provinces. Probably London gets far more telegrams from different points in and round China than we do in Peking. The Legations live in the midst of Palace gossip and 'camp rumours'; but of useful information as to the condition of the interior, they seem to have practically none.

What are we to think about the Chinese as a people? We have now been among them, from Mukden to Peking, only nine days. We are struck, first of all, by the complete difference of attitude and opinion among the European population as to the Chinese and Japanese respectively. The Japanese are universally and frankly disliked. No one has a good word for them. Everyone tells us horrid little stories about their doings, mostly absurd. On the other hand, every European and American man or woman professes to like the Chinese, and to speak well of them. When we proceed to ask what it is that they like in them, they do not find it easy to justify their admiration. We hear that the Chinese are honest, docile, industrious, sober; and it appears that our friends are thinking of them as house-servants! (As such, there is the set-off that they have no initiative, and cannot meet emergencies for which they have no orders; they are apt to leave suddenly without notice; and they practice to an extraordinary extent the art of getting commissions, the universal 'squeeze' of China; besides, somehow or other, one needs at least three times as many Chinese servants as would suffice with English servants.)

The Chinese-educated official class speaks English with extraordinary fluency and correctness of idiom and pronunciation — their fault is glibness — and the students are said to be hard-working, persistent and really capable intellectually, especially at *learning* mathematics and languages. But we cannot learn that they show any originality, or power of independent thought. They seem to be producing some translations, but practically no original works of any kind, in any language — nor is there anything to speak of being produced in poetry or painting or sculpture, or even artistic handicraft, in all of which they excelled some centuries ago. In everything that relates to administration, they are hopelessly inefficient.

We cannot make out that our European friends, even those who have been here for ten years, have made any close friendships with [the] Chinese, or indeed, have any really intellectual intercourse with them, even with the outwardly polished and English-speaking officials whom they receive at dinner. (Apparently the Chinese women never go out to dinner or receive visitors — except that the Manchu Princesses have lately begun to receive European lady callers.) Along with this professed liking for the Chinese, there is everywhere an openly-expressed contempt for them — which is given utterance to even in the presence at table of English-speaking Chinese officials — contempt for their inefficiency, their corruption, their cowardice, their cruelty as a race.

Our feeling is that the English and Americans have really so low an opinion of the Chinese that they habitually and unconsciously refuse to think of them on the same plane as themselves. They are never judging them by the same standards or really considering them as human beings at all. They like them as house-servants, because they are docile, and never resent being sworn at! (However, even in this capacity, it must be remembered that there are no other servants to be got.) It is part of this way of looking at them that they are not criticised for their sexual self-indulgence, or their general materialist sensuality – any more than a goat or a cat is. It never occurs to them to estimate the Chinese as a nation, on a par with European nations, having a civilisation of its own, and entitled to equality of consideration and treatment. And they are angry with the Japanese for insisting on being regarded and treated exactly in this way; they resent the extraordinary energy and persistency, the concentration of purpose and the undeniable efficiency, with which the Japanese have made good their position as the equals of the white race, and as its rivals in war and trade; even its successful rivals, before whose steadily-growing power the foreigner is losing ground in Japan itself, in finance as well as in commerce. The success of the Japanese comes as an unpleasant shock to the dignity or the self-conceit of the Englishman; and he has an uncomfortable feeling that the Japanese may actually beat him in some respects; as he actually does in intellectual curiosity and open-mindedness and in intellectual humility; even, perhaps, in family and national altruism and in patriotism. The Chinese offer the English no such shock. They accept their position of subordination and inferiority;[34] and they give the self-complacent Englishman or woman no such qualms and uneasy feelings – therefore, by contrast with the Japanese, he says he likes them! Really, he likes them for their manifest inferiority and shortcomings.

It is interesting to hear a very general opinion that the widespread revolutionary feeling, and the very general sympathy with it among the educated class, is due in the main to the Chinese students who have been educated in Japan. During the past ten or twelve years, there have been many thousand such, and these are now holding official positions all over the empire. Two years ago, the Government came to the conclusion that they were being thus corrupted, and stopped sending them. But the mischief had already gone far. We may disbelieve some wild statements as to the Japanese Government actually fomenting rebellion among them. What seems to have happened, as several thoughtful Chinese officials have told us, is that the students became aware in Japan of the difference between the European treatment of the Chinese and the Japanese. They saw their cousins, the Japanese, whose civilisation had been actually derived from China, treated by the Europeans on terms of equality. They saw them really possessing their own country, and maintaining its independent position against foreign powers. This made the Chinese students realise, as they had never done before, and as those who go to England and America are not compelled to do, the profoundly humiliating position into which China has been forced. They come back to Japan determined to restore to China its independence of foreign interference. And it is the Manchu Government that they blame as the cause of China's woes.

Dr. G. E. Morrison, the *Times* Correspondent, is an energetic and impulsive Australian Scotchman – a more steady and solid Garvin[35] – who is universally respected and liked by the Chinese, but whose position and influence with the Europeans is said to have been impaired latterly by his close intimacy with the financial group, of which more anon. He showed us his splendid collection of books and pamphlets relating to China (including a number of paintings on silk, etc.), which he is reported to intend to bequeath to some Peking institution.[36] But it is worth a large sum in cash, and it would not be surprising if he eventually converted it into a superannuation provision. He is just now intensely excited over the revolution, and is eager for its success, to such an extent as to impair his judgement. He says he wants to see an ocean of blood, as the only way of ridding China effectually from the Manchu incubus.

The financial group[37] consists of Willard Straight, an interesting young American of about 35, a student at Cornell when we were there in 1898, who became a Vice-Consul in Manchuria, etc., and is said to have been inspired by Shaw's *Major Barbara* (last Act) to go in for making money as the means of getting power.[38] He was taken up by Pierpont Morgan, and became his agent in China. With him, there is a certain Lord ffrench, a tall, aristocratic, languid Irish Peer, who here represents Pauling & Co., the railway contractors, whilst the local Manager of the Hong Kong and Shanghai Bank represents a group of English bankers. With Cazenave, of the Banque de l'Indo Chine, and a representative of German banks, Straight managed to get into line these four financial powers, and to get them to agree to make a loan of some millions to enable China to reform its currency. With great skill and energy, Straight got this 'Four Power Loan' through, and got the Chinese Government to agree to all necessary terms. He then married Dorothy Whitney, an enormously wealthy American girl of usual type; and they are just come again to Peking after a brief honeymoon. But alas!, the revolution has, for the present, upset the loan.[39] The Chinese Minister responsible for it was impeached by the National Assembly, just as we arrived; and he promptly took refuge against assassination with the American Legation, to be instantly sent down to Tientsin under guard of American soldiers. He was put on board ship for Shanghai; but we heard on Monday that a telegram had come from Shanghai saying that he would not be safe there, so that a hasty telegram was sent to Tsingtao, where the ship would put in, telling him to disembark in the German possession as his only chance of safety.[40]

The British Legation promised to send S.W. a ticket of admission to the Tzu-cheng yuan, or National Assembly, which is meeting daily; but no such ticket has come. Meanwhile, we have been furnished with a handful of tickets by our Chinese friends — this is typical of our experience of British Legations — and S.W. sat through a sitting. This Parliament, admittedly only on a provisional basis pending the full coming into force of the new constitution, consists of 100 Members nominated by the Crown (Princes of the royal blood, high officials, great landlords and wealthy men, and some distinguished *literati*), and about 100 Members representing the provincial assemblies. Each of these has to nominate about six members, three out of whom are thereupon chosen by the Crown to represent the province. The Assembly is meeting temporarily in the large hall of the Law Faculty, where the 200 Members sit in ordinary chairs at common tables, exactly as if they were candidates at the examination. The President, two Vice-Presidents and two Secretaries sit, like the continental 'bureau', on a dais. The Members speak usually from their seats, but go to [the] tribune to read any long document or make a set oration. They are said to be developing great oratorical powers; and one deputy from Shanghai was particularly noticeable in this way, his remarks eliciting volumes of hand-clapping.

[BW→] 5th NOVEMBER [1911]

We had a delightful two days visiting the Ming tombs and the Nankow Pass. A curious episode with the *ricksha* showed the lack of discipline and bad police of Peking. We had taken a guide from the hotel, and when we arrived at the station after about an hour's run in three *rickshas*, Sidney enquired what he should pay the three *ricksha* men. The guide said the correct fare was 50 c. each, but suggested 60 c., whereupon Sidney gave them 2 dollars, which was 20 c. more than the guide had suggested. Then ensued a scene of extraordinary rowdiness — two of the men began expostulating — they wanted a bigger fare. From mere angry words, one of them began to almost assault Sidney, actually pushing him about. There was a policeman standing close by to whom we appealed — but he looked quite helpless and said nothing to prevent the man from continuing to annoy us. At last, a superior officer consented to listen to the guide and the *ricksha* man, both shouting at each other; and in the end the official succeeded in sending the man away. The next day when we were returning, there was the usual crowd of *ricksha* men screaming at the top of their voices and scrambling for the passengers. But they were only gesticulating and were not breaking the peace. The policeman, however, struck at them brutally, and, I think, hurt one man considerably — without apparently producing any anger from the *ricksha* man! With such a population one understands the fear of a riot and wholesale looting, if there was any uncertainty as to the power of the Government.

Our guide turned out to be an illiterate man who barely understood English. We provided him with a mule, and took another for our wraps and lunch, and tramped off across the plains from Nankow to the Ming tombs. It was brilliant sunshine, bright air but still, and the twenty-mile walk was extraordinarily interesting and beautiful — the Ming monuments wonderful in their barbaric beauty, set in mountain ranges and harmonised by the autumn tints of the trees that surrounded them.[41] The next day we had a vision of the Great Wall[42] climbing from mountain to mountain; and from one of the towers we looked down on the plains of Mongolia and watched the long processions of camels wending their way along the ancient caravan way from the Far East to the plains of Russia. After the sophisticated atmosphere of the Legation Quarter, this glimpse of ancient China was extraordinarily invigorating. And it was interesting to walk through the country and actually see the Chinese villages with their mud-walled homesteads, their carefully-levelled mud floor for threshing — and with their little groups of men and boys smoking and lounging — their women and girls with feet that were barely big enough to stand on and quite impossible for walking. No temples, merely here and there the mean-looking and badly-kept little shrine for the burning of incense. The country population, like the coolies of the towns, are most unpleasant to look on — dirty and undisciplined [and] with that same mocking smile on the faces of young and old — sometimes cringing, sometimes hostile. At the tombs, we were surrounded by beggars and importunate caretakers — at every place you visit in China there seem to be hosts of men and boys perpetually holding out their hands. And one has an uncomfortable feeling that, if one were alone and if they did not fear the retribution that inevitably follows attacks on foreigners, the hand that is now held out would quickly pass to the hand which takes forcibly, property, and if necessary, life.

Yesterday, Saturday, Mr. [SW: G. K. Shen] of the Board of Foreign Affairs, who was to have taken us to lunch at the Summer Palace, sent his friend and colleague, Mr. Lo, to tell us that he had had to leave Peking hurriedly, as he had had bad news. The troops in the far-off province of which his father was Governor had mutinied, and Shanghai, where he had taken his wife and children for safety, had gone over to the Revolutionaries. So Mr. Lo was to call for us 8.30 on Sunday, and take us out to the Summer Palace and the Zoological Gardens.[43]

The expedition was very interesting, because we not only saw the old home of the wicked old Empress Dowager[44] with an intelligent guide, but we had some five- or six-hours talk with a thoroughly cultivated young Chinese official. Mr. Lo [SW: aged 24] was a son of a late Minister to England[45] and had been educated at Cambridge [SW: where he took the Economics Tripos in 1909. He had gone to England at 9 with his father in 1896, and had been there ever since until 1909. He had first been apprenticed to Armstrongs[46] as [an] Engineer, and had then gone to Cambridge. He] spoke English fluently, and had quite clearly observed and thought about political and economic questions. Like Mr. Shen, he had that strangely timid and nerveless personality which I think must arise from some sort of bad personal hygiene. He was perpetually smoking and drinking cups of tea, and his skin and eyes looked thoroughly unhealthy. But he was intelligent and frank and gave us a vision of the condition of the Civjl Service and of the daily life of the ruling classes.

Every Government office was overmanned and no one was expected to attend his office for more than half the working day. Some of the superior officials spent the whole of their lives eating dinners [SW: sometimes several in one evening] – at one house or the other, and were perpetually paying calls – so much so that it was said they killed their horses in one year! The family system meant that any successful man was a prey to his relatives and that when he died, numbers of people were left with nothing to live on, unless they could prey on his son. The great aim of life was to get two or three separate appointments – Shen had secured at least three different offices [SW: one at the Foreign Office, one at the National Assembly, and one in the Board of Communications], and had raked up an income of five or six hundred pounds a year – Mr. Lo had only one, so he had all his mornings free for study. All the students who went abroad became civil servants – and all the sons of important persons were pushed into one office or the other – generally into two or three. No one had any other purpose but to get some sort of livelihood out of the Government, for himself and his family. He was really very pessimistic about the condition of China, though he thought that the revolution would somehow or other alter things for the better. He believed the Revolutionaries would take Tientsin and Peking and that the Court would fly and the Manchu soldiers with them – and it would be, in some ways, a good thing if they did, as that would mean a bloodless revolution in Peking. On the other hand, the fall of the dynasty would practically mean the breaking up of China and each province would want its own nominee as Emperor or President. And then, 'the cunning and grasping Japan' would intervene and take everything they could lay hands on – certainly Manchuria. We asked him whether he would leave Peking if the Court fled. He said he would not do so – but as he had already left his house because he does not like to be left alone in the Tartar City with five servants and had taken refuge in the 'Hotel [SW: de Pekin', one of the two European hotels in the Legation Quarter], I have my doubts whether he will 'stay put' if the atmosphere becomes more troubled.

All the arrangements he had made for us were most generous of time and money, but quite oddly inconvenient and uncertain in time and place. He told us that of all foreign Legations, the Russian was the most considerate, and the officials learnt Chinese and associated with Chinese families. The American Legation had a large circle of Chinese who had been educated in America and to whom they were hospitable and kind. The Japanese tried to be friendly, but all Chinese suspected and feared them. The other Legations – and more especially the English – were very exclusive and took no trouble to get acquainted with Chinese officials and their families, even those who had been educated in England, or to know anything about Chinese literature or Chinese habits and customs. The one strong feeling that Mr. Lo showed was his dislike and fear of the Japanese Government and people; and he evidently regretted the times when Russia was the dominant power in the Far East. This depressed and gentle creature – with his weakly body and unhealthy skin, with an intellectual appreciation of the defects of his own race and with a total absence of any capacity or desire to alter things – with his absence of loyalty to the Government he was serving and his equal lack of fervour for the revolution which he was prepared to accept, seemed, to us, typical of the spirit of Peking.

[SW→] 5th NOVEMBER 1911

The news has become every day graver for the Manchu Government. Shanghai has gone over to the Revolutionaries, apparently without a shot being fired; and the Arsenal has also surrendered (our Chinese officials tell us that the bulk of its contents were removed a week ago). Yunnan and other provinces have apparently either gone over or declared their independence. The Viceroy of Canton has, we gather, come to some arrangement with the local Revolutionaries to the effect that, if they let that city alone, he will in due course accede to them when they prove to be the winning side. The soldiers in the province of which Shen's father is Governor are said to have mutinied. And the troops we saw leave Mukden, together with others, are said to have refused to proceed beyond some point on the line, where they extorted a month's pay from the Government and are now making other demands. The upshot of it all seems to be that it is touch-and-go whether the Court will not any day flee from Peking, and leave chaos behind. The Europeans regard as most serious the widely-published report of a massacre of Chinese men, women and children by the Imperialist troops at Hankow, where the fighting continues indecisively. The 'massacre' is probably exaggerated, and seems to be merely connected with a part of the town having been set on fire to stop street fighting, and with indiscriminate firing in the streets on the fleeing soldiers and inhabitants. But it is feared that the report will lead to reprisals. The fall of Tientsin is expected. Edict after Edict has been issued by the Emperor, each one fuller than the last of self-abasement and verbal concessions, which may be too late. We hear from Prof. Finlayson, who is tutor to Yuan, the son of Yuan Shih-k'ai, that the son says the father will not accept the Premiership — if so, there seems no one else of popularity. Our Mr. Lo admitted that Yuan Shih-k'ai had telegraphed a refusal, but said this was only Chinese etiquette, which requires three successive refusals of any high post, on the grounds of conscious unworthiness, before accepting. At moments of national crisis, such etiquette seems a little inconvenient, to say the least of it.

Tonight comes a further blow! The brothers Kungpah T. King and Soh-tsu King,[47] whom we had entertained in England some years ago, and who are the sons of a wealthy man in and near Shanghai, proved to be in Peking. They had never answered our letter, sent six months ago to say we were coming, in response to their very pressing invitation to stay with them; and we had written them off. But some of our Chinese friends telephoned to them that we were here, and they came to call, with effusive cordiality, bringing gifts of photographs of and by themselves. They spontaneously offered to take us out for the day, on Monday, to an old library and some temples. Now we get the annexed letter[48] to say that they really must flee to Shanghai by the earliest train! Really, these people are, beyond belief, nerveless. Here are two young men, with all their relations away in as safe a place as any in the whole Chinese empire, with which there is uninterrupted telegraphic communication; with all their valuables (as they told us) also placed in safety; and with no more to fear in Peking than any other of its millions.

They struck us as fundamentally unhealthy in physique; utterly mercenary and selfish in character; and without the slightest spark of religion and patriotism, or even an enlightened and far-seeing hedonism. We recall that we thought this of them in England years ago (as recorded in this diary at the time); and especially that the elder one said that his father had deprecated his going into the Army, because he should not like to hear of his running away! We gather that the elder is doing some legal work for the Government, and has been apparently at one time a Magistrate of some sort at Shanghai.

Dr. Yen Fu[49] came to see us, in response to an introduction. He is the great translator of English works in Chinese — he began with Herbert Spencer's *Study of Sociology*, and has done many other books. He has, accordingly, had to invent a whole new terminology, and is said to have been skilful in it. Now he is holding some Government post, in which his duty seems to be to find, or invent, Chinese terms for new European things or ideas. He spoke English fluently, but as usual, 'glibly' rather than intelligently — and that seemed to us to express his character! He confirmed the information that the Chinese were producing no original books at all, though there were some periodical magazines, and of course abundant newspapers, which seem of no account intellectually. (It is to be noted that he asked eagerly for the names of English books suitable for translation into Chinese; and of others, recommended for reading.)

There is nothing to be said about [the] other Chinese we have seen — Tong,[50] the head of the American Indemnity College and delegate to the Anti-Opium Conference; the Chinese colleague of Brewitt Taylor in the direction of the customs school; and Shih Chao-chi,[51] a Councillor of the Foreign Office, [and] others whose names and offices we did not learn, or do not remember. These English-speaking Chinese all give the impression of glib superficiality, of servile acceptance of their nation's inferiority to the white man, and of an insincere politeness. One does not feel in the least sure what they may not be saying behind our backs.

At Prof. Finlayson's dinner, we met Sir Robert Bredon,[52] an old official of the I.M. Customs service, the *protégé*, and an 'in-law', of Sir Robert Hart.[53] The British Government apparently vetoed his appointment to succeed Sir Robert Hart, and caused the Chinese Government to appoint his junior (Aglen)[54] on the ground, it is said, that Bredon was too 'pro-Chinese', and likely to be too subservient to the Chinese Government (whose official he is!). It may be, however, that the Hart régime had lasted somewhat too long for efficiency, and that new blood was required. Anyhow, Bredon is a critic of the British Embassy. But he was not at all embittered, and spoke cordially and sensibly; and he has evidently remained formally on good terms.

Aglen, his successor, whom we met at the Legation afternoon reception, is a solid, unimaginative official of the routine type, who will carry on the machinery but who could probably not have invented it and nursed it in its infancy by delicate negotiations with the Chinese Government, as Hart appears to have done. He professed to believe in China as a 'wonderful country', but could give no reason for his faith. He said that this dynasty had decayed just as the Ming dynasty[55] had done; and this seemed to him to explain the decadence or fall into sterility of the three hundred millions of Chinese. He said there would be a renascence after the present shaking up. He expected the fall of Tientsin within the next day or so, and evidently regarded the flight of the Court and the Manchu troops as both imminent and desirable, so that the Revolutionaries might have a clear field. He did not seem to have visualised what the result might be on the Peking mob; or what sort of substitute could be found for the Emperor.

He said that his Customs officers were sticking to their posts, and carrying on their work, undisturbed by the fact that their towns were in the hands of the Revolutionaries. They went on collecting duties, but there had ensued so complete a stoppage of trade that there was little to collect. They were not able to make any remittances at all from some of the ports. The financial problem was going to be very serious. He explained that the customs school was not under the I.M.C., but was a separate enterprise of the Chinese Government, designed in the long run to replace the European officers of the I.M.C. But the I.M.C. lent its officers and teachers, and was glad to employ its graduates.

We failed to go to a Chinese theatre, because ten days ago the Minister of the Interior had issued an order peremptorily closing all places of entertainment until the crisis was over! We could not gather the reason for this, which only increased the panic and led, we are told, to the immediate closing (and bankruptcy) of many restaurants.

It is to be noted that at Lady Jordan's[56] reception, we saw not one Chinese person; and we learn that there is practically no social intercourse between the British Legation and the Chinese, even the English-speaking or Christian Chinese (Lady Bredon said *she* had made no Chinese acquaintances). During the past year, some Chinese have been invited to the Legation as a new thing. The American Legation, it was admitted, did see something of the Chinese who had studied in America — we were told that they went there and played poker, which was evidently considered much worse than bridge, which the British Legation ostentatiously played!

At Prof. Finlayson's, we met also Simpson,[57] the ex-Customs official who was got rid of because, under the name of L. Putnam Weale, he published the *Indiscreet Letters From Peking* in which he gave so unpleasantly scandalous [an] account of the behaviour of the British colony during the Boxer siege. He was a talkative and somewhat conceited person, critical of all constituted authority, censorious and scandalous as regards all foreign dealings with China, whose sentiments about China (which he professed to admire and to sympathise with against the foreigner) did not impress us as either authoritative or intelligent. He is living here as a journalist and writer of books. He, too, was full of criticism of Japan's dealings with Korea and of its foreign policy. He professed great anxiety to keep the Japanese 'at the other side of the Yellow Sea'.

It is to be noted, to the credit of the Chinese, that the Director-General of the Imperial University — which we visited with our introductions on the day after we arrived — twice called on us (once we were out), in order to ask S.W. for suggestions how to improve the University; and how to get professors of economic subjects who had actual experience of banking, politics, etc. S.W. gave such advice as he could, especially as to getting single lectures out of *local* bankers, merchants, railway managers, etc., and as to a seminar arrangement of the library (as at Kyoto); he (the Director) also bespoke the further aid of The London School of Economics in getting professors and promised to send us some of his own students.

The University is at present a very inchoate affair with professors from England, France, Japan, Germany and America, as well as one or two Chinese, lecturing each in his own tongue; as the students have learnt one or other of these foreign tongues but not more than one, they are required to attend the lectures of the professor whose language they professedly understand, whether that is the subject they want to study or not! Thus, those who understand English may study economics and commerce, but those who know only French must study law and those who know only German must study science, because these subjects are what such professors as they can understand are teaching!

The Chinese professor we saw was an intensely intellectualised young man of remarkable expression, who had taken an extraordinarily brilliant degree at Berlin and was teaching mathematics, in which he was said to be highly proficient. The two professors whom The London School of Economics supplied (Finlayson and Cooper) seemed to be doing well; the former being, by the way, a sort of jackal to Morrison, *The Times* Correspondent, for whom he picked up news — perhaps from Yuan, son of Yuan Shih-k'ai, whom he was tutoring.

[BW→] NOV[r] 6th [1911]

We visited the Temple of Confucius[58] and the great Lama monastery.[59] The former was desolate in its emptiness and decay though no doubt of interest to the student of monuments; the latter was a repulsive sight, with its 1000 Lama priests and acolytes. To look at the faces of the men and boys, droning the *sutras* in the many temples or hanging about the courts begging from the foreign visitors, you would think you were passing through a convict establishment suddenly denuded of warders. Quite obviously this assembly of males, from little children to the hoary aged, was a mass of putrefying humanity − indolence, superstition and sodomy seeming to be its main characteristics. With regard to sodomy, ever since I came into China I have been wondering whether the vice did not prevail extensively because of the expression on the faces of the men − the vicious femininity of many of the faces. We are now told, on good authority, that in every Chinese town there are streets of 'boys' homes', and that this form of prostitution is far more popular than the more material and healthy one of men and women. It is this rottenness of physical and moral character that makes one despair of China − their constitution seems devastated by drugs and abnormal sexual indulgence. They are, in essentials, an *unclean race*.

The one pleasant impression left on our minds from our brief visit to China is of the beauty of Peking with its walls and gates and its picturesque grey-tiled roofs embedded in trees, and here and there, relieved by the golden, green, and blue-tiled edifices of the Imperial Palaces and the Temple of Heaven[60] and other ceremonial buildings. The walk round the walls looking down on the city,[61] and far-away over the plain to the mountain ranges, is one of the sights of the world − beautiful in its uniqueness. And when one lets oneself think of the Chinese race as a 'lower race', one is pulled up by the memory of the literature and philosophy of thousands of years ago, when our ancestors were savages. If one cross-examines the admirer of China as to the reasons of his admiration, he always adduces the artistic magnificence of its past and adds that, at any rate, 'it is a race that endures'. And it is possible that this quality of persistence, combined with the undoubted sensitiveness of the race (a sensitiveness shown in its liability to panic and to the good manners and grace of its educated class), might, if once the Chinese race could become healthy in body and mind, enable it to take its place in the great republic of nations. At present, it is clearly an outcast, and may any day find itself enslaved by a more virile people, or divided up among the great nations of the world as the hewers of wood and drawers of water in the lands of its ancestors − the same fate that has overtaken Korea.

I asked Mr. Cazenave − an ex-French diplomat who has lived in the East for twenty-five years − about the morality of the Chinese. He said that there was no morality and that no vice was unnatural in their eyes; all classes of Chinaman 'indulged in boys', exactly as other races amused themselves with women, so apparently I was right in my interpretation of their expressions. He also told me what I did not know, that Lama monasteries are maintained by the Imperial Court, as Lamaism[62] is the official religion of the Manchus. The Chinese Muslims are the best of the Chinese — better in class and conduct than the Christians. There are 36 mosques in Peking and some 50,000 adherents in the whole of China.

On our last day at Peking, November 7th, we lunched with Lord Li and his brother the Marquis, the only son of Li Hung-chang, who, with Lord Li (the adopted son), inherited the immense wealth of this great Chinese statesman.[63] Both these brothers are living in the Legation Quarter, though Lord Li continues to administer, as Vice-President, the Board of Communications, pending the formation of the new Ministry. We were therefore entertained at our own hotel, [with] Mr. Cazenave and another French diplomat and his wife and daughters [who] had been asked to meet us. Both these brothers Li talked English fluently and were accomplished gentlemen — both have that appearance of sensuality and that insincerity of manner which seem characteristic of the Chinese of the diplomatic world. This insincerity makes them wholly uninteresting to talk to — and the conversation resolves itself into polite words; whenever one asks their opinion they evade the question, or say that they really have no opinion. About the revolution, they appeared quite detached; and when I asked Lord Li, half in joke, to give me an introduction to the Revolutionary headquarters at Shanghai he responded cordially, remarking that the leaders were all 'their good friends' — one among them was even his cousin. So we have this introduction and intend to present it.

In the evening, we entertained three young Chinese officials — Lo, Tseng,[64] and [SW: Tyau][65] (who is married to an English lady who also came). They are depressed, but also detached — it was difficult to tell whether or not they were in favour of the revolution. Tseng — a former student of the School of Economics — sadly remarked that he did not believe that the Chinese were at present capable of governing themselves, and that the destruction of the Manchu dynasty would mean chaos and dismemberment. They told us, quite definitely, that the Imperial Court was leaving that very night — and implied that their office was making the necessary arrangements. The murder of the Chinese General Wu[66] by the Manchu soldiers had made Peking no longer safe for the Manchu dynasty. The Prince Ch'ing, and all the other Princes except Prince P'u-lun,[67] were leaving with the Court — Prince P'u-lun, a great favourite with the Legations and even with the educated Chinese, had volunteered to stay behind as 'caretaker' of the interests of the Imperial Court.

The next morning we went to the station an hour before the train was due to start. I shall never forget the scene. Every carriage and truck was crowded with Chinese families — men, women, and children were seated on the roofs of the carriages, and hanging on to the buffers between the carriages — whilst the platform was almost equally crowded with disconsolate ones, squatting on their household belongings. This crowd was quite orderly and silent — but they were haggard and deadly yellow, their black eyes seeming to start out of their heads with fear. The policemen and the officials who ordinarily are much in evidence were absent — no one seemed in command. The case seemed almost hopeless for us and our luggage. Tseng, who had volunteered to help us, ran about somewhat vaguely, trying to get us into this or that reserved carriage filled with Manchu dignitaries and their families. At last, the hotel porters managed to push us on to the platform of a carriage, and were struggling to get our luggage on — when the English conductor of the train came along and, recognising Sidney, completed the task and took me into the brake-van! Here were 2 or 3 English refugees from the place at which the Chinese General had been murdered, who entertained me with a gruesome account of the occurrence, and of their unsuccessful attempt to photograph the headless body.

From all that one has seen and heard, one gathers that the success of the revolution is mainly due to the *absence of resistance* [on the part of the Manchus], and to the gladness with which the Chinese officials and Chinese people have handed over the Government, in town after town, to some undefined people who call themselves the 'Constitutionalists'.[68] What exactly will happen when these forces come into conflict with Manchu soldiers who feel that their lives are at stake, one does not know. If the Manchus showed real fight the current of events might still be turned. Up to now, it has been the absence of resistance and not the presence of force, which has been the deciding factor — though this very absence of resistance has meant a deep-rooted objection to the Manchu rule on the part of the millions of Chinese who have been subject to it.

NOV^r 10th [1911] ON THE YELLOW SEA FROM TIENTSIN TO
SHANGHAI

We stopped yesterday at Chefoo, and went on shore whilst freight was being unloaded and loaded. We called at the offices of Butterfield and Swire,[69] and saw the local Manager (Beart). They were expecting Chefoo to be 'taken over' any hour [SW: It was 'taken over', quietly, at

3 a.m. on the 13th November]. The *Taotai*[70] was waiting until the Governor of the province had decided whether or not resistance was to be offered. Meanwhile, he had sent all his valuables away and was sleeping every night out of the city — either on his yacht or in a local Fort! We went through the narrow streets of the native town and actually called at the *yamen*.[71] Round about the entrance lounged men and boys, and two or three soldiers on guard were standing about in an unceremonial manner — there was no sign of any excitement, and a general look of amused indifference. The Chinese employee of Butterfield and Swire who accompanied us approved of the revolution and remarked that now 'China would be united' — but he did not know who were the Constitutionalists, and had only a vague sort of idea that 'numbers of them were already in the town'.

We went to lunch with the Manager [SW: Mr. Beart], a stout and prejudiced elderly man, who declaimed against the Japanese as 'scallywags' in the usual way and praised the Chinese as trustworthy, industrious, obedient, thrifty and honest. [SW: He had been keeping a loaded revolver on his desk for some days past!] The valour and efficiency of the Japanese Army and Navy was due to their 'Spiritualism' — a sign of their barbarism — and if they ever became commercially honest it would be because they wanted 'to do' the foreigner. As we threaded our way through the crowd of gesticulating and shouting Chinese labourers, he remarked (in support I suppose of his good opinion of the Chinese) that all these men could earn a good wage, but that when they had made 10 cents, they left work to gamble. He told us tales of the corruption of the resident *Taotai*, and on his table was a report of the Chefoo British Consul[72] which attributed the decline in the export of silk to the unwise action of Chinese merchants in sending out short lengths and bad quality. The port was crowded with Japanese steamers — which perhaps accounted for some of the virulence of the anti-Japanese feeling in the manager of the English line. His firm was no doubt stepping in to the trade lost by the Chinese merchants! Anyway, the wooden junks with their painted eyes were not likely to oust him from the export and import trade of China.

[SW→] SHANGHAI 17th NOVEMBER 1911

We arrived at Shanghai twelve hours late after a gale at sea in which our little coasting-steamer was tossed about like an egg-shell, to our great discomfort. We have now been five days in this great Foreign Settlement on Chinese soil — a unique and remarkable development, a city of 15,000 foreigners and more than half a million Chinese, entirely governed by a Municipal Council of foreigners elected by foreigners only, with an international police court for Chinese cases and extra-territorial consular jurisdiction for others, the Chinese Government being entirely ousted.[73] Adjoining is the old walled Chinese City of a couple of hundreds of thousands of Chinese, governed by the Chinese on Chinese lines. Staying in the luxurious house of the local Manager of the Hong Kong and Shanghai Bank,[74] we have lunched and dined out daily with the Europeans and Americans. But for our Chinese friend Hsu, and our Chinese introductions, we should have seen nothing else. Apparently, the resident foreigners see nothing of the Chinese socially, and take the very smallest interest in Chinese affairs or Chinese characteristics, apart from their trade and their 'house-boys'.

Hsu,[75] who was a brilliant student of banking and currency at The London School of Economics – we got him admitted as a volunteer into the Union and Smith's Bank branches and head office – is now Assistant-Inspector of Branches of the new Ta Ch'ing, a Chinese semi-Government Bank, and has just returned from a Currency Convention in London, where he was a delegate of the Chinese Government. He is the son of a rich Chinese resident of Shanghai and is lingering here instead of reporting himself for duty at Peking because, as he candidly confesses, he is afraid that (being without a pigtail) he would be massacred at Peking.[76] He went secretly to Lord Li, who seems to be the head of the Ta Ch'ing Bank [BW: We afterwards learnt this is not so.[77] Hsu had secured a second position at the Board of Communications, just as Shen and Tseng have done. Like all other influential Chinese, he is a dualist if not a pluralist] and stated this – returning immediately to the safety of Shanghai, and causing a paragraph to be put in the newspapers to the effect that he was still in America. He is an accomplished, refined and somewhat unhealthy man of about thirty; timid and undecided in his opinions; entirely sympathising with the anti-Manchu upheaval, but far too apprehensive and self-regarding to throw in his lot with them. He has been most kind and assiduous in his attentions to us, taking us through the Chinese City, escorting S.W. to institutions, interviewing with S.W. the Revolutionary leader, with whom he was anxious to make friends, entertaining us to lunch at a Chinese garden restaurant and at his own house, and taking us to the Chinese theatre.

The Chinese City, with its walls,[78] its narrow lanes between little open shops, where every kind of handicraft was being carried on, its crowds of pedestrians with no vehicles but small hand-carts (and a few *rickshas*), its muddy ditches, its smells and its entire absence of drainage, seemed to resemble with extraordinary accuracy the towns of mediaeval Europe of the fourteenth century (except for the *rickshas*, the new Chinese policemen, and here and there, an electric light). Certainly, any student of mediaeval social life would do well to visit this Chinese City, which (far more than Peking, or even Mukden) has preserved, as it were crystallised, the urban life before the Renaissance and the Industrial Revolution. Though the *Taotai* had fled and the Revolutionaries possessed the city, everything was as usual, except that the *Taotai*'s *yamen* had been burnt and lay in ruins; there was an abundance of flags of diverse patterns, all meant to represent the new Republic of China; and the soldiers and policemen wore a white rag bound round one sleeve as a sign that they were servants of the new régime. The most interesting thing to us was the guild-house of the bankers or money-changers, which we went over − a building four or five centuries old, consisting of a series of one-storied meeting rooms, interspersed with little courtyards which were queer 'rock-gardens' formed of sea-worn rocks which the surf had beaten into the strangest shapes, with a tiny pond full of gold carp and little bridges and passage ways − every wall covered with quaint wood carvings or paintings, and every gable and roof-ridge worked up into the strangest of dragons.[79]

There was also a temple, opening to the small open space in the centre of the city,[80] where brazen images of Buddha were behind burning candles and incense smoke, and were flanked by some fifty or sixty portrait statuettes of leading disciples and martyrs, and by half-a-dozen figures of guards or supporters, exactly like the human figures in the processional approach to the tombs. Whilst we were there a Chinese coolie approached, went on his knees, bowed his head repeatedly to the ground, then rose and threw a coin into the open money-box. The whole thing, with its dirt, its neglect, its squalor, and the absence of devotion [was] in marked contrast with the Japanese temples. But it *was* Buddhism, and not Confucianism.

At the lunch at a Chinese garden restaurant, Mrs. Hsu appeared in beautiful silken attire, resplendent in magnificent jewels, her fingers covered with rings, her breast hung with ropes of pearls, with other ornaments of jewels set in jade. She understood and spoke a few words of English, but was, so far as her husband's guests were concerned, only a dressed-up doll. Except for bird's nest soup, the meal was European in style, and intolerably long. Hsu's brother (a student of electrical engineering at the local university), and his cousin, were the only Chinese guests to meet us, Mr. Hunter (our host), Col. Bruce, the head of the Settlement Police,[81] and one or two other Europeans.

[BW →] We went in to tea in Hsu's house − our first experience of a Chinese house inhabited by Chinese gentlefolk. It was entered from one of the main Chinese streets of the Settlement − apparently most of the rich Chinese live in the Foreign Settlement – the front gate opening into a narrow alley between the high walls of other houses. Before the inner door there was the usual screen to keep away bad spirits. The guest-rooms were a series of dark halls with dirty whitewashed walls and bare deal floors, the furniture being a weird mixture of heavy Chinese ceremonial settees and tables and European ornaments in the worst taste – the whole appearance being almost squalid in its ugliness and discordant dreariness. Mr. and Mrs. Hsu gave us Chinese tea, sweets and cakes, and Hsu asked our advice as to whether he should return to Peking and what excuse he could put forward if he did not. The day after, he and his wife came to dine with us and our hostess of the Hong Kong [and Shanghai] Bank, in order to escort us to a Chinese theatre. It so happened that there were [also in the party] two sons of an Australian banker – colonial bounders of the most approved type – vulgar, talkative, ignorant and blatantly self-assertive. It was interesting to note the contrast between the newest product of Western civil-isation, with that of the oldest Eastern civilisation. Certainly, Hsu, with his refined expression, quiet dignity, culture and unselfconscious tact, shone in the comparison. But perhaps these Australian bounders would not have stuck to their office if there had been civil war in Sydney – anyway, they would have been on one side or the other in a virile and pugnacious fashion.

The play opened with an amazing acrobatic performance, amazing for the extraordinary rapidity and variety of movement. The play itself was modern Chinese, a commonplace melodrama with foreign black-guards waylaying wealthy Chinese citizens, slave girls, a detective, soldiers, officials, etc., with constant references to topical events.[82] Here again, what surprised one was the *movement* both of body and expression, the rapid succession of incidents and the vigorous acting. It was all extraordinarily dramatic and in a sense real. To Westerners, the noise and restlessness were exhausting and after an hour of it we had had enough. Looking round at the audience of men and women – some families of young people with their parents – one was struck with the intellectualism and mobility of many of the faces. Certainly the Chinese do not lack intelligence or quick response to rapidly-changing stimuli.

[SW→] S.W., accompanied by Hsu, called on Wu T'ing-fang,[83] a former Chinese Minister to the U.S. who is a leading member of the Revolutionary Government, designated as its Foreign Minister, to whom Lord Li had given us an introduction. We found him at his private residence, a large house in European style in the wealthy Shanghai suburb,[84] elaborately furnished with Cantonese carved chairs and tables, a Chinese carpet imitating Brussels, modern Chinese pictures after European style, and European ornaments in bad taste.

He turned out to be an elderly man of vigour, quick and loud of speech in fluent English, with aggressive and self-assertive manners which he had perhaps picked up in America. He at once questioned S.W. as to European opinion at Peking, said there could be no excuse for foreign intervention or even anxiety, declared that he would never consent to any negotiations or conference carried on in the vitiated mental atmosphere of Peking, which he said made him feel at once unenthusiastic and reactionary. He used to be in favour of constitutional monarchy and greatly admired the English constitution, declaring that it was far more free than the American. But now he felt that there was nothing for it but a republic; the whole Court and dynasty must be got rid of as the only guarantee for the future. S.W. observed that there would be difficulties in starting a federal republic for the three hundred millions of the eighteen provinces. 'But all great things involve difficulties,' he replied. 'We must overcome them.'

S.W. suggested that perhaps the retention of the boy Emperor, in the hands of a Regent whom they could trust, might prove an easier course; and asked why they should not get Yuan Shih-k'ai made Regent instead of Prime Minister? To this he said that Yuan Shih-k'ai was no good; he had never been out of China; he was not in sympathy with real reform; he was more popular among the foreigners than among the Chinese; he had commended himself to the foreigners, not so much by his actual merits as by contrast with the Manchus; and so on. S.W. suggested the Australian Commonwealth Act[85] as a good model constitution, if they substituted a President for the Governor-General. This interested him; he asked how the Australian constitution could be got in Shanghai; and eagerly accepted the suggestion that the volume of English statutes could be borrowed from the international mixed court, or British consular court. He said also that he would send to Melbourne for the report of the Australian constitutional convention.[86] He eagerly asked Hsu what the Ta Ch'ing Bank would do but Hsu naturally gave an evasive reply; and Wu T'ing-fang pressed him to come again. Altogether, for all his ''merican' shallow volubility and lack of appreciation of the depths of things, he struck us as a man of real ability and power of command; certainly, among the half-dozen ablest Chinese we have met.

The 'Nanyang University', the oldest of the Government educational experiments in foreign style, and said to be the best of the three Universities, turned out to be better in buildings and equipment than in any other feature. Established about 1895 under the direction of Dr. Ferguson,[87] it had quite excellent and imposing collegiate buildings in brick, and a practical engineering workshop [with] equipment on a limited scale. The science [building] was very poorly equipped and the library was contemptible — not better or bigger than that of a London elementary school. It had begun as a commercial school, and then was made into a science and engineering school; and is now to be a University. The Principal (who in many ways resembled Liu of the Peking University) was an ex-Minister in the Board of Trade at Peking, who may have administrative ability, but has evidently no notion of a University. Nanyang comprises a secondary school of several hundred boys, and a college of one or two hundred, nearly all resident in bedrooms containing three each; the language is English but there are only one or two American teachers (of English in the secondary school).

S.W. also visited the 'Shanghai Poor Children's Home', notable as a piece of enlightened, purely Chinese philanthropy showing initiative and invention. Started three years ago by donations of wealthy Chinese, it had taken in some two hundred boys and over 100 girls, selected for poverty (not orphanage necessarily), who were to be educated and maintained free for ten years. The Director (said to be unpaid), was a son of the principal donor; and seemed a philanthropic enthusiast of good type. He had devised the whole plan and curriculum himself, and invented every detail. The children, taken in at 5 to 10 years, did all the work of the establishment, and were largely employed in manual work so devised as to be educational and character-forming (this was the theory). For instance, the vegetables and chrysanthemums were grown by the girls and boys, not on a large scale under orders but by each child being in complete charge of so many plants each, and being encouraged by emulation (shows, etc.); other things made were boots, carpentry, cabinet-making and various kinds of needlework. A due amount of scholastic instruction was given, and there was a school orchestra (much individual violin practice was going on). Each (day)room was in the charge of one boy for cleanliness, etc. They slept on separate mattresses on the floor in large dormitories, a teacher occupying a curtained bed in one corner. The girls were in charge of women; but their instruction had to be given by men (except in needlework) owing to lack of qualified women. From top to bottom, all was exclusively Chinese — so much so that no European whom we met in Shanghai had ever heard of the institution. One more instance of the total lack of intellectual interest as to things Chinese! It was too early to see results; but the experiment is an interesting one in non-academic schooling, and in the hands of its intelligent and philanthropic Director, it may do well.

We were unlucky at Zikawei, the celebrated Jesuit observatory and extensive educational settlement.[88] S.W. went on a very wet day and saw only the Irish priest to whom we had a special introduction. He, unlike other Jesuits whom we have met, was an uncultivated, unintelligent, talkative, opinionated Irishman, who poured out an uninterruptible stream of barren facts and untrustworthy statistics as to the extent of the Jesuit work in China, which gave S.W. no insight into things. Curiously enough, he said it was impossible to associate with the Chinese; they had filthy habits in company, they showed no politeness to a lady, they were uncivilised, and so on (what would Jesus have said, or Paul?). The Jesuit Fathers sometimes wore Chinese dress, sometimes not (I saw several walking about in Chinese dress); it was convenient on journeys into the interior as exciting less attention and attracting less crowd, etc. The family system was a great obstacle to conversions, and to all progress; its resistance would be overcome only by getting a group of people to move together and support each other. The observatory work was carried on by twelve specially-trained astronomical Fathers who did no other work and were specially recruited from Europe as required. The R.C.'s divided China up by provinces, the English Jesuits being responsible for two out of the 18 (comprising 50 million); the other being undertaken by various continental R.C. orders. Father Martin Kennilly, whom S.W. saw, greatly regretted the abandonment of five-sixths of China to non-English R.C. influence; he thought it all ought to be brought under English R.C.s and had lately been in England to urge this. The English R.C. authorities gave him little encouragement, saying they had enough on hand; but he got more encouragement among the R.C.s of the United States, and he was hoping for their gradual penetration into the other provinces, either independently, or through the French and German R.C. Orders, in order to gradually oust French and German influence and make all China English! Altogether a most untypical Jesuit.

In the two provinces, they had already over 500 boys' schools, and over 500 girls' schools, with some 30,000 children, mostly under Jesuit-trained Chinese teachers, besides higher schools and colleges for Chinese and for Europeans. In all China, there were 1,300,000 R.C.s. By the way, he said the Muslims were 10 millions, now undistinguishable in race from other Chinese, living in separate quarters in each city, very obstinate in resisting any interference with their customs, so that the Chinese Government now left them alone; largely, the innkeepers and purveyors of meat.

The Municipal Council of Shanghai (of whom we met the Chairman, one or two other members, the Secretary, the Engineer and a clever young Assistant-Secretary) is a body of nine members only, entirely British in tone. By old habit (and for convenience) one of the nine is allowed to be an American and another a German; but the British majority insists on having all the other seven members, and an attempt by the German residents to elect a second German – still more an attempt of the Japanese to elect a Japanese – were overwhelmingly defeated as pieces of presumption. The only authoritative sources of law are the original 'land regulations' under the Treaty of 1842, and the by-laws made thereunder on all sorts of subjects by the Council, which have to get the approval of all the Consular representatives, the Legation at Peking, and the Chinese Government. There is an annual ratepayers meeting (and any 24 may summon a special meeting) at which the budget is passed. This sometimes deletes an item, and thus exercises some real control.

The Council appears to be efficient municipally, so far as concerns police, paving and lighting, water supply, electricity, etc., evidently applying itself just to those things that the European merchants and bankers wanted. It only maintains one or two schools, for poor Eurasians. Proposals for more effective education have latterly been made, but put off by failure to agree – some want schools by nationalities (partly in order to segregate the Eurasians, Portuguese and Japanese; partly out of German and French pride); whereas the dominant majority want a common system (for non-Chinese), where the only language should be English. We suggested the precedent of the English 1902 Act,[89] which seemed new to them. Meanwhile, the Japanese and Germans maintain schools for their own children, aided by their Governments; and the British rely on private-venture academies and refuse to believe that there are any poor Britishers whose children are growing up uneducated.

The Council seems to do next to nothing for the half a million Chinese within its own jurisdiction, beyond allowing them the use of the streets and the protection of the police – although a large part of its municipal revenue comes from indirect taxation in the form of licences, etc., and the Chinese pay a large part even of the rates on house property. As the Chinese Government has been ousted from jurisdiction, this seems unfair. 'No Chinese admitted except servants in actual attendance on their employers' is on the notice board of the public garden.[90] (There is another smaller, much less eligible garden, where 'any respectably dressed person' is admitted). It gives point to the complaint made by the present Revolutionaries, that the Manchu Government has allowed China to be degraded before the world, that the Chinese Government never protested against this intolerable piece of race insolence on what is, after all, Chinese territory.[91]

The Sikh police – tall, in red turbans – of the Settlement (there are also some English in their London uniforms and some Chinese) are a picturesque feature of the streets, and are said to be most efficient.[92]

It is a peculiar anomaly that the French Government refused to come into the International Settlement, and maintains its own little French Concession independently, with separate police, separate tramway service, separate *ricksha* and carrying licences, over a little bit of crowded city wedged in between the International Settlement and the Chinese City. There is a French Municipal Council, but with little independence, the Consul being its Chairman and having power of veto, etc.

It is another anomaly that these Municipal Councils have no jurisdiction over the *river*, even for police, smoke prevention, barge licences, etc. Once off the jetty and a criminal is safe from pursuit by the Settlement Police. A river police is maintained by the Chinese I.M. Customs. The whole arrangement is theoretically intolerable and could only be made to work by British practical common sense and disregard for form: and by the fact that British influence is *de facto* paramount in the 800,000 people congregated in the three different cities which make up Shanghai.

ON BOARD THE M.M. STEAMER 'DUMBEA' IN THE CHINA SEA 18th NOVEMBER 1911

Thinking over what we have seen and learnt in our glimpse of China, we realise that we have failed to give adequate weight to two things – the family system, and the prevalence of a system of collective responsibility. If the former is the substitute for a poor law (and indeed for most of the functions of internal government), the latter is a substitute for honesty. The family system seems to be more than the joint undivided family of the Romans, Slavonic peoples, etc. The living ancestor is indeed paramount, the sons on marriage merely bringing their wives into the undivided family. But even when an ancestor dies, the headless families remain associated for many purposes, and we gather that the eldest brother has considerable responsibilities. Our friend Hsu incidentally remarked that he might have time to write a book now, as his father was still alive and undertook all the family affairs; but when the father died, he himself would have a great deal to attend to. Exactly to what the clan system extends, and how far it goes, we do not understand. But that it imposes very real restrictions on individual freedom, initiative and enterprise, is clear. On the other hand, it affords mutual help, and support in adversity; and it exercises no small amount of jurisdiction in breaches of family convention. It is distinctly *piquant* to be told that it is the family that stands in the way of all progress!

The collective responsibility system is only revealed to the foreigner in glimpses; and we have seen or heard no systematic description of it. There are all sorts of guilds, often of great antiquity. But the man one hires a house-boat from in the Yangtze River will be guaranteed as to honesty and fulfilment of bargain by a society of boat-owners: the score of coolies hired to make a *portage* will be collectively responsible, through their headman, that no one [sic] of the innumerable articles will be stolen: even one's house-boy (so we were told) will be in some sort of society or group, the leader being often a house-boy elsewhere, by which any depredation should be made good. The Shansi men are often bankers in Shanghai and elsewhere; and this provincial co-citizenship is a sort of guild. They stand together and help each other, and any serious defaulter or breaker of their conventions disappears into the interior and is reported to be sternly dealt with, even unto death, by some domestic sentence for his offence.

It is to a great extent to this kind of thing that we attribute the reputation of the Chinese for honesty in trade. The foreign merchants at Canton a century ago were allowed to deal only with a selected group of a dozen Chinese merchants who mutually guaranteed and supported each other; and naturally did not default. To a great extent, this restriction of trade to a few firms has continued in one form or another. To this day, the foreign merchant does not enter into relations with the common Chinese village shopkeeper, or even with the multitude of Chinese small dealers who supply these little shops. The comprador[93] system works in a similar direction. In all the treaty ports, every foreign import or export merchant or banker or shipping agent has a trusty Chinese as comprador, whom he pays by salary and commission, and who is often also a dealer on his own account. The comprador is the sole medium of communication with the Chinese world. He selects the Chinese clerks and directs them; he arranges the buying and selling with Chinese firms; and he guarantees their fulfilment of their contracts. For his own fidelity and fulfilment of his obligations he usually gives heavy security. (We do not gather that there is any mutual guarantee by the compradors of each other.) The comprador of the Shanghai branch of the Hong Kong and Shanghai Bank deposits £30,000 of his own money as security; he guarantees all the Chinese firms to whom the bank makes advances in any form, and is paid a commission on all the business thus done. He recruits the bank's staff of 280 Chinese clerks (there are also 150 European) and directs their operations — all this gives, by the absence of losses to the foreign trader, an impression of honesty: but it is really evidence to the contrary! The ordinary Chinese trader is such that the foreigner cannot and dare not deal with him direct. We were told that attempts had been made of recent years (notably at Tientsin and Hankow) to save the expense of the comprador by dealing direct with Chinese firms; and that these attempts had led to disastrous losses. One man frankly said that it was impossible to give credit to the Chinese! The Japanese are said to be 'going into the interior'; and they are no doubt getting much nearer to the Chinese. The gradual 'opening' of trade and consequent increase in the number of Chinese firms dealt with, may account for the current impression that the Chinese are less honest than they used to be. It is only that those dealt with are now less select than of yore.

The question inevitably arises — a standing enigma for the sociologist — why are the Chinese so different from the Japanese? They are, for the most part, apparently of the same great racial group. They had once a common civilisation, all the arts and letters of Japan being derived (perhaps through Korea) from China. To this day, they have essentially the same written language, though their pronunciation of the ideographic characters common to them both has diverged to such an extent as to make them (like the different provinces of China itself) mutually-unintelligible orally. So far as they have a religion as distinguished from an ethical system, it is Buddhism which has influenced them both. Both have a highly-organised family system. They are separated from each other by no great geographical distance, and by no remarkable difference in climate. Both live predominantly on rice and fish and both indulge in (*sake*) the same form of alcohol. Even in little social details there is often a curious likeness: both, for instance, have their meals served up in an array of little porcelain bowls; both use chop-sticks, and the chant of the coolies bearing burdens seems to be identical on both sides of the Yellow Sea. Yet they stand today in sharp contrast, not only in such details as house construction, the posture in sitting down, cleanliness and clothes, but also in social organisation, in capacity for taking on the civilisation and accomplishments of Europe, in intellectual achievement — and above all, in the personal character and ethical qualities typical of the two countries. The Chinese are fundamentally egoistic hedonists of the most 'common sense', 'matter-of-fact', materialist type. As against any form of social organisation higher than the family, they are obstinate individualists, apparently incapable even of understanding any conception of the Common Weal. Of idealism, mysticism, or appreciation of anything not immediately reducible to terms of individual sensuous pleasure, they seem entirely devoid. They have no real reverence for anybody or anything, in the heavens above or on the earth beneath them. They are wholly lacking in intellectual humility.

The Japanese, on the other hand, who went into isolated seclusion three hundred years ago at a stage of development apparently not so very different from the China of the time (or for that matter, from the Europe of the Middle Ages), have shown themselves capable, first, of the momentous decision to emerge completely from that isolation, and to take on all the civilisation of Europe; and secondly, in the short space of fifty years, of constructing a social organisation able to claim equality (and to make good that claim) with the first-class Western powers, not only in military and naval strength, but also in wealth production, social intercourse and such highly-evolved products as medicine and physical science. What has made these wonderful achievements possible is the character of the Japanese people; its extraordinary idealism or mysticism which manifests itself in its all-pervading reverence — reverence for the parent, reverence for the teacher, reverence for the local land-proprietor, reverence for the official, above all, reverence for the Emperor which is seen in the amazing patriotism and self-sacrifice for Japan; and which is accompanied by a remarkable capacity for deliberate plan, persistent effort and subordination of the present to the future. The result is that whereas China seems incapable of industrial or governmental organisation on any large scale, Japan has become the most closely-knit, highly-concentrated, purposefully-centralised state in the world.

As to the cause of these differences, the sociologist can only confess his ignorance. It is impossible to believe that the inferiority of the Chinese is due to their having taken to eating pork! It is almost equally impossible to ascribe it to the pernicious doctrines of Confucius (besides, why did not Confucianism spread, like Buddhism, from China to Japan!). More suggestive may be the fact that the Japanese people, unlike the Chinese, were drilled and disciplined by centuries of a strict 'Feudalism', with its dominant note of universal obligation and self-subordination. This, on the whole, seems the most plausible explanation — just as Carlyle ascribes the national development of England to the stern discipline of the Norman Conquest.[94]

But we end with a further query. We have to note the fact that China has not merely failed to progress. It has positively decayed. Its ancient literature has come to an end, its art products have ceased to be produced, the whole 300,000,000 people seem, for the last two or three centuries, to have become intellectually and artistically decadent and sterile. The Japanese, who have certainly not become either decadent or sterile, are perhaps not far short of the Chinese in sexual licentiousness of the normal type. Is it possible that (a) the Chinese people are and have been for centuries honeycombed by 'unnatural vice', and (b) that this vice, as possibly among the Greeks, has some subtle deteriorating effect on character, far-reaching enough to destroy a whole civilisation?

Notes

1. But there is no entry for the elusive G. K. Shen in the LSE's *Register, 1895–1932* (London, 1934). He must therefore have been an occasional student, possibly related by marriage to another Chinese student at the School in the period, Yi Chen (b. 1885), B.Sc. (Econ) 1912, who in 1908 had married Moya Shen.

2. Chinese nervousness about the Japanese and (Russian) presence in North China and Manchuria should be seen in the context, say, of the 1910 Returns of the Imperial Maritime Customs, which give the number of resident foreigners for China as a whole as 141 868, with the Japanese (65 434) by far the largest national group, the Russians second (49 395), Britain a distant third (10 140), and further back still, the Germans (4 106), Portuguese (3 377) and Americans (3 176). The Chinese population, on the other hand, was estimated at some 342 million at the time. Compare this with the 1990 census figure of 1.133 billion people.

3. General Chao Erh-sun (b. 1846), Chinese Bannerman and widely experienced Manchu administrator, who had been appointed Viceroy of Manchuria in April, 1911.

4. Mukden, now Shenyang, capital of Liaoning Province, was the original seat of the Manchu Empire, founded by Nurhaci (1559–1626) in 1616. Mukden continued as a summer residence for later emperors following a dynastic change of name to Ch'ing in 1636 and the establishment of a new capital at Peking in 1644. It is unclear whether Beatrice is referring here to the tomb of Nurhaci himself, the so-called East Tomb or Tung Ling, or to the more accessible burial site of Nurhaci's son, the North Tomb or Pei Ling.

5. John Carey Hall (1844–1921).

6. R. Willis, British Consul at Harbin, and from October 1912, at Chefoo.

7. An adherent of the teachings of the French social philosopher Auguste Comte (1798–1857), founder of 'Positivism' – a nineteenth-century humanistic religion of science growing out of philosophy and culminating in sociology. Comte's teachings contributed to Sidney Webb's eclectic intellectual formation; but this 1911 passage suggests a rather more dismissive attitude on the part of Beatrice.

8. The American scholar-diplomat W. W. Rockhill, protesting 'the wholesale importation of Japanese prostitutes' along the line of the South Manchuria Railway in the aftermath of the Russo-Japanese War, termed it 'the most degraded traffic conducted by any nation in the world', while Sir Alexander Hosie, the British Commercial Attaché in Peking (1908–12), according to a letter written by *The Times'* China Correspondent, 'speaks strongly on this question in his report on Manchuria but the paragraph has been naturally enough in an official report suppressed by the F.O. He estimates the number of 'female goods' as the Chinese call them at 20,000.' Cf. Lo Hui-Min (ed.), *The Correspondence of G. E. Morrison*, vol. I, 1895–1912 (Cambridge, 1976) pp. 446 *passim*.

9. From the Russian *drozhki*, a low four-wheeled carriage.

10. A term dating from 1667 and signifying a coach with glass windows let out for private hire, as distinct from those on public stands.

11. The old imperial palace of Nurhaci, Chin-lan-tien or Jin-lan-dyen, in the centre of Mukden.

12. In his *Panopticon, or The Inspection House* (1791), the British legal reformer and utilitarian philosopher Jeremy Bentham (1748–1832) set out a scheme for a model prison based on his brother Samuel's idea of a workshop that would allow a single centrally-located inspector to observe his workers more closely and thus enhance their efficiency of production. Adding provisions for contracting out the management of prisons and other public institutions to private entrepreneurs, Bentham tried unsuccessfully for several decades to sell the British government on his scheme.

13. From the Mandarin *kao*, tall, and *liang*, millet, a sorghum-like cereal grain.

14. 'one Adderley', according to Sidney Webb, in a letter to George Bernard Shaw dated 29 October 1911.

15. Adjoining the southern wall of the Tartar City, Peking's Legation Quarter was set aside under the Boxer Protocol (1901) as a secure zone for foreigners and their Legations. The British Legation (the oldest, having been established after the 1858 Treaty of Tientsin) was situated here, in a leased building once the residence of the thirty-third son of Emperor K'ang-hsi (1654–1722).

16. I-k'uang (1836–1916), Manchu Imperial Clansman and Grand Councillor, who had been named by Imperial Edict as China's first Prime Minister earlier in 1911. 'Prince Ch'ing,' ran an article in *The Times* of 17 May 1911, 'has been for years the most conspicuous and the most notorious figure in China. The story of his life is the story of China for the past twenty-seven years – the story of the most disastrous experience in the history of the Empire.' As early as 1898 the article's author, *The Times'* China correspondent, had expressed the view (off the record) that Ch'ing was the most corrupt man in the government of the day; elsewhere, Morrison depicts Ch'ing as 'insanely avaricious', 'an opium sot of the worst kind'. See Lo Hui-Min, *The Correspondence of G. E. Morrison*, pp. 99, 398, 409–10, 607.

17. Na-tung, Manchu Bannerman, Associate-President of the Wai-wu pu (1903–11), Grand Secretary (1905–11) and Grand Councillor (1908–11).

18. Charles Perry Scott, D.D. (1847–1927), Church of England missionary, Bishop of North China at Peking (1880–1913) and Chaplain to the British Legation in Peking.

19. The Imperial Chinese Maritime Customs, which was for long the one reliable source of income of the Chinese Government.

20. Charles Henry Brewitt Taylor (b. 1857).

21. Li Ching Fang, Minister to Great Britain 1907, and Acting Senior Vice-President of the Ministry of Communications from January 1911. An adopted son of Li Hung-chang.

22. Marquis Li Hung-chang, or Chung t'ang (1823–1901), a leading Chinese statesman of his day. See note 63 below.

23. Maurice Cazenave, a financial agent and one-time Chargé d'Affaires at the French Legation in Peking.

24. Peking, or Beijing as it is now known, historically consisted of four cities within one. At its heart lay the walled Forbidden Palace City, surrounded by the Imperial City, outside of which lay the Tartar City to the north, and the Chinese City to the south. The Tartar City was restored and walled-off by the Emperor Yung-lo after the Manchu capture of Peking in 1644, to serve as home for Manchu soldiers and families of the eight Chinese troop banners or divisions who served the Manchu cause. Until the overthrow of the dynasty

in 1911–12, residents of the Tartar City received tribute rice sent to Peking from the provinces.

25. Strictly, the Emperor was P'u-yi or Hsuan T'ung (1906–67), whose reign had begun in late 1908 when he was a mere infant; in the circumstances, his father Tsai-feng, the second Prince Ch'un (1883–1951), who was the younger brother of Tsai-t'ien, Manchu Emperor Kuang-hsu (1871–1908), was named Regent.

26. In response to the rapidly-deteriorating political climate, a series of humiliating Edicts issued in the name of the infant Emperor on 30 October 1911 had declared a universal pardon of political prisoners and instructed the Senate of the National Assembly to draft a new constitution expressly excluding members of the nobility from the Cabinet, thus granting leave for the establishment in China of a constitutional monarchy.

27. G. E. Morrison (1862–1920), Australian adventurer, medical graduate of Edinburgh University, and Peking Correspondent of *The Times* already referred to in these notes, who was to become Political Adviser to the President of the Chinese Republic.

28. Lord ffrench, Charles Austin Thomas Robert John Joseph, 6th Baron (1868–1955), British agent of Pauling & Co.

29. Willard D. Straight (1880–1918), former American diplomat who was at the time acting as financial agent for the J. P. Morgan Harriman group.

30. Philip Halsey Patchin (1884–1954), who had from 1909–11 been Chief of the Division of Information in the US State Department, and was later to serve as Chief of the Division of Foreign Intelligence (1917–18).

31. Or, Yen Hui-ch'ing (1877–1950). Yen, a graduate of the University of Virginia, was to prove a remarkably resilient political figure, rising to the office of Prime Minister in 1925–26, serving as China's Minister to the United States and to Russia in the 1930s, and as late as 1949 heading an official delegation to talk with Mao Tse-tung and Chou En-lai in Peking, remaining with the Communists when the National Government fled to Taiwan.

32. Hsu Shih-ch'ang (1855–1939), previously Viceroy of Manchuria, and an eventual Republican President (1918–22). In May of 1911 Hsu had become Associate Prime Minister in Prince Ch'ing's Cabinet, but on the date of this diary entry he had accepted the office of Vice-President of the Privy Council.

33. Yuan Shih-k'ai (1859–1916), prominent imperial official who was to become the first President of Republican China. He had been appointed Viceroy of Hukuang on 14 October 1911; but before he could take up the post, he was named Prime Minister to succeed Prince Ch'ing on 1 November.

34. At this point in the original, in Sidney's hand but subsequently deleted, is the passage: 'The Chinese are not only mere imitators and adapters, as regards Western civilisation – they are incompetent imitators and adapters.'

35. J. L. Garvin (d. 1947), London journalist, long-time editor of *The Observer* (1908–42) and of the 1929 edition of the *Encyclopedia Britannica*.

36. But Morrison sold his library of 8500 volumes to the Japanese in 1917 and it is now part of the Toyo Bunko in Tokyo. His papers are at the Mitchell Library, Sydney, Australia.

37. The four financial powers in the background were: an American group representing J. P. Morgan & Co., Kuhn Loeb & Co., the First National Bank, and the National City Bank of New York (United States); The Hong Kong

and Shanghai Banking Corporation (England); Banque de l'Indo-Chine (France); and Deutsch-Asiatische Bank (Germany).

38. Act 3, Scene 2. Adolphus Cusins, donnish suitor to 'Major Barbara' (Barbara Undershaft, daughter of Lady Britomart and Stephen Undershaft, a millionaire munitions manufacturer and arms dealer), opts to join Undershaft's firm at a high salary, selling his soul 'for reality and for power'. Cf. George Bernard Shaw, *John Bull's Other Island and Major Barbara: also How She Lied to Her Husband* (London, 1907).

39. Two years earlier, a Straight–ffrench agreement with the Chinese had provided for the financing and constructing of the Chinchow–Taonanfu–Tsitsihar–Aigun Railway, one of a number of railway and currency loans in which the financial group were to become subsequently involved; but Sidney's allusion seems to run together this general point with more immediate events. With financial panic impending in Peking, the Banque de l'Indo-Chine had advanced a million *taels* to the Ta Ch'ing Government Bank on 15 October 1911 as a means of averting a run on the Treasury, repayable in six months at 7 per cent interest. Separate negotiations between Government officials and the 'financial group', involving the provision of a further loan of twelve million *taels* guaranteed by Imperial Edict and repayable in a year at 8 per cent interest, were overtaken by events.

40. An Imperial Edict had been issued on 26 October 1911 in response to a demand by the Tzu-cheng yuan (National Assembly) for the dismissal of the Minister of Posts and Communications, Sheng Hsuan-huai (1844–1916). Fearing for his life, Sheng escaped via Tsingtao to Japan, assisted by the diplomatic representatives of America, Britain, France and Germany. He was the architect of a controversial scheme for the nationalisation of trunk railway lines approved in an Edict of 9 May, cancelling previous agreements struck separately in the provinces. The aim was to increase administrative efficiency and discourage corruption; but the new policy contributed directly to the provincial unrest immediately preceding the first revolutionary uprising at Wuchang in October of 1911.

41. The Ming dynasty (1368–1644) was founded at Nanking by Chu Yuan-chang (Ming T'ai Tsu, 1328–98), who ruled under the reign title Hung-wu from 1368–98. His son, the Emperor Yung-lo (d. 1424), moved the capital to Peking. Yung-lo's burial site, the Chang-ling, and those of his twelve successors down to the last of the Ming Emperors, Ch'ung-cheng (d. 1644), are located in a beautiful six-mile-long valley some 45 kilometres north-west of Peking. The Webbs apparently followed the standard touristic route of the day, involving an initial two-hours' morning railway journey to Nankow, and thence by mule and foot to the tombs.

42. After an overnight stay at Nankow, an early morning train carried the Webbs to the Great Wall, begun by Ch'in Shih Huang in the third century B.C. as a defence against Tartar raids out of Mongolia. Some 1500 miles of the Wall, stretching out across the valleys and mountains at heights varying from 20–50 feet, have survived. The portion seen by the Webbs at Nankow Pass is an inner section dating from the seventh century A.D.

43. The two popular destinations were situated near one another a few miles beyond the Hsi Chih Men or north gate in the west wall of the Tartar City. The Zoological Gardens was based on a menagerie started by the Empress

Dowager with wild animals presented to her. The site also included an extensive Botanical Garden. The original Summer Palace, set in landscaped gardens and containing about thirty residences for princes and officials and smaller dwellings for servants and eunuchs (begun by Emperor K'ang-hsi but much extended by his successor, Ch'ien-lung (1736–95)), had been looted and burned by British and French troops in 1860 in retaliation for the Chinese seizure of envoys under a flag of truce. Near its ruins, a new Summer Palace, like the old one built beside a lake surrounded by hills and containing many pavilions, was built by the Empress Dowager T'zu-hsi in time for her sixtieth birthday in 1895. The cost was met by diverting some twenty-four million *taels* intended to be used for building up the Chinese navy.

44. The Empress Dowager's quarters were in the new dwelling-palaces clustered at the north-eastern end of the lake. The Empress Hsiao-ch'in (1835–1908), known as T'zu-hsi or Hsu-hsi, second consort of I-chu, Emperor Wen-tsung (1831–61), was a notoriously devious schemer who instigated a *coup d'etat* following her husband's death, in consequence of which she emerged as virtual ruler of China for many years afterwards. One of her last acts had been to secure the accession to the throne of the last of the Manchu, the child emperor P'u-yi.

45. Lo Feng-lu (1850–1903).

46. A British manufacturing firm.

47. Kungpah King (Chin Shao-ch'eng, b. 1876) and Soh-tsu King (Chin Shao-chi, b. 1886). The first had studied commerce and the second electrical engineering at King's College, London.

48. Pinned to the diary, Volume 30.f.150a, with a notation in the upper-left corner in Sidney's hand 'Peking, Received Sunday 5th Nov[r] 1911, King, Kungpah T.', is the original letter:

> Dear Mr. & Mrs. Webb   *Present*
> I hope you had nice trip to the Ming-ling and had found my letter upon your return, but I am very sorry that I will not be able to go with you to visit the sights tomorrow because my parents are at Shanghai and I feel we must go there so we are going to leave by the first train tomorrow and *do hope* you would excuse us for really regret very much but we can't help leaving now. I wonder Pekin is safe for any length of time now?
> Yours very truly
>
> Kungpah T. King

49. Yen Fu (1854–1927) had studied at the Naval College, Greenwich, and was the translator into Chinese not only of the English sociologist Herbert Spencer (1820–1903), a close family friend of Beatrice's youth, but of Darwin, Adam Smith, Montesquieu and John Stuart Mill. Though influential in disseminating Western ideas, Fu eventually reverted to a defence of traditional Chinese culture.

50. Y. C. Tong (T'ang Yuan-chang) or Tong Kai-son.

51. Otherwise known as Alfred Sze (1877–1958).

52. Robert Edward Bredon (1846–1918), from January 1898 Deputy-Inspector of the Imperial Chinese Maritime Customs.

53. Sir Robert Hart (1835–1911), autocratic British Inspector-General of the Imperial Chinese Maritime Customs. *The Times* said of him when he died that

his life would go down in history as among the greatest monuments of British administrative capacity, a view not wholeheartedly shared by that newspaper's Correspondent in China; and Peking's *Jih Pao* marked Hart's demise with an article high-lighting the employment of aliens in Government service and urging their dismissal when China could dispense with them. Cf. Lo Hui-min, *The Correspondence of G. E. Morrison* pp. 631–2.

54. Francis Arthur Aglen (1869–1932), who acted for Hart when the latter returned to England on sick-leave following a stroke. Hart died on 20 September 1911 and Aglen was appointed his successor as Inspector-General.

55. The last Ming Emperor hanged himself following the sacking of Peking by the bandit Li Tzu-ch'eng in 1644, eight years after the Manchus had proclaimed an imperial Ta Ch'ing dynasty at Mukden.

56. Anne Howe [Crombie] Jordan, wife of Sir John Jordan (1852–1925), British Minister in Peking from 1906.

57. 'Putnam Weale is in Peking a social pariah,' Morrison wrote candidly in a letter to his London editor. 'I think I am right in saying that he is not admitted – certainly not admitted confidentially – to any Legation in Peking. His relations with the Chinese are also as distant as they could be...' Cf. Lo Hui-Min, *The Correspondence...*, p. 801. Weale's real-life counterpart, Bertram Lenox–Simpson (1877–1930), had served in the Imperial Chinese Maritime Customs before becoming China Correspondent of the London *Daily Telegraph*. He wrote a number of books besides the 1907 *Indiscreet Letters From Peking*, and was eventually murdered in Tientsin, allegedly by Japanese spies intent on silencing his opposition to Japanese smuggling.

58. Situated at Hatamen Street and the north wall of the Tartar City, to the immediate west of the Lama monastery. The site, rebuilt on many times, is notable for the tablets, housed in an austere main hall and dedicated to the teachings of Confucius and his disciples, and, in a courtyard, a grouping of ten black stone drums inscribed some three thousand years ago.

59. Yung Ho Kung, or 'Lamasery of Eternal Peace', originally the home of the Emperor Yung Cheng (1722–35) before he came to the throne, who is said to have strengthened his hold on the loyalty of his Mongol and Tibetan subjects by dedicating the property to the Lamas. Famed for its huge gilded image (over seventy feet in height) of Maitreya, the Buddhist redeemer. Juliet Bredon's *Peking, A Historical and Intimate Description of Its Chief Places of Interest* (Shanghai, 1920) p. 164, refers to the 'unpleasant, unwholesome moral atmosphere' of the Yung Ho Kung, and notes of the monks' cells that 'The filth is indescribable from centuries of foul living, and one cannot help feeling that these hidden places have been, and still are, the scenes of unnatural piety and crime.'

60. Housing the most sacred object in imperial China, the T'ien T'an, or Altar of Heaven, the temple complex included a group of buildings in the Chinese City whose tiled roofs formed one of the most familiar landmarks of Peking. Site of a shrine since prehistoric times, the buildings, dating from 1420 A.D., owed their construction to the Emperor Yung-lo after he transferred the capital from Nanking to Peking. For centuries, Manchu Emperors prayed here semi-annually, following a ceremonial procession of thousands of ornately-clad officials, soldiers and servants from the Forbidden City to the temple, led by the Emperor seated in a yellow sedan chair borne on the shoulders of

sixteen carriers. Houses along the route were closed and no one was permitted to view the pageant. But with the siege of the Legations during the 1900 Boxer Rebellion, allied troops forced their way in and the First Bengal Lancers and a Punjabi regiment were quartered there, the officers' mess being pointedly installed in the Emperor's Robing Room in the Hall of Abstinence.

61. The Webbs' vantage-point was probably Chien Men, a tower on the south wall of the Tartar City not far from the Legation Quarter.

62. The Buddhism of Tibet and Mongolia, a Mahayana form, including non-Buddhist Indian elements as well as elements of the pre-existing Bön shamanism. See also Note 59 above.

63. Beatrice seems to have been misinformed about the family connections of the two Lis. Since Lord Li was an adopted son, Li Hung-chang's hereditary marquisate passed on his demise to his eldest natural son, Li Ching-shu. But when the second Marquis died only three months after Li Hung–chang, the title passed in accordance with Manchu custom to Li Ching-shu's son, Li Kuo-chieh, the figure here referred to as the Marquis. As the adopted son of the original Marquis, Lord Li was thus the uncle rather than the brother of the third Marquis, who was the grandson of Li Hung-chang.

64. Tseng Ching-yi, or Tseng King East, Chinese diplomat.

65. Phillip K. C. Tyau, or Tiao Tso-ch'ien (b. 1880), a Cambridge graduate who was head of the English Branch of the Information Bureau of the Wai-wu pu, editor of the *Peking News*, and lawn-tennis champion of Peking.

66. The diary entry reads 'General Weh' but the reference is presumably to the Japanese-educated General Wu Lu-chen, who, sympathetic to the Revolutionaries, was assassinated at Honan on 7 November 1911, allegedly by Yuan Shih-k'ai's agents.

67. The diary entry reads 'Tsu' but the reference is presumably to Prince P'u-lun, great-grandson of the Emperor Tao Kuang (d. 1850), twice proposed (in 1875 and 1908) as heir to the throne, but opposed by the Empress Dowager Tz'u-hsi. He was President of the Tzu-cheng yuan or National Assembly in 1910 and Minister of Agriculture, Industry and Commerce from May 1911 until removed from office by the revolution.

68. The 'Revolutionaries', strongest in the South, were outright republicans insistent on the absolute termination of the Manchu dynasty; the 'Constitutionalists', more prominent in North China and including in their numbers Yuan-Shih-k'ai, looked rather to retaining the infant incumbent of the Dragon Throne, P'u-yi, as the head of a new constitutional monarchy.

69. British shipping, engineering and insurance firm.

70. A Chinese provincial officer in a *tao*, or circuit.

71. A Chinese mandarin's official residence.

72. H. H. Fox.

73. Today China's largest city, Shanghai was first opened to foreign residence and trade under the Treaty of Nanking (1842) between China and Great Britain. By the time of the Webbs' visit, Shanghai had mushroomed into the commercial metropolis of the China Coast, at once a cosmopolitan city of the world and the locale of a notorious underworld of drug addiction and prostitution. Around the original walled Chinese City there had been laid out on reclaimed delta lands a separately-administered International Settlement

and a French Concession. The population of these was given in a census of October 1910 as 13 436, including the British, who made up the largest group (4465), followed by the Japanese (3361), Portuguese (1495), Americans (940), Germans (811) and Indians (804). By 1915, the Japanese had replaced the British as the largest contingent of foreign nationals resident at Shanghai.

74. H. E. R. Hunter.

75. Hsu Un-yuen (b.1884).

76. When the Manchu replaced the Ming rulers of China in the seventeenth century, the subjected Chinese were compelled to shave the front part of their heads and to braid their hair into queues as a visible mark of their subjection. The practice continued until the outbreak of the 1911 Revolution, when pigtails were denounced by the Revolutionaries as tokens of Manchu bondage. On 20 November 1911 the Tzu-cheng yuan formally adopted a resolution in favour of the abolition of the queue.

77. The Governor at the time was in fact a Mr Yih.

78. Dating from the fourteenth century, these brick-faced walls stretching for some three miles around the Chinese City were torn down as part of a modernising initiative in the years following the 1911 Revolution. The boundary of the old city where the walls once stood is today demarcated by the broad streets of Renmin lu and Zhonghua lu, though the labyrinth of lanes within the old city itself remain too narrow for vehicular traffic.

79. M. N. Gamewell, *The Gateway to China, Pictures of Shanghai* (New York, 1916) p. 143, comments of Shanghai's Chinese City that in it 'every trade has its guild which sees to it that the interests of its members are protected. Many of the guilds are wealthy and powerful, politically as well as commercially...They have their guild-houses, all more or less elaborately fitted-up with rooms for conferences and feasts, and attached to them are rows of long low buildings divided into small chambers, where, upon the payment of a rental, the coffins of deceased members may be deposited until a convenient time for burial.'

80. The Temple of the Town Gods and, behind it, the Garden of the Purple Clouds of Autumn.

81. Colonel (later Brigadier-General) Clarence Dalrymple Bruce (1862–1934), British Commissioner of Police, International Settlement at Shanghai, from 1907–14.

82. Cf. Carl Crow, *The Traveller's Handbook for China* (3rd edn, 1921) p. 113: 'With the growth of the big Chinese population in the Foreign Settlement of Shanghai, Western ideas made great changes in the drama of China and there are now in Shanghai a number of pretentious Chinese theatres conducted on Western lines...The native producer of today is quite as up-to-date as his foreign contemporary, and before the end of the recent revolution in China, the theatres of Shanghai were producing plays which portrayed the stirring battles of the revolution...'.

83. Wu T'ing-fang (1842–1922), who would serve as President Yuan Shih-k'ai's Minister of Foreign Affairs in China's first Republican Government.

84. Bubbling Well Road.

85. An Act of the British Parliament creating the Australian Commonwealth on 1 January 1901.

86. It required in fact two conventions to formulate a final draft for an Australian federation, the first of these the 1891 National Australasian Convention convened at Sydney in 1891, and a second National Convention held in 1897–98.

87. John Calvin Ferguson (1866–1945), American administrator and author of books on Chinese bronze and porcelain.

88. Established by French Jesuits in 1847 at the homestead of the Zi family, Chinese Christians for more than three hundred years, the settlement included a convent and a furniture and brass shop, as well as one of the most complete meteorological observatories in the world, providing twice-daily weather forecasts for the entire coast of China.

89. The Education Act of 1902 created uniform standards for elementary education in England and Wales, bringing both denominational and nondenominational schools on to the rates and subject to the authority of county and borough councils. Denominational schools could continue to provide religious instruction, subject to a conscience clause, and to choose teachers of their own creed provided that they were proficient in secular subjects. The Webbs' point is that some such approach might be useful in accommodating within a general educational system Shanghai's diverse community of resident nationalities.

90. Situated on the Bund, fronting the Whangpoo River, a branch of the mighty Yangtze. Today known as Huang-p'u Park.

91. According to M. N. Gamewell, *The Gateway to China*, p. 44, the rule was that 'Chinese are not admitted to the Gardens, except nurses with foreign children, unless dressed in foreign clothes or accompanied by a foreigner. This is to keep the grounds from being overrun by the coolie class.' But it was eventually proposed, at the 1927 ratepayers' meeting, 'That Jessfield and Hongkew Parks, the Public Gardens, the Bund Lawns and Foreshore, Quinsan Gardens and Brenan Piece be opened to the Chinese on the same terms as foreigners.' Initially postponed, a similar motion was proposed and passed on 18 April 1928. F. L. Hawks Pott, *A Short History of Shanghai, Being an Account of the Growth and Development of the International Settlement* (Shanghai, 1928) p. 303.

92. 'The picturesque red turbans of the Sikhs are conspicuous everywhere. These men are harsh but efficient preservers of the peace', observes Gamewell, *The Gateway to China*, p. 29, giving the make-up of Shanghai's police force as including 230 English policemen, 450 Sikh Indians, and over a thousand Chinese. To these, with the rapid growth of resident Japanese, were added a complement of Japanese policemen, starting in 1916.

93. From the Portuguese, meaning 'buyer'.

94. Thomas Carlyle (1795–1881), historian and essayist. See his *Chartism* (London, 1839) ch. V.

4

Hong Kong[1]

[BW→] ON BOARD THE P. AND O. STEAMER 'DALTA' NOV[r] 26th 1911 [SW: GOING TO SINGAPORE]

On landing at Hong Kong last Monday morning (Nov. 20th), we went straight to the Hong Kong Hotel – with its large and pretentious but dark and dirty premises – and there sallied out to present introductions to Government House and several big European firms. On our return, we found a pressing invitation from Lady Lugard[2] to come to lunch that day, which eventuated in our moving our belongings to Government House, and making it our headquarters for our few days' sight-seeing at Hong Kong, Canton and Macao.

We enjoyed these days at Government House, not only for its comfort and pleasant dignity, but on account of the attractive and interesting personalities of the Lugards. Sir Frederick Lugard[3] belongs to the best type of English administrator. Not a striking or dominant personality – he is in fact a modest gentleman – but a man of overwhelming conscientiousness, absolute integrity, slow but steady industry, the whole inspired by a broad, sympathetic, open-minded determination to make the world better. In political opinions he is what might be called a feudal Tory, believing in hereditary obligation and honour, doubting the value of democracy, but quite prepared for a due amount of collectivism when it can be shown to be feasible and consistent with the maintenance of an aristocratic organisation of society and the development of the British Empire.

Hence, in his treatment of subordinate races – whether in Africa or in China – he is essentially honourable and well-bred, considering that he has an obligation to raise their status and to respect their customs and conventions. Apparently, both in Nigeria and at Hong Kong, he has tried to govern the natives through the headman or the leaders, and has had a kindly and almost intimate relation to the principal native inhabitants. At Hong Kong, for instance, he has persuaded the leading Chinese to stop 'corpse-dumping'[4] and spitting and to begin to organise primary education at the Government expense, as well as themselves to

164

endow handsomely the new University – using these Chinese as the medium of communication with the whole body of 350,000 Chinese inhabitants. Just at present he was much preoccupied in keeping the partiality of the Chinese for the revolution from declaring itself too openly, whilst permitting his Chinese officials to give cautious advice. He had nothing to say that was illuminating about the Chinese. He repeated the usual preference for the Chinese over the Japanese (which has become a sort of shibboleth in the Far East) but he was really pessimistic about the immediate future of China. Intellectually, Sir Fred[k] Lugard was not interesting or suggestive, but sociologically – as a concrete justification for and explanation of the British Empire – this attractive, public-spirited Englishman was full of significance.

Quite otherwise with Lady Lugard. The intervention of the brilliant Flora Shaw in the affairs of the British Empire as 'Times' expert for South Africa before the War was at the best a dubious episode.[5] To some she appeared as an irresponsible evil genius who was excused, only because she was a woman, from the severest condemnation. And I confess I came prejudiced against her. And when Lord George Hamilton[6] told me – in the days when we were friends – that she and I were extraordinarily alike, I certainly did not feel complimented!

But certainly in the few days we spent together I was charmed with her dignity and grace, and also found myself quite unexpectedly sympathetic and interested. She is an almost ideal 'Her Excellency', with her tall and stately bearing and her careful elegance in dress and manner. Most of the time she was in bed,[7] so I saw her more intimately than if she had been entertaining many guests. As a conversationalist she is brilliant, tending a little too much to orations but with a lucid and vivid power of expression, derived no doubt from her Irish and French descent. She is of course an imperialist of the somewhat hard type – a Tory, combining her husband's feudal faith with the crude capitalist individualism of Moberly Bell, the Manager of the 'Times',[8] who promoted her to a position of unusual importance on the staff. All this is obviously unattractive to us. But her attitude towards men and affairs generally, and her general philosophical outlook, proved sufficiently near my own to make conversations stimulating. She has an intellectual curiosity and a subtlety of reasoning power which leads to a quick exchange of thought and feeling. I lent her Bergson's Creative Evolution; and her reflections were just that combination of longing and scepticism and a clear appreciation that she did not 'follow' all his flights of intellect which represents my state of mind – in her case expressed with brilliancy. She reminded me of another brilliant woman for whom I had a warm affection in days gone by – Marie Souvestre.[9]

[SW→] At Hong Kong, we saw some of the heads of the European business community — the local Managers of the widely-ramifying banks, shipping firms and merchants, having houses in every port, which are characteristic of European trade in the Far East. They live in great material luxury, often having expensive houses provided for them in addition to princely salaries (the Hong Kong Manager of the Hong Kong-Shanghai Banking Corporation[10] gets £10,000 a year, in addition to two houses and other emoluments). They were plainly men of great practical capacity but with amazingly little intellectual culture or curiosity, knowing and caring practically nothing about the Chinese or anything else but their daily work and their amusements (the latter taking a large place). They seem to be frequently moving from port to port on promotion, and to be therefore in each place only transients of a few years' stay. The comprador system (already described) [see page 152) is universal — with the one exception to be presently noted — though the details vary. At Butterfield and Swire's (the great shipping, dock-owning and sugar-refining firm, now the premier organisation of the Far East in succession to Jardine Matheson & Co.,[11] which, though still very large and multifarious in its interests, has failed to keep abreast) at Hong Kong, the comprador does not guarantee *every* Chinese firm; this wealthy corporation is now taking the risk as regards a few selected Chinese clients. The comprador's own income, though admittedly large, was said to be eaten into by the customary requirement that he should find places about him for every member of his family (which one would have thought cannot make for efficiency). Whether it can be true, as we have seen it stated in books, that the local Chinese official in the minor treaty ports insists that the comprador shall pay him a percentage on all the foreigner's business in order that no official obstacle shall be put in the way of trade, we cannot be sure. There is said to be a society of compradors which takes trade union action; and any firm dispensing with a comprador, or even dismissing its existing comprador in order to take on another, finds itself boycotted! Altogether, the use of the comprador in business seems to be like moving in a friction-brake — it must mean a diminution of net product somewhere!

It is, accordingly, interesting to find the great Japanese firm of Mitsui, as its Hong Kong Manager informed us, breaking through the custom. For six years it has, at Hong Kong, had no comprador. All its personnel, which (except for the coolies and 'boys', or servants) is exclusively Japanese, learns Chinese from the outset, from the Manager himself down to the youngest clerk. 'If I do not do it myself,' said the Manager, 'I cannot expect my juniors to do it.' From 5 to 6.30 p.m. *every day*, there is Chinese tuition on the premises, at the firm's expense, at which every member of the staff attends; and in the evening again, they are said to continue their studies. Mitsui, accordingly, now trades directly with the Chinese firms not only in Hong Kong but also those of Chinese towns; and the Manager declared that they found it answers admirably. There was *less* risk of non-fulfilment of contracts because there was less misunderstanding of what was agreed! And Mitsui is increasing its trade by leaps and bounds. Last year something like a million tons of coal were sold in Hong Kong for bunker coal and for South China. Of this, nearly 700,000 tons were sold by Mitsui, the Japanese coal thus replacing the English, to the loss of the English firms. The comment of one great English magnate on this Japanese success was that the Japanese Managers did not need such high salaries as the English firms had to pay; and we gathered that the Mitsui salaries were in hundreds of pounds as compared with the thousands of pounds of the English houses. But apparently the English quite failed to realise the Japanese assiduity, intellectual humility and deliberate purposefulness which made Mitsui's men learn Chinese and dispense with the comprador.

There seems to be practically no social intercourse at Hong Kong between the Europeans and the Japanese, who keep to themselves and have their own Club, or between either of them and the Chinese. At Government House, only some 25 Chinese – all men – are ever asked to dinner, and about 100 to receptions. A very few Chinese ladies accompany their husbands when asked to *tiffin*. They are never asked to dinner because the dinners to which the Chinese are asked are always men's parties; the Europeans, we were told, would often be intensely offended at their wives being taken in to dinner by Chinese men, even Chinese of the highest rank and greatest wealth! What happens, we gather, is that the two or three Chinese Members of the Legislative Council, those on the Sanitary Board, a few leading Chinese merchants and bankers, are occasionally invited to dinner in fours or sixes to meet the principal English officials, the other Members of Council, and any European visitors at Government House who do not object.

On the other hand, it must be noted to the credit of the Hong Kong Government that there is no invidious exclusion of the Chinese from the public gardens, any more than from the public medical service or the Legislative Council. And the new Hong Kong University,[12] to which Sir Frederick Lugard is devoting himself as the principal achievement of his five-year term, is primarily and essentially for the Chinese. The Government provides some schools of its own, and aids by grant many more, for Chinese elementary education; but substantial fees are charged, and there is of course no compulsion. The result is that, after seventy years of British rule, only a few thousand boys and only a few hundred girls in a population exceeding 300,000 are at school, and these exclusively from the middle class. This does not contrast well with Japan's universal primary schooling, and compulsory attendance.

Canton[13] was in the hands of the Revolutionaries and it was not even known by whom it was being governed. The Revolutionary official who had taken over charge when the Viceroy fled had himself quietly slipped away to safer quarters the week before; and whether he had a successor, and if so whom, was quite unknown in Hong Kong. The Revolutionary force in possession of the city was said to consist of 10,000 brigands from the mountains who had been bribed to enlist as soldiers. Our introduction to the Chinese Government officials had become useless owing to their flight; but as Cook's[14] did not demur to providing a guide and the Governor did not forbid it, we made up our minds to do the usual tourist round.

The Foreign Settlement at Canton, called *Shameen*,[15] a small island in the river joined to the shore by two carefully-guarded bridges, proved to be full of charm, with its avenues of trees, its broad sward of grass between stately buildings, with pale-faced European children at play under the protection of French and Indian police. But leaving our hospitable friends, we went in chairs borne by three or four coolies each, in and out of every corner of the crowded city, to all the usual sights. There was nowhere any molestation or disorder. At every corner and in nearly every temple and other public building, we saw groups of wild-looking, unkempt youths in more or less uniform, bearing the white rag of the revolution on their arm, with a hundred rounds of ball cartridges ostentatiously in their belts, playing with their rifles and still more with their bright new revolvers; and at one place, discharging them in the air as if they were fire-crackers! We heard afterwards of some of them handling dynamite bombs quite casually in fun. We were glad to get round the corner of the hill by the powder-magazine, so that any explosion would pass us by. When we came to the Five-Storied Pagoda[16] where they were quartered in strength, we passed through straggling groups without even being accosted. That same afternoon, just after our steamer dropped down the river, a bomb was thrown (or perhaps accidentally dropped) in the Provincial Assembly building, destroying it and killing or wounding more than a dozen people.

Apart from this replacement of Chinese Government officials and troops by these 'brigands', Canton seemed to be going on as usual. The narrow streets were densely crowded, the wilderness of shops were all open, the thousands of craftsmen were at work, the guardians of the temples were selling their charms and joss-sticks, women were worshipping, all just as if the Emperor was still in command. The only difference was that the men were queue-less! For the first time in three centuries there were, on all the hundreds of thousands of men in the Canton streets, no pigtails! In the preceding few days, there had been a universal cutting of them off, and any person who had delayed and appeared with one on had been roughly seized and subjected to summary docking in the street by means of the first axe, knife or scissors that came to hand. (At Hong Kong Government House, the Chinese servants had all cut off their pigtails on the preceding Saturday; they explained that to wear them meant to be jeered at and assaulted in the streets.)

Our impression of Canton is a sort of nightmare − this million of blue-clad human ants inhabiting apparently endless series of dark and dirty cells in which they lived and ate and worked amid gaudy decoration. Between the rows of these single-storied brick or stone cells open to the narrow street of eight- or ten-feet width, there poured an endless stream of pedestrian life as in an ant-hill, through which our coolies forced their way with constant shouting, bearing our cumbrous 'chair' (itself three feet wide) like a motor car through a crowd. The whole city gave us the impression not of distinct houses but of a single construction of brick or stone cells built adjoining each other, divided indeed only by the thickness of a wall, without courtyard or garden or so far as we could see any separate compound. In these cells, deliberately made dark to exclude the burning sun, the whole population, rich and poor, seemed to be burrowing with the animated motion, the uniformity and the perpetual repetition of identical parts of an ant-hill. Here indeed was (to outward seeming) the 'ant-like' activity to which Belloc[17] and others object. But Canton city is poles asunder from Japan, which such persons foolishly imagine to be what Canton seems − namely, not really a social organism but an ant-hill.

It was perhaps characteristic of China that the temples (in which, by the way, cavalry horses were in one case actually stalled) were horribly squalid, neglected, and of the lowest barbarism, the images grotesque, the appurtenances tawdry, and the rites of the few worshippers degradingly superstitious. We saw women offering incense to the image appropriate to the particular *age* of their children, shaking sticks in a vessel until one jumped out − this was eagerly consulted as bearing the sign of the particular medicine to be given to the sick child or the particular fortune to be expected − of course needing interpretation at a fee by the person at the receipt of custom. The pictures of the tortures of the wicked − in themselves not essentially different from analogous Christian pictures of the Middle Ages − were 'farmed out' by the Government to the capitalist who offered the highest rent for them – he recouping himself by his receipts from the charms sold and the fortunes told by palmistry and otherwise, by a staff which drew in the pennies of the frequenters.

One new temple, erected some ten years ago on the outskirts of the city by the Ch'an or Shun family,[18] deserves mention. This was a Confucian resting-place or place of deposit for the *tablets* bearing the names of deceased members of the family, the tablets typifying these ancestral spirits. A large number of members of this family had subscribed to erect this temple and many hundreds of tablets were already in position. Twice a year the descendants of those whose names were thus inscribed assembled to do reverence to them with feasts and ceremonies. The rest of the year the place was deserted. It was a gaudily-painted and fantastically-carved building consisting of a succession of arches, open courts, and covered halls open at the side, in which the tablets were placed. The whole thing was immensely costly – the huge slabs of granite, the lofty pillars, the wealth of carving and paint representing, we were told, a million dollars – and, as it seemed, a monument of merely conventional observances which we cannot believe to be more than conventional.

A night's steaming down the river took us to Macao,[19] a city of 50,000 Chinese governed by a few hundred Portuguese officials and soldiers. Here the houses, of Portuguese style, harbour a curiously degenerate Government which keeps the town clean and tidy but otherwise lets the Chinese do as they choose. The main industry is gambling – 'First-Class Gambling House' is the usual inscription in the principal street – out of which the Portuguese Government draws a revenue from the keepers of the houses which more than covers the whole cost of the Colony, pays the troops, and enables an annual sum of five thousand pounds or so to be remitted to Lisbon.

The most interesting thing we saw was the garden and summer residence of the principal Chinese gambling-house proprietor. Here, in a quite formal garden, were the usual beautiful flowers of the tropics, many of the bushes elaborately trained into the shapes of dragons, deer and lions. The house was a one-storied erection, the rooms filled with elaborately-carved blackwood furniture, tables with inlaid tops, and so on – without any books or pictures to speak of.

We found, on our return to Hong Kong, the Governor worried over the developing situation – trade completely stopped, the population excited, some mobbing of the police and now bad cases of piracy in the adjacent Chinese waters, a steamer bearing the English flag attacked, one English officer killed, many Chinese killed and wounded, the whole boat looted. This will lead to patrolling of the West River by British gunboats, and may be the beginning of intervention.[20]

We can hardly form a definite opinion of the product of seventy-years' rule in Hong Kong in the way of educated and wealthy Chinese. We met at dinner the two leading Members of the Legislative Council,[21] and two leading Members of the Sanitary Board. They struck us as somewhat cringing [*sic*] in their obsequious courtesy to the Europeans and (though undeniably up to standard in accomplishments) not taking a self-respectful or a really intelligent view of the relation between West and East. But we had very little opportunity of talking with them.

We saw more of one Kotewall,[22] a clerk in the Colonial Secretary's office who was deputed to take us about. He felt himself a Chinese and dressed as such; but we were told he had had a Parsee[23] father. He was a highly accomplished and polished little man of about 40 who had, as second wife, a Chinese lady of beauty speaking a little English. He took us to 'tea' at his house, which turned out to involve (at 5 p.m.) a very elaborate meal of half-a-dozen courses, all Chinese, eaten with chop-sticks − bird's nest soup, shark's fin, preparations of *vermicelli*, minced meat in dumpling crusts, and lotus-seed (a kind of apple jelly). But the interest of the home lay in the books. This little clerk had accumulated far and away the largest library in Hong Kong, possessing many hundreds of volumes of English works, poetry and fiction, but principally philosophy, science and travels − as well as an extensive collection of the Chinese classics. And he had read and thought over all these books, including Myers' *Human Personality*,[24] in an intelligent way. He had formed a great hero-worship for A. J. Balfour, whose bust he was sending to London for. We delighted him by promising him one of that stateman's books, with his autograph if possible.

We went over schools in Hong Kong, both Chinese and English, both 'private-venture' and grant-aided, to very little profit (carried about by the Government House coolies in bright scarlet linen jackets, which made us conspicuous everywhere, the policemen all saluting). The premises were dreadfully inadequate, the teaching seemed poor, the instruction was wholly copied from English without intelligent adaptation, and the attendance was in effect confined to children above the wage-earning class. We could not help thinking that the Japanese Government would have done it more efficiently.

More interesting was the Chinese Hospital,[25] a purely native philanthropic institution, run by a committee of leading Chinese who are expected to give large sums for the honour of office. Besides a hospital and extensive out-patients' department, it has developed into an institution of general utility for the Chinese − it repatriates stranded Chinese, buries dumped corpses, relieves indigence in extreme cases, and undertakes large collections of relief funds for calamities in China −

in all this having the entire confidence of the Chinese all over the world. The Government exercises a benevolent supervision over it and helps where necessary, without interfering. The intelligent young Chinese doctor who took us over seemed well-educated and efficient. But any patient, in- or out-, may ask for Chinese treatment or European treatment at his option; and a majority still ask for Chinese treatment. We saw two Chinese doctors (educated in Chinese medicine only) prescribing for out-patients: feeling the pulse, asking a few questions, and then writing a prescription — not essentially differing from the routine of the six-penny doctor at home, or for that matter, from that of the out-patients' department of a London hospital. There was an extensive dispensary for preparing Chinese medicines, including dried snake, crushed beetle, and so on, which were duly exhibited to us, all the extensive resources of the Chinese *pharmacopoeia* being utilised. On the verandah were three men bringing live snakes in baskets, one a yellow-banded cobra, out of which they proceeded then and there to extract the gall bladder and liver (whilst the snake was still alive) for use as Chinese medicine.

There was only one trained nurse to some 300 patients in bed. But the ward attendants kept the place clean and very airy, though [it was] dreadfully noisy from the closely-adjacent, densely-crowded Chinese tenement houses and theatre.

We ought to record the beauty of the view *on the other side* of Hong Kong, from the Peak or otherwise. The beauty of the harbour side is well-known, by photographs and travellers' enthusiasms. But no one mentions the early morning and sunset views of the Western sea, with its wealth of islands large and small, and its fleets of diminutive fishing vessels — a panorama of unrivalled beauty.

Notes

1. A British Crown Colony of some 400 square miles. The island of Hong Kong itself was ceded by China to Great Britain under the Treaty of Nanking (1842). Kowloon, on the Chinese mainland, was added under an 1860 treaty, and so too, under a 99-year lease agreed on 9 June 1898, was the peninsula south of a line drawn between Deep Bay and Mirs Bay, together with the islands of Lantao and Lamma. Recently, Britain has agreed to return Hong Kong to China in 1997. At the time of the Webbs' visit, Hong Kong was governed by a Governor appointed by the Secretary of State for the Colonies, in London. The Governor, who held his position during the pleasure of the Crown, was obliged to consult his Executive Council on all major policy decisions, but five of its seven Members were officials bound to

vote as he directed. There was also a Legislative Council empowered to make Hong Kong's laws, but its composition of seven official and six unofficial Members meant that here too the Governor exercised effective control. Two Members of the Legislative Council were Chinese. No Chinese served on the Executive Council until 1926.

2. Before her marriage to Colonel Sir Frederick Lugard in 1902, Lady Lugard (d. 1929) had been the newspaper writer Miss Flora Shaw, of the Colonial Department of *The Times*.

3. The British soldier and colonial administrator Sir F.D., later Lord Lugard (1858–1945), author of *The Dual Mandate in British Tropical Africa* (London, 1929). Lugard's career is chiefly associated with Uganda and Nigeria, but he also served as Governor of Hong Kong during the period 1907–12.

4. On Hong Kong island there were fewer than 14 000 non-Chinese at the time, and a shifting population of over 300 000 Chinese, living in crowded tenements along the rim of the island and a little way up the slopes at the foot of the Peak. Sanitation and social services were primitive, and upwards of 1000 dead bodies a year were simply left by the Chinese in the streets. Though successful in discouraging this practice, Lugard met spirited resistance when he published an order, regarded as dictatorial by the Chinese, that would ban spitting on pavements and, except in provided spittoons, in public places. Presented with a petition of protest signed by some 8000 Chinese, which he was told another 80 000 had tried to sign, the Governor gave way and agreed instead to the Chinese setting up (with mixed results) their own Anti-Spitting Committee of eighty of their leading men.

5. The 'War' reference here is to the South African or Boer War, 1899–1900. The 'dubious episode' was the ill-fated Jameson Raid of several years before, in which Flora Shaw, influenced by her friendship with business man and benefactor Cecil Rhodes (1853–1902), had played an embarrassing background role. At the time, Rhodes was Prime Minister of Cape Colony. Frustrated in his scheme to get the Transvaal Boers of the South African Republic to join in a customs union that would further both his imperialist beliefs and his financial interests, he had begun to encourage Uitlander settlers in Johannesburg to rebel against the Republic. Late in 1895, the British Government attached Bechuanaland to the Cape Colony, except for a narrow strip of territory along the Transvaal frontier that was instead turned over to Rhodes' South Africa Company, ostensibly for the purpose of launching an extension of the railway from Mafeking north into Rhodesia. Dr Starr Jameson was immediately despatched by the S.A.C. as 'administrator' of their newly-acquired land; and from there in late December, with a force of some 600 men, he struck out for Johannesburg, in a surprise raid planned to coincide with an insurrection by the Uitlanders. But the insurrection never took place, and the Boers, having learned in advance of Jameson's plans, defeated his forces in an engagement at Krugersdorp three days later. Jameson was handed over for trial in England, in the course of which he was condemned but given a light sentence. The episode became a political *cause célèbre*. Cecil Rhodes' heavy implication led to his resignation as Prime Minister. Flora Shaw had been privy to the plot and had written leading articles in *The Times* pointedly supportive of the Uitlanders' cause. She was in

telegraphic communication with Rhodes himself by secret code in the days leading up to the raid, and tipped off by Rhodes' agent, had published in *The Times* the morning after Jameson began his raid a manifesto the Uitlanders were to have issued *if* they had risen. She was called before a parliamentary committee of enquiry, and though 'excused', her reputation was under a cloud.

6. Lord George Francis Hamilton (1845–1927), Conservative politician and Chairman of the Royal Commission on the Poor Law, on which Beatrice had served.

7. According to Margery Perham, *Lugard* (London, 1956, 1960) (2 vols), Flora Shaw was susceptible to bouts of frail health, 'partly due to her ceaseless over-exertion'. She was also, at the time of the Webbs' visit, still recovering from complications attendant on an operation for acute appendicitis.

8. Charles Frederick Moberly Bell ((1847–1911), long-standing Egypt Correspondent before becoming Manager and later Managing Director of *The Times*.

9. The radical free-thinker Marie Souvestre (d. 1905), daughter of French Academician, Emile Souvestre. She ran a fashionable boarding-school at Wimbledon.

10. N. J. Stabb.

11. British shipping and trading firm.

12. The foundation-stone was laid on 16 March 1910, and the handsome first building of the University, occupying a site about halfway up the side of the Peak, provided a prominent landmark when viewed from the harbour.

13. Then China's largest city, situated some eighty miles to the north-west of Hong Kong on the Chinese mainland, at the delta of the Pearl River. The Webbs appear to have followed the recommended tourist practice of travelling there via the Canton–Kowloon Railway, and returning to Hong Kong by steamer with a stop at Macao.

14. Thomas Cook, the British travel agency.

15. An island separated from Canton's western suburbs by a canal 100 feet wide, the west and centre of the site was occupied by the British Concession, with a much smaller French Concession to the east.

16. A tower rather than a pagoda, situated near the Great North Gate of the Old City. Built between 1366–99 A.D., the tower's upper-stories provided fine views of Canton, the river and the surrounding country-side. In a hollow below the Pagoda was a Government powder-magazine.

17. Hilaire Belloc (1870–1953), poet and prolific author.

18. The Ch'an Ancestral Temple, located at Lai Chi Wan, built in 1890 at a cost of over 100 000 *taels*.

19. Situated on an 11-square-mile site 35 miles west of Hong Kong, its multi-coloured houses rising on a hill-side overlooking a beautiful crescent-shaped bay, Macao was the oldest European outpost in China, the Portuguese having arrived there as early as 1557. Eclipsed as a trading centre with the cession of Hong Kong to Great Britain, Macao became chiefly a pleasure resort known for its *Fan Tan* houses, its nickname 'the Monte Carlo of the Far East'. Macao reverts to Chinese control in 1999.

20. Concerned that an imminent end to Manchu rule might spill over into Chinese demands for an end to foreign domination, Lugard ordered soldiers

with fixed bayonets into the streets of Hong Kong and took measures to reinforce the garrison with two battalions of infantry and a battery of artillery sent from India. On 30 November emergency powers were invoked and a penalty imposed of up to twenty-four lashes with a cat-o'-nine-tails for a wide range of offences, and some fifty-one prisoners were flogged in the three months that passed before the emergency measures were rescinded. See Norman Miners, *Hong Kong Under Imperial Rule, 1912–1941* (Hong Kong, 1987) p. 4.

21. Kai Ho Kai (later Sir) (1859–1914), a Member since 1890, and Bosnan Wei Yuk (later Sir) (1849–1921), a Member since 1896.

22. Sir Robert Kotewall, of Parsee ancestry with a Chinese mother. A clerk in the Colonial Secretariat from 1896–1916, he later became a Member of the Legislative Council (1923–35), and thereafter of the Executive Council.

23. The Parsees (or *Parsis*) are adherents of the religion of Zoroastrianism, the oldest prophetic religion, originating in iran c. 1200 B.C. and later brought to India by Persians fleeing Muslim persecution.

24. Frederick W. H. Myers (1843–1901), Platonist student of the subliminal self and President of the Society for Psychical Research. In his 'Foreword' to a 1961 reprint of Myers' posthumously-published *Human Personality and Its Survival of Bodily Death* (London, 1903) (2 vols), Aldous Huxley writes: 'In this great book Myers brought together a universal store of information about the always strange and often wonderful goings-on in the upper-stories of a man's soul-house.'

25. The Tung-Wah Hospital.

5
Malay Peninsula

[SW→] PENANG 9th DEC^r 1911

We end today a nine days' run through the Malay Peninsula during which we have been able to see something of the administration of the Straits Settlements (Crown Colony) and the Federated Malay States (nominally, only a Protectorate in which the inhabitants are not technically British subjects but entirely British-administered under the Governor of the Straits Settlements as High Commissioner).[1] Through the introduction of Sir John Anderson, once a clerk in the Colonial Office with S.W.[2] and lately Governor of the Straits Settlements,[3] we have been most hospitably received by the Government – staying with the Acting-Governor or Chief Officer at Singapore, Seremban, and Kuala Lumpur respectively, and at Kuala Kangsur with a young Fabian who is second master at the Malay College there.

We need not expatiate on the beauty of the tropical vegetation, nor on the heat, nor on the amazing economic development in tin and rubber. At Singapore we were shown the whole working of the opium monopoly, which the Government has taken into its own direct administration.[4] The opium is bought through various intermediaries, mostly from the Indian Government (which insists on selling at periodical auctions only and refuses to make any special arrangements for the Straits Government) and, to a small extent, from Persia. It is then made into 'chandu' at a Government factory at Singapore (by a process of boiling and drying), done up into tiny packets at another Government warehouse, [and] there sold at a high price to the licensed opium shops. The object of the Government is mainly to get revenue; but the control of the production is useful also in controlling the opium shops and in keeping a finger on the public pulse, in the way both of diminishing the extent of the opium habit and in preventing resort to such evil alternatives as morphia and cocaine, of which there is unfortunately great danger. The chief administrative difficulty lies in preventing smuggling of so costly a product and in circumventing the efforts of the Jew [sic] wholesale dealers in opium (largely the

Sassoons)[5] to make a corner and drive the Government to pay high prices for the current supply. The Singapore Government factory supplies also the F.M. States. It seemed well-administered, though the young Director was puzzled when we asked him what was his test of the success of his department – was it maximum revenue or minimum consumption? What they are actually doing is to raise as much revenue as possible in a decorous way, at the same time raising the price (so as to get more revenue out of less consumption) up to the point at which the temptation to use substitutes, and to smuggle, would be irresistible. The opium department, by the way, is called the Government Monopolies Department, though there is no other than opium – not by way of prediction as to others being added, but in order to avoid using the word opium!

[BW →] Except for this morning over the opium monopoly, we saw little in our three days at Singapore. The three officials with whom we had to deal – the Acting-Governor, the Secretary of F.M.S., and the A.D.C. of the Acting-Governor – were not persons of much initiative. The Acting-Governor, Mr. Wilkinson,[6] was an attractively intellectual and reflective man – the son of an Englishman in the Consular Service who had married 'in the East', it was said, a Greek lady. He had tumbled up in all sorts of weird countries, but had finished at Cambridge and had entered the Civil Service through the usual Class I (Eastern Cadetship) examination, having failed by a few marks to get into the Indian Civil Service.[7] This foreign origin and training had certainly made him more interested in the natives, and his scholarly tastes had resulted in starting the first researches into Malay customs. But he suffered from a lack of the ordinary English capacity for 'getting on' with everyone, his very reserve and refinement and intellectuality and the slur of his 'foreign origin' – qualities which attracted us to him – making him unpopular in a service recruited from the ordinary English public school boy. His A.D.C. was just a nice young officer with no particular zeal or capacity.

The Secretary, Mr. Claud Severn,[8] made up for the somewhat negative qualities of his temporary chief by a bounding personality – a snob, a *bon vivant*, a *raconteur*, and I can quite well believe, a quite efficient organiser of an office. When we arrived he was full of his appointment to the Colonial Secretaryship of Hong Kong – a great and unexpected rise in the service. In opinion he was an ardent Anglican, a conservative and a *soi-disant* socialist or social reformer. But he was wholly uninterested in the natives or in any institution for their benefit – he knew and cared nothing about the characteristics of the Chinese or the Tamils,[9] now swarming into the Peninsula. What he liked to talk about was English society and all the persons of high degree with whom he was in some way connected. He and Wilkinson were not only uncongenial but mutually contemptuous, though Wilkinson said discreetly pleasant things about Severn whilst Severn quite clearly manifested to us by manner if not by word his low opinion of Wilkinson. All this is ungrateful, because it was Severn and not Wilkinson who looked after us — and he did it to the best of his ability.

We stayed at two other official residences — with Mr. Cecil Parr[10] at Seremban and with Mr. Brockman[11] at Kuala Lumpur, and we saw various other officials of one sort or another. All these officials live in large and attractive houses, with well-kept gardens and numerous servants, and with a meticulous elaboration of meals and clothes. The standard set is that of South Kensington if not Park Lane, and the hours (9 for breakfast and 8 for dinner) are all conventionally correct for the English climate. All these officials are obviously men of honour and *integrity*, fulfilling punctiliously all their official obligations. But outside the office hours, they live unto themselves, with their motors, their sports, and their social enjoyments. They do not associate with the wealthier Chinese or Malays and they are not interested in the condition of all these people beyond keeping law and order and giving facilities for capitalist development. The only really keen people we saw were the medical men engaged in research into malaria and beriberi. These men were really living in their work; but even here, the public opinion they were looking to was the public opinion of the London scientist and medical man and not the public opinion of the Peninsula, British or native.

We motored with Mr. Parr to Ramban to see the working of a sub-district under a young cadet, Mr. Pennington [SW: of the well-known London solicitor family].[12] The sub-district office consisted of an open court of justice and an office for administrative work, with Malay and Eurasian subordinates, close to the bungalow of the A.D.O. and in the midst of the jungle. Here the typical young Englishman — tall and athletic, with a well-bred, careless manner, was administering justice, not 'indifferently', but with an honest, slow, painstaking effort to interpret the F.M.S. statutes and the customs of the particular tribe.[13] This was the day for giving out the titles of the land to the small owners according to the new survey — and little groups of women, sometimes accompanied by men, were crowding round the office.

[SW →] The local custom of Rembow in Negri Sembilan (one of the four constituent States making up the Federated Malay States) puts all the land permanently in the ownership of the women, descending to the daughters. The man enters the wife's family, and is ruled by the mother-in-law, his wife, and even by the sisters of his deceased wife, until he marries again. It is the women who manage the cultivation of the little rice-plots, the man being put to perform the heavier tasks. How the custom arose, or what it signifies, we do not know, but it is universal throughout the State (of course, only among the Malays, who here predominate), and is fully upheld by the English courts. It is said to have the useful practical result of preventing alienation to the money-lender, as each plot is virtually in the position of being entailed (in the female line), and no individual can give a valid title. The women were said to be exceptionally independent and capable, and the few that we saw certainly bore this out (it may have been an accident that the men whom we saw were, several of them, minding the baby!).

This so-called 'Malay' Peninsula has ceased to be predominantly Malay — this is the governing feature of the situation. The Malays, themselves conquering immigrants from Sumatra of the 12th to 17th centuries, pushed back the scanty savage tribes into the hills but themselves succumbed to the influences of the climate and the jungle, remaining a soft, feeble, gentle, timid, unenterprising folk satisfied with their little plots of rice and groves of coconuts and bananas. To them there came in the 19th century immigrant Chinese who worked for tin and carried on trade; and casual European adventurers. The Malays were being more and more pushed on one side with robbery, murder and civil war among the Chinese clans and sections,[14] when (about 1870–5) the English Government intervened and, more or less with their consent, practically took over the Government. Now the Chinese form more than half the total population; another quarter is made up of Indian coolie immigrants.[15] The English are the capitalists and estate Managers, and the Malays, still preserving the form of ruling the country through their four Sultans (and the five other Sultans of the States still merely 'protected'), have fallen into the background. They have not sunk or suffered, as they remain just as they were. But the new wealth growing up around them in tin and rubber belongs to the Chinese and the English, who supply the brains, the capital and the labour (the latter, either Chinese or Indian indentured coolies who assume to go home again after two or three years).

The English administration has secured law and order and all that is comprised in 'justice and police'. The boom in tin and rubber[16] has given a superabundant revenue, so amazingly good roads and bridges, railways and steam-ferries have been constructed. The officials have provided themselves with luxurious and stately Government Houses and public offices. Latterly, something has been done in the way of public hospitals and Malay vernacular schools. Sanitation is just beginning (because malarial fever is becoming more serious now that hundreds of coolies are aggregated together on each plantation). One cannot help feeling that the English official has been in earnest only about maintaining law and order and administering justice in an amateur, country-gentleman way. He has not really tried to educate the Malay or even to make the country healthy for him. When revenue became abundant it was spent on magnificent roads on which presently the officials' and planters' motor cars were everywhere to be seen.

The educational system seemed to us rudimentary. There are no Government schools (in F.M.S.) for Chinese or Indian children, although by this time there are tens of thousands of such children whose parents are practically permanent citizens of the F.M.S. and large contributors to its revenue. For the Malays the Government provides a series of small elementary schools in the larger villages, where the boys attend (we are told) willingly without compulsion. They have Malay '*gurus*' or teachers who know no English and (to judge from those we saw) are little removed from illiteracy and incompetence.

In the Straits Settlements (at Malacca), there is a Government training-college where a younger generation of Malay teachers is now being trained – [but] not with very satisfactory results, we were told. The Malay school-house, in extreme contrast with the abundance of class-rooms in the Japanese schools, is a *single room*, bare of anything but a few maps and some rudely-made desks and forms. The hours of school are very short (ending at 11 a.m.), the holidays are frequent, and the attendance is very perfunctory. There is no census of children who ought to be at school and no apparatus for seeing that they are there; and the population statistics are so crude that no one has so far been able even to compute how many children need school places or what percentage of them are in attendance. The girls are usually totally unprovided for, and except in large towns, are not at school at all – this is after more than thirty years [of] English administration, for much of it with an abundant revenue!

Four years ago, the Government started a 'Malay College'[17] with the idea of educating the sons of the Sultans, Rajas and other big men on the model of an English 'public school' (meaning Eton or Winchester), where they should receive a training in 'character' and be 'made men of'! A fine building has been erected (at Kuala Kangsur in Perak), a headmaster and two assistants appointed, and over a hundred boys have been induced to come (mostly provided with Government scholarships of 12 dollars a month to cover the school fee of 8 dollars for board and lodging and tuition, and books, pocket-money, etc.). About a dozen sons of Sultans, etc. occupy separate bedrooms, dine at a separate table, and pay a substantial fee.

We stayed with the second master (a Fabian named O'May)[18] and saw a good deal of the school, the headmaster (Hargreaves),[19] the other English assistant (Stuart)[20] and the boys. The place has achieved a certain measure of success of a sort but it seemed to us a monument of blundering, amateur, inconsiderate empiricism. No curriculum had been thought out — there was absolutely no science, no drawing, no manual training, no swimming, no gymnastics, no music — and when we asked why not, we were told, first, that these things were not taught at an English 'public school' (which is no longer quite true), and secondly, that the staff was unable to teach them! Practically, the instruction seemed confined to English with a little history and geography (by the three European masters), arithmetic (by a Eurasian subordinate!),[21] and Malay (by the village schoolmaster called in for the purpose).

The boarding and lodging arrangements seemed miracles of ineptitude. The hundred boys varying in age from 7 to nearly 20 slept in large dormitories without any supervision whatsoever other than that of 'prefects' or elder boys appointed by the headmaster. In fact in the whole school building there was at night nobody except the boys themselves. The servants all slept out. The masters had their own bungalows apart. When we expressed surprise at this lack of supervision of the bedroom it was objected that no master could possibly be expected to 'sleep in'! (Of course, at the large school at Penang for Chinese and Malays run by the Christian Brothers, who know something about schools, we found that a 'Brother' slept (in a curtained-off bed) in each dormitory.)

The headmaster admitted that there was some immorality but said that there was not more than was inevitable and usual, and that he relied on his own 'personality' in looking after the boys (in the daytime!). We noticed that about a score of the boys were segregated in one dormitory, as he said, under special supervision by the prefect.

The boys were fed on rice and the usual vegetables, pickles, etc. in Malay style. We noticed with surprise that (except at the Sultans' table) there were no knives and forks; and we learnt that the boys ate with their fingers! This is Malay fashion, it is true, but it seems extraordinary to bring up boys 'on the lines of an English public school' in a way which prevents their having any social intercourse with Englishmen. Nearly all these boys are to enter the local Civil Service and two of them have already been appointed to be Assistant-District Officers. Moreover, the habit is uncleanly and unsanitary, and the doctor to whom we mentioned it condemned it in no measured terms as promoting some locally-prevalent disease. In answer to our criticisms, we were told (a) that knives and forks were too expensive! and (b) that it would be undesirable to give the boys habits that differed from those of their parents. They played games to some extent, but not much — a little cricket and more football and the elder boys had an embryo cadet corps.

The washing arrangements were quite inadequate, and there was no training in the bath or the toilet even for the little boys. There was no matron (in fact, no woman at all) as it was said that these Muslims would object to any woman (but then, boys of 7 were not sent to boarding-schools in Muhammad's time). Mrs. Hargreaves, the head-master's wife, did not enter the school at all, and devoted herself to her flower-garden.

Altogether it was rather a grievous picture of English amateur blundering. No one seems to have put any thought into it or made any enquiries as to what is done elsewhere, or to have got free from the self-complacent delusion that the English 'public school' was so good a thing that it needed only to be set up in Malaya to succeed. And of the three points of the English public school — the housemaster's family provision, the incessant games in which the masters participate, and the school's social equality — they have ignored the first and last, and only imperfectly adopted the second. All that had been done was to appoint prefects.

Through the whole range of education in the F.M.S. one felt that the officials had not really believed in it or desired to make it efficient. The money was spent perfunctorily, without expert advice or criticism. How differently the Japanese Government has gone to work! If the F.M.S. Government had really wanted an efficient education system, it would have set itself twenty years ago to train up Malay teachers. It would have established a normal school under European masters and put the necessary number of selected boys through a ten years' course. By this time it would have been turning out an annual crop of trained and civilised Malays speaking and reading English but able to run vernacular schools; there would have been inspectors conversant with European and American pedagogy; and there would have been a Director of Education running the whole machine. In the F.M.S., the matter is dealt with by an undifferentiated civil servant who has been made Director of Education because he was fit for nothing more important!

[BW→] We amused ourselves by gathering 'hearsay' about the three staple races of the Malay States and their characteristics. All the officials 'liked' the Malays; they were well-mannered without being servile, they were honourable and kindly and loyal to their own chiefs and Sultans, and to the British sovereignty. That they were idle and inefficient and lacking initiative was taken as a matter of course. No one had a good word for the character of the Tamils — they were merely regarded as useful animals who would work on small portions of rice, and would die without complaint. About the Chinese, there were many opinions, from the conventional 'they are a great race, and when they get a good Government, they will beat the world', said in tones of cheerful complacency by European capitalists at dinner, to the almost physical dislike of them as personally repulsive, greedy for gain, given-over to unnatural vice, and at times, grossly disorderly – the view of them which is taken by some harassed officials. Alone among the Eastern races in the Malay Peninsula, they have amassed wealth by productive enterprise, and their fine houses and magnificent temples are notable features of Penang. Under British rule they have developed a healthy *bourgeoisie*, which takes part in the municipal government and organises philanthropic enterprise of its own.

But we do not gather that even under British rule the Chinese have developed either business or social enterprise on a great scale – on the scale of the European or Japanese banking, shipping or mercantile houses. They remain individual profit-makers, often employing European contractors or Managers for technical processes such as tin-mining or smelting. Socially they are not accepted by the European community, being excluded from all the Clubs. When we asked the very able schoolmaster of the 'Free School' of Penang whether he associated with the families of his Chinese boys, he said that it was impossible because of their crude ideas and crude habits. This was remarkable, because these boys were the sons of wealthy men and, at school during school hours, were almost ideal students – intelligent, respectful, and zealous. When I tried to discover what he meant by crude ideas, he said that they had no idea of honour or public spirit, that they attributed low motive to everyone, and that their only idea of patriotism was 'To kill the Manchu', and sometimes, 'To kill the Japanese' – without being themselves prepared to fight. However, the Singapore Chinese have undoubtedly backed the revolution with very large sums and also by a certain amount of personal service to the Revolutionary forces.[22] Perhaps it is to their credit that though they accept British rule gladly in the Peninsula and grow rich and comfortable under it, they remain Chinese, and always think of the Chinese Empire as something to which they owe their allegiance and to which some day they will return. And this, in spite of having intermarried with Malay women and having adopted many Malay habits and customs – even to the extent of bathing every day and sometimes three times a day. As for the swarm of Chinese coolies who make up the bulk of the Chinese population and who remain for a few years only, they supply the steady industry which has opened up the Peninsula. They also supply the great majority of the criminals, and their recurrent outbreaks in gang robberies and disorderly secret societies, not to mention their 'secret vices', are the perpetual concern of the British Government.

At Kuala Kangsur, we had an interesting interview with the premier Sultan of the Peninsula — the Sultan of Perak.[23] This shrewd and kindly old gentleman enjoys a large allowance from the British Government, and also has considerable private means. He has three legal wives, two occupying two separate palaces of identical construction and furniture, whilst the youngest and dearest puts up with a modest bungalow at which the old man delights to live, and to which we were privileged to take tea with him and the son, who acts as A.D.C. He was feeble and talked little English. But his mind was occupied with three considerations — Islam, British rule in the persons of the King and Queen, and the welfare of his own people.

He was interested to hear about Japan and enquired, after listening to our panegyric, whether the Emperor of Japan was of as old a family as our King George who, he said, had 37 generations behind him (a fact that we did not know). He was dismayed to hear that the Emperor's family claimed descent from the Gods. Then what was their religion? Neither Islam nor Christianity. That seemed a further blow — he gave up Japanese success as inexplicable.

He was interested in public health — said that he had called in European doctors in order that his people should do likewise. He cross-examined us as to women doctors — what would it cost to have one out from England[24] — and were there any women doctors on the staff of the King and Queen of England, and if not, why not? He was interested in women's votes, and asked us how it had succeeded. He thought that if *any one had votes*, women might have, as they had just as good brains as men!

His son was a gentle-natured, well-bred, depressed sort of person. Neither the Sultan nor any of the Malays seem to have any feeling of common cause with Asiatics. Islam is their nationality, and just at present they are much concerned with the wicked infidel power Italy attacking the head of Islam — the Sultan of Turkey.[25] They dislike the Chinese and their dirty ways, and they have a thoroughgoing contempt for the Tamils and their servile manners. The British they accept as secular superiors who will expiate their dominion in this world by everlasting torture in the next.

[SW→] At Penang — which has been British territory for a century and a quarter but for a long time only as an Indian convict settlement — the population has grown to over 100,000, with [a] large shipping trade and many wealthy people, mostly Chinese. Here there are two large 'English' schools for boys and one for girls, conducted one by the Government, one by the Christian Brothers, and the girls' school by a convent. They are open to all races but are resorted to almost exclusively by Chinese and Eurasians, with a few Malays, all of the lower middle-class or upwards. (We did not hear of any Government or other elementary school for the Tamil or Chinese working class, among whom it is always carelessly assumed that there are no children, which is incorrect.) These schools charged substantial fees (of about £4 a year for tuition only). The Government school was called the 'Free' school, meaning that it was free from religion! It was started some twenty years ago when the Government confiscated the property of some Chinese secret societies and offered to use the money for some purpose desired by the Chinese.

This school was closed (being Saturday) but we inspected the other two and saw much of two nice assistant masters of the Government free school itself (W. E. Mann and one Cheeseman), who, being bachelors and pecuniarily unable to live up to 'European society' in Penang, had thrown themselves into study of their boys, of the jungle, of Malay character and folklore, and so on. They were rather attractive men (Mann especially) whose elementary teacher characteristics had been softened and refined by enlarged experience and the reflection for which they had time. They were evidently zealous at their work, doing a lot for their boys and throwing themselves heartily into it. The schools all worked up to the senior local examination, which their elder pupils passed; and one or two of the wealthiest Chinese youths passed on to England. (Dr. Wu Lien-teh, the Manchurian plague expert,[26] was one of them.)

Both the R.C. schools that we inspected seemed efficiently run, with great devotion by the 'Brothers' and 'Sisters', and great practical wisdom. The boarding-school in each was under the closest supervision in manners and morals, night and day, in contrast with the Malay College. The school-work seemed greatly concentrated on speaking, reading and writing English, to which predominating attention was given. (The convent also took in orphans and foundlings, mostly Eurasian, as an act of charity. These children were kept apart from the school proper, and whilst being well fed and looked after, were evidently put to work as soon as possible, with a minimum of instruction and less amenity of life than the paying pupils.) This extensive development of R.C. educational work in Penang was attributed to the favour of Sir F. Weld, a former Governor,[27] who was a Catholic.

Notes

1. Originally, the Straits Settlements (Singapore, Penang, Province Wellesley, the Dindings and Malacca) fell under the direct control of the Government of British India, but in 1867 they were declared a Crown Colony under the jurisdiction of Britain's Secretary of State for the Colonies. The structure of governance consisted of a Governor and Commander-in-Chief appointed from London, assisted by an Executive Council and a Legislative Council similar to those found at Hong Kong. The Federated Malay States (Perak, Selangor, Negri Sembilan and Pahang) were formed in 1896. A 1909 reorganisation created a Federal Council consisting of the Governor of the Straits Settlements (as High Commissioner to the Malay States), a Chief Secretary and four Residents, the four Malay Rulers, and four nominated unofficial Members representing commercial interests. In addition, the so-called Unfederated Malay States (Kedah, Perlis, Kelanta 1 and Trengganu, previously in Siam's sphere of influence) accepted British advisers (as did Johore, beginning in 1914) but did not enter the centralised administration of the Federated Malay States.

2. Sidney Webb had served in the Upper Division at the Colonial Office from 1883 to 1891.

3. Governor of the Straits Settlements and High Commissioner for the Malay States, 1904–1911, recalled to London as Permanent Under-Secretary of State at the Colonial Office, in which capacity he served from 1911–16.

4. Although more important as a money earner in the Straits than in the FMS (with their large revenues from tin and rubber), opium was a major source of government revenue. The Straits Settlements had set up a Government opium monopoly in 1910 based on the report of a 1908 Opium Commission, a system previously adopted in the Netherlands East Indies. These arrangements remained in place until the Japanese occupation of Malaya during the Second World War.

5. Bankers and mill-owners, descendants of David Sassoon (1792–1864), a Baghdadi Jew who founded David Sassoon & Sons in Bombay in 1832. Three of his sons, Abdullah, Elias and David, became respectively Chairman of David Sassoon & Sons; founder of E. D. Sassoon & Co.; and founder of the parent firm's London branch.

6. R. J. Wilkinson, CMG (1867–1941), Straits Settlements Civil Service since 1889 and Federal Inspector of Schools beginning 1903, author of *A Malay–English Dictionary* (1902 and subsequent editions) and other books on Malay culture.

7. Members of the Cadet Service, who were required to be of pure European descent on both sides of the family, sat the same examination in London as candidates for the Home Civil Service and the Indian Civil Service. Examinees with the best results usually chose the Home Civil Service or India, while the remainder 'usually opted for Ceylon, Hong Kong, or Malaya, in that order of preference'. Cf. Norman Miners, *Hong Kong Under Imperialist Rule*, p. 85 *passim*.

8. Later Sir Claud Severn, a Cambridge product, who left shortly after the Webbs met him to become Colonial Secretary at Hong Kong, a position he held until 1926. He served as Officer Administering the Government (OAG)

of Hong Kong in the interval following the incapacitation of the serving Governor, Sir Henry May, in 1918, and the appointment of his successor, Sir Edward Stubbs, the following year.

9. An Indian people of South India (and Ceylon), whence most of the Indians in Malaya had derived.

10. C. W. C. Parr.

11. Sir Edward Brockman, a long-service Malayan officer who entered as a cadet in 1886 and rose to become Resident-General in the FMS.

12. H. E. Pennington, recruited into the Unfederated Malay States service at Kelantan upon graduation from Trinity College, Oxford, later transferred to the FMS, killed in the First World War.

13. J. M. Gullick, *Malaya* (London, 1963) p. 40, notes that 'The sheer tact of the British Residents played its part' in winning the Malays over to British rule.

14. The two main Chinese secret societies in Malaya were the Ghi Hin, predominantly Cantonese, and the Hai San or Toh Peh Kong, mainly Hakka. Violent episodes involving the two groups over possession of tin-mine sites in Perak and Selangor were common in the early 1870s. Eventually a Societies Ordinance was enacted, the registration requirements of which effectively outlawed such secret societies.

15. In 1800 the Malays had made up 90 per cent of the population of Malaya; in 1880, two-thirds; and by the time of the Webbs' visit, some 51 per cent. The 1911 Census gives the total population of the Peninsula as 2 651 036, with 1 416 796 Malays, 915 883 Chinese and 287 159 Indians. There were 11 085 Europeans. In the ten-year period 1911–21, the overall population was to grow by some 26 per cent; but the Malays increased only 15 per cent to the Chinese 28 per cent and the Indian 76 per cent. On Indian immigration, see K. S. Sandhu, *Indians in Malaya, Some Aspects of Their Immigration and Settlement* (Cambridge, 1969).

16. In terms of large-scale production, tin-mining in Malaya dates from around 1830, when immigrant Chinese miners worked open-cast mines to depths of up to 40 feet, pushing production to some 6000 tons annual output through the 1860s, in advance of the opening of the largest tin-field in the world at Kinta. The replacement of steam-engines and centrifugal pumps by tin-dredge floats made possible further dramatic rises in average annual output to almost 50 000 tons by the date of the Webbs' visit. Rubber seeds had made their way to Malaya from Brazil via Kew Gardens in the last quarter of the nineteenth century, serving at first as insurance against the periodic fall of world prices on Malaya's coffee estates. But the arrival of the motor car and the invention of the pneumatic tyre caused a sharp upward trend in prices for rubber in the opening decades of the new century, with world consumption of rubber doubling between 1900–10 and trebling again between 1910–20, leading to frenzied development of rubber estates in Malaya.

17. Originally the Malay Residential School on its founding in 1905, but from 1910 known as the Malay College.

18. John O'May, Irish by birth and an Oxford graduate, assistant master at Malay College, 1907–18, and acting-headmaster 1918–19. His socialist beliefs appear to have cost him the headmastership. For anecdotal materials, see William R. Roff (ed.), *The Wandering Thoughts of a Dying Man, The Life and Times of Haji Abdul Majid bin Zainuddin* (Kuala Lumpur, 1978).

19. William Hargreaves, M.A., Trinity College, Dublin, who had previously held appointments at the Leatherhead School (Surrey) and, as headmaster, at the Penang Free School.
20. E. A. G. Stuart (d. 1927). Educated at Rugby and Cambridge, where he had been captain of the Football Eleven. Joined the Kuala Kangsar staff of Malay College in 1908.
21. R. C. W. Rowlands, a Ceylonese who remained at Malay College until 1926.
22. For background, see Yen Ching Hwang, *The Overseas Chinese and the 1911 Revolution, With Special Reference to Singapore and Malaya,* (Kuala Lumpur, 1976).
23. Sultan Idris of Perak, born Raja Iskandar, who reigned from 1887 until his death in 1916.
24. In fact, the wife of John O'May of the Malay College, Dr L. S. McLean, was a physician. A graduate of St. Andrews and the London School of Tropical Medicine, she was appointed to the FMS Medical Service in 1913, and transferred to the Straits Settlements in 1921.
25. On 5 October 1911 the Italians had landed a force at Tripoli but met spirited resistance from a small Turkish and Arab force led by Enver Bey. Eventually, under the Treaty of Lausanne, the Turks abandoned sovereignty of Tripoli; but the Italians agreed to recognise a representative of the Sultan as Caliph.
26. Dr. Wu Lien-teh (b. 1879), a Cambridge graduate and distinguished medical researcher who was at the time of the Webbs' 1911–12 Asian tour Chief Medical Officer of the Manchurian Plague Prevention Service.
27. Sir Frederick Weld, Governor of the Straits Settlements, 1880–87.

6

Burma

A stay of eight days at Rangoon and Mandalay gave us a glimpse of
Burma under the rule of the Indian Civil Service.[1] The Lieutenant-
Governor and all the heads of departments were absent at the Durbar,[2]
whither their wives had taken magnificent dresses; but we were
hospitably entertained by a Fabian I.C.S. of 16 years' service (C.
Morgan Webb),[3] who was temporarily engaged in the decennial
census of the whole province. At his table, or by his introduction,
we saw half-a-dozen other civilians, and several of the leading
Burmese, with whom we spent many hours inspecting pagodas and
monasteries.

Burma, whilst resembling the F.M.S. in having a great industrial
development in the hands of alien immigrants, differs from Malaya in
having no Chinese coolie class: its imported coolies, like all the house-
servants, are immigrants from India; and its Chinese are merchants,
traders and artisans. Moreover, these are mainly concentrated in
Rangoon and neighbourhood and on the railway, leaving three-
fourths of all the ten millions of Burmese to live to themselves on
their little ancestral rice-plots. To them the English Government has
merely replaced that of the Burmese tyrant kings. Government, to
them, is one of the five evils from which they pray to be delivered; and
it is not easy to make out whether they appreciate the great advantage
of the English over the Burmese rule! We have secured peace, provided
law courts and police, and introduced railways and post office – but to
the Burman in his native village, far away from the railway and the law
courts, it may well seem that we have merely substituted one tax
collector for another.

However, it seems that the net outcome is a great and almost
universal material prosperity. The great development of Rangoon as a
port, with its huge export-trade in rice, oil and timber,[4] and the
freedom of Burma from disastrous drought or river floods – coupled
with the fact that there is still ample land to be had for the clearing –
has so far kept the Burman on his rice-plot in easy circumstances, too

well off to be willing to engage in coolie labour, or as a domestic servant, or even a subordinate in the public service, at the wage that the Madrassee gladly accepts. Thus the Burman, if undeveloped, is at any rate unspoilt by British rule. He is, we are told, unwilling to submit to the 'discipline' involved in subordinate service, whether in household, office, factory or army. He cannot understand why he should not go to a '*pwè*' or entertainment when he feels drawn to it, even though this means leaving his duty undone. It is a corollary that he has never shown himself capable of organisation on any considerable scale: the tiny hamlet of a score of bamboo huts represents his highest form of social organism. (*With the Jungle Folk*, by E. D. Cuming, seems to us to give, almost with genius, an accurate vision of Burmese life and character which, we are assured, is as correct as it is vivid. The author was engaged in business in Bassein, not very successfully, it is said; and he drew from the life.)[5]

Certainly the Burmese are a people of charm — the first we have seen since the Japanese, which they in many little details resemble. They are gentle and courteous in manner, pleasing in countenance, and beautifully dressed. Every Burman man or woman appears in brightly-coloured, clean, silk gowns, with jackets or shawls of another colour, and the men with their heads done up in a brightly-coloured silk handkerchief. These silks (though spun, dyed and woven in the villages on rude hand-looms) represent no little expenditure, the gown-piece along costing ten to fifteen rupees (13/4d to 20/-). Thus, a Burmese crowd is a feast of bright, clean colours.

But the families thus attired reside in the rudest of huts — dark, dirty and devoid of furniture and convenience of any kind, rudely made of bamboo and bamboo-thatch, mere single rooms on piles, often without other flooring than a series of bamboo spars an inch from each other — and they live on 'rice and pickles', which they cook on the ground outside and eat with their fingers. Marriage is a mere civil contract of cohabitation, terminable by the man practically at will, though the women enjoy equal rights and separate property and are in practice well-treated, with at least equal influence. Something like two per cent of the whole population are monks vowed to celibacy and poverty, who live exclusively on the popular offerings and pass their time in meditation or idleness. Every Burmese boy goes to the monastery to learn, with a minimum of actual tuition from the monks, to read and write and figure. Moreover, by ancient custom which is universally obeyed, every youth enters the monastery actually as a novice, at 14 or 15, and dons the yellow robe, if only for a few days; and apparently, four or five per cent of these youths remain there permanently, to sally out each morning in the yellow robe, carrying the begging-bowl in

which to receive the day's subsistence. It is an extraordinary eccle-
siasticism, universally respected and supported not interfering with the
people's lives, not itself immoral or apparently in any way corrupted;
and yet, without any considerable intellectual development or output.
Most of the monks, we were assured, could not understand the Pali
scriptures[6] that they repeated.

Apparently the Burman cares nothing for material wealth. He does
not drink or smoke opium (though every man, woman and child is
perpetually smoking the very cheap, locally-produced, huge cigars,
containing very little tobacco, many chips of sandalwood, the whole
enveloped in white leaves). He never builds himself a better house. He
desires no more furniture, and not even more clothes than are actually
in use. He will not work harder or more persistently to get more than
enough for current needs. When he gets a windfall, he usually builds a
pagoda, or a monastery, or a 'rest house', or a well for public use — by
which he 'acquires merit' and secures a better reincarnation — or else he
gives elaborate entertainments in the form of '*pwès*', or singing,
dancing and marionette shows for the neighbours' enjoyment.

What is to be done with such a people! What the few hundred
English officials have done (in Lower Burma during half a century of
rule, in Upper Burma during a quarter of a century) seems to be to have
ensured peace, reasonably good protection for life and property, and
opportunity for the commercial development promoted by the English
and Chinese. We could not make out that the efforts or the results in
the way of education or sanitation amounted to much (though
vaccination had become very generally accepted and smallpox was
less prevalent). Malarial fever and infantile mortality remained apparently undiminished, whilst plague had spread from India to a serious
extent, something like one per cent of all the people in Mandalay
succumbing to plague each year!

We saw a good deal of a leading Burmese lawyer at Rangoon —
Maung May Oung[7] — who (perhaps with a trace of Indian blood)
belonged to a leading Arracan family with Calcutta connections. This
boy was educated at Calcutta for twelve years, principally at the R.C.
St. Xavier's School, and then proceeded to Cambridge where he took
the Law Tripos. He spoke English perfectly in every respect, with an
unusually large and correct vocabulary. He had throughout remained a
pious and sincere Buddhist, and was now a leading member of the
Young Men's Buddhist Association (which has 4000 members), and the
newly-formed Burma Research Society (of mixed I.C.S. and educated
Burmese). He struck us as an able, gentle-natured, refined and sincerely
pious man, whose first-class and long-continued English education had
in no way spoilt him and had, moreover, been completely assimilated

by him. He had a substantial though not very remunerative law
practice and was not wealthy. He had been nominated by the
Government as a member of the 'Educational Syndicate' (to control
the efforts at higher education) and he was a promoter of and
contributor to various journals in English and Burmese, which he had
helped to start to express Burmese opinion.

He said there was absolutely no sedition or even desire to upset
British rule, and very little active concern among the Burmese about
public affairs. But there was a good deal of quiet resentment by the
educated Burmese at the tone and manners of the English officials and
traders towards them; at the failure to provide at all adequately for
secondary, technical and university education; at the expenditure of the
public revenues too exclusively in ways that commended themselves
to the English and too little according to Burmese opinion; and at the
sending of a large annual surplus to Calcutta. He did not suggest that
there ought to be more Burmese appointed to civil posts. The Burmese
had never taken part in the Indian National Congress and they had no
relations and no sympathy with the Bengalese reformers.[8]

It was he who told us of the Great Shoe Question. The Burman, of
whatever wealth or station, habitually goes barefoot, with sandals
when he chooses. By old Burmese custom the sandals are removed
when entering the house of a superior, who is saluted by sinking down
on the knees, bowing the head, and joining the palms of the hands in
an attitude of prayer. King Theebaw's officers were, of course, 'shiko'd'
to in this abject manner.[9] The English officials had accepted this salute
which the Burmese had naturally accorded them; and so long as the
Burmese went barefoot, shod with nothing but sandals, there was no
objection to according it. But in a city like Rangoon (with 300,000
inhabitants, and stone foot-pavements), many Burmese clerks and
others, whilst retaining Burmese dress, had found it convenient to
wear European shoes and socks. They had then resented the demands
of some English officials that they should remove these on entering
their presence; and, in fact, resented being treated differently from the
Eurasian or Hindu clerk who dressed in trousers and shoes and neither
sank down on his knees nor removed his foot-wear. The Government
had issued a circular recommending that whilst only sandals were used
the ancient local form of respectful salutation should be required, but
that when European shoes and socks were worn it should not be
insisted on. But some of the more arrogant officials had been inclined
to resent any wearing of shoes or any departure from the most abject
form of salutation. Maung May Oung himself removed all covering
from his feet to enter the precincts of any monastery or pagoda even
when it involved walking hundreds of yards across dirty ground – this

is universally expected from everyone except Europeans. But though otherwise in Burmese dress he wore socks and shoes, and of course sat on a chair and saluted in European fashion only.[10]

The Young Men's Buddhist Association had been started principally to resist the somewhat aggressive proselytising of the American Baptist Mission. Its 4000 members were in some scores of branches throughout the country, which were steadily increasing. They had reading rooms and the beginnings of libraries, principally in the Burmese language; and they published a monthly journal. It is probable that the Association might develop into one for maintaining Burmese habits and customs, and for expressing Burmese opinion generally.[11]

At Mandalay we had the opportunity of visiting one of King Theebaw's Ministers, who still received a pension of £144 a year; and one of the Princesses, who had married his brother or nephew and who had herself a pension of £72 a year. These lived in bamboo houses built on piles, with bare bamboo floors, without furniture, etc., dark and dirty like the rest — the whole six or eight houses of various members of the family dotted about a large, untidy 'compound'. These pensions, originally 35 in number, had now died down to half-a-dozen — a natural diminution which was resented as almost a breach of faith by the pensioners' families and all that class — though the Government did its best to provide places for the sons, if they learnt English, as subordinates in the Government offices.

It is interesting that the officer (among the half-dozen that we met) who seemed to us the most satisfactory was a mulatto from Trinidad who was acting as plague doctor at Mandalay. (This 'Captain Hodgkinson Lack, M.D., of the Indian Medical Service',[12] whom S.W. met by chance, spontaneously recognised him as having been a friend of Lack's uncle when a bar student in London some seven-and-twenty years ago. S.W. had corresponded a little after the friend had returned to Trinidad, where he promptly died of phthisis, but not before he had talked about S.W. in the family circle!) He was a handsome, tall, well-built man, of light chocolate colour, speaking perfect English, with a distinguished medical student career in Edinburgh and a great local reputation for proficiency in his profession. He had had some years' experience at various Indian stations and had then come as plague officer to Mandalay, where he had been three years and where he thought he had got the epidemic under [control] by diligent sanitation and rat destruction. Now he was under transfer orders to proceed to another Indian station.

He was full of interesting and thoughtful observations on the problem of dealing with subject races — suggesting, for instance, that what would do more good than anything else would be the introduction of the 'Boy Scout' movement, as affording discipline, training in organisation, and interest in something outside the family. He had welcomed the circular asking English ladies to get in touch socially with Hindu ladies; and he deplored the aloofness of the average English official. (We learnt from an ingenuous junior I.C.S. whom we met, that Lack was accepted as a member of the Club, but that it was felt that he kept himself too much aloof from the others and was apt to be 'touchy' in thinking himself insulted. A distinguished (Raja) Hindu — Cambridge wrangler, who had got into the I.C.S. — was thereupon rejected, when his superior officer (Commissioner) had intervened and practically insisted on his being admitted on the grounds that all members of the I.C.S. must be accepted as social equals.)

What was interesting and satisfactory about Lack was his professional zeal, his love of his work, his keen intellectual interest in the larger problems with which he was brought into contact, and his desire for real self-improvement. He believed in there being evolved a 'West Indian' race out of the mixed blood that prevailed; and he looked forward to a 'Federated West Indies' taking its place in the councils of the British Empire alongside the Dominion of Canada and the Commonwealths of Australia and South Africa. He said that his experience was that the first generation of a mixed marriage was apt to be 'unstable'; there was danger that they would turn out badly, as often happened though by no means invariably; but that the descendants of this first generation became quite good and normal people no more unstable than others. If the original crossing was one having ameliorating effects on the strain, the later half-caste descendants were greatly benefited by being half-caste and not purely of the inferior race.

We gather that in Burma there is a good deal of intermarriage between the Chinese men and Burmese women, and that the off-spring are apparently benefited by the crossing. The boys usually grow up as Chinese (if the marriage is a durable one); but the girls usually grow up as Burmese and marry as such. The offspring of transient connections, whether of European or Chinese fathers, are brought up by the mother as Burmese. There is little sexual (or other) intercourse between the Tamils and the Burmese.

An interesting feature is the 'segregated vote' in the municipalities of Rangoon, Mandalay and Moulmein. The Town Councils consist of half–a-dozen officials *ex-officio* (the Deputy-Commissioner presiding), and perhaps a dozen members elected by the ratepayers in racial constituencies formed under rules made by [the] Government. Thus, the Burmese at Mandalay elected six Burmese, the Europeans five

Europeans, and the Muslims, the Hindus and the Chinese one member each. With the Europeans were included all who called themselves Europeans and dressed as such! Thus, all the Eurasians and every kind of mixture of blood, if acting as Europeans, are admitted as such. In some cases, as at Mandalay and Rangoon, the most numerous race — the Burmese — was further divided for election purposes into geographical wards, each electing one member. Mandalay had also a 'precinct' organisation (not so called), being further divided into 43 districts, each of which had its own headman chosen by common consent, serving for life, and formally appointed by the Government. He serves as medium of communication in sanitary and other matters but receives no pay.

The most hopeful feature of the whole Burmese administration is perhaps the village co-operative credit organisation introduced a few years ago by the zeal of Mr. English[13] of the I.C.S., and now steadily spreading. This is cutting out the Madrassee '*Chetty*', the money-lender who charges at least 36 per cent interest. There is a central bank which obtains money on deposit (and has to allow 7 per cent interest to get it). This lends it to the village societies at 9 per cent; and the village society lends it to individual members at 15 per cent! How far the villagers themselves are mutually subscribing, as in the German banks, and so freeing themselves from this still heavy rate, we did not ascertain. Certainly at present we are inclined to believe in (a) an extended Homestead Law preventing the seizure of the holding for debt; (b) co-operative credit organisations and (c) state loans at bare cost price to associations in order to reduce the rate of interest to a minimum, as the best means of keeping up these systems of small peasant properties and holdings.

It may be worth recording that in this particular year 1911 a convenient mark of the Far East, as distinguished from the East, is the *ricksha*. This useful vehicle prevails from Yokohama to Penang but practically no further. (We hear that there is, so to speak, an outlier at Colombo; and, at Rangoon, there are just a handful. The leaders of the Chinese community at the latter place prohibited Chinese from drawing *rickshas* — not wishing to have grow up any class of Chinese coolies there — and this has prevented their general introduction.) We shall find none of them at Calcutta. [There are some also at Simla, Mount Abu and other hill stations.]

[BW→] We have to record a certain feeling of disappointment verging on positive depression during our week in Burma. The idealistic description of Fielding Hall[14] of the Burman as not only a graceful and charmingly-clothed person but also as the finest type of Eastern mystic, are not borne out by the saner observers of Burmese life, and are certainly contradicted by the 'sights' of Burma. Religion is certainly always there, patent to the eye – whether in the swarm of yellow-robed monks or in the innumerable pagodas and monasteries all testifying to the devotion of the lay population. And possibly the refinement of manner and expression which distinguishes the Burman is due to the universality of religious education. But the religion of the multitude is largely made up of animism, with its accompaniments of sorcery, soothsaying, and astrology – and even, as the annals of the late Court showed, with the darker practices of human sacrifice. The strange sect or caste of 'Brahmins', emigrants or captives from India, seem to constitute the evil genius of the Burman race. It is part of the old eclecticism of the popular faith that it is to these foreign ecclesiastics and not to the Buddhist monks that the Burmese resorts at birth and death, and for all the practices of soothsaying and astrology by which he regulates so many of the acts of his daily life.

The Burman in fact is intensely superstitious. He is consequently wholly unaffected by modern science. His religious faith supplies him not merely with a purpose in life but with a ready-made explanation of all the processes of life. And even the purpose of the faith which he professes is the egotistic one of 'acquiring merit' – of saving himself from future punishment and gaining for himself future reward. More-over, the acts by which he 'acquires merit' are for the most part mechanical acts and do not seem to affect in any marked way his motives or his relations to other human beings.

To the Western mind there seems something extraordinarily unsatisfactory in the indolence and apathy of the whole body of Buddhist monks, though these men seem far more spiritual and more really ascetic than the debased religious orders of China and Tibet. Added to this equivocal character of the religious life of the Burman, we are saddened by the amazing futility and shoddiness of so much of their art – futility of form and meanness of material. This impression is summed up in Mandalay, a city barely as old as an old man and yet already, in its costly palaces and monasteries, falling into ruin – the gold leaf on the golden buildings peeling off, the elaborate carvings blurred and blunted, and the rough glass mosaic in a rapid process of disintegration, the whole seeming to reflect on the spirit which inspired the architects and artificers responsible for these hopeless monuments of mortal effort.

Notes

1. Burma, now known as Myanmar, was an entirely traditional society cut off from the modern world prior to the nineteenth century. But friction along Burma's border with British India led to two wars in consequence of which the British had gained control of Lower Burma (Pegu, Arakan and Tenasserim) by the 1850s. The Third Anglo-Burmese War of 1885 resulted in the British adding Upper Burma (Burma proper, the Shan Tableland and the surrounding hills) to their jurisdiction. On 1 January 1886 Lower and Upper Burma were annexed as a Province of British India, to be governed by a Lieutenant-Governor and a Legislative Council of officials and nominated non-officials.

2. The coronation *durbar* of George V (1910–36) held at Delhi on 12 December 1911, at which the new King-Emperor, accompanied by Queen Mary, presided over the transfer of the Indian capital from Calcutta in Bengal to Delhi, a more central geographical location and India's ancient capital.

3. Charles Morgan Webb (1872–1963), later Vice-Chancellor, University of Rangoon.

4. The opening of the Suez Canal at the close of the 1860s, combined with the building shortly thereafter of railways linking Mandalay and the interior with Rangoon, had been major factors in the growth of Rangoon's prosperity. By the turn of the century Burma's rice acreage had grown to 4.1 million acres, most of it in the Irrawaddy delta and in the lower valleys of the Sittang and Salween rivers. Some 1.5 million acres of this total were added in the five-year period 1895–1900. The Burmah Oil Company, founded in 1886, and the Bombay Burma Corporation in timber extraction (like the leading rice-millers, both British owned) experienced similar dramatic growth in the period.

5. E. D. Cuming (b. 1862), *With the Jungle Folk, A Sketch of Burmese Village Life* (London, 1897).

6. The Hinayana Buddhism of Burma (akin to that of Thailand, Cambodia and Ceylon and unlike the northern Mahayana form common in Tibet, China and Japan) employed Pali as its sacred or canonical language rather than Burmese or any of the other native languages and dialects.

7. Or, U May Oung (1880–1926), who was to become before his early death a Judge of the High Court and Member of the Governor's Executive Council.

8. Cf. J. F. Cady, *A History of Modern Burma* (Ithaca, NY, 1958) p. 193: 'Generally speaking, the overt efforts of Indian political agitators within Burma to extend their revolutionary apparatus to that country were singularly unsuccessful, and almost entirely so up to 1920 . . . the nationalist movement in Burma was never a part of the Indian Congress Party conspiracy, and the occasional Burman attempts to accomplish a union of effort were invariably anemic and spiritless.' Cady alludes to the more extremist element in the Indian National Congress, led by Bal Gangadhar Tilak.

9. King Theebaw, Burma's last king, whose reign was weak and corrupt, ruled from 1876–85. Easily defeated by the British in the Third Anglo-Burmese War, Theebaw was transported to forced exile on the Bombay coast of India, where he died in 1916. The elaborate Court protocol of old Burma required those seeking an audience with the king to remove their shoes and to sit on

the floor, taking care to avoid projecting the soles of their feet toward the King. Burmans were also obliged to prostrate themselves face downward before the King. With Western penetration of Burma, foreign dignitaries were usually excused this requirement. But Theebaw refused to see a British envoy unless he took off his shoes on entering the palace.

10. There are really two points here. In the first place, as Sidney suggests, the British, though regarding as 'barbarous and humiliating' the practice of having to go shoeless in the presence of the Burmese King, had themselves hardly discouraged – had indeed insisted upon – the Burmese removing their shoes on entering the offices of a British official. Then there is the matter of Europeans wearing shoes on pagoda premises. There were protests about this in 1901 and again in 1912; finally, in 1916–18, a group of radicals in the Young Men's Buddhist Association (YMBA) spearheaded a protest that produced a Government directive allowing pagoda heads to decide the question for themselves. J. F. Cady, *A History of Modern Burma*, p. 190, writes of the significance of this that 'This "no footwear" controversy was as close as most Burmans had got by 1918 to developing a popularly-comprehensible political issue. The question, although intrinsically unimportant, could and did unite all branches of the Y.M.B.A. in a common cause . . . the issue became a symbol of anti-British political sentiment. It provided an occasion in which the Buddhist Burman could tell the British overlord that there was something that the latter could not do . . . It was on such a religious issue that Burmese nationalism first expressed itself.'

11. The Young Men's Buddhist Association, its name imitative of the Young Men's Christian Association (YMCA), was founded in 1906 by a group of educated Burmese intent on encouraging the revival of Burmese religious traditions and culture. In 1909 it was joined by the Burma Research Society, dedicated to the study of all aspects of Burma's cultural past. Though British officialdom suspected the founders of these organisations of having political motives, the leading lights of the YMBA and the BRS were emphatic that their aim was educational and social rather than political, a position which by 1919, when the YMBA was merged into the General Council of Burmese Associations (GCBA) was regarded with growing impatience by a more nationalistic younger generation of Burmese intent on political independence from Britain.

12. Captain Lewis Albert Hodgkinson Lack, MD (b. 1880), Indian Army, commissioned 1905.

13. Alexander Emanuel English (1871–1962), Deputy-Commissioner, Burma since 1905.

14. Harold Fielding Hall (1859–1917), author of books on Burmese themes and religion, whose best-known work was *The Soul of a People* (London, 1898), a deeply admiring tribute to the village Buddhism of Burma.

7
India (1)

We were met on our arrival in Calcutta by Mr [SW: Minet],[1] representative of Messr^s Longmans, Green & Co. (who brought with him a personal servant for us), and by the Hon. [SW: Bhupendra Nath Basu][2] — the chairman of the reception committee of the Indian National Congress which we had come to Calcutta to attend. For the next week we lived in the patriarchal establishment of this distinguished Hindu gentleman. For the whole time I was ill, and I am still in a somewhat miserable condition. But before I forget I should like to record the impressions of a Hindu household.

There were three separate houses joined together by covered passages — a large handsome guest house of the ordinary European style of these parts, a house for women and children (somewhat like a respectable tenement house with balcony outside and another balcony running round an interior court), and a smaller and shabbier edition for the servants. The family consisted for our host and his wife, two widowed sisters and some thirty or forty young people of two generations — sons and nephews and their wives and their children. The ladies were *'purdah'*[3] and lived in seclusion, and never left their establishments except on pilgrimages, or in the case of the married ladies to visit their own mothers.

To this establishment I was taken by our host on the afternoon of our arrival and I paid three or four other visits during our stay. There was one decently furnished room — the library and office of our host — bare of all furniture but a writing table, some bookcases, two ordinary office armchairs, and a couch prepared for sleeping. All the rest of the house was made of dark and dingy bedrooms — one or two with little ante-chambers — each provided with a four post bed or a couple of single beds and with little other furniture. There was a singular absence of any little belongings and the place might have been inhabited by quite poor persons. It perhaps resembled most a conventual establishment — but a convent would have had images and altars and books and pictures. The internal court, which was the only place in which the *purdah* ladies could take exercise, was a bare dull yard, with no scrap of vegetation, and with iron netting over the top of it to prevent birds from descending into it. The sounds of children's voices gave a touch of humanity; but I have rarely seen such depressing surroundings outside grinding poverty.

But there was no sign of depression among the ladies themselves. Our host's wife is a woman of singular charm, with the expression of the Mother Superior of a Catholic convent – gentle, peaceful but with a look of command and with a certain shrewd humour. Among the young wives was a lively young person, who spoke perfect English and, either as interpreter of her aunt-in-law, or on her own account, carried on a lively conversation with me. Her aunt approved of *'purdah'* – 'only by this institution could the woman's energy be reserved for her family' – they were too busy with the children to be dull, and had they not the companionship of their own and each other's husbands – besides the pilgrimages to Holy Places, when they were 'out of *purdah*'. I am not sure that my clever little friend was of quite the same opinion and she signified that if her husband were 'to command her' she would go to England with him and thereby break for good and all her caste. Still, she would not like any of her husband's younger brothers to marry a *'Brahmo'*[4] lady – they would not receive her into the family. They had many friends who came to see them who were *'Brahmo'*, but they would not like one of their own men to marry an outcast. They were not permitted to appear before their husband's eldest brother except completely veiled, and they might not address him, but they laughed and talked as much as they liked with all the other brothers-in-law and with their cousins and nephews. The hardest part of the system was the life of the widows – they were debarred from seeing anyone outside the family, they could not eat rice and they had to fast both from food and water for twenty-four hours on the 11th of each month. Also she disapproved of the child marriages – the eldest girl of her uncle had been married at seven, and sent to her husband at nine years old. Sometimes the poor children cried so much that they had to be sent back home. Now her cousins were being married at 13 or 14. She herself had married very late – 17 years old she was when she left the convent school where she learnt her English. (Our host told us that he had selected her because his nephew had been many years in England taking his medical degrees and that therefore he wanted a companion as a wife). The other ladies were speechless – one or two had not only the inevitable bangles but anklets and nose rings which gave their pretty faces an unpleasantly barbarous look. All these ladies were light-skinned Hindus with graceful figures clothed in white muslin with coloured borders and with bare feet. In spite of the curiously disorderly bareness and gloom of the rooms – the absence of any personal belongings showing character and taste — the *purdah* establishment had a charm of its own, the charm of love of parent, mate and child, and the capacity of subordinating all personal desires for the good of the family. The discipline seems absolute. The male head of the family — our host — was obeyed in his lightest word or wish by all the grown up men and women. The grave and handsome men who every now and again appeared in the guest house always opened up communication with us with ' "My uncle" ' or ' "My father" told me to take you here or there'. These men never ate with us, but if our host was absent or late for a meal they always accompanied us to the table and sat and talked with us. Directly he came they either sat silent or left the room. Apparently they and their wives never spoke to each other in the presence of one of the elders — of their father or uncle, of their mother or aunt, or even in that of the widowed sisters of our host. Indeed, these widows of the first generation are joint directress with the wife of the reigning male, and are even given precedence on account of their widowhood.

There were about thirty or forty servants — 15 women (all widows of low caste) and about as many men — two Brahmins as cooks. All the property is held in common and cannot be alienated except with the consent of all the elders — both men and women. Where exactly this joint ownership ends, and what is the degree of relationship that entitles a person to support, no one quite knows. Probably every Hindu is entitled to be supported by his nearest relation having the means to do it.

With our host we had long conversations. He is a serious-minded, moderate man — tall and large and somewhat heavy-featured. He is a Pleader in large practice and has been a lifelong reformer of moderate views. He professed enlightened opinions on *purdah*, the seclusion of widows, and child marriages. He had married his first little girl at an early age because his mother insisted on it and he could not disobey her. He had asked his wife to come to England with him, but she had begged to be excused, and he had not liked to insist on her breaking caste and violating her religious feelings. Any of his womankind were at liberty to give up *purdah* directly they desired to do so — he put no restrictions on their actions — they settled everything among themselves. The family system was too deeply rooted in Hindu thought and feeling to make it possible to break through it. And it was clear that our host really approved of it. As for the widows, their life was hard; but then they were treated with the utmost reverence in high caste families and those of the elder generation were always given precedence in authority even to the wife of the male head — while even the younger widows were consulted and deferred to when the young wives would be expected to obey without discussion. The absoluteness of the authority of the head of the family prevented quarrels or troubles among the younger folk.

My general impression of this household was one of great happiness and considerable dignity and personal charm. Both men and women were tall, good looking and intelligent with grave and graceful manners. The servants were far more efficient than the Eastern servants of European households, and the steward was a sort of friend of the family who seemed on terms of equality with the sons and the nephews.

[SW →] The Indian National Congress, which we had come to attend (in order to have the opportunity of making acquaintance with Hindus and Muslims from all parts of India), proved rather a 'frost'. There were only between four and five hundred delegates instead of twice or thrice that number; the great *'pandal'*, or temporary Congress hall — a vast tent constructed for 6000 spectators — was seldom more than half full, and there was an element of listlessness and unreality about the eloquent speeches. The decline of the Congress was admitted by its managers, and it was (by one or other of them) attributed to a variety of causes, some transient but others lasting, viz. (a) the competition of the Delhi Durbar, which many delegates had attended, and were unable to afford another trip; (b) a feeling that by securing partially-elective Legislative Councils[5] the Congress had both done all that it could practically accomplish, and rendered its own continuance as the only exponent of native Indian opinion largely unnecessary; (c) the loss of energy and 'driving power' consequent on the secession of the 'extremists' at the Surat Congress some four years ago, which had never been made up; and (d) the growth, especially among the younger men, of discontent at the oligarchical management of the Congress by a little knot of 'old gang' who (for fear lest things should be said that would discredit them as being 'extreme' or 'seditious') always kept everything 'cut and dried'.

Certainly the Congress differed vitally in this respect from a great English popular conference, such as those of the Co-operators or Trade Unionists. All the resolutions were chosen and formulated by the 'Subjects Committee' (meeting in private, and having really no time); all the speakers were chosen beforehand by that Committee, and their names printed and announced beforehand; there was no room for any amendment (I doubt whether one would have been allowed), nor any chance for a mere delegate to rise to speak. Under these circumstances, although fifty or sixty eloquent speeches by as many different Indians from all parts of the country, of all races, all three religions, all shades of brownness, and all possible varieties of dress and headdress had some interest in themselves, they did not amount to a 'congress' or conference of opinions. It was impossible to gather anything of the real feelings of the rank and file of the delegates, or of those of the [speaker] delegates, or of those of the thousand spectators. Nor was there any attempt to put more than one side of a question – practically no more than a single section of a side – or to debate difficulties or objections.

There was a curious uncertainty as to the hours of beginning, adjourning for lunch, and concluding; a curious vagueness as to the arrangements for lunch, etc.; and a curious lack of explicit instructions to the delegates as to details. But the actual organisation of the meeting and the crowd was well done; and the vast tent, or rather awning on countless pillars open at all the sides, was quite free from the 'stuffiness' of an English meeting.

Our impression is that unless something is done to revive and reorganise the Congress, it will 'peter out'. This would be a pity as it does represent the only approach to a national opinion in India, and the very fact of men from all parts, all races, all religions, all castes, and all professions meeting together is a useful thing. It is no reproach to the Congress that it is 'all talk' – that is what it is intended to be. Nor is it any reproach to say that these five hundred highly educated, widely cultured and usually travelled gentlemen – predominantly lawyers and editors, with a sprinkling of landlords and business capitalists and such lecturers and teachers and medical men as not forbidden as government servants to take part – are not 'representative' of the 250,000,000 of peasant cultivators, petty retailers, jobbing craftsmen, artisans and labourers of India.[6] They do not claim to 'resemble' them, any more than an elected legislature of rich men and *bourgeoisie* resembles the millions of wage-earning labourers in whose name it legislates. The Congress is a very useful means of exposition of the real and growing discontent of the educated class of Indians at being virtually excluded from deciding on the policy of the Government of their country. It is an absurd calumny, as regards the vast majority of them, to say that they individually want Government posts. They are, nearly all of them, too old for first appointment to any branch of the Civil Service; many of them are too wealthy or have too good occupations of their own to be tempted by official salaries. [BW→] At Basu's house and that of some other members of the Congress we met a good number of these cultivated Hindus – also we steamed up and down the River Ganges for five or six hours with hundreds of them. Our impression is one of good looks, good manners, a quiet intelligence – a race that is, at any rate superficially, more attractive to Europeans than any other orientals whom we have seen. They are in fact more like South Italians than they are like the Japanese or the Chinese. They are brought nearer to us by their training in English history and English literature – by the fact that they are to a large extent accepting the public school university Englishman as the model upon which to mould themselves. On the other hand, you can perceive in them almost a contempt for organisation and a dislike for administration – no real interest in the problems of government apart from the sentiment of national home rule. They are, I imagine, all individualists at heart, and think our craving after governmental efficiency wholly disproportionate to its value. Their family, their caste, and their religion: these are still the threefold centre of their life in spite of a perpetual striving to take their part in European sports and European political life.

Among the most interesting and attractive Hindus are the *Brahmo* [SW: *Samaj*] ladies – ladies who have chosen to abandon caste and break with *purdah*. These are sometimes the wives of wealthy Brahmins and other high castes; they are frequently cultivated and able and, nearly always, pretty and well-dressed. They have started a girls' high school, and an educational movement among the *purdah* ladies. And, curiously enough, they are not treated even by orthodox Hindus as outcast or in any way objectionable – they are merely accepted as *another caste*. Indeed, the breaking of caste usually makes a new caste, which soon passes from the first stage of opposition into an orthodoxy of its own. The *Brahmo Samaj*, however, seems more likely to become, like the Unitarians, a general liberalising influence, and to lose its separate existence. These *Brahmo* ladies were all ardent nationalists – more outspoken than their husbands.

One of the most distinguished of the Hindus we met was Professor J. C. Bose.[7] He had made some remarkable discoveries in the nervous system of plants and explained to us his experiments, with interesting lucidity. He had an eager, graceful mind (more like an Italian than any other nationality); he was a moderate nationalist with a settled feeling that sooner or later the Hindu must govern his own country. His wife was a bitter nationalist – did not believe that the English would ever relinquish their hold as a governing race until they were forced to by the growth of militant Hinduism. We thought we recognised among all these Hindus a certain pessimism with regard to the practicability of their ideals – the fear that we had driven a wedge between the Hindu and the Muslim that would divide the Indian world; and that, even within Hinduism, caste was too strong to make popular government possible. 'How can you have democracy,' sighed [SW: Gokhale],[8] 'with fifty millions of Untouchables?'[9]

The unification of Bengal was received with real enthusiasm, but our Bengali friends were for the most part downcast about the removal of the capital.[10] Some of the younger men professed to rejoice even at that, because so long as the Viceroy of India was at Calcutta real autonomy for Bengal was impossible. But the elder men shook their heads over the removal of the Government of India from all popular influences. The higher the official the more sympathetic; and the central Government was more sympathetic than the local Government. They fear not having access to the Viceroy and the heads of departments.

So far as we could judge from the look of the crowds at all the great shows of the King's visit, the Emperor King was really popular and the people appreciated his coming to India and his free and easy way of going about. A Bengali crowd is an attractive crowd – eager, gentle, responsive and brimming over with enjoyment of the outing. The enormous number of *'gharries'* [SW: the native carriage] holding women and children inside and boys and men outside, that crowded on to the Maidan,[11] gave one the feeling of a great national celebration. Of course the cultivated Hindu professed to be bored with the whole thing, or to deprecate the expense; but I think he was a little bit 'put out' by the obvious enthusiasm of the crowd.

Throughout our stay in Calcutta I was invalided with chronic catarrh, which is still clinging to me. We saw little or nothing of the Government of India – which naturally enough was absorbed in the royal visit. They have given us a bevy of formal introductions to officials on our route and have arranged for us 'to Camp out' with a Collector. But they have shown no sign of wishing to see us. And we were not sent an invitation to the Government House Garden Party! But even such invitations as we got from the Europeans I was unable to accept; except a lunch with Sir Harcourt Butler[12] (Member for Education in the Viceroy's Council) and Sir Richard Carlyle[13] (Member for Agriculture [SW: brother of Rev. A. J. Carlyle of Oxford],[14] Viceroy's Council) – both able, and broad-minded men. They professed to agree that more Hindus must be taken into the higher branches of the [Indian] Civil Service [and] that the Army must be opened to them; but they were not keen on it, and they objected to any particular way of doing it.

[SW →] We saw something of an attractive, wealthy Hindu family – that of the Bonnerjee, who own land in Bengal. Bonnerjee is the son of the chairman of the first [Indian] National Congress 26 years ago;[15] he was himself educated at Rugby and went to Balliol; he is married to a highly-cultivated Hindu lady who is a member of the *Brahmo Samaj*; and they live in a large house in Calcutta which (unlike that of Bhupendra Nath Basu) had all the charm and drawing room comfort of an English home, coupled with the openness and magnitude of the oriental home. Bonnerjee's position exemplified strikingly the practical exclusion of the Indians from public affairs. This wealthy young landlord, a man of local position and influence, cultivated and travelled, thoroughly equipped for public life and apparently anxious to be of use to the world, had not been made of any use by the Government of India. In England, he would have been a member of his County Council, an active J.P.,[16] possibly a Poor Law Guardian in his own parish, and probably also an M.P. In India, he had no sort of public function to work at. It does not seem even to have occurred to a Governor-General, or a Lieutenant-Governor, that one of his many Private Secretaries and A.D.C.'s[17] might well be an Indian gentleman of education and position such as Bonnerjee. Of course there are now district boards and municipal councils in India having elected members, and there are even elected members of Legislative Councils to which Bonnerjee might aspire. But the former are still extremely unimportant, uninfluential and indeed 'unreal' creations; and the latter (where the Indian members have no real power) have been so hedged about by qualification requirements as to make ineligible for election not only Bonnerjee, but also such leaders as Bhupendra Nath Basu (whom the Government thereupon nominated) and S. P. Sinha[18] (who has the distinction of being the first unofficial Indian to be nominated a Member of the Viceroy's Executive Council − [but] he resigned shortly afterwards, finding it interfered too much with his law practice, and was replaced by Ali Imam).[19]

BENARES 10th JANy 1912

We were glad to leave Calcutta after twelve days' stay, as the distractions and crowds consequent on the royal visit made things extremely uncomfortable and gave us few opportunities of talking with representative people. We accordingly left on the evening of the pageant (5 January) for Gaya, in order to see Buddhgaya, the scene of Sakya Muni's meditations under the bo-tree, and now a renowned centre of pilgrimage from the Buddhist world.[20] After a night in the train, we turned out on the platform in the cold grey dawn at six o'clock, intending to drive to the *dak* bungalow[21] (there being no hotel). But a young official whom we had met at dinner at Calcutta had telegraphed to the Collector (to whom we had no introduction) with the result that we found ourselves accosted by a quite unintelligible '*Chuprassy*'[22] or Government messenger, and found a smart carriage and pair waiting for whom there were no other possible occupants than ourselves. None of the servants could explain clearly who it was they were to carry off but at last we decided to risk it. We were whirled away to the Collector's house, received by obviously expectant servants, invited to bedroom and bath and urged to begin breakfast – all without being quite sure who was our host or whether we were really his guests. He presently emerged from bed and made himself extremely hospitable – a man (Whitty)[23] of about 36 with 12 years' service whose wife was in England. He sent us to Buddhgaya (8 miles) in state, in his carriage with a large *tiffin* basket; brought the local Civil Surgeon (Conor) to meet us at dinner, and sent us to the station next morning in time to pick up the train at six o'clock for Benares.

Buddhgaya was not particularly interesting in itself, and cannot be recommended for architectural beauty. But this lofty pyramidal shrine, enclosing various images of Buddha and protecting the original bo-tree under which he sat (or rather, a tree descending by continuous 'shoots' and reproductions from that original of 2500 years ago), had a real historical attraction.[24] The remnants of the stone railing erected by Ashoka 1600 years ago are certainly authentic.[25] We saw pilgrims from Bhutan and Burma worshipping; and we made an attempt to see the *mahant* or abbot of the (Hindu) monastery in whose charge the shrine is. But all the monks were absent (the abbot at Calcutta!), and all we saw of interest were two elephants in the monastery compound and a Shan[26] Raja (Burma) who was a pilgrim distributing farthings in alms to each member of a vast crowd. On our way back we drove to the native town of Gaya (70,000 population) and walked through its narrow streets to the 'Vishnupad' temple (Hindu), with the usual hideous images and grossly superstitious observances by the crowds of Hindu pilgrims, on whom the Brahmans were levying toll.

In the afternoon we found a young official (Paterson),[27] who was 'Assistant Magistrate' temporarily living with the Collector and *who was in the first month of his service*, and was accordingly trying his "prentice hand' at the administration of justice, imposing fines up to 50 rupees and imprisonment up to a month. We were interested to see the I.C.S. thus in the making – the bright young Oxford youth with the public school manner, just beginning to develop into the bureaucrat. It is certainly a remarkable thing, this annual export of sixty or seventy young men to be posted to all parts of India, nearly all of identical school and university training, all cast in the same mould as to dress, manners, language and habits, and (to a great extent) also opinions and prejudices. India itself may be as diverse as Europe; but its administration and its governing bureaucracy can hardly fail to be, from Cape Comorin to the Himalayas, 'all of a piece', with infinitely greater similarity or uniformity than exists in England alone.

We spent five days in Benares, having tea with the Commissioner (Molony),[28] and dining with the Collector (Streatfield),[29] the latter turning out to be a brother of the supporter of [the] National

Committee who has just married Miss Lucy Deane.[30] But our chief
interests in Benares were unofficial. We had an introduction to a
wealthy old Hindu gentleman (Raja Madho Lal),[31] who had been given
the title of 'Raja' and made C.S.I. because of his wealth, loyalty, public
spirit and past service on the Legislative Council. He sent his grandson
and carriage to meet us, and called at our hotel, but by accident we
failed to see him that day, and then he had to go to Lucknow. So he
sent in his stead his son-in-law (Baldeo Das Vyas),[32] himself a landlord,
who on two separate days devoted himself to showing us how the
Hindus live. We first went over (a) his house in the midst of the city,
where his wife had just been confined, and then (b) the Raja's country
mansion some four miles off, on the Grand Trunk Road. These houses
had the same sort of combination of spaciousness and narrow dark
rooms of splendour and squalor, of elaborate native ornamentation and
the most childishly bad English oleographs and pictures cut from the
illustrated papers, that we noticed at Basu's in Calcutta.

Another day, he took us to see one of his own villages, where he
went to settle some estate business. After an eight-mile drive we
descended from his carriage, and were conducted by devious field
paths for half a mile to the little two-storied house built for his
accommodation on such visits. We were shown the working of the
well, and the primitive crushing of the sugar cane; we walked round
the garden which he kept up, and noted the mango and guava trees,
the pepper plants, and a tuber resembling a sweet potato (which
subsequently proved to be very good fried).[33] But much more
interesting was the group of peasants which collected to interview
their landlord. There was no common grievance, but sundry individual
applications and controversies which the landlord listened to, asked
questions about, discussed with his resident agent, and with all
kindliness and friendliness, peremptorily decided. One aged man, of
at least eighty (he said) who had been a tenant on an eleven-year
lease, begged to be reinstated. It appears that no application for
renewal of tenancy was made because his brother (a junior of some
sixty-five years) thought it clever not to apply, believing that the
landlord would be driven to ask the tenant to remain at a lower rent.
But after a long waiting another applicant had applied, offering five
per cent *more rent*, and had accordingly been promised the tenancy.
Now the aged man wanted this undone. The landlord (who said he
liked the aged man, who was an old tenant) eventually said he would
try to get the new applicant to take another piece of land, and then
reinstate the aged man. In another case a tenant had taken into
cultivation a piece of waste land and wanted his rent for that piece
settled. This was decided, after some discussion, to be three rupees per

acre per year. The third case was the most interesting. It concerned the desire of one tenant to extend his mud house in order to take in a nephew whom another uncle had turned out. The proposed extension would, however, bring the new household into closer contiguity with the open space surrounding a neighbouring mud hovel tenanted by another cultivator. Now, this latter was of the Brahmin caste whilst the former belonged to a lower caste, described as that of the 'Ascetics' (*Gosain*?).[34] Hence the Brahmin, a tall, spare handsome man, vehemently objected, pleading most vivaciously that the ladies of the two households would quarrel, that they would interfere with each other's cooking, and so on. So we all went to view the premises, in the village a quarter of a mile off. There seemed to us to be plenty of room round the mud hovels; and the 'Ascetics', who did not look quite so ascetic as the Brahmin, pleaded equally vehemently that any other way of extending their mud hovel would be inconvenient, owing to trees, access, etc. Eventually the landlord said he would reserve judgement and we came away amid the respectful and quite friendly salutations of the crowd of some thirty men — the women and children peeping timidly round the corners and taking to flight when Beatrice walked towards them.

After tea, biscuits and fruit, with fried potatoes as specimens, we walked back to the carriages escorted by men with sticks from another village belonging, it was said, to a caste of warriors who had come merely to greet their landlord. Baldeo Das Vyas, with whom we had thus long conversations, is a gentlemanly young man of about thirty-five, educated at the Queen's College, Benares, travelled all over India but not beyond; a loyal subject of the King and unhesitatingly preferring British rule to any native administration, but also patriotic in his Hinduism and complaining that the Government was not favourable enough to persons of proved loyalty among the Hindus, and that it was unduly partial to Muslims. He had applied for a commission in the Army, but had been refused (no natives of India are eligible) — he felt deeply this exclusion, and also the universal prohibition to any Indian to possess arms and their exclusion from all the higher posts. He complained also of the lack of facilities for the education of the cultivators — some hundreds of schools had actually been closed by [the] Government for lack of funds. [BW→] He disliked the native Christians and the Government patronage of them. They were mostly of low caste — some 'Untouchables' — and yet they would be given posts in the railways or the post office! He did not like the Bengalis and rather sneered at them and at the 'talk' of the [Indian] National Congress, which he said did harm to silly boy-students who had cast off respect for their parents and who hated the British

Government as part of [an] old established authority inconsistent with liberal ideas.

The vision of village life yielded us today brings into relief the dominance of caste as a disintegrating force, even of the village community. The little group of mud huts which constitutes a 'village', and which we visited with our landlord to settle the disputes described above, was divided sharply into the Brahmins and the Ascetics; and it was clear that if the dispute was not settled, there would be a village fight and a police court case. Another village was made up to the fighting caste;[35] and others of that caste were assembled together in the yard of our landlord and came with us to the said village evidently to talk over matters with members of their caste. Between these different castes there was no community of action; there was even hostility which had to be perpetually smoothed down by the landlord. Our friend himself, when discussing a proposed journey to Europe, mentioned incidentally that he would bring the matter before his community, promise to remain strictly vegetarian and not touch alcohol, and get their permission before he dared leave the country.

Another impression of village life was that of the grinding poverty of the people. There is no amenity and no comfort in the little groups of mud huts used indiscriminately for man and beast − all the appliances are of the most primitive and inefficient type; and there seems to be an indefinite number of human beings only half-occupied, and all in a state of semi-starvation; a vicious [SW: circle − a] low standard of nutrition and a low standard of effort. The Brahmins and other high castes are distinguished by the fact that they bathe daily in the village pool and that they do [SW: 'puja'][36] (i.e., religious observances) either at the village shrine, or in the case of the better off, at the family shrines in their own habitations. They are all particular about their food and the cooking of it. The lower castes have no daily observances, though probably they go on pilgrimages when they can afford it? From the western standpoint, the village community, as we saw it yesterday, is [SW: a] most depressing aspect of humanity − listlessness and discord being its two outstanding features − a listlessness curbed only by fear of starvation, and a discord checked only by the village 'chaukidar'.[37]

It would be a waste of words to describe the beauty of the Benares Ghats and the extraordinary picturesqueness of the narrow irregular streets, with their half-hidden temples and shrines, their palaces, and their indefinitely varied life of booth and marketplace.[38] Compare Benares with Canton, and Benares shines out as intensely human and in a sense spiritual − fascinatingly and weirdly spiritual, as against the hideous insect-like uniformity of the narrow streets of the Chinese town. The Hindus are a lovable race, with their indifference to this world and their emotional and lively care for the next. But their religion is, in itself, a perturbing and even a horrible sight to the western observer − the hysteria of the worshippers of evil gods demanding the sacrifice of life, the anarchic choice of gods to propitiate, the absence of any conception of right and wrong, either in the conduct of the god or that of his devotee − the strange combination of meditation, indolence and fraud in the ascetic, and the mercenary dealings of the professional priest. Above all, the intensely egoistic purpose of all religious rites − the 'acquiring of merit' and consequent advancement to a more enjoyable existence − and hence, the complete unconcern for the common good. The cultivated Christian missionary − a Rugby and Oxford man [SW: Rev. Frank Lenwood] − who took us over the Ghats, said that 'Christianity was the only hope for India'. (!) But those who have watched the effect of Christianity in its converts say that it loosens the obligations of family and caste without substituting the obligations towards the Kingdom of the Christlike God, or towards a Commonwealth of Fellow Human Beings.

We visited the Hindu Central College, affiliated to Allahabad University; and had an hour's talk with Mrs. Besant.[39] She is the centre of the 'New Hinduism', i.e., the attempt to appeal to the religious patriotism of the Hindu in favour of combining a maintenance of Hindu tradition and mysticism, with the power of conduct and a power of knowledge of Western civilisation. Owing to her personal magnetism she has established a successful educational institution with 1000 students (500 boys and 500 undergraduates), which has attracted the praise and the money of Maharajas and Rajas, and latterly, the approval of the British Government. She has 50 professors, only three or four European (I think all women for the younger boys), all the others Hindu men. Many of these Hindu professors work for love − out of enthusiasm for the New Hinduism − and it is clear that there is an intimate relationship between the professor and the pupil, which is lacking in Government institutions. Added to this peculiar atmosphere of Hindu patriotism and educational enthusiasm Mrs. Besant has, owing to the support of wealthy Indians, been able to give a good education at half the fees of Queen's College − the local Government institution.[40]

This university college, also affiliated to Allahabad, is presided over by Mr. Venis,[41] a well-known Sanskrit scholar, who took us over Sarnath,[42] and was delightfully lucid in his explanations of these wonderful relics of Buddhism. But he showed no inclination to show us over his College and quite clearly did not care for his job. He was of the same intellectual type as Sir Charles Eliot of Sheffield University[43] – an iconoclastic secularist who combined a great technical knowledge of Sanskrit literature with the most thoroughgoing contempt of Hindu philosophy, or as he would call it, Hindu mythology. He poured out bitter ridicule on the proposed Hindu University – how could you have a university without men of learning and how could you have a man of learning who believed in any of the childish barbarisms of the Hindu or Buddhist scriptures? How could *he* work with a colleague who tried to discover the doctrine of evolution in the Vedas![44] (I should have thought the difficulty would have come in if his Hindu colleague had tried to *disprove* evolution by quoting passages from the Vedas.) No exposition of the sacred books of the Indians was worthy of a university, or was to be *tolerated* in a university which did not proceed on to assumptions of modern physical science and modern historical criticism. He refused to express his opinion of the Central Hindu College, which would I think have been beyond polite words. With high fees and an unsympathetic Principal, the Queen's College is rapidly declining.

We saw something of C. S. Streatfield, the Collector. He is a talkative, prejudiced, middle-aged Englishman eager to go home directly his time is up. He has no standards of administration and is a passive resister to any liberal inspiration from the Government of India. He showed us a 'municipal free school' – a dark little mud shanty supposed to accommodate eighty-five pupils, with an illiterate Brahmin as teacher and no timetable or fixed time for coming or going: he showed it to us with no sense of the absurd inadequacy of this 'popular instruction'. He glowed with pride over the magnificent new police quarters, and was quite complacent over the neglected and squalid gaol. He talked, talked, talked. Doubtless he is honest and impartial in character and gets through the routine of his duty without failure. But he represents the low-water mark of administrative aim, if not of administrative execution. 'Damn the educated native and the Liberal Government', would, I think, represent his state of mind.

[SW→] Over every three or four Collectors there is a Commissioner, who naturally lives in the largest town (and therefore, in the same town as one of the Collectors). On asking whether this was not an extravagant duplication of the exiguous European staff, we were told by the Commissioner (Molony) that the work was quite distinct. But except that the Commissioner hears legal appeals from the Collectors – which perhaps ought to be done by a Judge – we still enquire whether the Commissioner might not also be the Collector for the district in which he resides, having a quite junior man under him. It is a question of principle of administrative organisation whether it is possible to get the best out of a District Officer if his immediate superior lives in the same district. In the Madras Presidency, there is no such grade as Commissioner.

ALLAHABAD 11–16th JAN^y 1912

In this great 'station' (the Club has 250 members), we have been fortunate enough to see a '*Magh Mela*', a great Hindu religious gathering or fair. The junction of the Yamuna with the Ganges is a specially sacred place for ceremonial bathing, and once at year at this season there is a great gathering of pilgrims; once every twelve or fourteen years, a huge concourse (the *Kumbh*); and once every six or seven years, an intermediate-sized crowd, the *Ardh Kumbh*.[45] This year it is the latter, and it is computed that a million people will attend in the course of the six weeks. We were lucky enough to see the sight on one of the greatest days, when eight separate processions of '*sadhus*', or men who have devoted themselves to the religious life, made their way to the spit of sand where the two streams meet.

This point is some miles from the city, and is not approachable by carriage, so we were fortunate in getting from the Collector (at the Club the night before) an order addressed to any officer entitling us to annex any Government boat. We started at 8 a.m., got to the riverside at 9, found a boat there (a paddle-boat worked by six men), and were taken thus down the Yamuna to the junction with the Ganges. There, on the sandy riverbed left uncovered, was a gaily-dressed crowd of many tens of thousands, amid hundreds of tall flags, each denoting the little wooden stage of the '*Pragwal*', or Brahmin having the prescriptive right to the attendance on the pilgrims of a particular district. There were to be eight separate processions – of which we saw three – an almost indescribable sight. Each procession included one or more native bands; half-a-dozen acrobatic performers who danced about to music with swords and sticks and sometimes did tumbling tricks; gorgeous silk banners borne aloft by men naked and clothed; camels with drums; capering horses; gaily-dressed abbots and monks in litters; idols carried in palanquins; and from 50 to 200 '*sadhus*'. These latter were mostly stark naked, smeared with ashes and often bedizened with yellow ochre. Others were clothed in various degrees, from the loincloth up to flowing robes. Some of the naked men sat on gaily-caparisoned horses. Others walked hand in hand by twos, or in irregular groups. Some played weird sorts of 'serpent' instruments but most of them chanted some invocation to the Ganges and the God Ram. With them were scores of (fully dressed) little boys who we were told were their pupils and apprentices, and some dozens of (clothed) female anchorites or nuns.

These 'sadhus' were sometimes grossly fat but usually emaciated; some were aged and some quite young men, but the bulk were in the prime of life. A few looked really pious and contemplative; but for the most part, their countenances gave them no good character for spirituality. After each procession had passed the crowd prostrated itself in the dust on which the 'holy men' had trod or took it up and put it on their foreheads. In front of the procession usually rode a young English officer in khaki followed by two Hindu mounted policemen; the procession was escorted by foot police and the road was kept clear and elaborate precautions were taken by the police to prevent the several processions jostling each other or being hindered by the crowd. All day long there rode up and down these young English Assistant Superintendents of Police in khaki, with the Collector and the doctor specially charged with the sanitation of the fair. Five hundred police were on the ground, all carefully picked out as being Hindus; and inside the fort, squadrons of cavalry and companies of infantry stood ready but concealed to come out the moment they were signalled for from the lookout platforms erected near the tent of the officer in charge. Inside that tent, his wife dispensed a scratch 'breakfast' to English friends, including ourselves, and discussed the incidents of the day.

It is impossible to convey any idea of the sights and scenes and sounds of the huge crowd of families among which we walked. The elaborate 'houseboats' from which the 'purdah' ladies bathed without entering the crowd or exposing themselves to the vulgar view. We saw in one case (that of the household of the Maharaja of Bettiah) the ladies descend from a carriage into a sort of movable square tent held up from the outside by retainers, and this moving tent enveloped them as they descended the sloping path down to the river and as they entered the 'houseboat' which was to take them to the bathing place. The ceremonial shaving of the head of men and women squatting on the ground without cover or screen, the barber receiving a fee high or low according as the operation was performed exactly at the confluence of the two rivers, or merely on the banks of the Yamuna. The hundreds of 'Pragwals', sordid and mercenary-looking Brahmins receiving rice and money from the pilgrims and reading aloud the sacred books or 'blessing' in this way or that. The voluminous books of family records carried by the servants of these 'Pragwals' in which the names of their particular pilgrims are recorded together with various items of family 'happenings' told on this occasion for recording in these books. The cows and calves tethered here and there among the crowd, partly because holding the tail of one of these sacred animals with due brahminical incantations has the same advantageous effects on a lately-deceased relative as if he himself held the tail and thereby got carried safely across the Styx, partly because the gift of a cow to a Brahmin is the most 'merit-acquiring' of gifts – and if you cannot afford a cow you can at least buy a cow for four annas off the Brahmin and then present him with the animal thus purchased, and so for fourpence acquire the merit of presenting the whole cow. The images of gods set up on the sands for reverence and to induce the gift of a handful of rice or a copper coin to the Brahmin keeping the idol. Or sometimes it would be a little boy dressed up to represent the god. The beggars everywhere asking alms. The family groups of pilgrims before bathing and after squatting down to eat or to restore their toilets. The individual *fakir* or *sadhu* carefully performing his toilet with grey ashes, with a little mirror which he repeatedly consulted so as to get the 'make-up' as artistic as possible.

[BW→] We have seen three leading Muslims [SW: Syed Ali Imam], the [SW: Legal] Member of the Viceroy's [SW: Executive] Council [SW: at Calcutta; Karamat Husain],[46] Judge [SW: of High Court] at Allahabad, and an able young lawyer [SW: Ibn-in Ahmed], who is local secretary of the All-India Muslim League.[47] The first two named personages were of the heavy, dull type. [SW: Ali Imam] professed himself in sympathy with the aims of the [Indian] National Congress – they wanted more Indians in the administration – but he objected to simultaneous examinations. He wanted a certain number of places reserved for Indians (Hindus and Muslims getting them in proper proportion) and these boys [SW: being then] sent over to England to be educated specially for the competition, either [as the] sons of wealthy men or on provincial scholarships. The elderly Judge at Allahabad was wholly mute but [SW: asked us to dinner at his house and] he arranged for us to see the young and energetic secretary of the All [SW:-India] Moslem League with whom we have spent the better part of two mornings.

He is a rather [SW: bitter] opponent of the Hindu – does not want any relaxation of British rule as this would inevitably mean if peace were maintained that the Hindus would govern the country and oppress the Muslims. He professes to think that if Great Britain withdrew her troops the Muslims would re-establish their empire over the Hindus. He did not care to associate with Hindus and their caste rules prevented any friendly intercourse. He wanted equal representation on all local bodies, even where the Muslims were in the minority – and if this was not accorded he wanted the British Government to be the arbitrator in all matters of dispute. He admitted that among the lower orders there was a good deal of amalgamation –

in the villages, the Muslims and Hindus would worship at the same temple. But in the higher ranks of society, there was no sympathy and no possibility of joint action.

He took us to see 3 or 4 Muslim schools. One, for the [SW: early] training of *maulvis*,[48] was rather a pitiable affair — some fifty little boys learning the Koran (in Arabic) by heart under the rule of some aged *maulvis* — honest and pious men no doubt but obviously of the most narrow-minded and feeble type. [SW: only or two would become *maulvis*; the others drifting into teaching!] The other schools showed a little pretence at teaching arithmetic and [SW: Urdu] reading and writing, but the education given to little boys who came and went when they or their parents chose, was obviously that of an uncivilised race. None of these Muslim schools received Government money. [SW: Some elder pupils were learning elementary Persian and Arabic.] All that could be said for them was that they were extraordinarily picturesque, these gatherings of gaily-dressed youngsters swaying their bodies to and fro, droning out the sacred words in the open verandah of the mosques with the grave old *maulvis* wandering up and down amongst them. But these young citizens of the Oriental empire were not learning anything that could be useful to them as independent members of a self-governing state. [SW→] Every mosque has its school at which children attend free and are taught by the *maulvis* as above. The question arises (as these thousands of mosque schools cannot be suppressed and will in the aggregate be attended by thousands of children) whether [the] Government might not make them a little more efficient by some simple form of aid. We suggested to our young lawyer (1) the free grant of suitable school books, maps, etc. (2) the free service for one or two hours a week or more of a trained visiting teacher, a Muslim whom the Government might appoint and pay to go round from school to school teaching English, arithmetic, geography, etc.

We had also been taken by a young Hindu lawyer to see Hindu schools. In the queer picturesque houses in the narrow lanes in the recesses of the native city we found four schools set going by committees of leading Hindus, getting fees and subscriptions and some minute Government grant and teaching several hundred boys and girls Hindi reading and writing and some arithmetic. The first (lower primary) consisted of some 40 little boys with half a dozen elders taught by a wild-looking Brahmin with dishevelled hair, not speaking a word of English or possessing any examination qualification. The girls' school was far better and in fact had elements of real efficiency. About a hundred girls from 5 to 14 were being taught by half-a-dozen women (all married but one, and that one a widow). The headmistress had been through a normal school; there were maps, physiological diagrams of the internal organs of a man, a globe, a sewing-machine, a shifting frame like a giant abacus for teaching the letters and numerals, etc., and some showy needlework was exhibited. Two other boys' schools were under a single committee, the lower and the upper standards being for convenience in different buildings. The headmaster was a graduate of Muir College, and his half-a-dozen assistants had all passed lower examinations. He himself spoke English well and seemed a capable man. This school was an 'Anglo-Vernacular Middle School', and sent pupils to the Government high school, some of whom went on to Muir College.

This Muir College we also saw, the principal Government university college (with Queen's College, Benares and Canning College, Lucknow) in the Allahabad University. It has 450 students, excellent buildings[49] and scientific laboratory equipment but a very poor library. There are four hostels − Hindu, Muslim and Christian, and one Government. The Principal (Jennings) had risen through the Indian Educational Service − Sub-Inspector, Inspector, Professor, Principal − and was a competent official but not an inspiring personality.[50] He said that what they had done hitherto was to 'turn out graduates': he hoped they might now do a little for learning! This College, nearly fifty years old, struck us as 'wooden' but efficient in a rather poor way. The professors were partly English − chosen in England by the India Office and appointed as professors at large − and partly Indian, paid at a lower rate, with good qualifications, sometimes from English universities. The students paid about 10 rupees a month (£5 to £6 a year) for tuition, and about 2½ rupees a month in the hostels for board and lodging (30/- a year!); or about £7 for the school year altogether.

We had some talk with the Director of Education for this province (de la Fosse),[51] an able and open-minded official under forty who was alive to all the shortcomings, but said he had been unable to get the Government to improve things partly from lack of funds, and partly because the Education Service was put in a second place, its head having no direct access to the Lieu[t.]-Governor but being subordinate to the Chief Secretary. All depended on whether the Chief Secretary was or was not favourable to education (and of course, in the end, the Lie[ut.]-Governor). The Public Works Department, and indeed all other departments, had direct access to the Lieu[t.]-Governor, but the Education Department not. But ultimately all turned on the amount of money that the Government chose to make available. The municipalities and district boards were naturally loath to levy local rates and the small funds allocated to them by Government were largely spent on roads, etc. by the influence of Collectors unappreciative of schools.

They were bound to spend five per cent of their income on schools but one big city had got it reduced to three and a half per cent. Altogether, de la Fosse impressed us as more keen about his job and more definitely thinking about how to overcome obstacles than any of the civilians we have so far met. He had a great admiration for Orange,[52] who had been head educational official for India and who retired, he said, largely because he could not get the Government to give more attention to his proposals.

At Lucknow, we were taken to see two Muslim schools, one a large mosque school of a hundred or so boys and young men picturesquely squatting on the floor in half-a-dozen circles in a series of open rooms next to the mosque in the great *Imambarah*,[53] taught – by half-a-dozen *maulvis* who understood no English and had apparently no academic qualifications – Persian, Arabic, and the Koran and lcgic (by a *maulvi* renowned for learning). (This latter seemed to be simple, the difference between genus and species, etc.) This school got no Government aid and charged no fees. Here, however, it seemed that some real education was going on. The second school had higher pretensions (Nadvatullama);[54] it had been established by the leaders of the faith as a boarding school for all India in which English teaching should be added to the usual religious and linguistic Muslim curriculum. It was in temporary buildings, but we were taken to see the large new building under erection on an extensive site (central hall and 32 rooms). This school had a hundred or so boys and young men present from 10 to 25, with half-a-dozen very able and thoughtful-looking *maulvis*, some of whom had small academic qualifications (the English teacher was a studious-looking Muslim who was a B.A. of Allahabad University). Here we saw real teaching going on (to judge from the faces and gestures and tones of the teachers) in Islamic law, philosophy, logic, literature, mathematics and English. To teach philosophy in Arabic they had got a man from Arabia. (Persian the boys knew when they entered, it was stated.) This school attracted boys from all over India and was said to be unique. It got about £400 a year Government grant, and the Lieu[t]-Governor had laid the foundation stone of the new buildings.

We lunched with the Principal (Rees) and [the] English assistant of the Colvin Talukdars' School (Lucknow)[55] – with them Professor A. W. Ward (Science, Canning College), brother of Prof. James Ward of Cambridge.[56] The Talukdars' School is established and run nominally by the *talukdars* or 'barons' of Oudh, great landowners of from £500 to £5000 a year income, part Hindus, part Muslims, for the education of their own sons and no one else. Really, we gather, it is a Government nursling, the Comm[r] being chairman of the committee. These boys –

there were only 40 or 30, between 10 and 25, half Hindus, half Muslims − are treated as plutocrats; each bringing his own three or four servants, and having his own set of rooms, his own kitchen, stables and his own horses, and providing and having cooked his own food to be eaten alone in his own apartments. (They are forbidden to visit each others' rooms). The school of only 40-odd had to be divided into ten classes of different ages, etc. which were taught by as many Indian teachers. (Such small classes were said to have the drawback of providing no stimulus and evoking no emulation.) The English Principal and his assistant seemed entirely occupied with administration and games (to which great attention is given). English is the medium of instruction and apparently the only language taught. It seemed an attempt to create an English boarding school for wealthy boys without infringing their caste or religious customs. But the atmosphere was necessarily disintegrating to Hindu and Muslim religion; and it is not altogether to be wondered at that *talukdars* (and especially their pious womenkind) are not very eager to send their sons. We were told of one lady who broke her *purdah* to come and kneel before the (late) Principal, begging him to 'let her son go'.

It is to be noted that though the idea is to give an English education and the 'public school training', the boys' rooms were lacking in all amenity and charm and were even squalid. Nothing in the way of personal habits seemed to be taught. The boys ate with their fingers in native style and were not taught to use knife and fork or to sit at table, so that they might associate with [the] English later on. No doubt the idea has been to avoid scrupulously anything that would be hostile to caste or custom. The boys paid some £20 a year each for tuition and lodging alone, all food and service being provided by themselves in addition.

This vision of educational organisation in the United Provinces (which we shall supplement by seeing village schools and also Aligarh College), joined with a perusal of the educational reports and statistics both for the U.P. [and] for India, gives rise to disquieting reflections. We have been at it for half a century (Muir College itself was founded in 1857); and only a tiny proportion of boys and a handful of girls are even now getting any decent education in the primary grades, let alone anything in the higher. The Government efforts seem to have been (and still to be) quite absurdly 'amateur' and spasmodic in their character. There has been no deliberately thought-out policy and no intelligently-devised adjustment of means to ends. This has been aggravated (as it is also explained) − [and] as we infer and believe − by a curious half-hearted indecision of the Civil Service as to whether they want to educate the Indians or not, and how they want to educate

them. An indistinctive dislike to the education of the Indian reveals
itself in the frequent oscillations of policy which successive administrations inspire or impose, in the alternation of preference between
English and vernacular teaching, and between the higher education of
the few and the elementary education of the masses.

It is less easy to suggest the remedy. If a strong Viceroy would
definitely mark out a definite policy, clearing up all ambiguity and
explaining what was negatived as well as what was approved, and insist
on substantial action being immediately taken to begin to put it in
force, a great deal would be done. Lord Curzon however tried this, with
only moderate success. The Education Department ought clearly to be
put on as high a position as any other department, with equal facilities
for explaining its own needs and developing its own policy. The whole
method of organisation and recruitment of the educational service
seems calculated to ensure and perpetuate its subordination to the older
departments of administration. It would almost seem desirable to make
it from the start an integral part of the 'covenanted' service, recruited at
the same time and by the same examination without distinction of pay
or title – in fact, simply assigning some of the successful men to
educational work (Sub-Inspector, Inspector, Director of Public Instruction, etc.) instead of making them Assistant Magistrates, Settlement
Officers or Collectors; and letting them specialise from the outset in
educational administration just as some others do (though at a later
stage) in judicial work. The same principle might be followed in other
(at present) subordinate services, whose technique is really not any
more 'expert' or difficult than that of the mere administrator. It is clearly
impossible to get as good men for education as for civil administration
unless they are given the same pay and prospects.

Coming to details, there ought to be (a) a much more determined
effort to train teachers, female as well as male, Muslim as well as
Hindu, supplying in the main secondary schooling with only a
comparatively small veneer of pedagogy; (b) a widely-advertised and
influentially-pushed system of grants-in-aid of municipal and district
board educational expenditure based on the principle of 'pound for
pound'; (c) whilst there need be no objection to giving similar grants to
'private venture' schools this should only be done where there is a
highly-organised, extensive institution; and the present plan of
(practically) subsidising the individual 'hedge-schoolmaster'[57] living
by his fees should be wholly abandoned; and there should be ingenuity
in devising forms of aid acceptable to the mosque and other religious
schools not adopting [the] Government code or rules; (d) the Government should be equally liberal in aiding vernacular schools and English
schools, letting either be established according to the demand and

certainly setting no limit to either; (e) the secondary schools should be differentiated and varied so as to allow room for greater attention to science, manual work, art, economics, etc.; (f) the universities should be supplemented by schools of economics and technology which might in some cases be run as postgraduate institutes for all India.

There seems no reason why Mr. Gokhale's Bill for universal and compulsory education for boys should not be passed, safeguarded as it is by the provision that compulsory powers are not to be put in force except at the request of a municipal or district board and only when it can be shown that 30 per cent of the boys of school age are already on the rolls.[58] Such enterprising and advanced places should be given greatly increased grants-in-aid. The law should be enforced in these — for a long time to come exceptional places — by school attendance officers, not the police. This omits consideration of certain obvious difficulties (such as diversity of language and the struggle between the Urdu (Muslim) and the Hindi (Hindu) forms of Hindustani) and also the standing obstacle of lack of funds. We cannot however believe these difficulties to be insuperable.

But the educational problem needs both inventiveness and public discussion, for neither of which there seems at present adequate provision. We cannot discover who is 'doing the thinking' — certainly not the Collectors or Comm[rs], hardly the Secretariat — we doubt whether the Inspectors of Schools and Directors of Public Instruction have time to think or ability to make their voices heard if they do think — and Sir Harcourt Butler, able administrator as he is, brings only an amateur and very imperfectly informed mind to bear and that distracted by Viceregal functions and Imperial Council duties. And there seems no machinery for discussing problems and projects with the native leaders of thought in the different provinces with a view, on the one hand, of gaining their consent, and on the other to promulgating to the public the views that it is desirable the public should adopt if there is to be the indispensable unofficial co-operation. One would imagine that it would be most valuable if the Viceroy could preside at public conferences all over India at which all educational questions could be freely discussed; or, as the Viceroy has much to do, the Minister for Education might take his place. The suggestion is doubtless revolutionary. Lord Curzon's educational conference at Simla consisted only of a small group of English Government officials, with one aged head of a Christian College in Calcutta and absolutely no Hindu or Muslim! The result was that he raised a hurricane of opposition and his schemes have made little headway.

An interesting episode at Lucknow was our visit by way of the Chauk Bazaar,[59] a long narrow street of Indian shops that picturesquely recalled to us Canton, to a renowned Muslim 'hakim', or medical practitioner qualified only in Islamic medicine. In a ramshackle, extensive ground floor, up a narrow lane in the native city, we found him (11.30 a.m.) squatting down just inside the open window dealing with a succession of patients. One by one they came up to be questioned as to symptoms, to have the pulse felt at both wrists, to have the abdomen fingered (query, for liver or spleen enlargement?) (there was no use of stethoscope, or clinical thermometer); and then, to receive a prescription which was dictated rapidly in a loud singsong drawl for the benefit of the kneeling students. For inside the room there knelt in two rows about a score of young men listening to the interrogations and noting down in a kind of shorthand the prescriptions given. Among the patients was one *purdah* lady who was brought in an orange-coloured curtained chair or palanquin out of which she protruded her pulse to be felt, and even peeped round the curtain at the physician or perhaps at us. Our Muslim companion remarked that a Muslim lady would not have lifted the curtain at all! The cases we were told were mostly cough and fever; and the prescriptions were nearly all herbal (though one contained sparrow brains and quinine was said to be prescribed by a few native doctors, also mercury for syphilis). It is interesting that all that we saw was gratuitous, the physician taking no fees either from patients coming to him or from the students. He was said to charge a fee when he was called to visit a patient (5 rupees plus carriage hire). In Delhi, the native doctors do not charge even for visiting within the city but only when called to patients outside the city. The Muslim tradition is that healing, like instruction, should be gratuitous, done in the performance of duty by those who have a gift. When we asked how doctors could live we were told that they often had received of old grants of land or had inherited family property, on the understanding that they were to practise; but also, that they got the fees for visiting patients.

The *hakim* whom we visited, who looked a man of ability and strength of character and might well be a magnetic personality, was said to make as much as £400 a year. He took us to see (a) his medicine shop, where herbs were being chopped and emeralds were being ground to powder whilst various messes were being boiled and steeped; (b) his little distilling place, where three or four rude stills were on the fires, the vapour from which was being condensed slowly into glass vessels; and (c) the free dispensary where the medicines were given gratuitously to the poor – all indescribably picturesque and primitive, with no attempt at cleanliness or accuracy. The practice was usually for the patient to take the prescription to a native medicine shop (the apothecary in *Romeo and Juliet*)[60] which we saw close by, where the prescribed ingredients were simply sold to him and he made up the medicine in his own home! The whole thing was singularly interesting as an unaltered survival from the Middle Ages.

On the other hand, the Muslim community was becoming alive to the advantages of western science and had extracted an incautious promise from the Government that in the gorgeous new medical college just erected, there should be courses of instruction for *hakims* in Islamic medicine. Against this some of the civil service were revolting on the ground that the Government ought not to encourage error! It does not seem to have occurred to anyone that even accepting that view (which we do not, for a Government which does not endow 'error' can never endow 'truth', since all truth is error to someone), there are heaps of things in chemistry, physiology, and hygiene which the *hakims* would be the better for knowing and which good and qualified Muslims might be hired to teach, without venturing on the dangerous ground of Muslim therapeutics. The difficulty in which the Government finds itself on this point, and the lack of ingenuity displayed by the Civil Service in finding alternatives, seem characteristic and typical of India.

We dined at Lucknow with the Commissioner (Lovett)[61] and lunched with two members of the Secretariat (Stuart and Burn)[62] — all men of good though not striking ability with real good will and desire to do the best possible, all working very hard but all giving the impression of amateurishness and lack of ingenuity in devising or remembering alternatives; all unspecialised, doing a hard day's work at a succession of different subjects about none of which they had expert knowledge or professional skill and about some of which (e.g., education and sanitation) they had only a half belief. More interesting were our successive interviews with groups of Muslim and Hindu gentlemen. We went first to the house of Aziz Mirza, a wise, shrewd, well-informed and even humorous Secretary of the All-India [Muslim] League.[63] There we met the Raja of Jehangirbad (a landlord worth some tens of thousands pounds a year), his dissolute nephew and a dozen Muslim barristers and *vakils*, with the secretary of the Nadva-tullama school (above described). These specially enlightened Muslims deplored to us the backwardness of their own community, the general lack of wealth among them so that they had still not got the money together for a new university, their unwillingness to spend money on education even of their own sons (a *maulvi* at 10 rupees a month seemed to many a *talukdar* enough for his sons and neighbour's sons): the special unwillingness of the wives to let their sons be educated properly; the absolute inability to get the women educated. They insisted on the necessity for separate representation and for their having equality with the Hindus (lest they should be outvoted) in spite of the fact that they numbered only 14 per cent of this province. They said that only in this way could they have assurance of fair treatment in schools, languages, etc., at the hands of the municipalities and district boards. They were insistent on Urdu being taught, not Hindi, because Persian had been the court language of Delhi and Oudh and Urdu was the real popular language (the imported words being from the Persian); whereas the literary Hindi desired by the Hindus was really made up from Sanskrit. They resented quite as much as the Hindus the social exclusiveness of the English and their occasional rudeness to Indians; and it was they who complained that the Collector did not return the calls even of most distinguished Muslims and that they had to take off their shoes on entering his presence. On the other hand, they wanted the British Raj and they strongly objected to Bengalis being put in authority over them. Ruling was their hereditary business. They had left trade and even education to the Hindus and now that they had been ousted by the English from ruling they felt very much their backwardness in the professions and business. But they were striving now to improve Muslim education.

The next day we went to tea with a young Muslim barrister (a Cambridge graduate), Naziruddin Hasan,[64] whose father was a retired member of the statutory (or Provincial) Civil Service, a District Judge in Central Provinces. There we met a dozen young Muslims, mostly *vakils*; and B.W. went to see the *purdah* ladies. She found a dozen or fifteen collected to meet her, extraordinarily backward and unintelligent, only two or three speaking a few words of English. One very clever girl of 14 not in *purdah* was the daughter (pure blood) of a Muslim mathematical coach at Cambridge and spoke English well. The Hindu group we met through the Hindu editor of *The Advocate*, a leading member of the municipality and a man of great ability and public spirit (Ganga Prasad Varma),[65] who was an advanced nationalist and had been a friend of Tilak.[66] We met apparently in the rooms of the 'People's League' or some such society and found a dozen or so of Hindus (with one Muslim nationalist). The best way to describe them is to say that they seemed to us in tone and temper and grievances and opinions to be almost identical with the Muslims except that they wanted Hindi and not Urdu and that they bitterly resented the undue representation conceded to and claimed by the Muslims. The Hindu community as a whole was apparently wealthier, more successful in trade and at the Bar and more eager for English education than the Muslim community as a whole. But between these groups of enlightened leaders there was no discernible difference.

24th JAN^y 1912 IN CAMP AT GAURA, DISTRICT OF GORAKHPUR, UNITED PROVINCES

We have now been three days 'in Camp' with a Collector on his progress through his district, which is the largest and most populous in all India, having over three millions of people and covering some 4,500 square miles. The 'Camp' is a collection of four principal tents and an indefinite number of minor erections for kitchen, stores, clerks, servants, etc. pitched usually in a grove of mango trees. We 'break Camp' at about 8 a.m. each morning and go by carriage and on horseback to the next halting place 10 or 13 miles off. There we find a duplicate set of tents, etc. already erected, with our trunks which have gone on in advance. Our beds and rugs and toilet requisites arrive by the afternoon. On the way we inspect a vernacular school or visit some particular village. In camp there is an assemblage of village headmen to the number of a hundred or a hundred and fifty whom the Collector harangues in fluent Urdu about the necessity of reporting crime, the advantage of anti-plague inoculation, and the state of the crops. We inspect the local police station and the village school. Yesterday we had a grand inoculation, the (native) Assistant Civil Surgeon being on his own progress round the district, and with the help of the presence of the Collector and his Assistant (who was inoculated to encourage the others), actually induced some 200 natives to be done. It must be added that they were most of them policemen or servants of officials or else boys at the school (whose willingness to undergo the operation was encouraged by a bribe of twopence each from a local Hindu landowner).

The Collector hears appeals in civil suits from the decisions of the Assistant Magistrates, mostly 'partition cases' where the land of a joint Hindu family is being divided up among the participating members, one of whom is dissatisfied with the allotment. His 'court' is of course the large tent which is our common dining room. He is attended by three clerks, and the litigants appear in person without formality and argue their own case one against the other, of course in the vernacular Urdu. The Collector listens, interjects questions, explains to us in English what it is about and then questions them again, and finally abruptly declares that the appeal is dismissed or else remits it back for some alteration to be made. The litigants seem on the best of terms with each other and their lawsuit, often about a matter of trifling pecuniary value, partakes of the nature of the excitement of mill gambling. Various people come to see the Collector – minor officials of the locality, a small landlord on horseback followed by an armed retainer on horseback carrying a quaint sword, a cultivator with some grievance against the Government, and so on – everyone having perfect freedom of access. During the day, trays of presents arrive in the form of beautiful flowers, fruit, vegetables, locally-made sweet-meats and even the fresh fish from the local rivers – all of small pecuniary value and as such difficult to refuse without rudeness (the regulations strictly prohibit all other presents whatsoever).

KASID 28th JAN^y 1912

We continue our progress 'in Camp' with unfailing interest, so unceasing indeed that we find but little time to read or write. At night the Camp is guarded by half-a-dozen or more *'goraits'* or village watchmen (holding land rent-free on condition of performing service, practically an hereditary office although if there is no fit son the zemindar[67] nominates and the Government appoints some other successor). These village watchmen armed with long staves squat about the outskirts of the Camp at night but in the early morning they gather together round a fire and carry on endless conversation.

The gathering of the *mouktars* or village headman at each stopping place is really most remarkable. These one or two hundred men (there are over 7000 villages in the district) gather by ones or twos during the day, to sit about and gossip until summoned to the meeting. Then they squat down in a semi-circle close around the Collector's chair, an outer circle standing up, flanked by a few other men and boys from the adjacent village and a policeman or two in khaki uniforms and red *puggaree*.[68] The Collector speaks familiarly to them with gestures, jokes and smiles. They interject freely, make comments and criticisms one against the other, without the slightest fear. When the Collector talks about the nuisance of the multitude of Brahminee bulls and asks whether compulsory registration would not be a good device, there is a hum of satisfaction although they will not commit themselves to approval. One intelligent-looking young man, with suggestions of fanaticism about his eyes, objects to any interference with these bulls on the ground that the cow is the salvation of Hindustan and must not be hindered. The Collector turns the laugh against him by instancing a village in which no fewer than 130 of these bulls are at large feeding on the crops and asking whether it was really suggested that the cows of that village required so many bulls. The Collector tells the meeting to take the suggestion of registration home to their villages and talk it over with their neighbours so as to report to him at his next meeting what the people think.

He talks to them about the plague and explains the rat-flea theory of its transmission and the benefits of inoculation. As soon as the latter point is reached there is a comical movement of the crowd. Those who are standing up, especially those on the outside of the circle, edge away — apparently by an involuntary movement of fear lest the Collector should suddenly inoculate them on the spot! The Collector notices this with a laugh and comforts the crowd by the assurance that no inoculating doctor is present and that, in any case, the matter is entirely optional. The Collector concludes with friendly enquiries about the crops, whereupon several persons assure him that things are very bad in their villages. The collector laughs at them, and calls on the others to witness that this year they have simply bumper crops which the crowd smilingly assents to; whereupon the Collector rises and, with frequently renewed salutations, dismisses the meeting in great good humour. These extraordinarily picturesque meetings seem to us of the greatest possible usefulness in all sorts of ways. We wonder whether all Collectors hold them, or hold them with the 'verve' and *'bonhomie'* of our collector.

The 'Brahminee bull' is becoming a very serious pest in many parts of the district. It is a great act of piety to dedicate a bull to the gods and it has long been customary for leading families of Brahmins to make this sacrifice on special occasions in memory of some deceased member or some thing of the sort. But now the practice has become common and it is being adopted by families of inferior castes who think by that to improve their status. The bull so dedicated is turned loose to wander at will. He is so sacred that he must not be killed or even struck, and as the fields have no fences he practically eats his fill of the growing crops. To have 130 of these depredators loose in one village seems pretty serious! But what is even worse is that as these bulls are naturally the worst and most defective that the owner possesses — for any bull will do for the gods — and as these wandering bulls serve the cows of the village, there is a tendency for the breed to deteriorate steadily. Yet neither the villagers nor the Government ventures to put a stop to the practice out of fear of stirring up a religious fanaticism fomented by the Brahmins. The suggestion of requiring registration (which we made) seems a possible way out. Registration, it is said, would in itself greatly diminish the number of bulls dedicated because the people would have a nervous fear that it might involve some dreadful unknown consequences.

On Sunday we borrow a motor car from a friendly Raja — a wealthy Hindu landlord who has also a sugar factory and much money out at 12 per cent interest — in order to pay him a visit at his 'palace' some 20 miles off. On the way we go to breakfast with the Assistant Magistrate (who is in semi-independent charge of the further end of this huge district). We find him living temporarily in the 'Inspection Bungalow' at one corner of his territory — this being a one-storied, brick erection available for any Government officer coming to the place. He is a quiet, refined Ulsterman of about 30, an LL.D. of Trinity College Dublin (Bennet),[69] who impresses us as a competent and careful executive officer, conscientious and plodding. There come in to breakfast two railway officials who are building a new line close by, a young Engineer and an Inspector. We breakfast extensively on five or six courses at 11 o'clock; and the Collector afterwards goes into an inner room to discuss the affairs of the district with his deputy — apparently, principally movements of the subordinate staff, whether this man had not better be sent there, and so on.

Eventually we go on to our Raja of Padrauna[70] — he is in siesta until 3 p.m. — and we find him waiting to meet us on the outskirts of his 'palace' in the midst of extensive outbuildings of one sort or another. He takes us to see his 'hospital', a free dispensary maintained by him, and his 'agricultural bank' which is not co-operative but is run by him as a sort of benevolent money-lending place to keep his tenantry out of the grip of the usurer. He started it with a free gift of 20,000 rupees which forms the nucleus of its loan fund, but whenever it needs more capital the Raja himself supplies it at 12 per cent which is the rate that the bank charges to its borrowers.

Then we inspected the coach-house with his second motor car and several stately landaus and barouches, his formal gardens, which were really rather attractive though bare to our eyes, his collection of animals, two magnificent cranes (whom the servant, with an umbrella as weapon, had to keep from attacking us), a whole array of birds in cages and of rabbits in a large barred hutch, and his sugar factory where he had installed a steam engine to crush the cane in a steel mill and a centrifugal sugar-crystallising machine of which he was very proud. It is perhaps characteristic that this centrifugal machine was set going for our edification without bearings, so that three men with giant bamboos had to hold it in position, and with an imperfectly-mended driving belt, which threatened to slip off the wheel and presently broke with a loud report that made us all scatter in alarm. However, some sugar was made and presented to us. The Raja was making, he said, £2 a day from this sugar mill, which represented a queer intermediate stage between the hand and the machine industry.

Finally we came to the 'palace', a rather attractive two-storied, battlemented, white-painted building which we entered by one of those strangely narrow, winding stone staircases characteristic of Hindu houses — like going up a cottage ladder to get to Windsor

Castle — and arrived at a drawing room full of carpets, furniture, ornaments and pictures in 'Early Victorian' English style! We were presented with perfume and cigarettes, B.W. with half-a-dozen excellent photographs and S.W. with a silver card case. Then we went to see the carpenter's workshop where the Raja's artisans were building a new 'howdah'[71] for use on his elephants, and also new chairs. Finally, we visited the temple built by his father at which he prostrated himself, built of costly marble, surrounded by a grove of trees grown in three feet of earth brought by his father from Muttra, a sacred place on the Ganges, and containing images of Krishna and Radigar, his wife. Our Raja is said to have an income of £20,000 a year clear, half derived from the rent of 400 villages (on which he pays some £6000 a year land tax) and half from money out at interest. [BW: But the Raja, in spite of his wealth and his Government title, has a skeleton in his cupboard: he is of low caste — a circumstance which not one of his fellow countrymen — Rajas or peasants — ever forgets!]

We finished our Sunday with a visit to an indigo planter whom we found living in great state in a charming house with lawns in English style. The estate is an old jungle-grant which has been cleared and put under cultivation. The business is a very fluctuating one, almost a gamble, and this planter is gradually taking to other crops — is contemplating indeed starting an up to date sugar mill.[72] Altogether we have motored 55 miles exclusively over country roads, unmetalled and sandy with ruts and hollows and ridges and culverts, returning close upon sundown after a ten-hour day during which we have seen a great deal of the country.

[BW→] There remains little for me to add to Sidney's description of our life in Camp except a word or two about the Collector, his Assistants, and the little world that surrounds him at his station at [SW: Gorakhpur] and his [SW: four] months in Camp. Hope Simpson[73] is not a remarkable man; but he is remarkably fitted for his work — to us he seems almost ideal as an administrator over an alien race. Tall and muscular with a strong but kindly face, splendid nerve and health, a genuine love of guiding and serving other people, he is the exact opposite of the bureaucrat. In fact, if he has a fault as an administrator I should think it consists of too great an independence of and indifference to the common rules of law and administration — a determination to give full play to the human side of each particular case without perhaps considering whether his decision was a safe precedent for other people. For instance, his intimacy with all his subordinate officials and with the Indian lawyers and landowners of his district is one of the strong points of his administration and results in a [SW: greater] measure of 'common consent' than is usual in the British administration. But this policy of intimate intercourse would be impracticable and perhaps unsafe for a man with less firmness of will and with less absolute straightness of purpose. He can afford to be good-natured with his subordinates because, owing to his energy and perfect health, he sets the pace so quick that they are kept up to the mark by having to work up to him. Also, being a man of genuine piety (he is a fervent Congregationalist), his easy and intimate manner is consistent with an almost puritanic hatred for looseness of life and conversation. And all this piety and integrity are prevented from appearing as prudishness and priggishness because they are tempered by his love of outdoor life and his devotion to sport.

It is interesting to note that Hope Simpson is the son of the General Manager of the [SW: Bank of] Liverpool and that his family both in the past and the present are of 'banking stock'. He is himself *par excellence* a 'general manager' and not a specialised officer. I doubt whether he has either the patience or the intellectual curiosity to be a good expert. Perhaps that is the reason that he is so fitted for the work of a Collector. The Collector of an Indian administrative district is essentially a general manager. He is expected to make roads and bridges, to carry on works of drainage and irrigation, to start and manage schools, to decide on appeals in both criminal and civil cases, to direct the education of great landlords who are minors, and if necessary to manage [SW: their] estates and settle their [SW: family quarrels], to detect sedition and prevent crime, to protect the religious life and stop the fanaticism of Muslims and Hindus, and to [SW: lead in local] society — white and coloured. And for all this multifarious work he has no [SW: responsible] Assistants more specialised than himself [SW: though there are very subordinate — usually Indian — Engineers, School Inspectors and Police]. He has moreover to put up with and make the best of the Assistants sent him by the Government of his province and the Government of India — and he is handicapped by the tradition that no man however incompetent can (so long as he is decently conducted) be in practice dismissed from the Government service. He can only be 'removed' either to another part of the district, or if the Collector is fortunate, to another Collector's district.

In our rides together I had long talks with our host and learnt something of his personal and professional life. 'Out of eleven years of married life I have spent five years with my wife and children.' And the man adored his wife and children — idealised the one and idolised the others. His wife was a Girton graduate and has an income of her own. From her portrait and his description of her she seems to be a homely, domestic woman whose whole existence is centred on her husband and children. With great *naïveté* he insisted on reading to us her long letter

from Switzerland, whither she has taken her [SW: five] children – four
of whom had had the plague! – and this letter, which the dear man
glowed over, revealed a gentle and charming nature absorbed in the
little pleasures of the children and eagerly awaiting his decision to
come home, if possible for good. And clearly Hope Simpson is now
being tempted in the prime of life to throw up his job. With his
pension [SW: of £1000 a year] and his wife's income, he could just
manage to retire [SW: he entered the I.C.S. at nineteen and is still under
forty-five] and [SW: yet send his] boys to [SW: Rugby and Oxford].
Should he retire this year, or should he remain on for another year, take
two years furlough and look about him in England before he [SW:
settled] not to return to India? When we arrived he had almost settled
to go home this year and to retire at the end of his one year's furlough.
When we left he had finally [SW: settled to] stay on another year and
thus take two years to consider whether or not he should break off his
Indian career – and I think that change of mind was partly brought
about by our immense interest in and admiration for his administrative
work.

   [BW/SW→][74] Part of his discontent was due to a sort of estrange-
ment between him and the Lieutenant-Governor (Sir John Hewett)[75]
and the lack of any connection with or encouragement from the
Government of India. We had heard him spoken of as a first-rate
administrator and quite clearly the Government of India, in selecting
him to entertain us, had considered that he would be likely to give a
good impression to two potential critics. And yet, in spite of this
reputation, Hope Simpson has been more or less left behind. Men who
are less able than himself and who are not senior to him are
Commissioners (a higher grade than Collector) or have got into the
Board of Revenue or Secretariat or into other places from which
promotion may be expected. Obviously Hope Simpson is not liked
by the Lieu^t-Governor and has not secured any kind of recognition
from the Gov^t of India. We suspect it is largely due to his
independence and to the fact that he is 'pro-native' and to the
homeliness and carelessness of society matters on the part of both
himself and his wife. Indeed the only time he showed any bitterness
was in his description of the inanities of Simla and the intrigues
reputable and disreputable that went on at dinner, at balls, during
games and sports, in the Government House sets of Province &
Empire.

   Hope Simpson had three Assistants in the covenanted Indian Civil
Service one Englishman, one Hindu and one Muslim. The Englishman
(Edye)[76] was a bright, energetic, clean young man of 28 – public school
(Harrow) and university (Oxford), the son of the chief accountant at

the Bank of England and belonging to a family of public servants —
naval contractors, army and civil service. He too had married a lady
with an income and did himself well. But he was not in the least slack —
on the contrary he seemed as successful in administration as he was in
sport. He was in fact of the same sort as Hope Simpson — a first-rate
'general manager' with a great capacity for 'despatching business' —
though he lacked his chief's human interest & religious inspiration. The
two Indian Assistants were not so satisfactory. The Hindu (Mehta),[77] a
Gujarat Brahmin married to a pretty little Bombay Brahmin lady who
was well-educated and out of *purdah* — he had been educated in India as
a boy but passed through Cambridge with distinction and entered the
Indian Civil Service by examination. He was a tall, pleasant-looking
man with somewhat servile manners and fluent talk — in his heart a
nationalist but very discreet in Hope Simpson's presence. His chief did
not really like him — he said he worked for show, that he wrote reports
which were patently inaccurate in their 'white washing' and defended
them on the ground that they would impress public opinion. Also he
was far too intimate with one of the subordinate officials. Worst of all
he lacked courage. When told to go round during the cholera epidemic
he developed a lame leg — and this was typical of other small incidents.
One felt in talking to him that it was almost inconceivable that he
should step into Hope Simpson's place without a gradual deterioration
of all branches of administration.

The Muslim Assistant — Ameer Ali[78] — was a raw recruit just out
from England. He was the grandson of a Minister of the King of Oudh
and a son of a celebrated Indian barrister and Judge of the Supreme
Court in Calcutta, now the first Indian Member of the Judicial
Committee of the Privy Council in London. But his mother was an
anglicised German (Konstam) with Indian connections and he had been
brought up in England — Wellington College and Balliol — he therefore
was technically an Eurasian. A delicate and somewhat pretty youth of
25 with dandified dress and manner, he did not impress us. Hope
Simpson, in whose house he lived, treated him with kindly contempt.
He was always talking of his father and his father's distinguished
friends and was always telling us rather stupid little stories so as to
show his knowledge of the great world. He professed to be an
enthusiastic sportsman. But he lived in chronic funk of plague, cholera
and enteric and the poor boy was evidently destined to be in a state of
perpetual terror about his health. He was *very slack* — showed no
inclination to exert himself physically or mentally. When not talking
about English society [or] glorifying sport he was abusing the Hindu or
the Italians and the Russians for their hostility to Islam. He frankly
confessed that he loathed India — regarded England as his home and

Islam as his faith. In this latter respect he compared unfavourably with Mehta — who for all his nervelessness was devoted to the country of his service. Altogether, we prophesied that Ameer Ali would not last out over the rains — some pretext would be found for leaving India and settling in London.

But Hope Simpson was more fortunate in his subordinate Indian officers. One of them, Kumar Prasad,[79] an Assistant Magistrate in the Provincial Service and a member of the *Arya Samaj*,[80] seemed to be a quite excellent person; & others impressed us favourably. Indeed this intermediate class of Indian officials (the Provincial Service), native-born and mostly native-bred, with a high standard of work and a low standard of [SW→] expectation, well-educated in Indian colleges but not spoilt by English university examination successes, seemed to us full of promise. They may not produce Hope Simpsons, or be able to take over the top executive posts. But their help already enables one Englishman to administer a district of one or two millions of people and they will enable the number of English to be further diminished.

Hope Simpson was inclined to be pessimistic and despondent about the English administration. There had been a marked improvement in the past seven or ten years in such matters as roads, schools and sanitation; and Lord Curzon, in spite of his insolence, had done much good in stirring up a service which had become wooden and mechanical in its routine. But there was no definite purpose or plan about the Government of India. Were we really trying to enable the Indian people to dispense with our guidance or did we intend to remain forever in command? To pretend the one and secretly to mean the other crippled and nullified much of the practical work. The bulk of the officials who thought at all — together with all who did not think, and all the Army officers — believed (and occasionally let it be known that they believed) that English rule would go on forever and that the Indians were inherently incapable of self-government. Hence the continued agitation, which could not fail to grow in strength. The Government would give way on one point after another as soon as it was demanded with sufficient agitation, but give way too ungraciously and too tardily for the boon to do anything but stimulate agitation for more. At length something would be demanded which could not or would not be conceded — and then he feared an outbreak, a popular rising, in which the smaller stations would be overwhelmed and the larger temporarily invested or paralysed, when we should find ourselves back at the position of the Mutiny of 1857![81] This however he said in a moment of pessimism. For the most part he believed in his work and went straight onward in faith and hope that somehow a definite policy would get itself adopted.

We have omitted to note that the whole expenditure on local government services in this huge Gorakhpur district having 3½ millions of people, is £20,000 a year. With this sum, the 'district board' – really, the Collector as its chairman *ex-officio*, for the Indian members show no initiative or independence – has to provide roads and bridges, schools and sanitation. The provincial government has taken over one high school, and provides school inspectors. It also supplies two or three doctors and a supply of quinine for free issue. With regard to roads and bridges, it maintains a few miles of main road and makes grants towards exceptionally big local works. With these inconsiderable exceptions the £20,000 a year, which is the whole of the district board's resources, has to provide schools, roads, medical attendance and sanitation for 3½ millions of people! And even this sum is something like twice as large as it was ten years ago. Though Gorakhpur has been British territory since 1803, its real administration in these matters does not seem to have begun until the twentieth century.

3/2/12 IN CAMP WITH P. H. CLUTTERBUCK,[82] CONSERVATOR OF FORESTS, NEAR SONARIPUR (KHERI DISTRICT)

We left Gorakhpur with regret after an agreeable ten days and travelled a day and night to this place, where we begin five days in Camp with the officer in charge of half the forest area (eastern circle) of the United Provinces. The forest area of India is something like one-fifth to one-fourth of the whole so that one ought not to leave it out of consideration, though apparently it has practically no visitors except those who come to shoot tigers or stags. We were met at the station by our host the Conservator (who has supreme charge of seven forest districts) and by the officer in charge of this particular forest district. With them came two elephants, which took our luggage and would have carried us, but after twenty-four hours train we preferred to walk. The 'Camp' here is around a forest bungalow in the upper floor of which we sleep and enjoy the comfort of a wood fire.

We began our experience of the forest by an afternoon ride on our elephants through miles of high grass and then miles of dense and trackless wood. The elephant stalks majestically at the rate of four or five miles an hour, picking his way skilfully through the jungle, down into *'nullahs'*[83] and up again on to steep banks, the *'mahout'*[84] seated on his neck, both guiding the beast so as to avoid tree trunks and branches too strong to be broken and warding off other branches by his hands – occasionally slashing them off with a heavy and sharp knife (a most formidable weapon) or telling the elephant to break down a thin tree or a branch by his trunk or foot. It is astonishing how easily a huge elephant goes through what seems a thick wood.

The next morning we started out at 7 a.m. on foot as it was cold and foggy and drenched with dew — the elephants following us — for the two forest officers to inspect two 'coupes' or felling subdivisions of the forest, in which the contractor who had bid for the timber had found too large a proportion of unsound hollow trees and claimed a rebate. After three miles walk along a forest road we mounted our elephants and penetrated into the dense mass, finally returning on foot a couple of miles by road. Forestry in India means, it appears, the conservancy and wise exploitation of existing self-sown forests. With one small experimental exception the Government of India does no planting or re-afforestation, having neither the requisite staff nor the pressing necessity. The huge area covered naturally with trees supplies all needs and demands all the available staff for mere preservation and management.

The problem is therefore quite other than that of the U.K., and the position is also quite different from that of Germany and France, where scientifically-planted forests are now in full and regular bearing. The Indian forests are only now beginning to recover from past neglect and the older trees now being felled date from a time when no care was given. Even so however the forests yield to the Government between one and two millions sterling net annual revenue, besides large free concessions to the local inhabitants of fuel, grazing, etc. Our enthusiastic Forest Conservator declares that the net revenue could be largely increased by merely increasing the forest staff; and he gives statistics showing that the revenue per acre of forest area in the different provinces varies almost exactly according to the expenditures per acre on staff. The tall grass that here surrounds the wooden area in broad belts and rising eight or ten feet high, is now burnt as useless for the sake of protecting the forest from accidental fires. But our Conservator has long had the idea that it could be made into paper and has more than once tried in vain to induce the Government to experiment with it. Last year he was put in charge of the forestry exhibit at the Allahabad Exhibition, and allotted a *lakh* of rupees (£6666) for expenses. He promptly took the opportunity of engaging a paper-making expert, and getting paper-making machinery with which he demonstrated at the Exhibition that paper could be made of this valueless grass. The Gov^t is now seriously considering how to turn to account this new forest product.

The timber is sold by auction to Indian sawing contractors from Delhi, mostly Muslims who come and camp in the forest for months and fell the trees marked by the Forest Officer, which they saw by hand on the spot and drag by bullock cart to the neighbouring railway which was constructed mainly for this traffic. The payment is in two parts, one (the 'monopoly' fee) a lump sum (say, 4000 rupees) for the privilege of all the felling in a given 'coupe' for one season, the other a fixed royalty charge per cubic foot for all that is taken away. But as no wisdom or care can estimate how many of the trees will be hollow and comparatively valueless the bid used to be almost a gamble. Our Conservator introduced the plan of a Government guarantee that the sound timber in a coupe should be not less than a specified quantity. This abolished the gambling element to a great extent and resulted in much larger biddings, as the contractor did not need to 'make himself safe'. But it involves the occasional allowance of a rebate when the proportion of sound timber turns out to be less than was anticipated; and then the Conservator finds some difficulty in explaining to a suspicious and unintelligent finance department at headquarters why any allowance should be made. There seems in fact to be no definite sanction for the arrangement, which the Conservator appears to have made on his own authority (though it has gone on for some ten years or so); and it has not been adopted elsewhere. Perhaps for this reason our Conservator decided today to satisfy the two complaining contractors by letting them cut more trees instead of returning the money!

Another day, we sally out in the misty morning as before, but proceed to our next day's Camp, making a long detour through high grass plains at the edge of dense wood, past swamps and bogs without end in order to settle exactly where 'His Excellency'[85] (who is coming in ten days to shoot stags) shall be placed. We see a score or two of graceful deer bounding away amid the tall grass, a herd of wild pigs rooting up the grass, monkeys now and then in the trees, a flight of wild peacocks and pea-hens, the jungle fowl from which all domestic poultry have been derived, beautiful white 'egrets' or goose-like birds, and in a swamp, a black object which our keenly-sighted *'mahouts'* (elephant-drivers) declared to be a crocodile. There are innumerable leopards, panthers and bears in the woods and a tiger to every 100 square miles or so; but these do not reveal themselves in the daytime to the casual visitor.

CHANDAN CHOWKI 4ᵗʰ FEBʸ 1912

This day's 'Camp' is on the very edge of the little river which separates India from Nepal; or rather, which used to be the boundary. As the river shifts its course constantly the Nepalese Government was induced to consent to the substitution of a demarcated land boundary a few hundred yards away. The foot-hills of the Himalayas rise rather abruptly a few miles to the North and over them we catch peeps of snow-clad mountain peaks which are in the Himalayas proper. The scene is here graceful and charming, with the silent flowing stream amid woods and glades and tiny villages of aborigines. We go for our afternoon walk into Nepal, across the new boundary, in order to consider whether the river can be prevented from cutting away the forest bungalow which is on its very brink.

We come to an idea in our talks with our Forest Officer which has been germinating in our minds for the past month. The Government of India is committing the sin of 'faint-heartedness' in more departments than one. It is desperately in need of more revenue to fill the void that is being left by the loss of its opium profits[86] as well as to meet the rapidly-growing demand for popular education, etc. It cannot raise money by death duties (as the joint Hindu family system stands in the way, and also intense feeling); its potentialities in income tax are limited by influential opposition and by the inability to discover Indian incomes; it cannot get much out of taxation on alcohol or tobacco because the Indian takes relatively little of them, and no tea or coffee; it dare not increase the land revenue by more than the periodic increment corresponding to increased productiveness; it is precluded by English opposition from raising its import duties, and moreover, as the Indians purchase few imported commodities, even protective duties would yield very little; it fails to bring to its aid with any effectiveness either local government or local taxation, because of the invincible reluctance of the local authorities to impose local rates on house property. The result is that its revenue is inelastic and insusceptible of increase.

There remains the resource of profitable Government enterprise. Unfortunately, the Government of India is averse from 'competing with private enterprise'; the English commercial interests in India and in England are quick to raise objection; the Secretary of State for India is naturally disinclined to sanction any Government commercial adventures; and the civil servants in India, who *are* the Government of India, are intellectually 'individualists', vaguely remembering the political economy textbooks that they crammed up twenty years before! Thus the railways, though often owned by Government, are nearly all leased to companies; the gas and electricity supply in the large towns is in private hands; the employment of the prisoners in gaol is restricted to a few articles which do not compete with English enterprises; and there is no advance towards profitable Government monopolies. The exceptions are opium (now disappearing under treaty), and salt, an indefensible tax on the poor which has rightly been reduced to a low figure. Fortunately, the irrigation canals have been kept as a Government service (because many of them are unremunerative) and these now yield a steadily increasing income. The 240,000 square miles of forests have also been kept in hand and these now yield nearly two millions a year net, a sum which should steadily increase as the trees which have enjoyed a generation of scientific conservancy come to felling point, and as the means of communication enable the sale of fuel and other by-products to develop.

There is a small Government factory of resin and turpentine and another of quinine. Here apparently Government enterprise stops. It is not that profitable concessions have been granted to capitalists. Partly out of treasury caution, partly out of past aversion to European exploitation of industries which might injuriously affect Indian agriculture, but mainly owning to the absence of desire on the part of European and American capitalists to embark on the difficult and unhealthy circumstances of India when more profitable fields lay open to them in Argentina, Canada, etc., and perhaps principally to the absolute indisposition of Indian capitalists to make industrial ventures, the field has (apart from jute and tea, the gold of Mysore, the coal needed by the railways and the Bombay cotton mills) remained as yet almost unworked. We cannot help thinking that it would be well for the Government of India to turn over a new leaf – to go in for tobacco and spirit Government monopolies, take over the railways and work them on a unified system for public ends, to put capital – perhaps attracting it out of native hoards by a 'patriotic national loan' – into the more complete and more rapid development of its 240,000 square miles of forest, to start Government factories for matches, for paper, for rope and string and what not, if only for its own enormous consumption in the first instance.

The Indians do better as minor Government officials than in any other capacity. They all desire Government appointments. The new movement might be made to appear essentially 'nationalist' in spirit and might even be made to seem to be inspired and demanded by the nationalists themselves. And the Government – like that of Japan – might in this way get large and growing new sources of revenue without appearing to tax the people, and indeed without really taxing them at all.

[BW→] Our host Mr. Clutterbuck has not so attractive a personality as Hope Simpson. [SW: In physical appearance and voice he is a cross between Michael Sadler[87] and John Kemp.] He comes from the landed gentry class — his mother became a Catholic and his four sisters have all taken to the religious life – [SW: one a] R.C. nun and two Anglican nuns, and the other the headmistress of a Catholic school, having been rejected by the convent because of her strong will! He is tall and muscular, a spare liver, and a good sportsman – or rather an ardent lover of the forest and the wild animal – for killing seems to be with him a minor consideration. I must add to this that he is an enthusiast, almost a fanatic, about the value of his profession; regards the wise exploitation of the forests as the central question of Indian administration. He has the reputation for being a hard and untiring worker at his jobs. He is in fact an excellent official within the narrow limits of the technique of his profession.

But outside his profession he has no knowledge and no wisdom – his sayings are really rather absurd in their ignorance of facts and strange medley of prejudices. And even with regard to his own subject he is wholly incapable of seeing its relation to general administration, and his proposals of reform are not likely to recommend themselves to his superiors because they combine good technical suggestions with foolish reflections on Indian Government in general. In explanation of this mixture of efficiency and unwisdom one must remember that for the last twenty-one years, ever since he became a man, he has lived in remote districts – for months at a time wholly solitary except for the native coolie, at other times cooped up with an inferior European or Indian Assistant. Also, his work does not bring him into any responsible relationship with the inhabitants of the district – he is merely an employer like any other employer or a trader dealing with native contractors on strictly business lines. Whether from circumstance or training he lacks the broad humanity of Hope Simpson – and directly one leaves the forest and its development his company is tedious.

His Assistant [SW: John] Tulloch[88] [SW: also of the India Forest Department, a few years junior to Clutterbuck] is I think Eurasian – married to a buxom English woman of lower middle-class origin. He is an unattractive but socially harmless person – silent and commonplace – suffering in health and activity from chronic overfeeding. His wife eats the same five meals a day without apparently spoiling her digestion; her eyes and her skin are bright and clear and she is a pleasant creature of the fat, fair and forty type. Clutterbuck lives with the Tullochs. Apparently he entertains them while he is in their district – a relationship we should think undesirable between a chief and a working assistant. He treats Tulloch as something between an intimate and a foreman. The relationship lacks the dignity which qualifies all Hope Simpson's friendliness with his assistant.

Clutterbuck's great hero is Sir J. Hewett, the Lieu^t-Governor of the U.P. It is interesting to note that though he has been 23 years in India,

Hewett is the first Lieu^t.-Governor he has ever known − and this acquaintanceship is due to Hewett's love of forest sport. (Among all the other officials of the U.P. whom we have seen, Hewett is unpopular, regarded as a self-advertiser, and condemned as a devotee of sport when he ought to be attending to business.) For the rest of the Government of India, Clutterbuck has nothing but abuse: the Viceroy is a useless figure-head, the Secretary of State a damnable nuisance, the Secretariat all selfish obstructionists, the Collectors amateurs who meddle with matters they don't understand. And yet when S.W. or I make some mild criticism of the Government of India our host fires up as if we had attacked him personally! As to England it is going rapidly to the bad − Lloyd George is a blackguard and Keir Hardie[89] ought to be hung, drawn and quartered. We cannot help suspecting that our host, in spite of his kind hospitality and his eagerness to make us realise the immensity of the forest as an asset to Indian finance, has a somewhat unfavourable opinion of his present guests. Anyway we perplex and irritate him − he cannot make out who and what we are or what are our political intentions.

[SW→] 5th FEB^y [1912]

This morning S.W. visited on an elephant the two aboriginal villages close by the Camp in company with the Indian 'extra-Assistant Forest Officer', who is permanently in this district under Mr. Tulloch. This Indian, a pleasant-speaking, efficient-looking man of 45, had had 27 years' service and had been through the Government Forest College at Dehra Dun. He had reached the highest grade open to him, but as he has only just passed his last examinations he is getting only £200 a year, though he could go on further by increments up to 800 rupees per month (£600 a year). He lived all the year round at Sonaripur with his wife but sent his son to a boarding school at Naini Tal.

The aboriginal villages, inhabited by '*tharu*' or dwellers of the Tarai,[90] the low-lying country on either side of the Nepal frontier, differ ethnologically from the Hindus of the Gangetic plain and it is said also from the hillmen of Nepal, who are definitely Mongolian. But they struck me as being probably a result of intermixture between these races. They are now Hindus by religion of a sort; they burn their dead by the river and they go on pilgrimage to Hindu sacred places. But they kill and eat fish and game of all sorts as well as domestic fowls and pigs, and they make no use of Brahmins or other priestly personages even on the most solemn occasions. They have no temples or obvious shrines or images but on being questioned, they said they 'did *puja*' in a recess of their hut. Their habitations were in groups of half-a-dozen or so only, often the households of relatives. They only marry one wife and within the tribe but they must choose outside their own little village. One girl who may have been 14 or 15 was described by her mother as lately married, but not being sent to her husband in the neighbouring hamlet for two or three years to come.

They are reported as being entirely chaste, honest, truthful, industrious, and almost completely free from crime of any sort. They cultivate each household a few acres of land which the Forest Department lets them have at nominal fixed land tax, on the understanding that they will labour at wages for the Forest Department when called upon (e.g., outbreak of fire, etc.). They have oxen and various tools; they crush their own mustard seed for oil and husk their own rice by foot-lever and pounder; each house has a 'go down' or open shed in which grain, tools, etc., are stored; their houses are elaborately constructed of white mud walls often worked into panels for ornament, surmounted by a good roof of regularly cut beams and well-constructed grass thatch. They grow wheat, rice, dal, mustard, pepper, potatoes, etc., and they make butter from the milk of their cows. They were well and decently clothed, the women in different coloured gowns and shawls with many silver and brass bangles, nose-rings, ear-rings, necklaces, ankle ornaments and toe-rings. Altogether they seemed to be quite as far advanced in 'civilisation' as the Hindus of the villages in the Gangetic plain. But though they make their rude pottery and their own carts, etc. and weave baskets and matting, they have no hand-looms for cotton cloth, which (with their metal pots, etc.) they buy.

They were said to be apt to shift their habitation without apparent cause — often on account of omens of one sort or another — and the population on each side of the Nepal frontier was thus constantly fluctuating. The Government makes them report births and deaths month by month to a forest guard who visits for that purpose; and it sends periodically a Hindu vaccinator (whom S.W. saw with his pony laden with vaccine, etc.) to operate on all the children thus reported. These hamlets have just been done and all the children had bad sores on their arms in consequence. The Forest Officer collects their land tax of a few pence per acre per annum and allows them unlimited fuel free, whilst some of them are licensed to have guns of a rude sort to frighten away the deer. This sums up the whole of their contact with Government. There is no thought of a school for them or of sanitation or of medical attendance. They make no use of the police or post or civil courts and they are practically never in the criminal court.

DUDWA 7th FEB^y 1912

We end our forest excursion today in an ideal 'Camp' in the very centre of this vast tract of wood, with seven straight roads radiating in all directions for ten or fifteen miles, with monkeys in the adjoining trees and wild pea-fowl roosting in the branches around us. Certainly it has been a most novel and interesting experience. And today come telegrams notifying that the Viceroy is after all the preparations unable to come owing to the serious illness of his brother-in-law, Lord Alington.[91] Fifty elephants are converging on this place from different directions and cannot easily be stopped or diverted, whilst preparations for feeding some five hundred persons of all ranks are in progress – all of which our host has now as far as possible to countermand.

[BW: CHHATARPUR, BUNDELKHAND, CENTRAL INDIA] 11th FEB^y 1912

[BW →] We stayed a night at Lucknow and another at Ghansi on our way to a visit with the Maharaja of Chhatarpur. Professor A. W. Ward [SW: brother of Prof. James Ward of Cambridge, whose daughter married our friend, Lawson Dodd],[92] with whom we stayed at Lucknow, is the senior professor at [SW: Canning] College, and is bitterly disappointed at not being made Principal. He is an example of how men of capacity but without professional zeal go to seed in India – especially if they happen to be of the sensual type. From his appearance we infer that he has come down from a talented man to a lounger whose habits have brought him under a cloud. At his house we met a young fellow [SW: MacMahon,[93] of Owens College, Manchester and Oxford] just out from England [SW: as lecturer in chemistry] who, if he stays in India, will certainly go the same way. From the slackness of these two men one would gather that there has not been a principal of any personality at Canning College.

At Ghansi we were met by the Collector, the Judge and the Railway Engineer: we were eventually carried off to the house of the Railway Engineer.[94] The brother and sister had a really well-appointed house – more luxurious and comfortable than that of Government officials. The sister (Miss Barnett) was a remarkably pleasant, able lady – much travelled – who deplored the futility of the lives of most Anglo-Indian women. 'They give way to the climate and lounge all day, and then wonder that they lose their health.' The brother was a hard-grained individualist – he seemed to be kept at work for long hours and had very little leave. They were the children of the General Manager of the railway and had been born in India and were thoroughly acclimatised. But they [SW: knew] nothing of the Indians except as servants and subordinates and were not interested in the Government of India or in any of its problems.

The Collector Mr. Silberrad (who dined with us and took us round the fort in the morning) was a distinctly able, open-minded man — said to be one of the ablest administrators — well thought of by the Government of the U.P. and of India. He was a harder and more reactionary person than Hope Simpson and though pleasant and sympathetic in manner, did not really believe in raising the Indians to a higher level. His excuse for the negative policy was that English civilisation was doubtfully good — why then 'impose it' on the Indians — why not keep them in a state of primitive bliss! He looked [SW: so] efficient, so healthy, and so agreeably self-complacent and so energetically happy that one could hardly believe that he was honestly doubtful of the civilisation that had produced [SW: him! In his] attitude towards Indian unrest and Indian aspirations he reminded one of Alfred Cripps[95] when he assures you that the labourers of his estate are on the whole more happily contented than his own class. In both cases the wish is father to the thought and is a mere excuse for a sort of passive resistance to the upheaving forces.

[SW→] Ghansi, normally a city of 36,000 inhabitants, was reduced in population by one half (and half the remainder only came in by day and slept in rude shelters in the adjacent plain). The people have fled from the plague. The remainder were dying at the rate of forty per day! (43 was the statement for the day before we arrived.) Nothing practical could be done except watch the sanitation, remove the dead bodies of rats and men and inoculate the living. Some 3000 had been inoculated there within the last three months. At Cawnpore, where we stopped between trains, we drove to the memorial gardens which surround the consecrated tomb, once the well into which the women and children were thrown at the Mutiny.[96] This tomb, with its somewhat meretricious Marochetti statue, is quite properly fenced in and only opened by a soldier to visitors. But what is most objectionable, no *Indians* are allowed to enter the beautiful ornamental gardens, which are kept up out of public taxation. This dates from the Mutiny days and is really an invidious piece of vengeful feeling. The soldier on duty defended the exclusion on the ground that if the Indians were admitted they would picnic all over the grounds and make a mess — but this is a mere excuse. The clerk at the Bank of Bengal to whom we mentioned the matter said that he thought the continuance of an invidious race exclusion was a mistake.

[BW→] FEB^y 14th [1912]

The journey from Cawnpore to Ghansi revealed a new India – an India of rocky fortresses and walled cities and villages – reminding one of the internecine warfare devastating the continent before the British Raj. The state of Chhatarpur seems to be a place of temples, the little capital where the Maharaja has his palace and guest house being almost Burmese in the number of its temples in all stages of decay and smart newness. Very wonderful are the temples of [SW: Khajuraho],[97] whither we were motored by the Dewan on the second day our of visit to the Maharaja of Chhatarpur.[98] Situated in a remote part of the state – 52 miles from a railway station by a decent road and 30 miles by a bullock wagon-train – they are seldom visited. They are reputed by experts to be one of the finest groups in northern India – some say in the whole of India. To antiquarians and art dealers I suppose these temples [SW→] have not only interest but also charm; but to the Philistine and puritan mind they are spoilt by their incessant repetition of lascivious figures – some being most grossly indecent in their representation of 'unnatural' lust. Their beauty is confined to the attractiveness of a surface made up of innumerable carvings. But their location is also picturesque in its wild isolation.

We were motored out to them from Chhatarpur – doing the last mile or so in bullock carts for lack of a road – by the Dewan or Prime Minister of the state (salary £600 and house, etc.), an able, attractive and outspoken Hindu [BW: all these Hindu officials – even Mehta of Sonaripur who is accused of cowardice – are controversially outspoken in their criticisms of British rule and their desire for complete self-government. As they must see that we are on intimate terms with their official superiors, it shows commendable sincerity and courage] who had been Deputy Superintendent of Police and Deputy Collector in the United Provinces (Provincial) Service, and who was now 'lent' to his present office (Misra).[99] He was an 'enlightened' Brahmin of Lucknow whose nephews were being educated in America and England and whose son (aged 8) was destined for England. He described to us how he had felt his career in the Provincial Service baulked by being denied promotion owing to the places being reserved for Englishmen, although they could not say he was unfit; and how he consequently accepted the Maharaja's offer to make him Dewan although he would greatly prefer a Superintendentship of Police or a Collectorship in British India. Notwithstanding his present great power of executing improvements he did not like the attitude of servility to the Maharaja nor the uncertainty caused by the absolute rule of a capricious person.

He described to us also in detail how his official career was once nearly wrecked – [a] warrant for his deportation without trial may perhaps have actually been out – because a subordinate whom he had reported got a venal informer who had actually been convicted of forgery to lay a secret charge against him of having subscribed his name (as a donor of 20 rupees) to a fund for upsetting British rule. Elaborate secret enquiry was made by the highest officials and troops were even got ready. At last one of the officers confronted him with the charge and produced the incriminating document, which he denounced as a clumsy forgery. He fortunately got the officer to order an instant search of the informer's house where they found all the apparatus of forgery, which led to the conviction of the informer. It is clear that the U.P. Government was in the most credulous mood and prepared to swallow the most absurd delations. He had in his 18 months of Dewanship succeeded in greatly increasing the revenue, decreasing the waste and peculation and doubling the number of village schools. The state had been suffering for a decade from bad and incompetent Dewans, with the result that it had sunk near bankruptcy.

The Maharaja himself was rather a pathetic figure; a man of 45, sickly and weak, who had been married at 16 to the young daughter of a neighbouring little Maharaja like himself who had borne him no children and who (like his own mother) was superstitiously religious in Hindu fashion, and without education. He himself had had Theodore Morison[100] as tutor and had taken to reading Comte and Herbert Spencer and G. H. Lewes[101] (alternating with Marie Corelli).[102] Without children, without anyone to talk philosophy to, without friends, without faith, he had (we were told, and he almost confessed it to S.W.) taken to sexual malpractices and was profoundly unhappy and unable, as he said, to 'find peace'. He had found utterly useless the Anglican chaplain of the nearest cantonment. He went every year on Hindu pilgrimages (perhaps to please his ladies) but bathing in the sacred Ganges did not, he said, bring him peace of mind.

'Where can I find God?', he asked us. 'Where can I discover the ideal like Buddha or Jesus?' – 'How could Comte find this ideal in Clothilde de Vaux?'[103] he demanded at each of our three interviews. S.W. could only urge the way of work and duty and quote to him 'We live by admiration, hope and love'; B.W. captivated him by explaining the difference between science and religion – the one demanding a perpetual striving after making our order of thought correspond with the order of things; the other supplying the purpose of life to be gained by aspiration or communion or prayer whereby our order of thought in the realm of purpose is brought into harmony with a higher order of thought, the great spiritual force that we hope and trust is above and

behind all the worlds. He was familiar with translations of Plato and
Hegel, and had been satisfied with Spencer until G.H. Lewes'
materialism had sapped his faith. We could only recommend Bergson
and Father Tyrrell and William James[104] (which books he instantly
ordered from London) together with a sincere effort to do his duty by
the 160,000 subjects in his charge.

Certainly it was an odd position — to be recommending Bergson and
Father Tyrrell to a little Indian kinglet ruling over the area of an
English county in the most backward and secluded part of India, the
only white folk in the whole state. He was profusely grateful to us for
coming to see him and childishly eager to detain us longer. Poor
prince: he had no one to talk to, no one to confide in. It is a terrible
problem how to bring up these native rulers. They must have some
sort of education and once educated they can hardly escape an
intolerable loneliness. We wonder whether a determined man might
not make a Weimar out of a little Indian state, develop the best
possible high school, graft on to the local hospital a miniature medical
college and on to a state printing press and engineering works the
nucleus of a science faculty and technical institute — calling to him the
ablest men from all parts of India and thus at the same time making his
little principality a centre of intellect and securing congenial society for
himself. It might not cost more than dissipation or sport or building
extravagant palaces.

We accidentally met at the guest house the 'Political Agent', who
has charge of all the twenty-two ruling Chiefs of Bundelkhand under
the 'Agent to the Governor General' at Indore, who has responsibility
for all the states in the 'Central India Agency'. This 'political', an ex-
officer of the Indian Army (Colonel Impey),[105] was touring round
Bundelkhand with his sister and we had one evening together very
pleasantly. He was much more of the polished and cultivated
diplomatist than the typical Collector. It is interesting that when we
tried on him the suggestion of the 'Boy Scout' movement for India as
tending to give the boys manliness and vigour and discipline and
manners he instinctively objected lest it might lead to a demand for a
volunteering movement in India, or at any rate, to a training which
might one day be found dangerous to British rule! The question arises
always, are these officers really desirous of improving the character and
capacities of the people of India? Col. Impey (as we heard next day) is
to be the new Resident at Baroda, a great promotion for him.

We gather that the relation between the Government of India and
these Native States is a peculiar one. Practically nothing is published
about their goings on. (Col. Impey said that Tupper's 'Political Practice',
a secretly-printed official book in four volumes,[106] contained most

interesting precedents but that it was kept strictly confidential.) The relation varies with size and importance of the state. Those big enough to have separate Residents (like Hyderabad, Mysore, Kashmir, Baroda, etc.) were treated very carefully and not interfered with except in extreme cases. The smaller states were more summarily dealt with. They did not all have the power to inflict death sentences and most of them had to submit them for confirmation before they were carried out. The officer in charge of them was always open to receive petitions and complaints and these were either simply filed (if frivolous) or forwarded to the Dewan for him to act on as he chose (if unimportant) or else sent 'for favour of a report' (if they disclosed any *prima facie* injustice or malpractice). The 'political' would comment informally on anything bad in the way of administration that he noticed and might make suggestions for improvement in an unofficial way. But mere inefficient administration, mere customary peculation or waste, mere ordinary cases of capricious favouritism or injustice, mere common extravagance in expenditure, would not be interfered with any more than consistent lack of improvement, or personal immorality.

On the other hand, any glaring and serious tyranny of a gross kind, any actual bankruptcy of the state as well as serious, persistent, long-continued drunkenness in the ruler, led to summary deposition, the seating of the next heir on the throne and the deportation of the erring ruler to some obscure corner of India, there to live on a fixed allowance under the eye of a vigilant officer. The Maharaja of Datia, a neighbouring kinglet, had lately been deposed.[107] He was addicted to drink and used to extort money from his richest subjects. One unhappy victim went home and slew all his family and then committed suicide rather than comply with the tyrant's whims. This led to instant deposition.

The legal position is peculiar. These native rulers are in law independent sovereigns and their people are not British subjects. But they are under a definite suzerainty which deprives them of all foreign relations, defines and limits their criminal jurisdiction, prohibits wars and sets arbitrary bounds to the number and quality of their armed forces, receives complaints of their administration and actually entertains appeals against their action in internal affairs, keeps a tight hand on their raising loans, watches and to some extent controls visitors to their states and themselves, and makes them personally liable to trial and punishment — even to summary deposition at the hands of the British Government for gross maladministration, crime or grave misconduct.

In confirmation of our impression as to the idea of Boy Scouts for India, we have just learnt that one chaplain did start a corps but has been told by the Government of India *not* to recruit any further — the reason alleged being that it was not yet decided whether there should be an organisation for India or a branch of the English organisation — or (as we suspect) any at all! (See further confirmation from Sir Louis Dane at Lahore, March 3rd.)[108] [BW: Dane, L.G. of Punjab, who on B.W. suggesting Boy Scouts, said that he himself had favoured the idea & had actually praised the native rulers for starting Boy Scouts. The Government of India however had issued a confidential Minute to the L.G., ordering him not to encourage the est. of Boy Scouts & to disband any that had been started!]

BHOPAL 17th FEBy 1912

We have been two days in this state — about seven times as large and five times as populous as Chhatarpur — on the invitation of the Begum, an exceptionally energetic and enlightened ruler.[109] In the luxurious 'guest house' in which we were entertained we found an Anglican chaplain and his wife (Martin),[110] who were touring round their extensive 'parish' of many hundred square miles, in which he dealt only with the few Anglican Christians. He reflected the usual 'Army' prejudice against the 'niggers', which he owned to sharing though he was open-minded enough to recognise it. He said that discontent with English rule was universal and increasing and that there would be grave danger in the future. When it was put to him that the Government of India had no clear purpose he said it seemed to him that their purpose was to develop the Indian to manhood and nevertheless keep him in leading strings after attaining manhood! He admitted and defended the English race-exclusiveness whilst recognising its invidiousness. He approved of excluding Indians from the English clubs. The exclusion was occasionally relaxed for money. He related a case which he admitted to be one of rather mean behaviour, as to the new Club at Indore which is the seat of the Agent to the Governor General for all these Central India Native States. As the new building cost money, the Club Committee actually asked all the native rulers for donations which many of them gave, and these were then, with much heart-burning, personally and exceptionally admitted as members. It did not seem to strike him that any such application for donations under the very peculiar relations of the English officers with these native rulers was quite unwarrantable.

We have seen the jail, with a couple of hundred male and dozen female prisoners under the superintendence of the state Engineer, the son of a previous (Scotch) state Engineer. This prison was well-built and sanitary; the men prisoners were all (lightly) ironed and were at work in the open at carpet-weaving, gardening, the kitchen, and tile-making outside the walls. A large proportion (a quarter?) were under life sentences for murder and there were only five belonging to a criminal tribe. (We infer from these facts that mere petty theft does not usually lead to jail.)

Under the guidance of the energetic lady doctor employed by the Begum (Mrs. Dissent Barnes),[111] we inspected her own hospital for women and children, and also the men's hospital (under Dr. Sarabji, a Parsee). Syphilis is said to be almost universal and unnatural vice as well: there is, in fact, no idea of sexual morality among either Hindus or Muslims. The most interesting feature was the attempt to regulate midwifery. The Begum had ordered the *'dais'* or native midwives, who were to the last degree ignorant and superstitious, to attend classes held by the lady doctor; and the police were now stopping the practice in Bhopal city of any who had not received a diploma or who being qualified had been suspended (by the lady doctor) for malpractice or carelessness. We have heard of no such attempt in British India.

One thing we notice about all these Central India States — Chhatarpur, Bhopal, Gwalior and the intervening British territory — is the very large proportion of land lying waste and unproductive. Vast stretches of sparse scrub and bushes, plains covered with a scanty natural herbage of the coarsest kind, little bits of self-sown woodland of no pecuniary value, acre upon acre of boulder-strewn rock surface weathering into brick-making clay — all indicate that there is here at any rate no pressure of population on the soil. In Chhatarpur, for instance, the Dewan was fully conscious of the need for more population, which would actually increase the yield per head. Wells and tanks — even more than irrigation canals — would apparently well repay their cost. The Begum of Bhopal is reported to be keenly alive to this need but we did not learn what was being done. In Gwalior, much is being spent in irrigation by the state.

[BW→] We spent the afternoon with the Begum of Bhopal — at least we ladies did (the wife of the chaplain and two relations of officials and myself), Sidney and the other men being restricted to an hour's interview — during which Her Highness kept her veil down, just showing her eyes. The conversation was chiefly between the Begum and myself as the other ladies were shy; and before the afternoon was ended, we were on very friendly terms.

The Begum of Bhopal is the one woman among the native rulers of India and she is the third or fourth (?)[112] woman in succession in the State of Bhopal (the eldest child whether boy or girl inheriting the chieftainship). She is now an elderly woman with two grown-up sons

[SW: and another at the day school. She] has a great reputation as perhaps the most [SW: dutiful] and statesmanlike of the Indian Chiefs. And certainly her personality fully bears out her reputation. She is small and thick in stature, but when she threw back her veil on the departure of the men I was surprised and attracted by the strong fine features and humorous and kindly expression (somewhat like the portrait of George Eliot),[113] and with the total absence of any self-consciousness either as a woman or as semi-royalty. A wise old mother and an able business woman − not a bit of the great lady − clad in austerely simple garments − far more simple than those of the Muslim dames we afterwards met at her *purdah* club. She is obviously a masterful woman who is her own Prime Minister, having direct relations with each head of department. Her officials are devoted to her but they record that she checks every penny of expenditure and insists perhaps overmuch on getting full value for her money. We talked about women, their position and their education, about the education of Chiefs' sons, about the sphere of religion, about Turkey and Egypt and their reform movements, about European society. She has recently been on a tour, beginning with the Coronation in England and ending with her reception in Constantinople by the Sultan. She seemed to take the British Dominion for granted and to have an almost naïve respect for the King Emperor and the British Raj. But she did not wish the Indians or the followers of Islam 'Europeanised'. 'The English are very "habile" − Europeans know a great deal − when they are evil they are powerful for evil. If our young men go there when they are young they may get into bad hands, they may learn to abuse India and their own religion. I go to a house of a Duchess in England and see all the magnificence, and though I am an old woman, when I come back here I think my own palace very plain and I am tempted to abuse it.'

And certainly when one followed her eyes round the homely and almost bare room − more like the parlour of a very large farm house − one saw what she meant. So she was against Chiefs' sons being sent to England: she was dissatisfied with the Chiefs' colleges as too luxurious and not sufficiently advanced in learning − she wanted her sons to go to an Indian public school where they would have to compete with boys who were going to be Pleaders and medical men and civil servants and engineers. 'I want my youngest son to go into business so that the race may become rich'. About religion and its relations to the state she was depressed. 'Our *maulvis* are too conservative, they are against English education and science, and our clever young men despise them and throw off religion − that is not good. The young Turks abuse religion: we shall not prosper unless we are true followers of our Prophet.' Apparently, the old lady is a strong believer in Islam;

what money she can spare from the temporal wants of her people she is lavishing on a new mosque which is to be more magnificent than any at Delhi. But at the same time she refused to give to beggars and is a sworn critic of the idle *maulvis*. 'My mother used to give to beggars: I always send them away saying that "I pay teachers and doctors and nurses and not idle ones"'.

Her main preoccupation is the education of women. She wants the Muslim woman to become highly trained before she leaves off *purdah*. She even approves of *purdah* as a permanent institution – at any rate the modified *purdah* of never going unveiled among men. 'The Turkish ladies are breaking *purdah* before they are fit for it. They are reading bad French novels and they do what is wrong'. So she has started a first-rate girls' high school – said to be one of the best in India – and she is trying to educate the married ladies by a *purdah* club where they have lecturers and talks once a week. As to the position that women should occupy, her views are somewhat conflicting. She is dead against the suffrage movement but she thinks that *all rulers should be women*. 'My mother and my grandmother were rulers before me: I lost my two daughters and now a son will succeed me. It is a great misfortune. Men care for their pleasures; they must have sport and races. A woman ruler is the mother of her people: her whole life is spent in thinking what is best for them.' And she seems to have been as good as her word. Not merely in education but also in public health she has been more advanced than the Government of British India. Three English lady doctors and one Parsee medical man and an assistant are engaged in hospital and dispensary work at Bhopal. At present they are trying to educate the native midwife and the Begum has practically adopted the English Midwifes Act for Bhopal city. Any energy she has [left] over from the supervision of her Government she spends in translating English text-books and school books. 'I want to start a department at Bhopal for translating and publishing good books for all India in the vernacular – I have tried to get a clever young man to come and live here and do that work but I have not yet found one. What we want in India more than anything else are good books in Urdu and Hindi. You cannot teach children in a foreign language; they only pretend to understand what they read.'

She took us to the *purdah* club held in one of the old palaces. Here were some twenty Muslim and two Parsee ladies – the Hindus had not joined the club. With their bright coloured and elaborately embroidered satin leggings and soft silk gauze veils they made the dear old Begum with her cotton leggings and knitted woollen shawl look more than ever the wise old woman, too wise and careful about the good of other people to care how she looked herself. She was treated with

great deference, but with no kind of servility — more the difference
shown to age and knowledge than that shown to social position. She
chatted some half hour with them and then, as the lecturer failed to
come (a lady doctor who was to have lectured on 'First Aid' but who
was detained by the dangerous illness of an infant), she rose and left
saying that she must go back and do her gardening. For the Begum has
one or two relaxations — gardening, 'Sketching from Think' she calls it
(i.e., driving out and seeing something and then trying to reproduce it),
and playing on the piano with one finger tunes she had heard played
by the English teacher to her little grandsons. She has also adopted a
handsome little grand-daughter. I doubt not she would like to make her
the Begum — for quite clearly she adores her. The little girl is
extraordinarily handsome and intelligent looking — more like a north
Italian than a typical Hindu. Her youngest son's wife, a girl of 13 not
yet allowed to live with her husband, was also under the care of the
Begum and was being carefully educated.

FEB^y [SW: 17/19th] G[SW: WALIOR]

We are staying here in the hotel — we had no introduction to the
Maharaja, and the Political Agent to whom we had a letter was not
'on-coming'; but the Muslim Minister of Gwalior (an old pupil of
Theodore Morison) and the Hindu physician to the Maharaja to
whom we had a nationalist introduction, have been most kind and
helpful. Gwalior is the most wonderful Indian city that we have yet
seen. In all the cities of British India, the 'native city' is always
'slummy' in character — narrow alleys dirty and ill-paved, such fine
houses as there are tumbling into decay or degraded by being used as
warehouses or tenement houses. But at [SW: Bhopal], and still more at
Gwalior one finds broad streets, beautifully carved balconies, doors
and latticed windows, mosques and temples, old and new palaces, all
telling of the Indians in possession of their own country, making for a
civilised India 'without the English'. And so far, as one gets a glimpse
of the actual administration, one can hardly say that Indians show
themselves incapable of the art of government. Of course the officials
have often been educated in England or taken from the ranks of
Indians in the Government of India's service. But there is certainly no
sign of these officials being inherently weak or corrupt or partial
between creed and creed or caste and caste. In fact, in all of the three
native states that we have visited there has been no kind of tension
between Muslim and Hindu, and each ruler, Hindu or Muslim, has
officials of the other creed.

We were interested in talking to two energetic young Hindu business men, one of them having a workshop in Gwalior and another in Bombay and both of them being ardent nationalists, to learn that on the whole they preferred living under British rule to that of a native chief. 'We are more free in British India,' they both exclaimed, 'we can say more what we like and we know that there will be no arbitrary government. Here we can be imprisoned without appeal and tried in secret. We are not secure. Anything may happen.' The old physician, who was the uncle of one of them, disagreed – but then he was a court functionary. On the other hand, the Englishman who was acting as Director of Education preferred working in a Native State as he had more scope for initiative and was not tied down by rigid rules or limited by the necessity of elaborate reports to the Government of India.

We met at the Minister of Justice's house some half-dozen of the other Ministers [SW: all Hindu or Muslims except the Director of Education, though three out of the four Chief Engineers are English also.] One gathered from them that the Maharaja, an active man of thirty-five,[114] is a good administrator and really concerned to make improvements. His palace and beautiful gardens are open to everyone, and from the tasteful and sober internal decorations of both the public and private rooms one would gather than he is a man of refinement. He pays great attention to the performance of religious rites and keeps Muslim as well as Hindu festivals. Just now his domestic affairs are in a state of confusion. His present wife has borne him no children – his subjects desire his re-marriage and he himself is courting the daughter of the Gaekwar of Baroda. But the young lady is making elaborate conditions – she refuses to keep *purdah,* insists on six months in Europe and even, so reports say, demands the key of the treasury besides a written guarantee that any boy of hers shall succeed to the throne.[115] Meanwhile there is a left-handed lady who is doing her best to stop the marriage, though the legitimate wife – a pious and popular woman – has given her consent to the Maharaja's second marriage. Altogether one imagines that the palaces of the native rulers are veritable hotbeds of intrigue – usually revolving round a woman. [SW→] As a contrast to the elaborately civilised palace and capital city of the Maharaja, there came a glimpse of his mental attitude towards his deceased father. That potentate, long since dead, is still treated as living. In a palatial tomb on the outskirts of the city his life-sized statue in black marble sits on a couch, fully dressed in his royal habiliments. On either side is said to sit similarly attired a statue of his two wives; but these were behind a *purdah* so we did not see them. Before him twice a day is spread a varied repast, which is offered by attendant Brahmins with appropriate incantations. And every evening in the great hall below his raised chamber there is performed, from six to eight p.m., an entertainment for his delectation of singing and music and (we were told) dancing. The whole daily celebration is organised and performed by a hundred Brahmins. It was not the Minister of Justice who told us this – he seemed a little ashamed of it and refused to accompany us though he kindly sent us in his carriage. Nor is it mentioned in the guide book. But the hotel keeper put us on the track of it. Certainly the scene was strange. Putting off our shoes, we ascended steps in the dark to the great hall which we found brilliantly lighted. Four performers (three men and a gaily-dressed girl) were singing and playing as if to the Maharaja, whose black figure one saw in the raised inner chamber, before which a great sculptured bull was kneeling. Inside the Brahmins were offering food, chanting sentences, and lighting incense. A score or so of other persons, presumably Brahmins, sat around and listened to the weird music. Day by day this barbarous rite is repeated.

AGRA 19/23rd FEBy [1912]

The wonderfully beautiful buildings here[116] – far more beautiful than we had ever imagined, of a charm and grace that no photograph gives any idea of – compel the reflection that only 250 years ago these people were capable of conceiving and executing work of quality unsurpassed by anything of any race in the world. Not only in conception and design, but also in craftsmanship, the Indians of the Mughal Court (1550–1650) stand unrivalled. In England at that date we were building St. John's College, Oxford and the Banqueting Hall at Whitehall, and to this day we have no building which in grace and charm and beauty of design or workmanship comes anywhere near the work of these 'niggers', as the Army officer calls them. It is clearly a case for the recognition of 'reciprocal superiority' as the proper mental attitude between races.

[BW →] And from some of these beautiful creations of Indian art – the mosques and palaces inside the Fort – all 'natives' are excluded since the Mutiny unless they procure a special pass – though all Europeans, foreigners as well as English, go in and out as they choose without let or hindrance. This is all the more detestable as Indians delight in visiting famous and beautiful places, and their behaviour at the Taj[117] or at the ancient city [SW: Fatehpur Sikri][118] where we graciously admit them without question, are most decorous and even reverential.

We spent a morning with the John brothers [SW: Sir Edwin John and Mr. Ulysses John], the great capitalists of Agra employing 7000 workpeople in cotton and corn mills and miscellaneous works such as ice-factory, brick-fields, etc.[119] This family is of Greek (?) origin (some say Eurasian) and R.C. religion. It claims to have been settled here for over one hundred years, always marrying Europeans, usually British women. Sir Edwin John and his brother were real 'bounders' – self-indulgent and commonplace – but apparently energetic and enterprising in investing their money to win. We saw most of the younger brother who took us over the mills, and after a sumptuous lunch in a luxurious bungalow drove us out to [SW: the Dowla Tomb, across the Jumna.][120]

He and his brother had the most unutterable contempt for the Indians – Hindu and Muslim – and quite clearly thought that their right position was that of slaves who could be beaten if they did not work. In the course of our conversation I hardly think there was one bad quality that they did not accuse them of. And – though their most acid criticism was reserved for the educated native ('a damnable mistake to educate the native') – they were equally angry with the cultivator and the coolie. 'We employ no natives in positions of responsibility – they all [SW: rob] and lie and cheat. Come to the mills and see for yourself how the native works – he never works more than 4 hours in the 24 and he is away every other day.'

And certainly the scene at the mills seemed to give colour to their statement. At some building operations not a single man had turned up at 9:30, the unfortunate contractor saying that they had all absented themselves without notice, he supposed to attend a wedding! In shed after shed half the mechanics were idle. We learnt afterwards that a quarter to a third of all the hands had not turned up during the whole day. In some cases the machines were running without an attendant and the output was littering the floor. For it was not only a case of absentees – the men and boys who were there were in many cases sitting outside the mill or eating or sleeping near their machines. In one case a youth was fast asleep between two looms. After several kicks from Mr. John he started up and with the usual servile attitude of folded hands remarked that he 'had not slept last night' – another way of saying that he had been amusing himself! All the hands seemed in fact to be deliberately skulking and even wasting the material and their attitude was hostile and sulky.

It must be added that John swore and cursed them and would have struck them if he had not feared the consequences. 'They put us into court if we try to punish them – and if we scold them, they simply don't turn up the next day.' 'Oh! it is cruel,' he went on saying. 'Look at them, they are eating all day, and when they are not eating they are gambling or smoking or sleeping.' When I asked which were the worst, the Muslim or the Hindu, he replied that 'the Muslim could work if he chose – two Muslims would any day put an end to 20 Hindus. But then, he was a real 'budmash',[121] he stole and he lied. The Hindu had usually no brains – when he had brains, he was far too clever, and cheated and lied'.

We tried to find out on what method these hands were paid – he told us they were all paid piece-work but the Scotch foreman told Sidney that only one man out of nine [SW: the chief 'minder' of the self-acting mule] was paid piece-work, the rest (i.e. piecers) were on a daily wage. In fact, all John's statements were vague and inaccurate. He told us that 4000 out of the 6000 were boarded and lodged in a compound but when we went to inspect it turned out that they were only given cheap rooms [SW: paying 4 to 6 annas per month rent] – he had apparently not understood our question. The families living in these houses – or rather holes – looked as sulky and hostile as the hands in the mill. They were all low castes, John Brothers refusing to employ Brahmins *in any capacity*, 'if they knew it', apparently because they thought Brahmins were centres of sedition against the Johns' firm and the British Raj.

One interesting sidelight they gave us – Japan was becoming a formidable competitor in cotton piece-goods in Calcutta because of the *first-rate quality* of her cloth. They had a great admiration of the Japanese business man.

They were bitter critics of the liberal policy of the present administration, but curiously enough they talked just like nationalists about 'the drain'[122] and said that India was better off before railways made the export of corn easy. From the John brothers' bad tempers I should gather that their enterprises are not going well and that the rebuilding of Delhi is making their labour market even more unsatisfactory than usual.[123] What is quite clear is that these old-standing European inhabitants of India have not acquired the art of managing the Indians. What is equally clear is that the Indian is sometimes an extraordinarily difficult worker *to sweat*.[124] He does not care enough for his earnings. He prefers to waste away in semi-starvation rather than overwork himself. However low his standard of life his standard of work is lower – at any rate when he is working for an employer whom he does not like. And his irregularities are baffling.

[SW→] (At Gwalior, the wages of highly-skilled stone carvers and painters were 8 annas per day (15 rupees per month). In Agra a *punkah* coolie[125] who used to get only 3 to 4 rupees a month now gets 6 rupees a month, which is 3 annas a day.)

We had, in Gorakhpur, jumped at the chance of attending a Hindu wedding which Gokal Prasad, an Assistant Magistrate of the Provincial

Service, was going to attend at Agra on 20th February. We heard no
more of it; but on the morning of the 20th no fewer than six members
of the family, introduced by Gokal Prasad himself, called upon us and
formally invited us to come at 8 p.m. There were various weddings
going on – the season is the favourite one – and the Indian city was
alight here and there with primitive illuminations. Avoiding with some
difficulty a great *bunnia*[126] wedding, we at length reached the house to
which we had been invited, the whole street being lit up with primitive
oil lamps. Entering the courtyard we found it covered by a huge
awning and arranged with long tables for the two or three hundred
guests. Presently the bridegroom's procession arrived, the bridegroom
himself arrayed in the customary gorgeous robes and bearing on his
head the gilt and jewelled crown appropriate to his position. He as an
intellectual-looking, spectacled young man of pleasing countenance, an
assistant civil surgeon of Delhi, who had brought with him forty or
fifty men friends.

This was a wedding of a Kayastha[127] family and the Kayasthas have
made for themselves a reforming regulation limiting the number of
guests introduced by the bridegroom at their weddings. We understood that there were three classes limited to 75, 50 and 40 guests
respectively (or something like that) and this particular family had
elected for the second class. The bridegroom had so far never seen the
bride, who had of course been selected for him by the negotiations of
the two families. The bridegroom was seated on the seat of ceremony,
and half-a-dozen Brahmins performed the *'darwaza'*[128] ceremony,
which consisted in the presentation to him of various things including
some family presents and much recitation of Sanskrit formulae. The
odd thing was that this was not made in any way a central feature. It
was done in a corner of the covered courtyard whilst the guests sat at
the long tables and ate and talked, paying no attention to the
ceremony – even a gramophone was playing hideous Hindu tunes
part of the time.

After this was over we went upstairs and had refreshments apart
from the crowd and B.W. was taken inside to see the women, including
the bride, most of them never having seen at close quarters any
European woman. The actual marriage ceremony at which the bride
would be presented to the bridegroom was not to take place until 2
a.m., that being the hour pronounced by the Brahmins to be auspicious
according to the horoscopes of the parties. These people were all of the
Kayastha caste, mostly in the Government service or Pleaders They
sliuck us as extremely intellectual, refined and courteous – in their own
way highly civilised – but both unwilling and unable to free
themselves from superstitious uses and the conventions which in

India are both social and religious. Some however had joined the *Arya Samaj*.

[BW→] The women of the family were introduced to B.W. in the refreshment room (their quarters, which I had peeped into, were merely dark bedrooms) by one of the English-speaking men of the family; he had however to retire when the younger women appeared, and his place was taken by a relative of the second generation, but even he had to turn his back before I could speak to the wife of the third generation. The women were prettily-dressed and looked happy and intelligent. The bride was [an] especially pleasant-looking little girl of 13 – she was not yet in bridal dress, as that had to be put together at the last moment.

[SW→] At the wedding, an *Arya Samaj* member had pressed us to attend a meeting or service of the Agra branch of that organisation, which we agreed to do the day after tomorrow. They seem thereupon to have hastily summoned a special meeting and at 5 p.m. six members, including the secretary, came to the hotel with carriages to fetch S.W. to the function. (Whether or not they expected B.W. also is not clear but she was too tired to go.) The meeting place was a small plain house having a large paved courtyard in which, under a wide awning, the meeting took place. Something like 150 men were squatting down under this awning facing a table and three chairs. But first four of them went and sat apart facing each other and gradually made a fire in their midst, piling on stick after stick and then pouring on salt and clarified butter and incense, the whole being accompanied by Sanskrit recitations and incantations. This was 'havan', a ceremony prescribed for morning and for the beginning of every service or meeting according to the prescription of the Vedas. It was expressly explained to be no more than an act of purification of the atmosphere, the substances burnt having purifying qualities with the purpose of remedying as far as practicable the involuntary fouling of the atmosphere which human life involves.

Here again what was noticeable was that it was only a 'sideshow'. It was not made the central feature of the service but went on in a corner of the compound without the waiting crowd (squatted under the awning) even turning round to look at it. Presently one of the crowd arose in obedience to a call from the chairman, and recited a long Sanskrit prayer or invocation from the Vedas. Then another man read an essay entitled 'Is God a Reality?' in English, proving the existence, the omnipotence, the omnipresence and the permanence of God, a paper of no intellectual value or logical strength. Finally, after brief speeches of welcome of S.W. and reply by him, the meeting terminated with another Sanskrit recitation. It was noticeable that every quotation from the Vedas was chanted or intoned, never spoken naturally.

The meeting consisted almost entirely of intellectual-looking, cultivated *young* men under 30 or so, there being only half-a-dozen grey heads among the whole hundred and fifty. This was explained by the hour of meeting, arranged for S.W.'s convenience, being too early to allow of attendance by men in business or Government service, so that the bulk of those present were said to be the student class or else superannuated persons. It was remarkable that such a meeting should have been got together at such short notice. They were obviously devout and apparently full of sincerity and zeal. At one point a dozen little children were brought in, being some of the orphans that the society had rescued from death and undertaken to support and educate. Each member pays 1 per cent of his income as subscription.

We saw in Agra at dinner or otherwise four civilians – Reynolds,[129] who was just handing over charge as Commissioner on final retirement owing to age limit; Mardon,[130] Collector, who received temporary charge as Commissioner, F. C. Chamier,[131] Joint Magistrate about to act as Collector, and Dacres[132] (cousin to Sir Sidney Olivier),[133] a youthful Assistant-Magistrate. Reynolds was old and worn out by 34 years' service and seemed a routine person, 'wooden' and uninteresting. Chamier was a young man of charm and refinement, somewhat silent and modest but apparently able and sympathetic. Dacres, on the other hand, was a mere 'Society' rattle, a handsome, well-dressed youth interested in nothing but dancing and sport, snobbish in opinion and anti-Indian in prejudice, who served to remind us that even among the youngest and newest civilians there are some who have all the class and racial prejudices of the worst of the old generation.

HARDWAR 24/26th FEB[y] [1912]

Our three days here as the guest of R.C. Hobart[134] (a sub-divisional officer virtually acting as Collector of this sub-division of 350,000 inhabitants under the nominal supervision of the Collector of Saharanpur) have been full of interest. We stay with him in the 'Municipal Bungalow', a building erected for his accommodation when visiting Hardwar (from Rurki, his headquarters) as chairman of the municipality.

Hardwar is an immense pilgrimage centre though just now only a few are coming. We went first to see the *gurukula*,[135] a college established by the *Arya Samaj* for education according to the prescriptions of the Vedas. The boys enter at 7 years old and they must remain until 25, never once visiting their homes or families or their native villages, and living day and night under the closest scrutiny of and in company with their teachers. The idea as explained is to protect them against the polluting influences of the world including the average Hindu home! No woman is even allowed to see the boys and B.W. had to stay outside until they had been carefully packed away. Their parents are allowed to visit them, not more than once a month, but such visits are not encouraged except at long intervals or in emergencies. The institution has been started only some 15 years so that the effect of this 18 years' rigid monasticism cannot yet be seen. Two youths however are being this year 'graduated as M.A.' and finished, they having started 15 years ago at a somewhat higher age than 7. The greatest attention is paid to personal character; a teacher sleeps with the boys in each dormitory, eats with them at each meal and plays games with them. (Nevertheless, during the year 23 are noted in the medical report which S.W. saw as suffering from 'onanism and debility'.)

The curriculum is a carefully-planned combination of Sanskrit language, the Vedas, Vedic logic and philosophy, on the one hand, and English, western philosophy and elementary science on the other. There was a really extensive library including good collections of English philosophy (and English translations of German, Greek and French) – they had Bergson's *Creative Evolution* for instance, though it was only just published, and it was actually being read by one of the teachers – and also of English and American economics and history. There were chemical and physical laboratories, and a practical elementary knowledge of chemical, physical and mechanical processes seemed to be imparted. The lectures were given in Hindi, the English and Sanskrit books being used for reference and independent reading. The teachers, who all seemed to give their services free (or for bare subsistence), appeared generally intelligent and zealous.

Altogether we were much impressed by the place. It was stated that it was hoped that the students would become *Arya Samaj* missionaries and lecturers or teachers in similar institutions. They were all nominally admitted gratuitously and maintained out of the donations and subscriptions of the members; but money was taken from wealthy parents, in the beginning actually as fees and now in the guise of donations, this fact being bitterly complained of as inconsistent with the Vedas by their critics and rivals, as all learning ought to be imparted freely to anyone. This institution has been in the past an object of the most absurd Government suspicion and has been watched by police to see if it was not secretly drilling the boys and training an army!

The Government seems to have been unable to understand why so much devotion should be put into an educational institution and it certainly presents a contrast with the Government colleges or with

Aligarh, with their exclusively English teaching, total absence of personal supervision of the boys at night, practical freedom to come and go at will, government by masters of an alien race and creed, and (except at Aligarh) complete secularity and absence of religion and a curiously superstitious reliance on the games and prefectoral system copied from 'the English public school'!

They boys looked exceptionally healthy and happy. During the whole 15 years only 20 out of the 300 had been lost by expulsion or resignation. Over 200 applied for admission this year though only 20 could be admitted. And one at any rate of the two new 'graduates', who was to become a professor in the college, seemed a very charming and promising youth (who proposed to spend a year in England). The other, less prepossessing, was already editing his father's vernacular newspaper with, it was said, remarkable success.

Another day we visited two rival institutions set up in the same place in opposition to the *gurukula*. One, the Mahavidialey at Jawalapur, was also *Arya Samaj* and we could discover no assignable ground for its establishment or its hostility. Its fifty or sixty boys were being taught nothing but Sanskrit language and philosophy (though other subjects were said to be going to be added) and it was being run by a dismissed Hindu Sub-Inspector of Police, Atma Ram,[136] a man of bad character and unpleasing servility of manner. Its domestic arrangements were as good as those of the *gurukula* but the teaching seemed very poor; there was no library or laboratory and the note of personal devotion seemed lacking. The other was an imitation started by the orthodox Hindus in opposition to the *Arya Samaj*, with exclusively Sanskrit and Vedantic teaching without English or science. It was only a few years old and perhaps other subjects will be added later, as the boys grow up. It was important only as showing how the *Arya Samaj* is stimulating Hinduism to rivalry.

We had a long day on the Upper Ganges, going by train and carriage ten or fifteen miles up stream and then walking three miles along its banks amid the huts of the *sadhus* and the '*dharmsalas*', or pious lodging houses erected for their accommodation. These *sadhus* come and live here in the cold weather and migrate to Hardwar in the rains and travel further down to Muttra, etc. in the autumn. They seemed to us, in their simple reed huts, to be enjoying a pleasant holiday camp and not in the least to be meditating! Some were nearly naked and smeared with ashes, generally half-stupefied with hemp; others were clothed in yellow robes and seemed fat and jovial. At Lakmansjula Bridge we embarked on *saknais* to float down stream for five hours, shooting innumerable rapids. These are simply the hides of *nilgais*,[137] a horse-like cow, inflated with air and the holes tightly

fastened up. An Indian 'charpoy' or bedstead is laid across two of them
and thus a safe raft is made, so buoyant that it rises on every wave.
Two men, each astride his own nilgai, floated on either side and
holding on to the raft by their hands moved their legs in the water like
paddle-wheels. Thus mounted, we floated down the stream only a few
inches above the water from 1.30 to 6.30 p.m., going through gorges,
past wide shallows and down the most alarming rapids, disturbing
flights of hundreds of small black herons, wild duck, beautiful swifts
and other river fowl — finally getting into an iron rowing-boat with a
picturesquely attired crew of five men to be rowed swiftly in the
gloaming past the lengthy esplanade of Hardwar itself, with its lofty
lodging houses for pilgrims, its lighted temples and its long bathing
ghats — just in time for S.W. to dress and go to dinner with no fewer
than eight officers of the irrigation service, most of whom had met here
to consult as to how to make a great dam across the Ganges in order
to impound more water for their canals.

[BW→] We omitted to give any account of our brief visit to Aligarh
College. This College was started by a great Muslim leader [SW: Sir
Syed Ahmed][138] as the first English educational institution for Muslim
wealthy men's sons. One of the first Principals was our friend
Theodore Morison. Now it has 1000 pupils and will be the centre
round which the new Muslim University will grow. We had heard that
there had been trouble between the English Principal and the Muslim
teachers, owing to 'strikes' among the boys and the complaints of
parents leading to the resignation of the late Principal Mr. Archbold,[139]
and we understood that the college was no longer what it used to be.

We saw very little of the boys as we came on a Friday, the Muslim
Sabbath. But the Principal, with whom we stayed, drove us round the
buildings and talked extensively to us. The buildings are scattered over
a large site and make any kind of discipline with regard to coming and
going of boys wholly impracticable. Mr. [SW: Towle] did not seem to
us the right sort of man to be head of a big institution. In appearance
and in manner and still more in conversation he was a colourless,
evasive person. One could quite believe what we afterwards heard on
good authority, that he had lacked loyalty to his chief and had in fact
been chosen to succeed Archbold just because he had offered to do
anything that the trustees decided on. He was full of discreet but bitter
criticisms of the trustees, of the boys, of their parents, of Muslims and
indeed of India and its inhabitants. He was in fact a hireling — perhaps a
conscientious hireling — and no doubt fairly capable of the job of
getting boys through examinations — but lacking any kind of personal
influence over his staff or his scholars. So when we saw at Lahore a
leading Muslim, who was a trustee of the College and would be largely

concerned in appointing the Principal of the new University, we begged him to select a man of personality as Principal, and we suggested Hope Simpson. [SW: Towle] was only another instance of the poor kind of personality that is in the Indian educational administration.

At Hardwar we saw a great deal of two Indian officials, one the Secretary of the municipality, and the other the M.O.H.[140] Both these men were Brahmins and belonged to the orthodox school though approving much of the *Arya Samaj*, and both were particularly upright and intelligent — zealous — wholly devoid of servility or even of 'plausibility'. The Secretary of the municipality told me that he could not join the *Arya Samaj* because they neglected the worship of ancestors and advocated inter-caste marriage but that he was wholly with them in their objection to *sadhus* and to idolatry, and in their strenuous puritanism. He though Hindu society was on the whole improving, though he feared that *family obligation* was disappearing even before the larger public spirit, which should take its place, had developed. He did not believe that at present there was sufficient public spirit to run local government satisfactorily, leave alone provincial or national government. 'At present every Indian is for himself and his family — he cares little for the public good; he does not even understand what you mean by it. He understands family obligation and religious obligation. But the idea that he has any duty towards persons because they inhabit the same town or country is strange to him. Indians who have had an English education or who have mixed with Englishmen are getting this idea; but it is only limited to a few.'

The [SW: Hobart] brothers (one a civilian [SW: acting as sub-divisional officer, i.e. virtually as Collector for the Rurki sub-division under the nominal supervision of the collector of the whole Saharanpur district], the other an officer in the R.[SW: E.][141] (acting with a native engineer regiment) with whom we stayed for [SW: three] nights, were exceptionally sympathetic to Indians and men of great personal charm. The civilian brother (Charterhouse and Oxford) was able and energetic though somewhat hasty — even slightly scatter-brain. They had been born and bred in Indian public service either military or civilian, and though conservative in home politics, were extraordinarily appreciative and evidently much beloved by their respective Indian subordinates. After Hope Simpson, Hobart, the sub-divisional officer for Hardwar and Rurki district, is the best civilian we have met for the executive work of a district.

[SW→] At Amritsar we stayed only for the middle of a day, primarily to see the extraordinarily picturesque Sikh Golden Tem-

ple.[142] We were taken over it by a Hindu Fabian (Mabeshwarry), a
Rajputana *'bunnia'* by caste who was a barrister and an orthodox
Hindu. He (who had been in England and had joined the F.S. through
the South London Ethical Society[143] – he had lodged with Gunning,
then Assistant Secretary to the A.S.E.[144]) and his cousin, the leader of
the local Bar, were the first of the *'bunnia'* or trader class whom we had
consciously met to talk to. These two at any rate were quite
distinguishable from the Brahmins and Kayasthas: keen and alert
intelligence without aristocratic distinction, as if sharpened by generations of money-lending and trading. He was the first of the
Mabeshwarry clan or section of the caste to go to England and he
had not yet quite overcome that venture, several of his caste fellows
still refusing to meet him, though most had done so. He thought it
important to walk warily and to be very conciliatory to them or else no
other member of the clan would practically be able to enjoy the
advantages of English education. He had therefore remained strictly
orthodox, and did not favour the *Arya Samaj*. He was interested to
point out the multitude of orthodox Hindu shrines and images all
around the Sikh temple as demonstrating that the Sikhs were really
only a section of the Hindus.

After visiting his law office and his cousins he took us, at our
request, to a wholesale dealer in Cashmere shawls, up a narrow stair to
an upper-storey of a house in the crowded 'bazaar' street, the
establishment of a family of Bikaner Jains[145] who had many tens of
thousands of pounds worth of stock in that flimsy building, unpro-
tected (as we learnt on enquiry) by fire insurance. Here we turned over
beautiful things and bought a shawl and a tablecloth for under £10 on
his assurance that these were lowest net wholesale prices. The
headquarters of the firm is in Bikaner in the Rajputana Desert; they
have hundreds of Cashmere families virtually in their employment,
making them advances, and collecting from them periodically their
handwoven products.

We then went to tea with a Muslim Member of the Punjab
Legislative Council (whom Mabeshwarry declared to be an almost
penniless person who supported himself, in all probability, by the gifts
made him in the believe that he had influence with the Government –
but this was we imagine merely the *nouveau riche bunnia's* way of
suspecting everyone of destitution who is not plainly wealthy). This
dignified and courteous old gentleman sent a good carriage for us and
lived in a spacious flat above a narrow street in the native city. He had
the good common sense shrewdness of the educated Muslims but did
not show any particular ability or distinction. We learnt from
Mabeshwarry what no one English or Indian had so far told us, that

there exists throughout India a network of local associations of *sadhus* of orthodox Hinduism, each place having its own independent society and the whole being in some way affiliated to a society at Benares of which the wealthy Maharaja of Dhurbanga is president. This organisation has for its object the protection of the interests of Hindus and Hinduism; it evidently was in antagonism with the *Brahmo Samaj* and the *Arya Samaj* and it has incidentally maintained asylums for decrepit old cows which are thus saved from death!

LAHORE 29th FEB[y] – 3rd MARCH 1912

Arriving at Lahore at 6 p.m. we were met, to our surprise, by Rambaj Dutt Chaudhuri,[146] the *Arya Samaj* Pleader whom we had met at Calcutta and whose wife we had so much admired. It is all part of the extraordinary politeness and courtesy of these educated Indians of all sections. As we preferred to stay at an hotel rather than with him or with English officials so as to be free to see all sides, and as his wife was temporarily absent, we have spent hours with him, driving to the sights. He has been president and is still vice-president of the head or central branch of the *Arya Samaj,* and his clever wife, we believe, conducts some vernacular journal. But a certain simplicity of character and plain honesty of purpose, even to naïvety, has perhaps saved him from prosecution, though he went on a lecturing tour to England. He is quite convinced that the *Arya Samaj* is the true religion and the only one and that, without limitation of race or colour or creed, all the world will one day come over to it. To him it is not specially a Hindu or an Indian religion, though incidentally, he is a strong nationalist. He has thrown himself with energy into its philanthropic side, busying himself in forming many local branches or societies having for their object the raising up of the 'untouched' castes, the maintenance of orphans and the management of elementary and other schools. All this perplexes the English official who cannot believe that it has not some underlying political motive. [BW→] Without being personally bitter, he is estranged from the Government of India and regards the Punjabi officials as hostile to the race in education and self-reliance. He mentioned that the words underneath the statue of Lord Lawrence, 'Will you be governed by the sword or the pen', had given dire offence to Indians – the students of the university refusing to walk in that part of the gardens. We tried to explain that here they had taken offence without reason, the saying exemplifying the preference of the Englishman for civil over military government. But he clearly believed that the emphasis was entirely on the word 'governed' and that it was meant to signify that Indians had to submit to one or other form of the British Raj.[147]

We have had two long talks with Lajpat Rai,[148] a member of the *Arya Samaj* who was actually 'deported' without trial on suspicion of 'tampering with the native troops'. He is a short, thick-set man with a bullet-shaped head, bright, intelligent expression and somewhat thick lips and dark colour. A *bunnia* by caste (trading caste), and Pleader by profession, he is quite clearly an agitator by preference. He has not an attractive personality — though he is pleasant-tempered and open-minded, he has at times an unpleasant expression of successful intrigue. He looks [SW: a *bunnia*!]. With us he was apparently quite frank in his denunciations of the Government — especially the Punjab Government for its arbitrary proceedings and persistent desire to suppress the development of the race. He instances their suppression in the schools of the teaching of English history on the one hand, and their steady prohibition of any heroic history of early Indian civilisation. 'They want to withdraw any subject that might stimulate the courage and patriotism of the Hindu — whether it is the love for his own race and religion or his growing desire for western political freedom.'

In their colonisation policy of the lands rendered fertile by irrigation, in all their land legislation, Lajpat Rai contended that the B.G. had legislated with the express object of excluding the Hindu as compared with the Muslim from the ownership and occupation of land. They suppressed free speech and free press — tried in every way to emasculate Indian life. They threatened officials who belonged to the *Arya Samaj* and persecuted private persons who preached the doctrine, the police always telling the people that the Government would be angry if they attended the meetings and sent the children to the schools. About the religious side of the *Arya Samaj* Lajpat Rai seemed more or less indifferent, except that it freed the people from superstitions and fanaticism.

The second morning he brought another *Arya Samaj bunnia* — a more spiritual-minded man — and with him we discussed the prospects of *Arya Samaj* as a proselytising religion. I suggested that nowadays it was difficult to maintain the Infallibility of the Book: and the fact that it had originated in the dim and distant past did not increase its authority: and that the absolute reliance of the *Arya Samaj* on the inspiration of the Vedas above and beyond that of all other scriptures would eventually alienate the most intellectual Hindu from the *Arya* creed. The reply was that every Hindu was born and bred to faith in the Vedas and that the infallibility and comprehensiveness of the Vedic teaching was always assumed. We also suggested that in Hinduism in general, and even in the writings of the *Arya Samaj*, there was little or no direct teaching of *conduct* — nothing comparable to the Ten Commandments or to the Sermon on the Mount. 'We assume that a man who has reached a certain stage of spiritual development will necessarily be moral — all our effort is to get to this stage by spiritual exercise. If the modern Hindu lacks conduct — and we admit that he does — it is because he has departed from the truth of the Vedas and has become an idol-worshipper.'

There was in their conversation the usual reference to 'spiritual science' and 'knowledge' — by which they always mean a sort of mystical metaphysics or metaphysical mysticism. And they were quite assured that the ancient Hindus had a sort of monopoly of spiritual development and that all other races and creeds were what they called 'primitive' — a stage in which 'ethics frequently submerged true religion'. We are struggling with books and pamphlets — mostly highly controversial — explanatory of the doctrine of the *Arya Samaj*; but to us they are very unreadable, as they are elaborate explanations of [SW: every] apparent inconsistency or blemish in the Vedas and long arguments as to the *Truth* of all the dogmas — very much in the style of the commentary on the Bible by the old-fashioned evangelists who believed in the literal inspiration of the Christian scriptures. The only difference is that these Vedic 'Protestants' have read the theology and the criticisms of the Christians and use quotations with considerable skill and plausibility — they are in fact far more cosmopolitan in their culture than the analogous people among the Christian races. I doubt whether this side of the *Arya Samaj* will survive — visitors half-suggested that the time had not arrived when patriotic Hindus could afford to indulge in the 'Higher Criticism'! To fight orthodox Hinduism they must offer something that was equally dogmatic and exclusive — faith in the absolute inspiration of the Vedas.

On our way to Peshawar we stopped off at [SW: Gujranwala] in order to attend the conference of the *Arya Samaj* at this *gurukula*. The ceremony had that strangely informal, even disorderly picturesqueness characteristic of Hinduism. Round the purifying fire were squatted the little boys clothed in yellow with shaved heads, who were being 'instructed'! An outer circle of older boys (with hair intact and more ordinary costumes) were acting as a sort of chorus in the responses. A Brahmin instructor was reading passages out of the Vedas and he and some of the boys were pouring *'ghee'*[149] or throwing sweet-smelling wood and herbs into the fire. Meanwhile, some twenty mothers clad in white seated on a raised platform were talking with each other; some 100 male parents, visitors and governors of the *gurukula* seated European-fashion on chairs, were on the other side — the space between the men and the women being filled by *Arya Samaj* converts from the 'Untouchables' who were thus listening to the Vedas and taking part in the ceremonies from which they would be rigidly excluded by orthodox Hindus.

The ceremony consisted in the vows of chastity, obedience and 'self-study' during the eight years residence at the *gurukula* — the boys being given a symbolic cord wherewith to gird up their loins (signifying activity), and a staff to protect them from wild animals when they went out into the jungle 'to relieve nature' instead of making use of fellow human beings as 'sweepers' to remove night-soil! The boys then went round the company 'begging their bread' — a very perfunctory ceremony performed in memory of the old Vedic doctrine of the vow of poverty of the learned ones.

This *gurukula* only takes boys up to the age of 16 and though it separates them from their parents for eight years, it does not prevent the parents from visiting them. The boys are supervised closely by a tutor (for every 25) day and night — the instruction seems inferior to that of the Hardwar *gurukula*, less money being forthcoming. The headmaster, with whom we had a long talk, was a young spiritual-minded intellectual (favourite philosopher, William James) — a charming personality, disinterested and refined. The Principal was an elderly man who had retired from the Government service in order to devote the whole of his energies (unpaid) to the establishment and working-up of this *gurukula* — a strong man of sturdy independence — rather the type of the 18th century Quaker.

After the ceremony of initiation there was a religious address by a young '*guru*' — of the simple, spiritual type — and a fervent address by an able young official of the Baroda Government, an Inspector of Schools who had sent two of his boys to the *gurukula*. We could not understand either the one or the other, but as was clear from the wrapt attention of some 200 persons, including the 50 Untouchables, the address was eloquent and persuasive. A collection was afterwards taken and a list of contributors of large sums given, making some [SW: 2000 rupees (much of it, by the way, in sovereigns, showing how these are getting into circulation).] We talked with some other of the professors and governors and were shown round the buildings and given tea and fruit in a tent set apart for us. Like the [SW: Hardwar] *gurukula*, there was the same note of disinterested devotion and patriotism — but as an educational institution, it hardly looked efficient.

At Peshawar and again at Lyallpur, we heard a good deal about the *Arya Samaj*. Every British administrator fears it as a political force. The Chief Engineer at Lyallpur told us that practically all his Indian officials and contractors were *Arya Samaj* and had managed to raise rates — wages and tenders — by at least 30% owing to their solidarity. He told us, too, something about the '*Hindu Sahib*' — a purely political organisation started by the *Arya Samaj* to unite all Hindus in one body. A very intelligent Muslim, a Government Pleader who came to see us at Lyallpur, also complained that the *Arya Samaj* was now trying to *consolidate* Hinduism. This, he said, was illegitimate since their original aim had been to *reform* Hinduism, i.e., to make another sect in antagonism to the orthodox Hinduism.

We have been studying '*The Light of Truth*', a weighty volume [SW: dated 1882, of] doctrine by the founder of the *Arya Samaj* — the famous '*guru*' or 'Ascetic' [SW: Dayanand,[150] who died shortly after its publication.] This book is the most extraordinary jumble of Vedic lore, modern culture, and acute and sometimes subtle original philosophy and reflection. Certainly, there is no lack of dogmatic teaching about *conduct* — since this work lays down not merely general moral maxims but also detailed instructions on [SW: sexual] acts, the duty of parents, the religious life and also on the 'Arts of War and Government'. Incidentally, it reveals the evils of the lascivious and idolatrous practices of modern Hinduism.

In this work you find the dogmatic insistence on the infallibility of the Vedas, the insistence on extreme austerity in restraint of animal passions, the inculcation of public spirit and patriotism and the proselytising fervour of the *Arya Samaj* in their most authoritative forms. Idealisation of the religious and social organisation of ancient Hinduism is combined with a measured and incidental denunciation of an alien government. It is however difficult to convict the author of 'sedition' since the whole argument of the book is against political agitation *until the Hindus have made themselves fit for it by a purification of their religion and an advance in personal character — in truthfulness, in public spirit, in energetic industry.*

In this work you find the same combination of intellectual subtlety, wide culture with an almost childish lack of sense of perspective or of scientific critical faculty, that is so common among the Hindu gentlemen whom we have met. Some parts of the work — notably the chapter on the practice of 'Yoga', are not to be understood by the ordinary western mind, and may be treasures of spiritual development which are fast locked to us. The curious rules laid down for holding the breath and concentrating the attention, seem to the Philistine mind of the western instructions in the art of self-hypnotism — a pathological process rather than a spiritual exercise. But that is only another way of saying that one does not understand it.

The account of our Peshawar and Lyallpur visit will be found in another volume.[151] We use these last pages to continue our account of the Lahore *Arya Samaj*.

On our return to Lahore we went to dine with [SW: Rambaj Dutt Chaudhuri], whose clever, energetic wife had meanwhile returned. Their house is a somewhat strange mixture of European and Indian furniture and the dinner, tho' vegetarian and including Indian dishes, was served in strict accordance with European fashion, from the hour, 8.30, to the disposition of the fruit and flowers on the table. The company consisted of ourselves and Alfred Ollivant, whom we had introduced, and some dozen men and two Indian ladies − mostly but not exclusively *Arya Samaj*. It was not a social success − the two ladies and most of the men talking English with difficulty and Ollivant being shy and reserved. Lajpat Rai and Chaudhuri and I kept up some discussion, but we were none of us at our ease.

Far more interesting was a garden party at the house of [SW: Harkishen Lal,][152] a big Hindu capitalist [SW: who had begun as a Pleader] a friend of both the *Arya* and *Brahmo Samaj*, though not actually a member of either. He was an able man of the world, with strong but moderate nationalist views, believing that the British occupation had had its uses, but that it ought to be superseded by a purely Indian administration. Indeed, one of the remarkable facts about India is that *all Hindus are nationalists* and − except for their jealousy of the Hindus − nearly all Muslims believe in government of India by the Indians as the ultimate ideal. [SW: Harkishen Lal] differs from the *Arya Samaj* in thinking that Indians have to adopt European education and in attaching really very little importance to Indian thought and Indian religion − he has, in fact, the same outlook as the little group of Japanese statesmen who caused the Japanese revolutions and have built up modern Japan.

We have seen a good deal more of Lajpat Rai, and the more we have seen of him, the more we like him. He is certainly not 'loyal' to the British connection—but why should he be! He is dead against bombs and assassinations but believes in converting all classes of Hindus to faith in their power of self-government. At present he is going slow − he feels that it is useless to fight the British Government − all that can be done is to keep within the law and go on as straight ahead as it is possible, with a black wall of suppression always appearing when the direction of the movement becomes known. It is this suppleness of policy which makes the English official fear and dislike him, and call him 'not straightforward'. But obviously, given his purpose and the hostile force of the British rule, his course cannot be straightforward. Certainly with us, trusting to our good will, he has been absolutely frank both about his objects and his methods.

He took us to see the [SW: Dayanand Anglo-Vedic] College [SW: (D.A.V. College)], affiliated to the [SW: Punjab] University but receiving no grant. It was the policy of affiliation which produced the split in the ranks of the *Arya Samaj* 14 years ago — its dissentients leaving the governing body and founding the Hardwar *gurukula*. This college, with [SW: 700] undergraduates and a preparatory school of [SW: 1500] students, is the most live educational institution in Lahore. Its principal and founder has laboured 18 years without pay or reward — being maintained on a small subsistence allowance [SW: 50 rupees per month] by his brother. The professors were most of them men of attractive personality and wide culture, and the science equipment was certainly superior to the Islamic or Christian College [SW: of the Punjab University (though probably not to the Government College, which we did not see). This] college contributed [SW: ¼] of its [SW: whole] yearly crop of graduates in an apparently successful attempt to combine an elaborate education in Hindu learning with the modern requirements of the Punjab University. The elementary school is divided into two departments — the first two classes being held in [SW: various] branch schools [SW: throughout] the city and the remainder in a large [SW: central] school with good classrooms. The [SW: percentage of] attendance of the boys seems exceptionally good [SW: but the Punjab rule is that] failing to attend for six consecutive days [means] being struck off the registers [SW: and this improves the percentages].

As to this College and school, we were amused to hear little malicious stories from Sir Louis Dane, Lt-Governor, with whom we lunched. He professed to admire the *Arya Samaj* and had reversed the policy of his predecessor [SW: Sir Denzil Ibbetson],[153] of blind suspicion and suppression. But he could not resist telling me that the College had been proved to be a centre of lawless sedition — two boys belonging to it having been discovered with pistols and with a press for printing violent leaflets, just before the Durbar. When I enquired, I found that [SW: seditious leaflets were discovered but that] the boys were not living in the College and that only the younger brother [SW: who was not proved to have any share in the printing] was [SW: even] attending as a day scholar; and that the pistols were ancient weapons belonging to the boys' deceased father — a Government official with the right to have them; and that the police had [SW: eventually] withdrawn [SW: all] charges (this was in the newspaper of the day following).

Also, he told me that the college authorities were fighting among themselves and had kicked out the Principal and founder. As the Principal had shown us round himself and had told us that he was presently retiring, *to become president of the governing body,* I was a little surprised. It is curious how all the British officials talk loosely about

Indians or Indian institutions [SW: on] the supposition that as a tourist
you will not have heard the other side. When you cite your
information, they shelter themselves behind some equivocal restate-
ment of the case. Certainly we have found the British officials more
inaccurate and more disingenuous than the Indians – the Indian
nationalists showing a most laudable desire not to mis-state facts. Of
course this must be discounted by the fact that we appear important
persons to the Indian, whereas the officials think that anything will do
for two globe-trotters who have no particular right to official
information.

Interesting to note that Lajpat Rai and many other nationalists
object altogether to the present system of government of the Native
States and would like to see them absorbed in British India. 'Under
Native State rule we have neither the reign of law of the British
Government nor the sympathy of an Indian administration. Many of
the Chiefs would like to administer their states on progressive
nationalist lines, but whenever they try to do so they are stopped
by the British Resident. On the other hand, as their authority over their
subjects is autocratic, they can be more capricious and arbitrary than is
possible under the red tape administration of the British officials.' He
quoted the recent persecutions in Patiala – the Maharaja was really
against them but he was in deadly fear of displeasing the [SW: British]
Government, by whom he might be deposed. Once his ministers
started on the path of suppression they were not restrained by the
routine of British administration, and some [SW: 100] officials [SW: and
others] were [SW: arrested and] kept in prison on mere suspicion of
being seditious, for about a year without any kind of trial or conviction
– which could not have happened without public scandal in British
India. The hope of the nationalist lay in an appeal to the Liberal and
Labour Party of the British Parliament – in so far as they had any hope
from sources outside themselves. The native Chiefs were bound to be
hangers-on of the B[SW: ritish] G[SW: overnment], and like all hangers-
on would be more intolerant than their chiefs.

I ask L[SW: ajpat] Rai what Act of Parliament he would like best – if
he were limited to one – and he answered after a moment's thought,
'liberty to educate the people', by which of course he meant liberty to
agitate among all sorts and conditions of men!

Our admiration of the *Arya Samaj* brought us into a heated
controversy with a Christian missionary in Delhi in which I certainly
lost my temper and became readily abusive! Andrews[154] [SW: an
ardent member of the Cambridge Mission at Delhi], to whom we had
an introduction from Bishop Talbot,[155] had been [SW: cited] to us as
the most 'nationalist' of Englishmen in India, and that reputation threw

us off guard. He is a somewhat 'saintly' and disingenuous missionary bent on the redemption of Indians through Christianity. Like all the missionaries we have met, he is subconsciously bitter at the ill-success of missionary [SW: effort] in actual conversions. So, when we began to admire the [SW: *Arya*] *Samaj*, expecting agreement from him, he started off by damning them – not with faint praises but with little malicious stories of their sedition and association with political crime – and complained of their underhand attitude towards Christianity – 'they take all its teaching and ascribe it to the Vedas'. By this time, we had already become heated and had asked him for chapter and verse proving that Lajpat Rai and the *Arya Samaj* had 'tampered with the soldiers'. He maintained that as all the [SW: Punjab] cultivators had relatives in the Army, any conversion of these to nationalist sentiments must mean disaffection in the Army! 'It is a crime to make a soldier disloyal to the Colonel whose salt he takes.' 'What do you mean by that?' we exclaimed hotly. 'The salt of the soldier, like the salt of the Colonel, is paid for by the natives of India. Not a penny that is spent on the Army of India is British money. How dare you say that the soldier is unfaithful to the country that supports him when he becomes an Indian nationalist.'

Afterwards I felt I had misbehaved myself and was sorry. But these missionaries, with their perpetual assertion that they 'love the Indians' and their equally perpetual malicious abuse of them [SW: to our English people] as immoral and unworthy, are not attractive controversialists. The nationalists, on the other hand, are curiously indifferent and even kindly disposed towards the Christian missionaries as providing a great deal of education – especially [SW: as] pioneers – which would have otherwise been absent. Perhaps it is easy to be generous when you are getting the best of the bargain!

The Christian missionaries, hoping to get converts, have offered free education – the Indians [SW: like the Japanese] have taken the education but have ignored the Christianity. Hence the bitterness. [SW: Now] the *Arya Samaj* are threatening the only preserve of the Christian missionaries – the depressed classes – and therefore, in spite of the obvious self-devotion and piety of the *Arya Samaj*, they are in real disfavour with earnest Christians. The *Brahmo Samaj*, on the other hand, with its idealisation of Christ and the Christian scriptures, its detachment from Hinduism in all its forms and, be it added, its incapacity to proselytise, is in high favour as the only 'pure movement' in India. (One of the leaders of the *Brahmo Samaj*, by the way, when he heard that I came of Unitarian family, introduced me to a group of *Brahmos* as belonging to the European branch of their Church!)[156]

Notes

1. Mr J. B. Minet, Educational Representative, Longmans, Green & Co., the Webbs' London publisher.
2. Bhupendra Nath Basu (1859–1924), Indian lawyer and nationalist politician, President of the Indian National Congress in 1914.
3. Figuratively, the Indian practice of secluding women of rank; literally, 'curtain', from the Hindu and Persian *pardah*.
4. The *Brahmo Samaj*, a universalist theistic society influenced by Unitarianism, was founded at Calcutta in 1828 by 'the father of modern India', Rammohun Roy (d. 1833). The *Brahmos* were pioneers of liberal political consciousness and nationalism in India. See David Kopf, *The Brahmo Samaj and the Shaping of the Modern Indian Mind* (Princeton, NJ, 1979).
5. In 1909 the so-called Morley–Minto reforms were incorporated in a new Indian Councils Act responding to demands by the moderate mainstream of the Indian National Congress for the reform of Indian political institutions and in hopes of blunting the appeal of more radical elements whose aim was complete independence for India. The powers of India's Legislative Councils were enhanced and a majority of unofficial Members made elective, with an Indian to be appointed to the Viceroy's Executive Council and two others to the Secretary of State's Council in England.
6. The population of India now exceeds 800 000 000 and is expected to surpass that of China early in the next century.
7. Later Sir Jagdish Chandra Bose (1858–1937), he was Professor of Physics at Calcutta University when the Webbs met him.
8. Gopal Krishna Gokhale (1866–1915) joined the INC in 1889, and had founded the Servants of India Society in 1905. He served on both the Bombay and Imperial Legislative Councils.
9. Under the traditional system of Hindu castes, the Untouchables were believed to be polluted by their association with the crafting of leather goods and the disposal of excrement and human corpses. The post-independence Indian constitution formally guaranteed the rights of these so-called Scheduled Castes, but in practice they remain to this day economically underprivileged and subject to ritual discrimination.
10. With a mixed Hindu and Muslim population of eighty million administered by a Lieutenant-Governor and Council, Bengal was the locus of recurrent breaches of law and order and growing political unrest in the early years of the new century. By then, as Henry Dodwell sardonically observes, in *A Sketch of the History of India from 1858 to 1918* (London, 1925) p. 271: 'It had long been recognised that this was more than one man could manage'. In 1905 the then Viceroy, Lord Curzon, had partitioned Bengal, creating a new province of East Bengal comprising Assam, Chittagong and fifteen other districts with a total population of some thirty million (predominantly Muslim but with a large Hindu minority), with Dacca as its capital. The partition triggered outbreaks of violence and sustained nationalist opposition from Bengali Hindus who viewed Curzon's move as a cynical scheme of divide and rule. The partition was reversed in the course of the Delhi Durbar.

11. The *Maidan*, a two-mile-long plain or park at the centre of Calcutta, with Government House, residence of the Governor-General, facing it on the north, and Belvedere, the residence of the Lieutenant-Governor of Bengal, on the south.

12. Sir Spencer Harcourt Butler (1869–1938), ICS, Member of Lord Hardinge's Viceregal Executive Council from 1910–15 and thereafter, Governor of Burma and of the United Provinces of Agra and Oudh.

13. Sir Richard Warrand Carlyle (1859–1934), Indian civil servant and scholar.

14. Dr A. J. Carlyle, a friend of the Webbs, was at the time rector of St. Martin and All Saints, Oxford. He was the author of *A History of Medieval Political Theory in the West*, 6 vols. (Edinburgh, 1903–36), the fifth volume of which was co-authored with his brother Richard. A. J. Carlyle was the founder in 1909 of 'The Political Philosophy and Science Club', for teachers in Cambridge, Oxford and London, revived as the Carlyle Club by a distinguished LSE figure, Professor Michael Oakeshott, after the Second World War.

15. W. C. Bonnerjee (1844–1906), a Calcutta lawyer, had been among the founders of the Indian National Congress and had chaired its first meetings at Bombay in December 1885.

16. Justice of the Peace.

17. Aides-de-camp.

18. Satyendra Prasanna Sinha, Lord Sinha (1864–1928), Legal Member of the Viceroy's Executive Council (1909–10) and later Under-Secretary of State for India and Governor of Bihar and Orissa.

19. Sir Syed Ali Imam (1869–1932), active in the All-India Muslim League, had succeeded S. P. Sinha as Legal Member of the Viceroy's Executive Council and was to become first President of the Executive Council of the Nizam of Hyderabad.

20. It was c. 528 B.C. at Bodh Gaya in present day Bihar that Siddhartha Gautama (c. 563–483 B.C.), the Buddha, is said to have attained enlightenment, following a six-week meditation under the Bodhidruma, or 'tree of enlightenment'.

21. An Anglo-Indian term meaning an inn for travellers on a *dak* route, the Hindi *dak* signifying a relay of men or horses carrying the mails as well as passengers in palanquins.

22. Hindi *chaprasi*, an attendant.

23. John Tarlton Whitty, ICS, appointed 1898, Joint Magistrate and Deputy-Collector, Bengal, from December 1908.

24. The much renovated shrine, a brick structure, dates from the sixth to seventh century.

25. Ashoka, who reigned c. 272/268–232 B.C., was the most celebrated of the Maurya monarchs and played a key role in the spread of Buddhism.

26. The third largest of Burma's indigenous peoples, traditional inhabitants of the northern Shan States bordering Thailand.

27. George Alfred Paterson, ICS, appointed 1891, District and Sessional Judge, United Provinces, from 1908.

28. Edmund Alexander Molony, ICS, appointed 1884, Magistrate and Collector, United Provinces, from 1899.

29. Claud Arthur Streatfield, ICS, appointed 1889, Magistrate and Collector, United Provinces, from 1906.
30. Miss Lucy Deane, a London friend of the Webbs and a researcher for the National Health Insurance Commission, 1911–12, was married to Major Granville Streatfield.
31. Raja Madho Lal (b. 1840), a wealthy landholder and banker elected to the Legislative Council of the Government of India in 1906.
32. Baldeo Das Vyas, Honorary Magistrate, Benares.
33. Possibly cassava.
34. A caste of Hindus in northern India, or alternatively, a religious mendicant.
35. The Warriors of the classical *varna* class-system, along with Priests, Merchants and Peasants.
36. To 'do *puja*' was Anglo-Indian slang for 'say their prayers'.
37. A watchman.
38. Varanasi (Benares) in Uttar Pradesh is one of the seven sacred cities of traditional Hindu religious observance. The Ghats, from the Sanskrit *ghatta*, are flights of stone steps descending to the Ganges from the most famous buildings of the city. Pilgrims make a six-day circuit of the Panch Kosi Road, commencing on the Manikarnika Ghat, proceeding by the Asi Ghat and returning by the Barna Ghat.
39. Annie Besant (1847–1933), one of the contributors to *Fabian Essays in Socialism* (1889), had abandoned socialism and left England for India in 1893, where she started the Hindu Central College in Benares' Kamachcha quarter. Founder of the Indian Boy Scouts Association and the Women's Indian Association, Besant became President of the Indian National Congress in 1917 and was also President of the Theosophical Society from 1907–33. As the 'New Hinduism' allusion suggests, theosophical teachings, a blend of Tibetan and Theravada Buddhism, Advaita monism and Christianity, encouraged Hindu and Buddhist reform and contributed indirectly to early Indian nationalism.
40. Housed in a handsome building constructed by Major Kittoe of the Bengal Engineers in 1847–52, Queen's was renowned for the *pandits* of its Sanskrit Department.
41. Arthur Venis, Professor of Post-Vedic Sanskrit at Allahabad University and a Member of the Legislative Council of the United Provinces, had been Principal of Queen's College since 1897.
42. Dating from the third century B.C., the Buddhist sculptural artifacts of Sarnath near Benares are noted for their non-naturalistic and abstract renderings of surface.
43. Sir Charles N. E. Eliot (1864–1931), then Vice-Chancellor of Sheffield University, who in 1913 became Principal of the University of Hong Kong and was later British Ambassador to Japan.
44. The Vedas, 'knowledge' or 'wisdom', the entire corpus of sacred Sanskrit texts of Brahminism generated in the long period from 1200 B.C. or earlier down to the middle centuries of the first millennium B.C., signifies the authoritative canon for all subsequent forms of orthodox Hinduism.
45. The *Magh Mela* occurs annually from mid-January to mid-February during the Indian month of *Magh*, in conjunction with a prescribed religious ritual of bathing daily before sunrise at the confluence of the Ganges and Yamuna

near Allahabad. The *Purna Kumbh Mela* referred to celebrates at twelve year intervals the mythical return of Jayanta to paradise with a pitcher (*kumbha*) containing the nectar of immortality, his route of passage marked by lesser festivals held in a three-year rotation at Nasik, Ujjain, Allahabad and Hardwar. The *Ardh Kumbh Mela* (*ardh* signifying half) which the Webbs witnessed at Allahabad, occurred every six years, at the midpoint of the twelve-year cycle.

46. Syed Karamat Husain (1852–1917) was at the time a Judge of the Allahabad High Court and Member of the Legislative Council of the United Provinces active in the All-India Muslim League.

47. The Indian National Congress had from its foundation failed to attract Muslim members. The All-India Muslim League, founded at Dhaka in December of 1906, would eventually lead the movement for Pakistan.

48. A *maulvi* is an expert in Islamic law.

49. Muir College, like Lahore's Aitchison Chiefs' College, occupied a fine building in the '*Saracenic*' style near Allahabad's Alfred Park and Government House.

50. J. G. Jennings had been Principal of Muir Central College at Allahabad since 1895.

51. Claude Fraser de la Fosse, previously Professor of English Literature and Logic at Queen's College, Benares, had been Director of Public Instruction in the United Provinces since 1906 and a Member of the Lieutenant-Governor's Legislative Council.

52. Hugh William Orange, ICS, Director-General of Education for India, 1902–10, and thereafter a member of the London Board of Education.

53. From the Persian: a building to which the Shias carry the *tazias* or biers in the *muharram*, often the tomb of the founder.

54. The *Nadwah-ul-'Ulama*, founded at Lucknow in 1894.

55. Mr J. C. Rees was Principal, and Mr F. A. James Vice-Principal, of the Colvin Talukdars' School, Lucknow.

56. James Ward (1843–1925), philosopher and psychologist, Professor of Mental Philosophy and Logic at Cambridge, 1897–1925. His younger brother 'A. W.' Ward is not to be confused with his better-known contemporary, Cambridge historian and Master of Peterhouse, A. W. Ward (1837–1924).

57. Literally, a teacher in a poor, low-class school where instruction, as in Ireland in the early nineteenth century, was conducted by a hedge-side or in the open air.

58. Gokhale's Elementary Education Bill had been first introduced in the Governor-General's Legislative Council in March 1911, with the aim of establishing a system of compulsory elementary education financed in part by a local education tax. It was again before the Council at the time of the Webbs' visit, but was defeated in March 1912.

59. The *Chauk* was the principal street of the Indian city at Lucknow.

60. Act V, Scene 1.

61. Later Sir Verney Lovett, author of *The History of the Indian Nationalist Movement* (London, 1920).

62. L. Stuart was Judicial-Secretary to Government, and R. Burn Financial-Secretary to Government, United Provinces.

63. *Maulvi* Muhammad Aziz Mirza (1865–1912), Hyderabad Judge and Muslim politician.
64. Dr Naziruddin Hasan, M.A., LL.D. The *'vakils'* the Webbs met at the house of Mirza and Hasan were Muslim Pleaders.
65. Ganga Prasad Varma (1863–1914), editor of *The Advocate* and member of the INC.
66. Bal Gangadhar Tilak (1856–1920), a leading nationalist politician and journalist of radical views, and one of the founders of the Fergusson College at Poona: see 'Poona 8–10th April [1912]' on page 325. At the time of the Webbs' visit to India, Tilak had been deported to Mandalay in Burma and was serving a six-year prison sentence there.
67. Or *zamindar*, an Indian landlord required to pay land taxes to the British authorities on the rents received from his peasant tenants.
68. A light turban, from the Hindi *pagri*.
69. Dr Edward Bennet, author of *Idylls of the East and Other Poems* (London, 1912).
70. The Raja of Padrauna was a *tehsildar*, a collector of revenue from a *tehsil*, an administrative unit of roughly one hundred villages within the larger district of Gorakhpur.
71. A canopied seat for two or more fitted to an elephant's back, from the Persian *haudah* (Arabic *haudaj*), a litter.
72. In nineteenth-century India indigo had been a major and very profitable export crop for use in the European textile industry; but with the introduction of synthetic dyes demand fell dramatically and estate-owners shifted to other crops.
73. Sir John Hope Simpson (1868–1961) retired from the Indian Civil Service in 1916 and was later a Liberal MP. Many years after their first meeting, when Sidney Webb was Secretary of State for the Colonies in the 1929 Labour Government of Ramsay MacDonald, he was to appoint Hope Simpson to a special mission to Palestine.
74. Although the initial entries at Volume 30, ff. 370–2 are in Beatrice's hand, these are so extensively overwritten with inserts and clarifications in Sidney's hand as to render them virtually joint entries.
75. Hewett held the post from 1907–12 and subsequently saw service in Mesopotamia.
76. Ernest Henry Edye, ICS, appointed 1907, Assistant-Magistrate, United Provinces, from 1908.
77. Vinayak Nandshankar Mehta, ICS, appointed 1905, Assistant-Magistrate and Collector, United Provinces, from 1906.
78. Waris Ameer Ali, ICS, appointed 1910, had only arrived in India on 20 November 1911, to take up his first post as Assistant-Magistrate and Collector, United Provinces. The 'celebrated Indian barrister' was the Rt. Hon. Syed Ameer Ali (1849–1928), law professor and Judge.
79. Kumar Jagdish Prasad, Assistant-Magistrate and (3rd grade) Assistant-Commissioner, United Provinces Provincial Service.
80. A sect of *Samajists* especially influential in the Punjab. *Arya Samaj* teachings were more popular in spirit than the implicitly elite *Brahmo Samaj* modernism of Calcutta's essentially Westernised Indian intelligentsia. *Arya Samaj* reformism, couched in expressly Hindu forms and usages, appealed to a broader audience of non-Westernised intellectuals.

81. The mutiny of the garrison at Meerut and other northern stations in May and June of 1857, ostensibly occasioned by fear of pollution from the animal grease on the cartridges of the new Lee Enfield rifle, but as well by growing resentment at the introduction of lower castes into the Bengal Army and by the recent annexation of the princely state of Avadh from which many of the soldiers hailed, lasted until November, and led directly to the abolition of the East India Company the following year and the passage of the administration of the Indian Empire to the British Crown.

82. Sir Peter Henry Clutterbuck (1868–1951), India Forest Department, United Provinces, later Development Minister for Kashmir.

83. From the Hindi *nala*, a ravine or watercourse.

84. An elephant-driver, from the Hindi *mahaut*.

85. The reference is to Lord Hardinge, Viceroy of India from 1910–16.

86. Defeat in the Opium Wars of the nineteenth century had forced upon China the official recognition of opium imports through the treaty ports, chiefly originating in India and including in practice a good deal of smuggling. But in the final decade of the Ch'ing dynasty, a series of measures aimed at China's modernisation had included Edicts for the extinction of Chinese cultivation of the poppy and a 1907 agreement with Great Britain that would extinguish imports as well over a ten-year period. The 1911 Revolution reinforced the anti-opium mood; and just at the time of the Webbs' arrival in India, a conference held at The Hague from December 1911 to January 1912 had concluded an International Opium Convention which led to the control of production and distribution of raw and prepared opium and a ban on the import and export of prepared opium, with an eye to a gradual elimination of opium addiction. One consequence for the Government of British India, as the Webbs here indicate, was that in areas hitherto under opium cultivation, chiefly Bengal and the princely states, government revenues from taxes on 'exported' opium were falling dramatically.

87. Sir Michael Sadler (1861–1943), Master of University College, Oxford, who was to serve as President of the Calcutta University Commission in 1917–19.

88. John Cromarty Tulloch, joined the IFD in 1891 and was Deputy-Conservator, United Provinces, from 1901.

89. Keir Hardie (1856–1915), Scottish miners' leader and working-class socialist hero, founder of the Independent Labour Party.

90. The *Tharu* are a tribe of the Himalayan Tarai region of Uttar Pradesh.

91. Humphrey Napier Sturt, sportsman, 2nd Lord Alington, who succeeded to the title on the death of his father in 1904. Before that he had been MP for East Dorset.

92. Frederick Lawson Dodd (b. 1868), a London dental surgeon, first Chairman of the Fabian Society's Summer School.

93. P. S. MacMahon, M.Sc., Professor of Chemistry, Canning College, Lucknow.

94. The Collector at Ghansi (or Jhansi) was Charles Arthur Silberrad, ICS, appointed 1893, Magistrate and Collector, United Provinces, from 1911. The Judge was Henry Edward Holme, ICS, appointed 1888, District and Sessional Judge, United Provinces, from 1906. The Railway Engineer was W. G. Barnett, AMICE, District Engineer, Great Indian Peninsular Railway.

95. Alfred Cripps (1852–1941), later Baron Parmoor, was married to Beatrice's sister Theresa. Himself a member of both the 1924 and 1929 Labour Governments, he was the father of another prominent Labour Party politician, Sir Stafford Cripps (1889–1952).

96. A memorial church in the Romanesque style was consecrated in 1875 near the site of General Wheeler's entrenchment during the 1857 siege of Cawnpore. A small garden enclosure surrounded the nearby well in which 250 of the garrison killed during the siege were buried.

97. Khajuraho in Madhya Pradesh is the site of a magnificent group of temples dating from the seventh century.

98. Maharaja Vishwanath Singh Bahadur, 'the Maharaja of Chhikrapur' in J. R. Ackerley's *Hindoo Holiday* (London, 1932).

99. Pt. Shyam Behari Misra, M.A., PCS.

100. Sir Theodore Morison (1863–1936), educationist.

101. G. H. Lewes (1817–78), English journalist and philosopher, and companion of George Eliot.

102. Pseudonym of Mary Mackay (1855–1924), English romantic novelist encouraged by George Meredith as a musician but not as a writer. *The Reader's Encyclopedia* (New York, 1948) vol. I, p. 242: 'A pretty little blonde woman who wrote torrentially and died of her 28th novel in her 70th year...'.

103. At forty-six, two years separated from his wife, Comte had fallen in love with Clothilde, whose husband was serving a life sentence for embezzlement as a tax collector. When she died only a year later, Comte considered taking his own life before resolving instead to love the human race, a conversion to which he thereafter bore witness through the adumbration of a new humanistic religion, the philosophy of Positivism.

104. William James (1842–1910), Harvard philosopher and psychologist, brother of Henry James. Author of *The Will to Believe* (1897), *Varieties of Religious Experience* (1902), and other works.

105. Lieutenant-Colonel Lawrence Impey (b. 1862), Indian Army, and from 1883, Foreign Department, Government of India. Political Agent, Bundelkhand, from 1911.

106. C. L. Tupper, *Indian Political Practice: A Collection of the Decisions of the Government of India in Political Cases* (1895).

107. In 1907, when he was succeeded by Lokendra Sir Govinda Singh.

108. Sir Louis Dane (1856–1946), Lieutenant-Governor of the Punjab, 1908–13. The 'see further confirmation' remark refers to the diary entry for 'Lahore 29th Feb^y - 3rd March 1912' at page 271 below.

109. Her Highness Nawab Sultan Sir Jehan Begum of Bhopal (1858–1930), who had succeeded her mother in 1910.

110. Reverend F. W. Martin of Sangor, Central Provinces.

111. Mrs F. D. Barnes, MD, LMS.

112. She was, in fact, the third woman to occupy the throne.

113. Pseudonym of Mary Ann Cross (1819–80), one of the greatest of English novelists. There is a portrait by M. d'Albert painted at Geneva in 1850 but the allusion is probably to the Frederick Burton drawing in the National Portrait Gallery.

114. Maharaja Madhav Rao Scindia of Gwalior (1876–1925), ruler of the largest Maratha state and one of four Indian princes entitled to a twenty-one gun salute.
115. Even so, the Princess Indira of Baroda eventually married instead Jitendra Narayan, the Maharaj Kumar of Cooch Behar.
116. Islamic architecture, its greatest contribution the development of the tomb garden, reached its climax under Mughal patronage at Agra, Lahore, Delhi and Fatehpur Sikri in the sixteenth and seventeenth centuries. Amongst the architectural highlights of these cities are the red sandstone and white marble Friday Mosques or *Jami Masjid*.
117. The Taj Mahal, the white marble mausoleum and tomb garden of the wife of Shah Jahan (r. 1628–57).
118. The most completely preserved palace city of the Mughals, including among its unusual buildings the Diuan-e Khass.
119. Sir Edward and A. Ulysses John of Messrs A. John & Co., Agra, descendants of Anthony John, a dealer in precious stones who had migrated to India from his native Greece in the early nineteenth century.
120. Itmad-ud-Daulah, the tomb of the father of the Mughal empress Nur Jahan.
121. An untrustworthy person, a rascal.
122. Cf. Dadabhai Naoroji, *Poverty and Un-British Rule in India* (1901). Naoroji's thesis that economic exploitation in India entailed the 'drain' or export of indigenous wealth to England was taken up by prominent Indian nationalists of the day. See also 'Peshawar 4/6th [March 1912]' at page 288 below.
123. The construction of the new capital at Delhi had meant the employment by the Indian Department of Public Works of some 30 000 workers drawn from Agra and elsewhere.
124. That is, given a large pool of available labour, to employ at low piece-rate wages for long hours.
125. Strictly 'punkah' (Hindi, *pankha*) signifies a portable fan made typically from palmyra leaf; here the reference is to an unskilled labourer whose employment consisted of working a large cloth fan.
126. Anglo-Indian for a trader or shopkeeper, from the Hindi *banya*.
127. A high caste referred to as a so-called writing caste in British India, since Kayasthas were often employed as clerks.
128. From the Persian, signifying a gateway or door.
129. Herbert William Ward Reynolds, ICS, appointed 1875, retired March 1912, his last posting, from March 1905, as Member of the Governor-General's Legislative Council.
130. Evelyn John Mardon, ICS, appointed 1886, Inspector-General of Registration and Commissioner of Excise and Stamps, United Provinces, from 1904.
131. Francis Capper Chamier, ICS, appointed 1903, Assistant-Commissioner, United Provinces, from 1904.
132. Leonard Seymour Dacres, ICS, appointed 1907, Assistant-Commissioner, United Provinces, from 1908.
133. Sydney Olivier (1859–1943), one of the original Fabian essayists and a lifelong friend of Sidney Webb, the two having met as young civil servants in the Colonial Office. Olivier was to serve as Secretary of State for India in the 1924 Labour Government.

134. Robert Charles Hobart (1881–1955), ICS, Assistant-Commissioner, United Provinces, from 1905.

135. The *Gurukul Kangri*, established in 1902 by the *Arya Samaj* to serve as a centre for the revived classical Hindu system of education.

136. Lala Atma Ram, M.A., Clerk to the Dayanand Anglo-Vedic College, Lahore.

137. Or nylghau, a short-haired Indian antelope (from the Persian *nilgaw*, blue ox).

138. Sir Syed Ahmed Khan (1817–98), educational reformer, founder in 1877 of the Muhammadan Anglo-Oriental College, which subsequently became the Aligarh Muslim University.

139. W. A. J. Archbold, M.A., LL.B. (Cantab), Principal, Muhammadan Anglo-Oriental College, Aligarh, succeeded in 1911 by J. H. Towle, M.A. (Cantab).

140. Medical Officer of Health.

141. Lieutenant P. C. S. Hobart, Royal Engineers, 1st King George's Own Sappers and Miners.

142. Rebuilt in 1764, the celebrated Sikh sanctuary, known as the *Darbar Sahib* or the *Harmandir*, stands in the centre of a pool or tank and is accessible by means of a long marble causeway. In 1802 Ranjit Singh roofed the great shrine with sheets of copper gilt, hence its name as the Golden Temple.

143. One of a number of London societies for the discussion of radical political and religious thought that flourished at the turn of the century and briefly published *Conduct: A Monthly Journal of Ethics*.

144. Amalgamated Society of Engineers.

145. The Jainist sect comprises less than half of one per cent of India's population but is heavily overrepresented amongst its *mahajans* or business men.

146. Pandit Rambhaj Datta Chaudhuri (1866–1923), nationalist politician and a prominent *Arya Samaj* leader in the Punjab.

147. Sir John, later Lord Lawrence (1811–79), was a leading figure in nineteenth-century Anglo-Indian administration, a Lieutenant-Governor of the Punjab, and from 1864–69, the Viceroy of India. The inscription on the statue alluded to an incident during Lawrence's stay in the Punjab when, faced with an incipient insurrection, he issued a proclamation indicating that 'I have ruled this district three years by the sole agency of the pen, and if necessary, I will rule it by the sword. God forbid that matters should come to that.' His officials proffered pens and swords to the headmen of villages throughout the district, asking them to choose one or the other; and not unsurprisingly in the circumstances of the time, the move elicited a general view in favour of the pen. But eventually, with the rise of Indian nationalism, British officials were to substitute the word 'served' for the word 'governed' on Lawrence's statue at Lahore.

148. Lala Lajpat Rai (1856–1928), since 1888 a radical member of the Indian National Congress and a leading figure amongst nationalist politicians. Deported to Mandalay prison, and on other occasions reimprisoned for resistance to British rule, he was to die from injuries sustained while participating in a demonstration in 1928.

149. Or *Ghi*, a clarified Indian buffalo-milk butter resembling oil.

150. Swami Dayanand Saraswati (1824–83), founder of the Dayanand Anglo-Vedic College at Lahore and author of *Satyarth Prakash* or *The Light of Truth*, a book attacking the superstition and ritualism of contemporary

'traditionalist' Hinduism, and urging a return to the original, more enlightened religion of the Vedas. Dayanand had begun the *Arya Samaj* in 1875.

151. That is, in Volume 31 of the manuscript diary, the third devoted to the Webbs' Asian travels. 'These last pages' refers to the final sheets of Volume 30.

152. Harkishen Lal (1864–1937), banker and business man who eventually served in the Punjab Government.

153. Sir Denzil Ibbetson (1847–1908), Lieutenant-Governor of Punjab in 1907, when political agitation by nationalists had led to the deportation of Lala Lajpat Rai.

154. C. F. Andrews (1871–1940), at the time a missionary attached to St. Stephen's College, Delhi, and in due course, a close and well-known associate of Gandhi in the cause of Indian independence, dating from their first meeting in South Africa in 1913. See also 'Delhi, 12–16th March 1912' at pages 301–2 below.

155. Edward Stuart Talbot (1844–1934), Bishop of Rochester, Southwark and Winchester.

156. End of *Mss Diary*, Volume 30.f.476. On the reverse of folio 478 there is a list in Beatrice's hand of nine apparent chapter headings under the title 'What is Socialism?'

8
India (2)

We begin this book[1] on the north-western edge of the Indian Empire, to which we are paying a flying visit. Arriving at 6 a.m. we sallied out after tea and a hot bath to call on the Director of Public Instruction, the only person to whom we have an introduction (the Deputy Commissioner, to whom we sent on a letter, had just left on promotion to the Secretariat at Calcutta − this constant shifting being typical). The Director (Richey),[2] an energetic man of about 35, has only been here a year, having come from an educational post in Eastern Bengal. And the matter is made worse by the absence of anything in the nature of specialist journals which should make known to all India what is being done in each part. Thus, we have been inspecting the *muktabs*,[3] or common mosque schools where Muslim boys learn the Koran by heart, in various places in the United Provinces. There (and as we learn also, in the North-West Frontier Province), they are quite outside Government aid. As there are throughout India thousands of these schools attended by perhaps hundreds of thousands of boys, and as they cannot be abolished (seeing that the religion of Islam makes them obligatory), we have been exercised in our minds as to what could be done.

It is impossible to force them into a Gov[t] system and it does not seem either creditable or administratively expedient to leave hundreds of thousands of Indian boys without any real education, even elementary. We have therefore been asking what could be done, and suggesting the possibility of the Gov[t] leaving the schools under the *maulvis*, but offering (1) to supply them with books, maps, etc., and (2) to provide peripatetic visiting teachers, being Muslims, who should teach secular subjects if invited by the mosques. None of the officials in the United Provinces and none of the prominent Muslims whom we consulted were aware that in the Province of Sind in the Bombay Presidency this very problem was tackled in 1873, thirty-nine years ago, and after various experiments and checks (due very largely to the constant shifting of officials), a system of very loose Government recognition and inspection, with liberal grants-in-aid for instruction in

284

secular subjects over and above the teaching of the Koran, has resulted in some 12,000 boys in such schools in this one province being brought under instruction in reading and writing their mother tongue, in arithmetic and in geography, under a very simple code. We have learnt this today only from a confidential memorandum by the Sind Director of Public Instruction of which the Director here happened accidentally to have got a copy. The Sind plan though, after 39 years of effort so far successful, leaves unsolved the problem of what to do for the boys in the mosque schools which will not adopt even this simple code, and are thus in the position of all the mosque schools in the U.P. and N.-W.F. Province and probably elsewhere in India, for all of which our own suggestion stands.

What these (and other) facts suggested to us is the desirability of there being a weekly or monthly journal devoted to popular description of new administrative experiments in the different provinces of India, for the information of all the other provinces. In this country it is not possible for such a journal to be run by private enterprise and it is clearly a case for a Gov^t publication, to be run perhaps semi-officially without Gov^t responsibility (like the Colonial Office List), or actually by a Government department (like the Board of Trade *Labour Gazette*). The editorship might very well be held by an Indian official of education and discretion.

We went to see the Church Missionary Society (Edwardes) College here, an excellently-built structure elaborately furnished up to English standards, with living rooms for the students in quadrangular form. The three or four English clergy are engaged in teaching about 24 Muslim youths up to the 'First Arts' examination of Lahore University (now being extended to the B.A.), without any science laboratory or science teaching and with only the nucleus of a library. There are simple Christian services each morning, but otherwise no proselytism; and the youths in fact do not become Christians.[4] It is difficult not to feel that this work, which seems typical of Christian work in Northern India, is not what the British public subscribes for. Useful as it may be in supplementing the educational work of the Government and the independent efforts now being made by the Hindu and Muslim communities, it is a dead failure from the standpoint of the Christian missionary. This fact may account for a certain lack of straightforwardness, and a disagreeable attitude of dislike for the Indians and of contempt for their views and aspirations, that we find characteristic of such missionaries as we have met (who happen all to have been Anglican or Congregationalist).

These missionaries are in a false position with regard to the mission-subsidising folks at home. They seem to be secretly irritated with India and really annoyed at any attempts at Indian progress such as the *Arya Samaj* outside their own panacea, and none of those we have seen manifests any admiration or love for the people whom they are professedly trying to influence. We feel that the first and fundamental requisite for successful missionary work must be a genuine admiration of the people among whom it is to be carried on, a real appreciation of the good qualities of their race and a generous recognition of those special excellences which make possible a sincere attitude of 'reciprocal superiority'. If a man cannot feel towards the Indians that 'best form of equality', as John Stuart Mill termed it,[5] he is not fit to come out here as a missionary. We have not found among such missionaries as we have seen any glimmering of appreciation that the Indians may be in certain race qualities actually equal to the English, let alone their superiors – in spirituality, in subtlety of thought and in intellectual humility or national modesty, for instance. The theological representatives of England in India seem to be as cocksure as our military or civilian or commercial representatives that we are in all respects the superior people, kindly vouchsafing to stoop to administer, at liberal salaries, the affairs of an inferior 'subject race'. (We have not seen any Roman Catholic missionaries in India, and things may be different even as regards Protestants in the Madras Presidency, where most of the Christian converts are to be found.)

We have met here Alfred Ollivant,[6] the author of '*Owd Bob*' (who has been a couple of months in India chiefly with soldier and civilian cousins and other relations), and have spent a pleasant day with him at the Khyber Pass meeting and passing the caravans, escorted by armed soldiers, which traverse the pass in each direction on the Tuesdays and Fridays when the 'truce of the road' prevails, and (what is perhaps the greater security) when it is picketed at intervals by the Khyber Rifles, who at other times merely occupy the dozen small forts and blockhouses that we garrison between Jamrud (at this end) and Lundi Kotal (near the true Afghan border). The wild and desolate hills between the two frontiers are sparsely inhabited by Afridis,[7] who live in fortified mud castles each sheltering a family group with walls and towers, and who intersperse the cultivation of their little patches of arable land and the herding of their goats with promiscuous plundering of passers-by and almost continuous blood feuds between families – the Corsican vendetta – when they lie in wait for each other and shoot at sight. It is a lawless land where every man goes armed, and over which there is no magisterial jurisdiction.

This belt of mountains, a sort of 'No mans land', seems here to exist all along the border. The N.-W. Frontier Province Government has now settled down to a policy of mingled bribery and reprisals, so as to secure (1) that there shall be no raids on British territory or attacks on the British officials and soldiers who garrison isolated forts or traverse the passes; and (2) that no person shall actually be attacked on the road itself, though he may be followed and attacked on the road if he merely takes refuge on it. Otherwise, the Afridis are left severely alone to murder and plunder each other as they will. Their adhesion to these conditions is secured by (1) the enlisting of several thousands of them in the Indian Army, especially the Khyber Rifles; (2) the regular payment to them of subventions in compensation, so to speak, for their loss, by abstaining to plunder the caravans on the road; (3) occasional employment at wages in road-making, etc., and (4) stern reprisals on any tribes which make raids or infringe these conditions. Reprisals seem to take the form of secretly and simultaneously arresting and detaining all persons of a particular tribe together with whatever camels, oxen or other property they have about them, who are found in British territory or within grasp of British forces on a given day; and then informing the tribe that unless they pay a fine there and then imposed on them, the property detained will be sold. In graver cases, the tribal villages will be invaded and captured by a punitive expedition.

The British forces claim to do as they like whether in keeping the peace, erecting forts, maintaining garrisons or road-making along the Khyber road itself and for fifty yards right and left of it; but whether or not even this much is technically British territory is not clear. Visitors are allowed up the Pass even on Tuesdays and Fridays only by special permit, and are now stopped at Ali Masjid, half way up — chiefly so as to shorten the day for the pickets who are withdrawn practically as soon as the two caravans have got through. Apparently no European is allowed to go through to Afghanistan unless he has a special permit from the Amir. He would be turned back at the Afghan frontier and therefore the Indian Government's prohibition is not questioned. We were told by the officer or Commissioner of the Khyber Rifles (Bickford)[8] that when some years ago Pierre Loti[9] was in India, the Government of India believed he would try to pass through the Khyber in the caravans disguised as a woman; and severe orders were given that every person was to be closely scrutinised so as to detect and arrest him. But they never found anyone like him; and presently, he was authentically known to have returned quite unromantically by steamer to Europe.

The 'caravans' consisted of four men of the Khyber Rifles marching in front, then a straggling crowd of one or two hundred men with a few women, walking, then several dozen pack donkeys, several score of laden camels, some shaggy creatures from the Bactrian Desert, others lean and bare, and finally, four more men of the Khyber Rifles, the whole dragging out to something like a mile. The outward camels were laden with sheet and rod iron, petroleum and packing cases and bales presumably containing cotton goods and miscellaneous European products. The inward camels were less heavily laden but they were bringing skins, bales of wool and nondescript bundles which may have contained carpets. It looked as if we were witnessing in tangible form part of the 'drain' of excess of exports over imports which the Indian patriots complain of! The outward caravan was swollen by Afghans returning from service or peddling in India during the cold weather, and some of them were driving young oxen and cows which they had apparently bought out of their earnings. It was noticeable that hardly anyone rode except a few young children. The animals were used almost exclusively for the transport of goods; and the wild, unkempt, curiously-garbed figures of all ages strode along gossiping or silent, sometimes quarrelling and wrangling, often looking like our idea of Abraham, Isaac and Jacob.

Opposite Jamrud Fort is a well-built four-square *caravanserai* where the caravans halt for the night and pay a fee or toll for each animal, which is taken by the Government as part of its revenue. We went to tea with the officer commanding at the fort (Bickford), a healthy and clean but unintellectual soldier who had (we were told) been somewhat unduly advanced by the favour of the present Chief Commissioner of the N.-W.F. Province (Sir George Roos Keppel)[10] under whom he had served.

In the evening we dined with Maffey,[11] the 'Political Agent' for the Khyber, an I.C.S. of charm and ability. (From him we learnt that J. A. Spender,[12] the editor of the *'Westminster Gazette'* who was out here for the Durbar, had just written privately to say that the Liberal Government would be 'out' within six months, wrecked by the unpopularity of the Insurance Act and the difficulties of the Home Rule Bill!) On the following day, we lunched with two other civil servants (Richey, Director of Public Instruction of an educational service, and Howell, I.C.S.,[13] temporarily acting in revenue administration).

We are amused at the universal praise of the wild Pathans[14] (= Afridis and Afghans) of these parts. Everyone says they are fine fellows, far superior to the Hindus! We learn on cross-examination that they are cruel and treacherous, shockingly addicted to unnatural vice and habitually given to stealing each other's wives, that murder and robbery are so common as not to be deemed crimes, that the men do little work, leaving their agriculture and the care of their goats mostly to the women and boys, and that the only occupation considered worthy of manhood is the promiscuous shooting at each other taken unawares which they call war. When we ask why a people is admired which breaks nearly every Commandment, and is apparently of no earthly use in the universe, we are told that they are fine manly fellows, 'good sportsmen' with a sense of humour! Verily our English standards are peculiar. The fact is that the British officer likes them because (1) they admire and respect him and his special qualities (2) they make good soldiers under him, and (3) they in no way compete with him or 'claim equality' or excel in directions in which he feels himself deficient. When we ask a thoughtful civilian whether he sees any reason to believe that even in a couple of centuries the Pathans will have developed into anything like a civilised people, or into anything else of use in the world, he is bound to admit that there is no sign of any such possibility.

Peshawar itself is a picturesque and crowded walled city full of little square shops opening on the streets, nearly all exactly alike, each with its occupier, his son or his apprentice squatting on the floor plying their handicrafts — here the coppersmiths in a group, there the primitive shoemakers or the tailors working Singer's sewing-machines, with innumerable sellers of coffee, sweet-stuffs and fruit interspersed among them, and a whole narrow lane of butchers' shops, the first we have noticed in India. The first day we traversed its crowded streets, they were thickly picketed by armed police, though there was no sign of disturbance; but we learn that, two years ago at this season, when a solemn Muslim commemoration of the death of Ali coincided with the Hindu saturnalia called 'Holi',[15] there was a serious riot and fight between the two religions, with loss of life. So this year special precautions were taken. Only a few years ago, the wild Afridis made a successful raid on the richest bazaar in Peshawar itself, and got clear away with much loot. This carefully-planned exploit, done by a few dozen men, was organised by a youthful recruit of our own Army who induced 'Rahab the harlot', who, as in the Old Testament story,[16] dwelt 'on the wall', to let the men be drawn up into her dwelling. They then erected barricades at each end of the bazaar they had chosen for plunder and set them on fire! These fires kept out the stray police who appeared, long enough to permit the band to secure their plunder and escape by the way they came!

With Richey, the Director of Public Instruction, we have inspected (1) the Gov^t normal school, temporarily housed in a modern palace built to accommodate the Amir of Afghanistan and other distinguished oriental visitors (2) the municipal high school, with some 450 boys under an Anglicised German headmaster housed in quite insufficient buildings, and (3) a Hindu high school of 600 boys in still worse accommodation. These were all in their several ways surprisingly good, the normal school small but having its own practising school and turning out astonishingly well-drilled teachers; the municipal high school admirably organised and administered and doing real educational work; and the Hindu high school, up to now despising any grant from Government and maintained by private subscriptions by local men of means, being under an eager, zealous and pushing young headmaster, a member of the *Arya Samaj*, and achieving good examination results with very poor school appliances.

Altogether, we get a vision that the N.-W.F. Province, hitherto much neglected, is seemingly making more actual progress in education than any other province of North India. The Chief Commissioner (Sir G. Roos Keppel) is very keen on making up leeway; Richey, the Director, is an able, energetic, zealous and resourceful man; both Hindus and Muslims are now eager for schooling; and, alone in India, the provincial Government has abolished school fees. Richey, by the way, from Rugby and Balliol, was one of 'Milner's young men' in South Africa[17] and married there a rather pretty and charming girl who was apparently teaching in a normal school, her people being English and Scotch, at Johannesburg. On retrenchment he was found a post as Assistant Director in Eastern Bengal whence he has, a year ago, been promoted higher.

It may be worth noting that the formation of a separate N.-W.F. Province, so keenly pursued by Lord Curzon, has by no means universally commended itself. In the desire to get a Government specialising on frontier problems, which involve so largely political and military considerations, the revenue and general administration of the by no means trivial strip of territory taken out of the Punjab is said to have suffered. Moreover, what was created is not an independent province as autonomous as that of the Punjab or the U.P., but an administrative district very directly subordinate to the Government of India. We learn that the officials of the N.-W.F. Province do not constitute a service by themselves but are reckoned as part of the Political Department of the Government of India, and they are interchangeable with the political agents etc., in and for the Native States. A considerable proportion of them seem to be military officers who are now engaged in the work elsewhere done by the civilians.

LYALLPUR 6/8th MARCH 1912

A flying visit to this centre of the great Chenal Canal colony[18] has given us a vision of the most extensive and reputedly most successful of the Indian irrigation schemes. A tract of some 5000 square miles, a quarter of a century ago almost barren desert inhabited by under 100,000 wild nomads, has been turned into a highly productive wheat-field (with cotton, sugar-cane, oil-seeds and vegetables as subsidiary crops) having something like two million inhabitants who are extremely prosperous and quite free from danger of famine. This has been done by a great scheme of bringing water from the Chenab, and distributing it all over the area by ramifying distributary canals. Owing to the Deputy-Commissioner being down with enteric, and other officers' bungalows being full up, we were sent to the *dak* bungalow, where we found the rooms far more commodious and comfortable than that we occupied at the hotel at Peshawar or at the hotel at Allahabad, though the food and cooking were more primitive.

We spent the morning going over a fragment of the colony, tramping from canal to canal under the guidance of one of the Canal Engineers (Yeoman)[19] and one of the Indian canal officials. The Indian spoke no English, and the English engineer, who may have been good at his technical job, neither knew nor cared anything about the people or their social and economic arrangements and was, indeed, after more than twenty years in India, as ignorant of and as uninterested in the country that he was serving as the ordinary sailor is about the ports at which he touches. All he had picked up were the common prejudices and dislikes of the English community. Certainly, from the three 'Cooper's Hill men'[20] whom we have met (Yeoman, Clutterbuck, Tullock) and the half-a-dozen others with whom S.W. dined at Hardwar, we can only derive the impression that 'Cooper's Hill' failed to produce any cultivation of mind or to turn out men of real education or breadth of view. They have for the most part proved far inferior to the members of the I.C.S., prejudiced and snobbish and unenlightened as some few of these are.

The Chenab colony is clearly a success in the main essentials and thus reflects credit on the engineers, though it seems that at the start the levels were very roughly taken, so that some of the first settlers found that they could get no water and threw up their allotments; and some of the allotting was badly done. But we were not so much impressed with the colony as a social and economic experiment as its repute had led us to expect. We have enlarged and corrected our impression from the official reports (gazetteer of the colony and '*Punjab Colony Manual*').

We were taken first to an inconceivably squalid mud compound housing half-a-dozen families with their buffaloes, in one hideous confusion. These turned out to be tenants — paying half of all their gross produce in kind, as well as bearing all the Government demands

for land tax, canal charges and local cess – of a small landlord owning
six 'squares', or 160 acres. The Government, whilst wishing to have a
majority of peasant owners, had given some land to capitalist owners,
thinking it desirable to have 'leaders of society'. By common consent
they have been a failure. Yet we were told that Sir Louis Dane, the
present Lt-Governor of the Punjab, was in favour of having them in
the new colonies.

We went next to a regular canal village, laid out officially at the
outset and inhabited by sixty families cultivating thirty squares, so that
each family had about 13 acres for which it was said to pay to the
Government, altogether, about 75 rupees (£5). This was more
prosperous in appearance than the tenants' mud huts. The mud
dwellings had extensive compounds; they were equipped with
elaborate wooden doors and the house of the headman, into which
we were allowed to peer, had a good deal of household possessions.
They had built themselves a small mosque and they supported a *maulvi*
whom we saw, and who taught the boys the Koran. But the people
looked very wild and barbarous; the cattle and children were very
promiscuously mixed up in the dirty compounds and there was, after
some twenty years of colonisation, no sign of education, sanitation or
medical aid – scarcely even decent roads or any really effective police
(as regards protection of village property) being provided by the
Government which attracted all these people to this spot. We learn
that at the start there was no thought of doing anything at all but allot
the land. No provision whatever was made – hardly any is yet made –
for the conditions of civilised life. It was regarded exclusively as a
question of water engineering and land allotment – neither the
educational nor the medical officers were asked to report what such
a colony required, and no one seems to have planned out anything like
a model settlement.

Truly, Indian Government is a thing of contrasts. In the afternoon,
we visited the Lyallpur Agricultural College, some four years old. Here
we found a very extensive, handsome, really well-built [facility] of
good quality 'oriental' design, splendidly equipped with science
laboratories, apparatus and library, with its own oil-gas plant making
electric light, having excellent lodging accommodation for over 100
youths under an able English chemist of expert skill, with two other
English professors and several Indian assistants working its own
extensive farm and experimental grounds of hundreds of acres – the
whole done apparently regardless of cost and containing only some 45
youths, half of whom were bribed to come by scholarships covering
their whole maintenance. On this College the Government had spent
between fifty and a hundred thousand pounds and was incurring a

heavy annual charge, whilst ninety per cent of the boys even on its own colony could not be provided with elementary schooling, on the plea there was no money available! Barnes,[21] the Principal, struck us as an able scientist and ambitious for discoveries – not really interested in teaching and least of all in teaching Indians. It appears that the small demand for agricultural instruction is rendered even smaller by the refusal of the Government to admit any Hindu students not belonging to an agricultural caste! Professedly, part of a policy to prevent the alienation of the land to *bunnias* and money-lenders, but (the Hindus said) really part of the policy of retaining the land for the Muslims.

In the evening, we dined with Gwyther,[22] the principal local Engineer, a quiet, able man who had been born in India and trained at Rurki. There we met Gibbs,[23] a Cooper's Hill man superior in distinction to any yet seen, inventor of 'Gibbs' Module' (a water measuring device) and ridiculously like Sir William Ramsay.[24] We had seen in the afternoon Abdul Kadir, a Muslim Pleader (getting the Government briefs), who was like other educated Muslims in quiet charm, but like them also, servile in dependence on the British Government and horribly conscious (in spite of claiming to be a ruling race) of inability to organise or initiate or maintain anything without Government aid.

LAHORE 9/12th MARCH 1912

Our second brief stay in Lahore was, besides visits to the Fort and the Shardara tombs,[25] marked by (1) a Hindu dinner party (2) an interesting meeting with a score of leading Muslims at a Judge's house (3) a garden party at a Hindu capitalist's to meet the leading Hindus (4) lunch at the L[t].-Governor's (5) a visit to the Islami College (6) a long visit with Lajpat Rai to the *Arya Samaj* school and college (7) a visit to the Aitchison Chiefs' College (8) dinner party of officials at the house of the Director of Public Instruction and (9) tea with the Agnews (District Judge)[26] – no bad record for three days! We failed to find time to utilise our introductions to the Anglican bishop and the leading Anglican deaconess.

The dinner party at Rambaj Dutt Chaudhuri's has been already described.[27] These dozen Hindu gentlemen and ladies (one 'enlightened orthodox', two *Brahmo Samaj* and the rest *Arya Samaj*), together with the garden party of similarly-mixed Hinduism, left on our minds the impression that the Hindus of Lahore, as compared with those of Calcutta, were a little 'provincial' in manners and ideas, much as Manchester and Newcastle would compare with London – perhaps a little sturdier, but with that, somewhat 'rougher'. They were at least equally 'nationalist'.

There seems to be a vigorous branch of the *Brahmo Samaj* at Lahore quite independent of Calcutta and Bombay, small in membership but having substantial endowments which support a local newspaper (*Tribune*)[28] and a local college. From the editor of the one and the Principal of the other, and from the Cambridge wrangler who was prof. of mathematics at the Government College (Chowla,[29] with a refined and educated wife from Kashmir way, as white as any Englishwoman), we gathered that the *Brahmo Samaj* here, though thus relatively wealthy (again, like English Unitarianism), was not really more 'alive' or popularly influential than those at Calcutta and Bombay. The individual members were people of grace and charm and refinement who found in their abstract religion a resting place and freedom to contract legal marriages, but hardly desired propaganda or proselytism.

The Islami College, housed in a new brick building without amenity, provided a hundred or more Muslim youths with the means of getting a Punjab University degree without resorting to Christian or *Arya Samaj* colleges, on the one hand, or the completely secular Government College on the other. It had had a succession of Muslim Principals who had more or less failed, partly because of the inveterate habit of the Muslim governing body of interfering with internal discipline; and it was now under a somewhat second-rate English Oxford man (Martin), who had been promoted from being an assistant master at Aligarh. It struck us as a place poor in spirit, with inferior Muslim professors concerned only to get its youths through the B.A. examination. But it aspired to become a constituent college of the new Islamic University. It had however a department in which the '*Unani*' or Muslim medicine[30] was taught by *hakims*, which might usefully be developed into a practical teaching of hygiene and physiology alongside of the weird '*materia medica*' and traditional therapeutics of the Muslim doctors. We have however found no one prepared to accept, or even to understand, the idea of such a development.

The Aitchison Chiefs' College, a Gov^t foundation of a generation ago,[31] lived in the most magnificent college buildings that we have yet seen, built in charming 'Saracenic' style with gorgeous amplitude of space, amid groves and gardens and playing fields of opulent magnitude. Here about a hundred sons of native Chiefs, either ruling or practically noble, were educated from 7 to 17 or 20 up to matriculation standard. Each had his own servants (from 3 to 25!) and horses and provided his own food. (A common dining room had lately been started as an innovation to increase corporate feeling.) It was the young Raja of Faridkot,[32] a tiny independent state, who had

25 servants for himself and a brother. The family had asked that he should have sixty! The college authorities compromised on 25 including a domestic tutor, a *'manloi'* to attend to devotions, cooks and coachmen, etc. and a special *'chaukidar'*, or watchman.

The boys were reading and playing games as they chose, it being Sunday. Our host (Cornah),[33] an energetic and vivacious young Englishman, was Assistant Principal, whose vocation was school-mastering, which he probably did well. (Practically no supervision over the boys at night, though they slept in twos and threes in adjoining small rooms.)

The Director of Public instruction (Godley)[34] was a 'stick' — a dull, wooden, though doubtless honest and conscientious cousin of the late Under-Sec[t.] at the India Office — probably 'jobbed' into his present billet after coming out as professor in the Gov[t] College. He seemed to have no particular knowledge of educational administration, and was certainly unaware of the expedients being tried in other parts of India — indeed, he appeared unconscious that there *were* any problems to be solved. To him it was merely a question of getting enough trained teachers and of securing from the Lieu[t.]-Gov[r] sufficient money to pay them. The brightest of the company at his house was G. A. Wathen,[35] a professor at the Gov[t] College (married to a connection of the Buxtons[36]) who deplored the obstruction which the Deputy Comm[rs] usually offered to educational progress (thinking roads much more necessary and much more certainly useful than schools) and the fact that the Government always consulted these Deputy Comm[rs] on educational problems, yet never the Principals and professors of colleges nor the heads of schools. For instance, Gokhale's Bill was sent out broadcast for opinions (which, as expected, were usually hostile) to the civilian officers, but not to anyone concerned in educational work. He strongly advocated making the educational service an integral part of the I.C.S.

The Muslim party at the house of Mr. Justice Shah Din[37] was distinctly interesting. B.W. went an hour earlier to meet the *'purdah'* ladies, several dozen of them in gorgeous raiment, one a Begum of high rank in magnificent jewels, several speaking English, having been (or actually being) pupils of the English Anglican girls' school, which gains their presence by having a *maulvi* to teach the Koran. The score of men whom we both talked with later included the leading Islamic Pleaders and barristers, an editor or two, professors and Gov[t] officials. They all wished British rule to continue, for fear of succumbing before the Hindus, they would be glad if Government would aid the *muktabs* by peripatetic teachers; they nearly all desired a prompt modification and gradual cessation of the *purdah* system, though none of them would begin; they despaired of getting their girls educated (only a tiny few being rich enough to go in carriages to a school even if their families would allow this). Here again, the Muslims were despairing of achieving anything without Government aid. They said that, until quite lately, no Muslim above the labouring class would take to any occupation other than war and government; even now, there were far fewer Muslim lawyers than Hindu lawyers; and there were hardly any in business. Nor will the landowners take up agriculture as a profession and devote themselves to developing their estates — they like to be mere rent receivers.

We are struck by the enormous value to the Muslim community in India of the work done by Sir Syed Ahmed in founding and building up Aligarh College.[38] It looks as if, but for Aligarh, there would today be scarcely any Muslim in India able to rise above the rank of an artisan or a subordinate of police. The Hindus would perforce have held not only the whole legal profession but also the whole Government service. We meet practically no Muslim judge, barrister, or civil servant of standing who is not an ex-student of Aligarh. It is instructive to remember that Sir Syed Ahmed was, almost to the end, opposed by the bulk of the *maulvis*, and by a very large proportion of the wealthy Muslims. And to this day they don't like 'western learning' or anything else not emanating from Islam itself. Their present thirst for education is avowedly only in order that they may not be ousted by the Hindus.

A garden party of Hindus was given for us by Harkishen Lal at the instance of Lajpat Rai (who has already been described).[39] Harkishen Lal is a Hindu barrister who has gone into business on a large scale — government contracting, banking, flour-mill owning and what not. He seems to be in all the big business undertakings of the Punjab, where English capitalism does not seem to prevail to any great extent; and he may be anything between a millionaire or (as Agnew somewhat maliciously suggested) a manipulator of balances among his manifold undertakings. He seemed to us a shrewd and able business man, free from prejudices or enthusiasms, cool and a little cynical, good friends with both the *Brahmo Samaj* and the *Arya Samaj* but not actually a member of either body. His wife, a pleasant-looking, silent Hindu, was not '*purdah*' and appeared to welcome us when we called and was present also at the garden party to meet some fifty Hindu men and half-a-dozen *Brahmo Samaj* ladies. The men were Pleaders, editors, professors and Gov[t] officials; exclusively Hindus and mostly *Arya Samaj* or *Brahmo Samaj*. The conversation turned on the same points as with other educated Hindus: they were all 'nationalist' in sympathy and they had the usual grievances. Among the ladies was the Maharaja

Dhulip Singh's daughter, who had married a local Hindu 'bourgeois' and was supposed to hold distinctly 'seditious' opinions!

We were distinctly glad that we had not accepted the Agnews' proffered hospitality, though Mrs. Agnew seemed a nice woman, with intelligence and open-mindedness. He turned out to be the officer who as Magistrate had begun the proceedings against Lajpat Rai which led to the latter's arbitrary deportation without trial. It would have been awkward for us, if we had stayed at Agnew's house, to have had our four separate meetings with Lajpat Rai! He told us that Penton, the Financial-Comm^r of the Punjab, had suggested the expedient of deportation and had drawn attention to the long-forgotten power to deport. The Gov^t, as Agnew admitted to us, never formulated any charge against Lajpat Rai or revealed the cause of his deportation, or made any excuse or apology or explanation of their high-handed proceedings. Agnew, who talked loosely and carelessly (relying on our ignorance), made out that Lajpat Rai had suffered nothing! 'He had the time of his life: he was taken to the station in a motor car and given a pleasant holiday in Burma.' 'Treated like a King,' said Bosworth-Smith,[40] a Deputy-Commissioner of the Punjab, to us on board the boat. As if it was nothing to carry off a lawyer for six months away from his practice; to exile him from his wife and family; to make no allowance for their maintenance and to keep him a prisoner under close custody (never allowed out without a warder) during the hot weather in Mandalay!

What happened was that Sir D. Ibbetson, the L^t.-Governor, asked half-a-dozen people who were the people most influential in fomenting discontent, and they all gave Lajpat Rai as a leader. When we innocently enquired what was alleged against Lajpat Rai, Agnew mysteriously said that this was strictly confidential and had never been published – he seemed to think of it as of no consequence that Lajpat Rai accordingly had no chance of denying, disproving or explaining – but Agnew accidentally let out that the Gov^t thought that Lajpat Rai was tampering with the troops. Of this, we can discover no sort of evidence. But as we have had it put to us by naïve Englishmen, it comes only to this, that the Punjab furnishes the mainstay of the Indian Army (apart from the Gurkhas); and these Punjabi soldiers are nearly all themselves cultivators or of cultivators' families; so that any stirring up of discontent among the Punjabi cultivators excites discontent among those Punjabis who are serving in the Army – *hence any* agitation in the Punjab is in effect to excite disaffection among the soldiers!

This has been quite seriously urged upon us more than once as a reason why all agitation in the Punjab must be stopped at once, however peaceful and constitutional, and whatever the grievance. In confirmation of this we may record the gossip that when the new Canal Act was arousing great discontent in 1907–8, as an infringement of the promises made to the colonists (it was on this that a foul-mouthed agitator, Agit Singh,[41] was operating when he was summarily deported at the same time as Lajpat Rai), Lord Kitchener is said to have insisted on the Gov^t of India vetoing the Act (which it did), saying that otherwise he would not answer for the loyalty of the Sikhs in the Army. Agnew of course did not explain this to us; but we believe it to be the view on which the Punjab Gov^t acted. We learn that Lord Morley telegraphed out that there were to be no prosecutions for the vague crime of 'sedition'; if the Government prosecuted, it was to be for some definite offence. Agit Singh, by the way, appears to have been a person of no importance who railed at everybody in turn; a mob orator and journalist quite unconnected with Lajpat Rai. The English officials were ignorant of what had happened to him and told us all sorts of stories. The truth is that when brought back from deportation he discreetly went away to avoid police persecution – first to Persia, where he embraced Islam, and then to Constantinople where he is now editing a local newspaper.

Agnew was curiously like Sydney Buxton in physical appearance, manners and speech and had even the same kind of narrow precision of intellect; but he lacked Sydney Buxton's fundamental liberalism and fair-mindedness. We talked to him about the tremendous powers of imprisonment without conviction given to all Magistrates in India by their power of requiring anyone to find sureties, or in default, to go to prison ('rigorous imprisonment') for as much as two or three years. This is habitually used with regard to people whom the police report as 'of bad life', and it is not infrequently employed for 'political' agitators or lecturers. The Magistrate may even stipulate that the two or three sureties to be found, for some quite large sum, shall be residents in the locality, of known loyalty and good character and payers of so much in direct taxation. He can thus make it quite impracticable for the prisoner to find the sureties, *and he habitually does this*, intending and wishing to send him to prison for a year or so in default – without conviction of any offence!

This procedure appears to be regularly used throughout India with regard to reputed 'bad characters' – who are of course usually humble folk – when crime is rife and evidence cannot be obtained. Agnew said it was a very 'successful' device. *Dacoity*,[42] or cattle stealing, would be prevalent; no evidence could be obtained; the police ran in a dozen men; the magistrate committed them to prison in default of finding sureties; and the crimes ceased! He admitted that it was theoretically indefensible and said, of course, that the Magistrate ought not to impose plainly impossible conditions; but he asserted that the Indian Government must have some such power of summary imprisonment owing to the difficulty of getting evidence. When we pointed out that it was used in cases where full evidence was available (as in the case of the *Arya Samaj* lecturer at Jhansi), he evaded the issue. Someone ought to ask for a return of men imprisoned without conviction merely in default of finding sureties. It is a case of oppressing the poor and weak when rich men do not suffer; and it lends a very potent handle to police persecution of unpopular persons.

Our lunch at Gov^t House was the usual formality. Sir Louis Dane seemed a kindly, genial administrator of common sense and practical judgement in avoiding trouble. He had retired from the I.C.S. ten or twelve years ago and became an R.M.[43] in Ireland; but his wife found this intolerable after India and he asked and was given the post of Resident at Kashmir, whence on Sir Denzil Ibbetson's death he was made Lieu^t-Govr of the Punjab — apparently as a man capable of smoothing down things after Ibbetson had stirred them up. But though out of practical English common sense he smoothed things down, he had all the usual Anglo-Indian prejudices and he had even more than the common Anglo-Indian disingenuousness in talking to inquisitive tourists whom he thought ignorant (*vide* the story of the two *Arya Samaj* students & the pistols, already given). Lady Dane thought that no friendly intercourse with Indians was possible because they had nothing to talk about! We have never quite understood this complaint seeing how much we found to talk about with both Hindus and Muslims.

The conversation at the luncheon table between the two A.D.C.'s and the daughters made us realise what was meant. It turned exclusively on lawn tennis, polo and the various race meetings and tournaments. Now, it may be that races are separated from each other more by their amusements (and as regards the English, by their incessant talking about their peculiar amusements) than by their differences of religion, of language, of dress or even of cookery. Because the educated Indians don't talk tennis or polo the average Englishman thinks they can have nothing to talk about! Whereas it is *he* who is conversationally destitute. The educated Indians seem to us as ready as we are to talk about public affairs, about social and economic problems, about music and art, about philosophy and even about religion. But then, all these topics are banished from a large section of English society.

DELHI 12–16th MARCH 1912

We were disappointed in Delhi which, fine as some of its things are,
does not come well after Agra. But we were whirled to the Qutb
Minar[44] in the Commissioner's motor car, and spent an hour
wandering about these wonderful ruins with great satisfaction. It is
perhaps the best column of victory in the world; and the neighbouring
village had various interesting sights. On our way back, among other
sights we were interested in Humayun's Mausoleum as the forerunner
of the Taj,[45] of which it exhibits nearly all the features, missing only
the perfection of the whole. This disposes of the characteristic story,
repeated by Anglo-Indian after Anglo-Indian, that the Taj was built by
Italians! There is not a fragment of evidence that any 'Italian' of artistic
competence was ever at the Mughal Court; and the Italians at the time
the Taj was built were putting up the terrible Renaissance churches
denounced by Ruskin.[46] The idle story is only an instance of the
English lack of generosity to the Indians and of inability to recognise
any point in which Indians could conceivably excel Europeans.

We saw at Delhi, as usual, some leading Muslims, who were as
elsewhere. Out of a local Bar of fifty or sixty only six or eight were
Muslims, though Delhi has nearly as many Muslims as Hindus. The
bank where we got money had only Hindu clerks. The majority of the
Gov[t] officials were Hindus. The business is nearly all in the hands of
Hindus. The Muslims are mostly artisans, labourers and cultivators.
There is no Muslim college, only one (inferior) Muslim high school for
all Delhi, and apparently very few primary schools (apart from the
dwindling *muktabs* at the mosques). Our Muslim friends deplored all
this but seemed to despair of altering it. The most attractive of them in
many ways was Latifi,[47] an Anglicised Indian (St. John's, Oxford) in the
I.C.S., married to an educated Indian wife out of *purdah*. He was
officiating as District Judge but had lately spent a year in describing all
the industries of the Punjab, published as a book – quite ably done,
with many minor suggestions for Government aid in their improvement. He attributed the Muslim backwardness in business to their
inability to accept interest. When pressed as to how that interfered
with the ordinary commercial enterprise, which needed to borrow but
never had occasion to lend money, he said that the Muslim in business
was at a disadvantage in borrowing because he could not usually find
any willing lender who knew him intimately, or as a friend – such
being usually his co-religionists and therefore unable to lend at interest.
He thus always had to pay high interest to a stranger instead of the
low rate that an intimate knowing his character would be willing to
lend at. (He said they were unwilling to lend without interest and

hence did not lend at all, but always invested in land to get the rents.) This disadvantage seems to us unsubstantial. The explanation may be psychological.

We were interested to find that both the Comm[r] (Dallas)[48] and the Deputy-Comm[r] (Beadon)[49] of Delhi were ex-officers; the Punjab service seems to be full of these Army officers and this goes far to explain to us the ill-success of its administration compared with that of the U.P. Certainly those we have met or heard of at Lahore, Amritsar and Delhi appeared most unsympathetic administrators, neither understanding nor caring about the feelings of the educated Indian, and blandly unconscious of there being anything to study in the art of administration, of which they were entirely ignorant. They were doubtless upright Magistrates and honest officials incapable of being bribed, though not at all incapable of being prejudiced.

The Deputy-Comm[r] of Delhi was giving a garden party to 'natives' to which we were invited, as it was understood that we 'wished to meet natives'. It appeared that there were two garden parties on successive days, one for the English and their wives and one for the 'natives'. Latifi (being of the I.C.S.) and his wife were the only 'natives' present at the former. At the latter, the only English present were the Deputy-Comm[r] (Beadon) and his wife as hostess, the Comm[r] (Dallas) and his wife; the editor of the local newspaper, and the chairman of the local (English) Chamber of Commerce, both rather ineligible, lower-middle class men; a missionary (Andrews)[50] and a couple of clergy, who had been specially told to come; and ourselves. Among the Indians were the descendant of the Mughal Emperor and one or two other 'princes', various great Muslim 'nobles', all the Indian officials of a certain status, and Pleaders, lecturers, etc. For their amusement, an Indian conjuring performance was provided which no one attended to. The whole arrangement seemed a monument of invidious race distinction and snobbishness which does the English administration no credit.

We dined and also went to tea at the Cambridge Mission, which carried on practically the only university college at Delhi[51] (there is one other, a feeble Hindu college of inferior grade only recognised up to the intermediate arts examination and always on the point of being closed),[52] besides [inspecting] schools, dispensaries, and *zenana* work.[53] The Principal (Allnutt),[54] who had been 32 years at his post, was pathetically like a tired mill-horse wearied and worn out by his perpetual grind, but genial, kindly and broad-minded to the last. His 200 college students were more than half Hindu, less than a third Muslim and about an eighth Christians. No attempt at proselytism was made, though simple Christian services were held and only an infinitesimal fraction had ever been converted in all that time. He had thus brought up innumerable masters for Hindu and Muslim schools all over the Punjab. They had had some successful girls' schools for Muslims conducted by lady teachers *with a maulvi to teach the Koran*; but it was decided (by whom?) that this latter piece of toleration was going too far for a Christian mission, and when the teaching of the Koran was dropped, the attendance at once fell to nothing. Now they were trying to re-open one school, and with great difficulty they were getting three girls to promise to attend.

The other man in whom we were interested was the [missionary] in command, Andrews, who had been greatly commended to us by various people as the only enthusiastic 'pro-native' among the missionaries. He proved to be a somewhat 'smooth' and disingenuous 'ecclesiastic', clean-shaven and celibate, of the 'priestly' type. We unfortunately fell out with him straightaway as he proved to be full of rather malicious slanders against the *Arya Samaj*, Lajpat Rai and others whom we knew and respected – the statements being plainly, to our knowledge, loose and even disingenuous aspersions, which it was, to say the least of it, uncharitable to pass on to presumably ignorant enquirers. At our subsequent meeting we avoided this dangerous topic; but Andrews manifested the same '*mauvaise langue*' about the Indians and their character and characteristics – making us feel that he had the same jealous annoyance that we have noticed in other missionaries in North India.

JAIPUR 17–19ᵗʰ MARCH 1912

A night journey brought us at five in the morning to the British Residency here, to which we had been spontaneously invited by Col. Showers,[55] to whom the Impeys had written from Chhatarpur. The Residency is a two-centuries-old marble palace in wide and pleasant grounds, with large and lofty rooms somewhat splendidly furnished in quite good taste, apparently at the expense of the Jaipur state, to which it belongs. Col. Showers turned out to be a kindly, genial and simple-minded soldier so deaf that he could hear only when he put up his ear-trumpet to one's mouth, an excellent host so far as letting us do what we liked is concerned; but not able to be very communicative. As usual the wife is in England.

We gather from him that Political Agents at the Native States tend to interfere less rather than more as time goes on, and to interfere very little indeed with the larger states, unless invited to give advice, which is not often the case. He sees the Maharaja regularly, once a week on Thursday afternoon. He tells us that only Hyderabad, Mysore, Kashmir,

Nepal and Baroda have Residents all to themselves: all the others, even Gwalior, Jaipur, Bhopal and Patiala, are grouped with other and smaller states – perhaps to diminish the invidiousness of there being a 'Resident' in a state. The principal business is now the conduct of correspondence between the states and the Gov[t] of India. But the 'Resident' has summary magisterial powers over all British subjects in the state; he was not sure whether he had over European foreigners.

[BW→] We did not see the Maharaja[56] – an old gentleman of bad reputation, selfish, sensual and intensely superstitious – like so many Chiefs, childless and refusing to nominate his heir. Colonel Showers suggested that the childlessness of so many of these ruling Chiefs is deliberate, because they are so intensely jealous and fearful of an 'heir apparent' – and he pointed to the fact that this man has numerous illegitimate children and three legitimate wives, but no heir. The P[SW: rime] M[SW: inister] was a Muslim – an Aligarh boy to whom Morison introduced us, a great landed proprietor in the U.P. – a dignified and sensible elderly man, but not interesting.[57] Sidney saw also the Private Secretary [SW: to the Maharaja], a cultivated and plausible Bengali Brahmin. Perhaps we learnt most from the refined and intelligent young Brahmin student who was deputed to attend us. From what he said and implied, we gathered that the Maharaja's Government was priest-ridden, narrow-minded and despotic – no new movements being tolerated – enormous sums being spent on priests, *sadhus* and religious mendicants, and such education as is given being entirely in the hands of men brought up in Jaipur.

The *Arya Samaj* had some dozen members among officials and professors, but they had to keep very quiet as the Maharaja objected to them on religious and political grounds. To Muslims and Christians he was cordially tolerant. No beef was allowed in the state: to kill a cow meant imprisonment for life – exactly the same punishment as for the murder of a man. We visited two *Rajput*[58] noblemen's houses – one a comfortable European bungalow, the other a more resplendent and distinctively Indian residence with fine formal gardens, tanks, and running water channels with innumerable flower pots alongside them. In both cases our hosts were tall, handsome, accomplished men, speaking English fluently, devotees of sport and polo, with a large family of boys surrounding them – handsome, smartly-dressed little urchins with pretty manners. But these *Rajput grandees* seemed to be leading somewhat aimless lives – they ought all to have been in the Army but this the B.G. denies them except in subordinate positions, which their rank and wealth makes impossible to accept; and all part in the Government of the country is denied them by the constitution of the Native State.

[SW→] We learnt that it was felt as a drawback by the young student & by his class that they were excluded, as being not British subjects, from eligibility for the I.C.S., and indeed, also the Provincial Service. He said that only two Jaipuri men had ever got into the Indian Medical Service, and that only by making out that they were British subjects — perhaps as the sons of British subjects. He admitted that as regards subordinate posts in the Provincial Service, no great strictness was observed and a very short term of residence in the province might suffice to qualify. We learnt afterwards that the technical disqualification was often ignored or got over in cases where, through influence, it was really desired to appoint — though this does not make the matter any better! The result is to make it rather hopeless for clever and ambitious young men in backward Native States. At the Jaipur College (which is a full B.A. and B.Sc. college affiliated to Allahabad University), the hundred-odd students nearly all hoped for Jaipur Government employment, which most of them would fail to get. Our informant himself thought of going to the Rurki Engineering College, in order to get an engineering post. He had thought of medicine but had been unlucky; he was simultaneously a candidate for admission to Lahore and Lucknow Medical Colleges and failed to pass at the former. For the latter he did pass, but was rejected on the ground that he had sat also at Lahore. We thought that probably (as his father was a retired Superintendent of Jaipur Customs and his relations were in Jaipur Government employ) he would also get a small appointment.

It is part of the state feeling that all the nine professors at the Maharaja's College (except the Principal whom we saw, who had gone to Muir College to get his M.A.) were of that college only. Two of them taught between them all natural science, and others mathematics and the arts subjects. We took the opportunity of suggesting the establishment of post-graduate scholarships tenable elsewhere, and in particular, of sending new professors to see the other colleges of India at least. There was also a Sanskrit College with a hundred students, a high school of several hundreds and lower schools — all for boys — together with a small nobles' school (of 15) for the sons of great folk. We heard also of Jain schools & Muslim schools so that Jaipur city seems rather well-provided educationally.

ADAIPUR 23–25th M^{ch} 1912[59]

We came here *via* Chitorgarh which we stopped to see, involving a night in a quite comfortable *dak* bungalow. We found the state elephant which came to meet us at the station altogether too slow a method of progression – the poor beast had an open sore on the leg which made it whimper when it knelt down – so we hired a *tonga*[60] to go up the Fort, which is a great hill like that of Gwalior. The two towers, one Jain and one Hindu, were well worth seeing, as was also the confused mass of ruins of palaces, temples, tanks, etc.

At Adaipur we had the state guest house to ourselves & enjoyed two days' restful driving out morning and evening and browsing over an armful of books borrowed from the youthful Scottish missionary in the heat of the day. Of this State (Mewar) we saw only a youthful Private Secretary, a Bengali Brahmin whose father was a judicial officer in the service. The Maharana, as the ruler is styled, was away tiger-shooting, to which he devotes every possible moment.[61] He is a man of 65, intensely conservative and priest-ridden, opposed to all innovations, scoffing at those Hindus he calls 'knife and folk wallahs', spending the revenue on his amusements and doing nothing for progress, though his state seems [to be] getting more and more barren, and a great scheme of irrigation is (we were told) well within his power. Here there is no college and no educational or other opportunities for the young men – the place seemed to us dead, partly because the population was diminished by flight from the plague which was mildly raging. The Scottish Presbyterians have had a mission here for thirty-five years and have gradually won their way into the Maharana's favour by the medical skill and tact of Dr. Shepherd, who is an M.D. and runs a free hospital. He told us he had in the whole state 140 Indian Christians. A nice young Aberdonian (A. C. Grant) had just come out as his assistant and it was from him that we borrowed books.

The British Resident (Col. Kaye)[62] was away 'in Camp', visiting his other states. His wife entertained us and nearly all the other English residents to dinner – the Agency Surgeon, the Railway Engineer, the Adjutant to the imperial service force here and their wives – a rather 'terrible' party, the hostess and her lady friends in extremely *décolleté* and ultra-smart gowns, the conversation more than usually 'Anglo-Indian' in its contempt for the 'natives', its concentration on petty grievances and its snobbishness. But these English in such Native States as this have nothing to do and it is just as well that those who are fit for nothing better should be sent there.

AJMERE[63] 19–21st Mch 1912

We omitted to describe our two nights' stay at Ajmere, where we slept at the railway station refreshment rooms as the British Resident was

away and the Waddington's house[64] was full. When the train arrived at
10.30 p.m., an hour late, we tumbled out into a crowd of a dozen
Hindu gentlemen bowing and salaaming; these turned out to be the
leading members of the *Arya Samaj* who had come to welcome us and
(as we rather feared) for a talk! We were dead tired and could only
dismiss them abruptly and sit down to our belated dinner. Next
morning, one of the principals among them (Har Bilas Sarda),[65] a man
having four shops selling piece-goods, a Municipal Commissioner,
drove round with us for two hours to the sights. We spent two hours
more inspecting the *Arya Samaj* institutions. And in the evening half-a-
dozen of the deputation of the night before came and talked to us for a
couple of hours.

These educated and progressive *Arya Samajists* are certainly
remarkable men (Pleaders, officials and businessmen) who, in Ajmere,
have shown great organising and managing ability. They have a
successful printing and publishing establishment where they were
producing cheap editions of the Vedas and of Dayanand's writings,
as well as school books and pamphlets. The compositors worked only
45 hours per week. The adjacent orphanage provided for some two
hundred and more boys and girls who were being brought up and
educated. This was rather a crude sort of 'institution', the girls
especially looking depressed and unduly docile. But the upbringing
of girls is a difficult problem in India. These girls were apparently
'married by advertisement', so to speak, the bridegroom being required
to deposit some 2000 rupees as security that the bride would not have
to be provided for again by the orphanage. Some of the boys, the
mentally dull ones, were being taught carpentering. Otherwise, the
education seemed commonplace. It was rather an 'amateur' orphanage
dealing with the most hopeless class of waifs and strays, foundlings
abandoned by their parents, and so on. But its officers seemed devoted,
the management economical and the intention excellent.

The *Arya Samaj* day school has grown into a large affair, including
altogether some six or seven hundred boys and reaching up to the
entrance examination of Allahabad University. It was attended by boys
of all creeds and classes, three fourths of them not being children of
Arya Samajists. Here too the school seemed to have a good spirit,
though it did not strike us as particularly advanced educationally.
There was only a tiny nucleus of a library.

We gathered that the actual membership of the *Arya Samaj* in
Ajmere was small — a couple of hundred or so — and that it was not
increasing, though the society counted a large number of sympathisers
who preferred not actually to join as members. A voluble Pleader
(author of '*Hindu Superiority*', a somewhat worthless, because indiscri-

minate and uncritical compilation of extracts proving the greatness of Hindu civilisation in the past) who was among our evening party, said that the first apostolic fervour had passed away, and that the society now suffered from dissensions and splits between those who wanted to observe, verbally and precisely, the letter of Dayanand's writings, and those who claimed freedom to progress in their spirit – the latter being termed the 'flesh-eaters' because one of their innovations was to eat meat if they chose.

We lunched and spent the afternoon at the Mayo College, the best of the four 'Chiefs' colleges' of North India, now under a man of mark, the first educational personality we have met in India (Waddington). The really beautiful buildings, for which Sir Swinton Jacob[66] is responsible, were built partly by the Government of India, partly by the ruling Chiefs themselves, each state having its own house (Jaipur, Adaipur, Jodhpur, Kashmir, etc.) – some nine or ten in all – and sending free of charge as many pupils as it chooses, in return for an original donation. The boys, from 7 to 25 in age, have their own horses and servants and eat each by himself (even those in each state house not messing together). A few have English guardians who are in charge of them, living in houses of their own (including a son of the Gaikwar of Baroda, after being successively in half-a-dozen schools in England). Waddington himself had the young Raja of Idar (grandson of Sir Pertab Singh, now Regent of Jodhpur[67]) living in his house.

The hundred or more boys were playing cricket and tennis in the beautiful and extensive grounds. No 'chapel' was visible but we were pointed [out] a Hindu temple right away in an obscure corner, to which all the Hindu boys were compulsorily taken every afternoon to enable them to 'do *puja*' for a few minutes. There was a Brahmin whose duty it was to instruct them, but we gathered from Waddington that the whole thing was perfunctory and that, although the Chiefs insisted on the performance of the necessary rites, they were not keen on anything more. There was one Muslim house (that of the State of Tonk) which had its own *maulvi* and mosque.

The schooling is not very thorough or advanced, the boys finding some difficulty in intellectual work, and are not spurred onward by parental pressure. The assistant masters seemed undistinguished young men interested in cricket and sport. But Waddington is fully conscious that it is not enough, and he has gradually, after 37 years existence of the College, managed to develop a 'post-diploma course' for boys who have already passed the entrance examination. This he now hopes to see split off into a separate 'Chiefs' University', which some of the Chiefs wish to establish at Delhi, the new capital! He was pessimistic as to the education of the Chiefs, could not say what was the best course to pursue, was definitely against English schools for them, thought on the whole that Mayo College, with the proposed new Chiefs' University, was the best that could be done for them – with perhaps a year's post-graduate study in England at an advanced age, or better still, a year's leisurely travel with a wise *begleiter*.[68]

It is noteworthy that Waddington, though a man of exceptional force and personality, was not really interested in India or Indian problems, and applied himself solely to his job of directing a school for the sons of these proud Chiefs, without apparently any ulterior thoughts. We did not gather that he had a high opinion of the Chiefs, either for capacity, conduct or ability to do business.

[BW→] AHMADABAD MARCH 28–APRIL 1st [1912]

We had a delightful two days at Mount Abu seeing its fantastically beautiful [SW: Dilwara][69] temples and journeying in two Indian *rickshas* (far inferior in comfort and common sense to the Japanese) right into the mountains, with wonderful views of the great desert plain to the ruined temples of [SW: Achilgarh].[70] We were staying with an attractive, refined and sensible political officer – Sir Elliot [SW: Colvin][71] – the Agent of the Governor-General [SW: for] Rajputana, and controlling about thirty states. He confirmed our other information, that the B.G. was interfering less and less with the government of these states. He also thought that all natives of India, even those of Native States, should be eligible for appointments. He was a somewhat stiff conservative in general opinions, with the usual nervous dread of criticism of the British Government as a kind of sedition which must not be played with. Like Colonel Impey, he was not much interested in the problems of British India apart from the Native States and wholly unsympathetic to nationalist aspirations. All the same, his modesty and general good sense and personal charm made the atmosphere of his home quite sympathetic, even to two such obstreperous reformers as ourselves.

Here in Ahmadabad we are living in quite a different atmosphere. The Commissioner of the place [SW: Barrow[72] – a grand-nephew of Charles Dickens] telegraphed to Mount Abu to ask us to stay with him and we drove out, some three miles from the station, and found ourselves in a roomy old [SW: Muslim] palace [SW: or garden house] with a broad terrace on to the river, now meandering within its broad, dried-up basin. The situation is picturesque and the establishment most comfortable. But our host is [SW: a problem]. He is a tall, thick-boned, somewhat coarsely-featured man – the remnants of a fine countenance which has quite obviously grown coarse with the experiences of life. His wife is a confirmed invalid and lives in England with the three daughters. Our host seems to live a life of isolation — both from the 'natives', whom he despises, and from the few English people with whom he seems on very distant terms. We rather suspect some 'skeleton' stored away in the roomy old palace or in a humble establishment near by. He is most hospitable and quite anxious to tell us everything and refreshingly frank. For instance, he implied and even expressly admitted that 'Commissioners' were no longer wanted. He showed us all the papers with which he had to deal — all cases which did not seem to us or even to him to require his intervention between the Collector and the Government of Bombay.

There are [SW: only] three Commissioners [SW: for all] Bombay Presidency. [SW: He] has himself six Collectors and two Political Agents more or less under his direction — [SW: the three] Commissioners meet regularly during the year to discuss questions which arise in the Presidency and to send reports to Bombay. Our impression is that Commissioner Barrow is biding out his extreme limit of time with the minimum of exertion, rather than take his pension to live in retirement with his wife and daughters. He is hopelessly out of sympathy with anything Indian — looks on all natives, except a few British-educated aristocrats, as 'niggers' who have to be kept in their proper place. He violently resented the suggestion that the day might come when an exceptionally accomplished Indian might be appointed as Lieu$^{t.}$-Governor, or even as Governor of one of the presidencies, and he thought it had been a mistake to let Indians rise to the rank of Commissioner or even Collector. In fact, Barrow in general attitude on Indian affairs, and I suspect in private life, represents the old Anglo-Indian officer of fifty years ago. As might be expected, he complained that the young men who are now coming out are of a lower social status and 'no good' as a governing race.

[SW→] We have mostly spent our mornings and evenings in driving about, seeing the very large number of beautiful mosques and tombs and Jain temples. But one afternoon was devoted to an 'At Home' given by the Gujarat branch of the National Indian Association[73] to meet us. Here we shook hands and said a few words with one or two hundred Indian men and women — mostly Hindus, Jains and Parsees — the men being Pleaders, professors, officials, mill-owners and retired pensioners, and the women mostly Parsees or enlightened Hindus who have no *purdah* (common in Bombay Presidency), or members of the Bombay analogue of the *Brahmo Samaj*.[74] All spoke English more or less, and the party was just what it would have been in an English provincial town except for more graceful manners, somewhat greater intellectuality and more idealism; and on the other hand, somewhat greater shyness and diffidence among the women and somewhat less of 'forcefulness' among the men.

One morning we spent in going over the great cotton mills of Sir Chinubhai Madhavial, established some sixty years ago and now employing 4000 hands, mostly men and boys.[75] The owner is a Brahmin, a millionaire, very benevolent with his wealth, and he seemed to us a man of quiet power, calm wisdom and wise moderation of opinions. The machinery and organisation seemed excellent: there was one Lancashire 'mill-manager' and two other English employed in some other capacities, the rest of the 4000 being Hindu or Muslim. These operatives were working well and regularly, in marked contrast with those in John's mills at Agra. But they were largely the descendants of past operatives and not newly gathered together as in John's mills. They seemed also much more self-respectful and independent. They worked 12 hours a day in summer (13–1) and 11 in winter (12–1),[76] but the new Factory Act would prevent women working for more than 11. Boys began 'when they passed the doctor', said the Lancashire manager, or from 9 years old, said Sir Chinubhai. The latter agreed that the hours were too long and suggested that they were too early in beginning, especially in the summer, as it was difficult to get any sleep before midnight and the men came to the mill only half-awake. Sir Chinubhai wanted a tariff against foreign imports, with free trade within the Empire. He was beginning to feel the competition of Japanese imports. There were 40 mills in Ahmadabad, all in Indian hands; none of them boarded or lodged their hands.

Another morning we spent with the Collector (Painter,[77] a man of 40, strong, energetic and practically commonplace, without idealism, imagination or (as it seemed to us) much knowledge of India outside his daily work), visiting his 'cattle-kitchens'. The famine here is mainly a 'fodder famine' & the cattle, the renowned Gujarat breed, would die by thousands but for help. The Gov^t is distributing fodder, subsidising the railway to bring it in at a quarter freight and making cash advances. In addition, this Collector has got up a charitable fund and a voluntary committee which is feeding over 3000 cattle in 5 or 6 Camps, the cattle being brought in and attended to by their owners but remaining with these permanently in the Camp, which supplies only the site, organisation and food. It has proved very successful in calling out the people's own energies and saving the cattle without involving the Gov^t in the purchase and care of thousands of animals.

Ahmadabad, with a population of 185,000, with great wealth and many rich people, is strangely free from English residents or English business. There seem to be only two or three civil servants, two or three railway officials, two or three soldiers, and two or three banking people — not a dozen in all — together with half-a-dozen clergy or missionaries and not a single business man. There is only one 'English' bank, and apparently no 'English' shop whatever. It is a new experience to us in India to see all these wealthy villas and carriages and mills entirely in Indian hands. [BW→] It seems equally free from all 'movements' for the redemption of India — both the Commissioner and the Collector explaining this absence of sedition by the fact that the people were too busy, and successfully busy, in getting rich. The *Arya Samaj* hardly exists, the nationalist organisation is very weak and sends no delegate to the N. Congress; the *Brahmo Samaj* alone has one or two small philanthropic institutions. There is no bad feeling between the Hindus and Muslims — in fact very little movement whatsoever. The municipality had to be quashed and a nominated body put in its stead. The Collector would have preferred one man — an official — and evidently thought any attempt on the part of the Ahmadabad people to interfere by act or thought with the work of the Government was a [SW: dire] mistake.

GODRA[78] APRIL 1–3rd [1912]

'Ghosal is not Indian — he is British — in education and in manners — we should not regard him as a native,' had said Commissioner Barrow of his Collector. That surprised us, as we knew he was the brother of the ultra-Indian nationalist Mrs. Rambaj Dutt Chaudhuri [nephew of the Indian priest Tagore], and belonging to an old Brahmin family distinguished for its learning & its patriotism.[79] Moreover, he had married the daughter of a ruling Chief — the Maharaja of Cooch Behar. However, when we came here we realised the truth of the Commissioner's commendation. Ghosal has modelled himself exactly on what he *believes an English official ought to be*. He is silent and reserved, ultra-conservative in opinion, zealous and industrious in the executive business of his district [SW: devoid of intellectual curiosity] and sumptuously clothed [SW: according to fashionable English standards] for each part of the day's work — indeed he overdoes the part in this respect — his dress is too immaculately correct and his manners too perfect — a reproduction of the most conventional public school university man. When one remembers the [SW: fervent and inconsequent talk] and the slummocking and dirty garments of our friend the good-hearted Hindu Pleader — his brother-in-law — one realises why his sister never mentioned her connection to the Admirable Crichton.[80] The *Arya Samaj* and all its works he evidently holds in detestation —

though he is far too discreet to express his feeling in so many words: 'India is going too fast' is the only remark he has let fall of a general nature. He expresses no general views and vouchsafes no general information. But he has done his best, in a well-bred, taciturn way, to give all the information we have had the energy to ask for – and I should imagine that his facts were generally correct, though his judgement is devoid of any illuminating insight.

His wife is a pretty little lady who appears as a picturesque Hindu girl in the early morning, as a beautifully-attired Hindu princess for *déjeuner*, and as a neatly-garbed English tennis player in the late afternoon and a fashionable lady at dinner. There are no books in the house beyond third-class novels – Marie Corelli figures largely – no newspapers beyond the *Times of India*, 'The Pink-un' and a few illustrated London prints; the furniture is ultra-European and the walls are covered with portraits of English officers, society ladies, Maharajas, inscribed with 'Darling Babs' or 'from loving . . .'. Curiously enough, the husband talks English with a strong foreign accent and with difficulty, though he was seven years in England – the wife talks it as an Englishwoman. There is a French governess for the two children – boy and girl – and the boy goes this autumn to a preparatory school for Eton.

As our Commissioner said, the Ghosals mean to be more British than the British. What his real feelings are it is impossible to say. But it is dull work talking to him as one dare not assume that he is an Indian and one knows he is not an Englishman – the result being that we have felt less free to discuss Indian problems with him than with anyone else, except perhaps the effete Colonels and Mayors who act as civil administrators in the Punjab. All this is ungrateful, as the house is extraordinarily comfortable, and the Ghosals leave one alone in the hot hours and have the great advantage of two good motors. He has two English Assistants – the one I talked to was rigidly Anglo-Indian. Altogether, this glimpse of Bombay administration – of a Commissioner, three Collectors (two Indian) and two Assistant Collectors, does not reveal the sympathetic side of the British Raj.

[SW→] The famine relief works that we had come to Godra to inspect were both minor operations – one the making of a road on which some 1100 persons had been employed, and the other the deepening of a dried-up tank which was occupying between 400 and 500. But the 'famine' was itself a minor affair existing, as regards human distress, only in this one district of the Panch Mahals (and in some parts of the State of Baroda). It is a local scarcity due to an almost complete absence of rain in the last rainy season. The lack of fodder for cattle is a little more widely spread, as we saw at Ahmadabad; but the rest of India has had a good year.

The relief works had the usual features of crowds of men and women engaged in the simplest manual labour, the men digging soft earth and the women carrying it in small baskets to where it had to be dumped. The operations had been planned in advance as relief work to be resorted to when necessary. The work was set out by the P.W.D.[81] and supervised by (Indian) subordinate officials temporarily borrowed from different departments. There were hospital tents, casks of water under reed roofs, shelters for nursing mothers and their infants, latrines — all of the simplest and flimsiest kind. The Assistant Surgeon (a Goanese who had studied at Dublin and Edinburgh) visited all the works frequently, on the watch for cholera.

The special feature of these works was the absence of any arrangement for lodging the workers. These primitive tribes flatly refused to sleep away from their huts and preferred to starve rather than do so — partly from blind conservatism, partly because they feared to lose their little possessions whilst absent, and partly, we were told, from the not unjustifiable fear of disease and death if they herded together in a famine relief camp. (It appears that in the great Gujarat famine of ten years before, cholera played havoc in the camps.) So the Government had had to start numerous small works to and from which the starving men and women walked night and morning, four miles, six miles, and in some cases even ten miles each way. Those too old or too weak to work or prevented by *purdah* were relieved by doles of food distributed in the villages themselves. But none who were adult and able-bodied were given such doles; these had to come and work at piece-work rates for wages calculated so as to be just sufficient for bare subsistence at current prices — the men getting $1\frac{3}{4}$ annas per day and the women $1\frac{1}{2}$ annas per day. Or rather, a whole gang of about 50 being given a task to do which was calculated to yield such a wage if the task was completed, and the sum payable being reduced in proportion to every part of the task left undone at the end of the day. The grouping of the men and women in gangs was largely left to themselves, each village keeping to itself; and it was left to the gang to appoint its own ganger, a man of influence among them who got a fractionally larger share and directed instead of digging.

But the Gov^t object not being economy, but relief, the regulations were evidently not very precisely adhered to; and the gang was paid each night enough for its members to live on for twenty-four hours, the elaborate calculations of task and rates being used as a means of getting the work done and of affording some check on the total expenditure. Indeed, the whole 'Famine Code' that we studied, an elaborate printed volume the outcome of a whole generation of experiment, reads much more like a guide to relief so that no one should be permitted to die of starvation, than like any precise checking of the 'labour cost' of each work. We did not see in it anything applicable to English conditions; nor did we pick up from it any hint or suggestion for dealing with our own 'unemployed'.

The Indian administrator has to deal with (1) workers homogeneous as to occupation, all cultivators of the soil, (2) under purely temporary distress, from which it is certain that they will presently regain their normal occupations, (3) without fear of the workers being swamped by numbers of 'underemployed' or loafers attracted by the Government wage, and (4) without being subject to pressure to raise that bare subsistence wage to the 'trade union rate'. We learnt that the weaver or other artisan was not expected to come to these relief works and that wherever necessary other relief was afforded to him – sometimes the Government bought his unsaleable product or ordered more, using it to clothe the naked; sometimes, as with the bangle-makers, the Government advanced him subsistence whilst he went on working for stock. The part of the problem which most nearly resembles that of England was therefore outside the *'Famine Code'*! It is interesting here to remember that we were told that the Ahmadabad cotton mills had never in all their half-century of existence had to go on 'short time' or shut down altogether.

The men and women on these relief works looked well-nourished. We saw no signs of semi-starvation and no dreadful living skeletons. Hardly any boys under 14 were at work, though they might have got their penny a day; and we were told that the families preferred to leave them at home to look after the cattle, etc. This was a matter of policy – the Collector, with Government approval, as he explained, thinking it better to relieve *before* the people had been brought low in health in order that they might not succumb to disease. This policy has so far been justified by the death rate of the district being actually lower than usual, so the doctor told us, though he lived in dread of cholera. Those whose clothes had worn to rags had only to ask, when they were given new ones out of charitable funds at the Collector's disposal. We heard several complaints, all to the effect that the pay was not enough because it left nothing over for the little luxuries to which they were accustomed.

BARODA 3–5th APRIL 1912

A few hours' railway journey brought us to this capital of a Native State – to be met at the station by our *Arya Samaj* friend the School Inspector (Atma Ram), and by minor officials on behalf of the Gaekwar and his ministers. After dinner S.W. saw the Dewan (B. L. Gupta), the lifelong friend and son-in-law, and the biographer, of R. C. Dutt,[82] whom (after retiring from the I.C.S. as High Court Judge) he accompanied into Baroda service. He proved to be an able, genial, hospitable but uncommunicative man of about 62. (His daughter and another young Indian girl with her husband, a young Indian man (Mukerji, who had been an Oxford Fabian) and another (an Indian officer in the Gaekwar's Army) were just then, at 9.30 p.m., starting out on a magnificent elephant on some pleasure jaunt – which showed how little *'purdah'* there is here!) Gupta said that the condition of the Indian cultivator had undoubtedly improved within his recollection; his standard of living had gone up considerably, wages had risen more than prices and various social advantages had been added, in the way of hospitals, schools, etc. He was quite clear that India would always wish to remain part of the British Empire for obvious self-interest, however much self-government it obtained.

Masani,[83] the Minister for Education who had introduced compulsion, took us the next morning to see the boys' and girls' high school, the technical institute and [an] elementary school for girls, the training college for women, the state free library, and two palaces. The palaces were both furnished entirely in European style. In the one now in use we were shown into every room, including the bedrooms of the Gaekwar, his Rani, the young princess, the young princes, etc., even to the dressing rooms in which their clothes were laid out and their baths were being prepared for their momentarily-expected arrival. There were practically no books in the so-called 'library' and very few in the intimate living rooms; but it is noteworthy that we saw in the princess's room a copy of Pierre Loti's *'L'Inde, sans les Anglais'*, of which the very title strikes the Anglo-Indian as seditious and which we have accordingly found to be quite unknown to the officials and their wives.

The various educational institutions that we saw were somewhat primitive – the Principals were mostly absent for one reason or another, the classes were thin, the apparatus was poor and it seems as if the schemes were ahead of the capacity or integrity of the subordinate officials available. But the elementary school for girls was a reality. These hundreds of girls from 6 or 7 up to 12, and a few older, had been gathered in by the compulsory law alone. They were under the direction of a competent woman knowing no English, who had been 'trained' five and twenty years before and now had several women and several men teachers under her. She was drawing 60 rupees per month (£48 a year), a good salary as Indian teachers' salaries go. Baroda now has 94.3 per cent of its boys in school between

7 and 12 and 66.3 per cent of its girls between 7 and 11 – comparing the actual number of pupils with the children of school age revealed by the Census of 1911. Out of 3095 villages, more than 2138 have got schools, most of the others having fewer than 15 children of school age. About 94 per cent of the whole population have schools accessible to their children. All this is enormously ahead of the rest of India and reflects great credit on the state, even if the average attendance is only something like 60 per cent of the school roll and even if many of the schools and teachers leave much to be desired. The total gross expenditure (1911–12) for education is 16 *lakhs* of rupees or £107,000 a year for a population of two millions, which would be equal to £13,000,000 for all British India or about three times as much as the Government does spend. The Education Minister hopes to get his budget up to 20 *lakhs* or £133,000 a year, which would be [the] equivalent of 15 or 16 millions sterling for British India.

[BW→] The following morning we journeyed out to the summer palace and to a neighbouring village to see the schools. Here we found the school divided into three buildings – the headmaster [SW: an intelligent and trained Hindu], who was also the postmaster, holding the higher classes in the post office, an assistant master taking the lower classes in an adjoining building, and a separate school for the 'Untouchables' in the isolated group of cottages belonging to these outcasts, in the house of one of them, and taught by a member of this strange community [SW: who had passed the seventh standard and got 7 rupees a month.] A very small proportion of the students were attending in the two first classes we came to, but by the time we got to the third, a good attendance had been evidently whipped up. There were a good many children of school age in the streets, and quite clearly Baroda is only at the beginning of the task of getting the children [SW: actually to attend] school [SW: even if it gets them on the school roll]. The Minister explained the low attendance by the lowness of the [SW: castes (not a single Brahmin among the children)] – they did not care for education and it was not wise to push compulsion too far. He told us that he had started medical inspection, but as the parents were too poor to make up deficiencies – glasses for defective eyesight and extra food for anaemic children – it was useless to go on with it. For the same reason he had stopped physical exercises, as the children were not strong enough to do them after their mental work. Altogether, he was quite aware that primary education in Baroda had only just begun, and that universal education was still only on paper.

Masani [SW: who had begun service in Baroda as professor of biology at the college and then became Secretary to the Gaekwar] was a Parsee from Bombay – a strong, able, good-looking man with what seems to be the typical Parsee attitude, detached but benevolent, feeling that Parsees are not *of India* but are *in India* for their own advantage and have therefore an obligation towards India – not in the least nervous or [SW: touchy] about getting their rightful share of influence – assured that their superior enlightenment and education will give them as much influence as they deserve. His son is science professor at the college – an attractive and alert young man who is coming to England to get his D.Sc.[84] and hopes to find superior employment in British India.

We went over the college and high school. The high school had a Parsee as headmaster – a man of the same strong, virile type as the Parsee Minister of Education. The classes were full [SW: over 700 boys present and two or three Parsee girls] and the boys looked very [SW: intelligent] and the masters competent. The college has as Principal – Clarke[85] – an Englishman [SW: Cambridge] who had been twelve years in the Baroda service. He was a strong [SW: rather handsome] man, with [SW: a hard] conceited and unpleasant expression [SW: and he excited our antipathy.] He was clearly not on very cordial terms with the Minister of Education. We were left with no particular impression about the college [SW: 300–400 students mostly in arts] as Clarke was uncommunicative in the presence of the Minister and, though polite to us, was not in the least anxious to see us again. We heard afterwards from the headmistress of the girls' school and also from Mr. Gohkale and other official sources that Clarke was a notorious slacker and that he was merely hanging on for his pension, and that the Gaekwar had been 'taken in' in his appointment for twenty years.

On our return to the guest house we found a letter from the Maharaja asking us to breakfast at 11 a.m. The Gaekwar impressed us very favourably[86] and the Rani was extraordinarily attractive and charmingly clothed. The family is now under a cloud owing to the 'Gaekwar incident' at the Delhi Durbar,[87] the assumed disloyalty of the Rani, and the scandalous rumours about the daughter. We should gather, from what we have heard from the different Indian officials of Baroda, that the Gaekwar had been fretting for some time under what he considers the unjustifiable interference of the British Resident with regard to the internal administration of his dominion; the Rani is said [SW: to be bitter] about the [SW: probable] inheritance of the [SW: throne] by the [SW: little] grandson of the late Rani, which she believes will be insisted on by the British Government; whilst the whole family is sympathetic to the nationalists' aspirations and feel themselves born to be leaders of the Indian people. However that may be, the Gaekwar and his consort struck us as real enthusiasts for social reform.

The Gaekwar is not what one would call a gentleman – he is a clever and ambitious, sympathetic man, emotional and appreciative, liable to be led away by a stronger personality. [SW: He is said now to suffer from chronic indecision.] He talked quite frankly and was delighted that we admired the *Arya Samaj*, and asked Sidney whether he would be right to employ them as educationalists and whether he should ask the Government of India's permission. 'Employ them without asking,' was Sidney's reply. The Rani is charming to look at and very intelligent. But though she was also frank her frankness was tinged with bitterness. I can quite believe that 'India without the English' is her ideal. But at present the Gaekwar is on his good behaviour. He has made a mistake – a bad mistake. If he had paid elaborate respect to the British Raj whilst trying in his own kingdom to build up a self-governing race, the B. Gov^t could not have seriously interfered with him, or diminished his prestige in India. By bad manners he has risked the substance as well as damaged the form of his sovereignty. And the whole family seem to have suffered from an absence of self-restraint and domestic respect-ability [SW: their personal conduct is in a state of unstable equilibrium, the clash of two hostile codes of manners].

All the same, we like both the Gaekwar and the Rani – both seem to us genuine in their devotion to India and he, at least, was taking his disgrace in good part and not relaxing the vigour of his efforts to raise the standards of his people. The sons of his present Rani, like her daughter, seem to be somewhat addicted to 'irregular conduct'. [SW: One, just returned from Harvard, looked rather stupid and dissipated. We had seen a younger boy at Mayo College who had been in succession at several English schools.] The son of the first died at 24, it is said from dissipation – the little grandson is being watched over by the widow and a devoted nurse, and rumour is busy as to the precautions that have to be taken to safeguard him from the ill will of the charming lady. But these rumours would be rife in the court of an Indian ruler whether or not there was any reason for them. [SW: The Princess Indira, about whom were the negotiations for marriage to the Maharaja of Gwalior,[88] did not appear at breakfast.]

The city of Baroda, though possessing no old buildings, has the charm and good order of the cap[SW: ital] of a Native State, as distinguished from the squalor and disorder of the native cities of B. India. Ghosal, the [SW: Collector] of [SW: Godra], told us that even the villages in the Baroda State were distinguished by amenity and that the police were superior – life and property being more secure. He attributed the latter generally to the better administration of justice – all sorts of technicalities preventing the discovery and punishment of crime in British India. That is of course only the other side of the greater respect for personal liberty under the British Raj and the greater difficulty of good government by alien rulers.

Among the other institutions that we visited was a boarding school for the most promising students of the *Antaryas*[89] (Untouchables), in order to train them as teachers for their own community or as leaders to raise their fellows. The boarding school, though a Government institution, was under the charge of our friend the *Arya Samaj* Inspector of [SW: Schools (Atma Ram), whose salary is 110 rupees per month − £87 per annum]. He and his wife and [SW: 6] children, with a young Brahmin teacher (also *Arya Samaj*), were living with these 30 boys and 12 girls. They were being brought up in the rites of the *Arya Samaj* [SW: *culte*], and looked models of attention and careful physical and mental training. This little group of enthusiasts were evidently inspired by deep religious-humanitarian feeling, and the experiment looked more promising than similar work by the Salvation Army, as the religion the children were being taught and the customs and habits they were learning were in no way a breach of their own race-feeling and were in fact an intensification of it on the highest lines. If the [SW: Gaekwar], instead of being rude to the Viceroy and the King Emperor in order to assert his own sovereignty, had introduced *Arya Samaj* teachers in all his schools and established [SW: Boy] Scouts, he would have done a good deal towards making possible the ideal of 'India without the English' and yet not given the B. Government the chance of administering a [SW: big snub] to the most [SW: progressive] ruler in India.

[SW→] With regard to the compulsory education experiment, it appears that there is as yet practically no attempt to secure *regularity* of attendance as distinguished from occasional attendance. Until a child has failed to put in an appearance for six consecutive days (at first it was 10) nothing is done. Consequently, the 'regular irregulars' are suffered to pull down the average attendance without check. (We suggested notice from the teacher after two absences and a personal visit after four.) After 6 consecutive days' absences, notice is sent by the teacher to the village headman and the machinery of prosecution and fine is set going (usual fine, 2d or 4d). There are no school attendance officers but the headman is supposed to make out annually a list of children liable to attend school. The occurrence of the Census was naturally used by the Minister to check these lists with the result that many girls were found omitted. The Minister did not think there was much bribery or oppression, but he had summarily dismissed two or three minor officials and could only hope that his Assistant Inspectors would keep things straight. The Gaekwar offered 50 per cent increase of salary to Hindu teachers who would go to 'Untouchable' schools, but practically none accepted, so strong is the prejudice. They had to rely for such schools on a few Muslim teachers and on teachers sprung from the 'Untouchables' themselves. It is certainly a wonderful achievement to have got going no fewer than 300 schools for these 'Untouchables' and to have brought thousands of them on the school roll.

We learnt that since Lord Curzon's time there had been much less interference by the British Government. But the Resident toured through the state and therefore inevitably had complaints poured out to him, besides derogating by his very presence from the Gaekwar's position. Every detail about railway, telegraph, telephone and postal business had to be specially submitted to him. The British Government insists on the excise duty being levied on the mills in Baroda State and prevents the export of salt from the Baroda ports. It appears that the Baroda-born are precluded (as not being British subjects) from English Government employment; books published in Baroda do not thereby gain copyright in British India. Hence Baroda authors, whom the Gaekwar tries to encourage, have to get their books published in Bombay or Ahmadabad. This exclusion of the Native States from copyright seems wanton rudeness.

[BW→] Before leaving our description of Baroda, we may add what we heard [SW: about the Gaekwar] at Bombay Government House, and from [SW: Mr. Gokhale] whilst staying with him at Poona. Sir G. and Lady Clarke were, both of them, contemptuously bitter and suspicious about the Gaekwar and the Rani. It appears that Sir George[90] and his former wife and his daughter (who died lately) were on intimate terms with the Baroda family, and that Miss Clarke had stayed, for a fortnight at a time, actually with the Rani. Now, nothing is too bad to be said about the Gaekwar and the Rani and the children. Lady Clarke told me the long tale as to the discovery of a centre of active and violent sedition (bombs, etc.) in Baroda, which she asserted must have been known about by the Gaekwar [SW: this was never alleged to be more than a printing press], and she represented the Gaekwar as being quite ready to take arms against the British and the [SW: incident] at Delhi [as] being his way of testing the feeling of the other native rulers.

Mr. Gokhale, who is friendly to the Gaekwar, attributed the [SW: incident] to [SW: a combination of causes] — a certain amount of ill will brought about by the [SW: vexatious] interference of [SW: successive] B[SW: ritish] Residents, [SW: to] the [SW: unduly] great consideration [SW: that] the Barodas had received from foreign courts, which made them resent [SW: their treatment] as subordinates by Viceroys and British officials, [SW: & lastly] by genuine absent-mindedness or nervousness on the morning of the Delhi function due to the fact that the Gaekwar had *that morning* received notice of the pending divorce proceedings brought against him by an English solicitor [SW: Statham], with whose wife he had been on too friendly terms. (This case was dismissed – the Gaekwar's plea of being a sovereign ruler and therefore exempt from the jurisdiction of courts of law being upheld.)

[SW: Gokhale] gave us a dramatic account of the episode [SW: which he had seen]. The 'disloyal' rudeness to the King Emperor had been complicated by the Gaekwar's refusal to stand up at the entry of the Viceroy on a previous occasion – the B. Resident, Cobb,[91] having practically forced him to rise for a moment and having reported his behaviour to the Viceroy. It appears that the day after the Durbar, Gok[SW: hale], who was in the Viceroy's camp, heard that the Government of India was actually considering his deposition. Anxious to save the Gaekwar, Gokhale hurried to his camp early the next morning and had [SW: him] roused from his slumbers. Seddon,[92] his Prime Minister [SW: an I.C.S.], who was [SW: immediately] afterwards withdrawn [SW: by the Government of India], had also hurried to the Gae[SW: kwar] camp and [SW: Gokhale], he, and the Gaekwar had a consultation about what should be done. The Gaekwar was wholly [SW: unaware] of the [SW: gravity] of his offence but he was induced to sign the letter of apology which Gokhale and Seddon drafted there and then. The Viceroy sent a stiff answer refusing to accept the apology as a sufficient explanation of the [SW: two] incidents [SW: & asking] whether he could publish the Gaekwar's letter. The Gaekwar answered with equal stiffness that he could do as he pleased, and the letter was published. Since then, the relations have been very strained and the Gaekwar has been forced by Cobb to dismiss two officials who had connections with extreme nationalists and to issue a proclamation against sedition. He is in fact still in a precarious position. I doubt whether the Government of India would be so foolish as to make a martyr of him – but one can understand his state of nervousness and the Rani's state of anger.

[BOMBAY]

Arriving at Bombay in the early morning of the 8th, we were met by [SW: one of the A.D.C.'s] and escorted in a motor to Government House. It is a most attractive residence, consisting of various bungalows in beautiful, wooded grounds overhanging the sea, with one central suite of reception rooms. Our bungalow (No. 1 India) was actually [SW: perched] on the rocks, and from our verandah we could watch the waves of the Indian Ocean dashing against the very wall of our abode. Very delightful were the moonlit nights — I sleeping on a sofa on the verandah, and alternating the hours of [SW: sound] sleep with intervals of watching the fishing smacks sailing close under me — so close that I could distinguish the voices of the fishermen — perhaps discussing the white ghost appearing just above them! The charm and luxurious quiet of this official sanctuary was enhanced by the cool breeze of the homeward sea — refreshing after the parched heat of Baroda and Ahmadabad and reminding us that we should soon be sailing away to our home and our work.

But the [SW: etiquette] at Government House was stiff and the company not congenial — less so than we expected. Sir G. Clarke, whom Sidney knew twenty years ago and who had the reputation of a liberal-minded and progressive administrator, has grown old and bitterly reactionary, both as regards home politics and what is more important, as regards Indian affairs. Poor man, he looked unhappy; his eyes had that lifeless, sullen, and suspicious expression which betokens disillusionment. Since he came to India as Governor of Bombay, he has lost his wife and only child and though he has married another lady to whom he seems very much attached, she has not evidently filled up the blank. The former Lady Clarke and the daughter had been both enthusiastic devotees of the task of 'bridging the [SW: gulf]' and were much beloved by the Indians. The present lady is of the worldly-widow mould, no doubt sensible and devoted to her present lord but stupid and [SW: snobbish] (more than once she talked of *birth* as a requisite for the art of government), and disliking 'lower races' and 'lower classes' and resenting their desire for self-government. She complained with asperity of a Governor being 'shackled' by Legislative Councils and talked of India as a veritable volcano of sedition.

As for Clarke himself, he was somewhat taciturn; when he did talk, he uttered the usual commonplaces. 'Hindus were mere talkers'; and when I referred to the capacity for organisation and self-devotion shown by the *Arya Samaj*, he dismissed this activity as 'political', as if *that* necessarily damned it morally. There were one or two stupid but harmless A.D.C.'s and one or two able and alert secretaries and politicals — one Enthoven[93] [SW: formerly Secretary to the Gov^t of Bombay, now Secretary to Commercial Dep^t of the Gov^t of India under W.H. Clark[94]], of whom Clarke spoke highly but who was [SW: a bad type of] pedant and bureaucrat — and showed a good deal of nasty temper about Gokhale or any other Indian who claimed a share in the Government. [SW: He] denied that the Indians of the present day had any capacity whatsoever — except the capacity of making themselves troublesome to the British Raj. When I suggested that whatever were the rights of the case there would be in fifty years time more Indians in the Government of India, he flatly denied it. They had reached 'saturation point' and any further admission of Indians would be inconsistent with British rule and would be reversed even if it were introduced. He even resented my using the word 'Indians' instead of 'natives' — there was no *race* of Indians! [SW: Claud Hill,[95] now Member of Exec. Council, Bombay] — was equally reactionary but more discreet and outwardly sympathetic to and respectful of Indians. Altogether, we came away grateful for the hospitable kindness of the Clark[SW: es] — all the more so because they could not have liked either our reputation or ourselves — but not impressed with the prospects of a rule represented by Clarke and his entourage.

Staying at Government House was a very anglicised native ruler [SW: the Jam of Nawanagar], formerly [SW: the] noted [SW: British cricketer 'Ranjitsinhji'] and, as the Governor told me, much bored by his relegation to the rule of an Indian state after victories on an English cricket field.[96] He is now somewhat in disgrace, having overspent himself scandalously. He has now been cut down to an allowance of £10,000 a year and told to live in Europe whilst the British Gov^t administers his state. It is interesting to note that *both evenings* he sat on the left of His Excellency — Claud Hill taking precedence of him, apparently as a Member of the Executive Council of Bombay. Indeed this well-bred, quiet but uninteresting Indian gentleman, in spite of his position as a ruling sovereign [SW: & his title of His Highness], was decidedly kept 'in his place', and made to feel his unimportance, the Governor [SW: barely] speaking to him. [SW: Our] impression of the Clark[SW: es] was confirmed by the wife of the editor of the *Times of India* (Stanley [SW: Reed)]. She said that they were even more unpopular with the Europeans than with the 'natives' and that their staff was equally so. It appears that the stiffness of the etiquette at Government House, and Lady Clarke's assumption of regal airs, is ridiculed — especially as the lady is known to ha[SW: ve] 'liv[SW: ed in] a cottage' prior to her third marriage — and that Clarke, whatever may be his abilities, does not belong to the aristocracy. So says the tittle-tattle of British society! Moreover, Clarke has 'stood up' to the Europeans both as regards the granting of fresh sites for their sports and in his Bill for the suppression of bookmakers on the race course.

[SW→] Sir G. Clarke agreed that the Government of India was faint-hearted, especially about borrowing capital, dreading the incubus of heavy fixed-interest charges in lean years. This greatly retarded desirable Government enterprise even if estimated to be productive.

He agreed that the forests could be further developed, as well as irrigation and railways. He had himself recommended that the companies and shareholders should be got rid of and especially the obstructive and costly board of directors in London. But on the whole he said very little, always diverging off into irrelevancies which frequently included depreciations and aspersions of the nationalists.

We may put here what we learnt at Government House and elsewhere as to the King's visit. No one will ever realise the nervousness of the Government about his safety or the extent of the precautions taken. Sir Edward Henry,[97] late of the Indian Service and now Commander of the Metropolitan Police, came and took special charge. The precautions began months before. For instance, special reports were laid before him relating to all the various organisations in India, including the *Arya Samaj* and Mr. Gokhale's 'Servants of India',[98] so that he might decide what steps should be taken with regard to each of them when the King arrived; many hundreds of people were quietly arrested and kept in custody until he had gone — not that they were accused or even suspected of any designs, but merely as being people who might make a disturbance. Lady Clarke said that 400 were thus arrested in Bombay alone. Every 'native' house on the line of route had a policeman posted inside it (this was probably none the less annoying because these men were English clerks sworn in as special constables, who thus got a good view for nothing — so one of the English told us; and the householder was informed that he would be 'held responsible' for the good behaviour of all its inmates.

At Delhi, in the big procession on the first day, the Queen had all the usual insignia of royalty, but the King rode in the midst of a group of officers so that no one should be able to pick him out. Something similar was done at Delhi (as at Bombay) with regard to policemen being stationed in every 'native' house. We were told in the U.P. that the Gov[t] telegraphed that A. and B., well-known nationalists, had left Calcutta for Delhi. The officer in charge telegraphed back asking what was meant, should he arrest them? In reply he was told that this was for him to decide; and he thereupon arrested them and detained them in custody, remarking to us that 'he was not taking any risks'. After the first few days, when the immense popular approval was perceived, the precautions were relaxed until, at Calcutta, the King drove freely among the crowds. What had been feared was not so much an attack on the life of the King, which it was believed that Indian superstitious reverence for a king would prevent, but some attack on an officer in the King's presence as a protest and a demonstration unwarranted; and it merely serves to prove how little the officials know of the Indian mind.

POONA[99] 8–10th APRIL [1912]

We went straight from the luxurious and materialistic and intensely 'official' atmosphere of Gov[t] House, with its ungenerous belittling of the whole Indian people mingled with innuendoes and aspersions even of the most distinguished of them, for a brief visit to Mr. Gokhale at the home of the 'Servants of India'. We of course made no concealment of our destination; but 'Gov[t] House' is far too self-satisfied and is also far too obtuse to have any sense of the extent to which the contrast jarred upon us, and how it made us ashamed of our official representatives in India. For Poona is not only remarkable as an educational and intellectual centre, having evidently far above the average of Hindu intellectualism; largely under the influence of Gokhale, it has become the centre of two remarkable Hindu organisations, both of them extraordinary in their spirit of devotion and in their practical achievements.

The first of these is the Fergusson College (named after Sir J. Fergusson, who was Governor). This, in spite of its misleading name, is not a Government institution. It was started some thirty years ago[100] by a little band of highly-educated Hindus, high caste Brahmins who felt that what was specially needed was higher education under Hindu control. They had no money and no position but they set to work, themselves becoming the teachers and living from hand to mouth on such fees and subscriptions as they could get. They formed themselves into a sort of brotherhood (having twenty members) which took vows to serve the college for twenty years without remuneration beyond the subsistence allowance that they permitted themselves to draw from the funds – at first 30 rupees a month, then raised to 50 and now to 75 (£5), as funds came in. This is not to be increased. For this £60 a year each, these twenty professors, who are all married, their families living in modest little huts close to the college, run what is now one of the greatest Colleges in India, having over 700 undergraduate students, besides still more extensive school departments.

They form a republic of equals, their weekly meeting assigning work to each of its members and practically governing the College. For official purposes one of them is styled Principal; there is a board of management consisting of twenty of the subscribers and the twenty professors, and there is even an executive committee of three subscribers and three professors. But the whole thing is in the hands of the brotherhood, for without their virtually gratuitous service it would come to an end. They recruit their number by admitting a promising graduate of distinction on probation. Apparently there is no difficulty in attracting clever young men, whose devotion makes them willing to bind themselves for twenty years. The vow, we are told, is never broken. But the brotherhood itself has released a few and has offered to release others (who declined to be released). Thus the present Principal is an attractive young man of thirty or so who went to Cambridge with a Government scholarship and became senior wrangler. He could have had very high official appointments and the brotherhood spontaneously offered to release him. But he elected to remain with them at £60 a year. Gokhale was among the founders and was one of the leaders. As great public opportunities opened out to him the brotherhood offered to release him. But he resolutely served out his twenty years like the rest and only on its expiration did he give himself to his own political career and his own great project. And he does this on the modest superannuation allowance of 30 rupees a month (£24 a year) which the brotherhood accords to those who complete their term of service.

We met the Principal and all the other members of the brotherhood, and were much impressed with their personalities, their great culture, their gentle and attractive natures, their obvious intellectual ability. So much disinterested zeal and such a life of combined devotion and practical work reminds us, of course, of the best of the Catholic orders. Yet these men have done it for thirty years under the inspiration only of 'nationalism'. They are of course Hindus by religion and we should infer not particularly pious or orthodox Hindus. They have found a religion in their cause. The curious thing is that no official, no Englishman, even tells you of this organisation which is perhaps unique in the world. Sir George Clarke told us to see a Government normal school at Poona and to call on the Commissioner and the Collector. But he did not mention Fergusson College and did not seem to be aware of its remarkable and peculiar organisation. The Anglo-Indian apparently cannot take in the self-sacrifice and devotion of these people even when it assumes so practical a form as a great and flourishing university college. Accordingly, as a part of parsimony and 'early Victorian' administrative nihilism, the Government policy has been to do directly as little for secondary and university education as it could but to encourage private enterprise. This has led, on the one hand, to the missionary schools and colleges that we have repeatedly described, which seem to us to be to the great bulk of the Indian students, virtually secular institutions; and, on the other hand, to the upgrowth of great and influential colleges (like Mr. Surendra Nath Banerjea's at Calcutta,[101] the D.A.V. College at Lahore and the Fergusson College at Poona), *in the hands of the Indian nationalists.*

Thus, by the very policy of Gov^t itself a large proportion of the educated men are year after year actually moulded by the nationalist party. This is going on all over India. This is what Lord Curzon really wished to curb and prevent by some of his educational reforms. But after thirty years these colleges are in too strong a position to be uprooted, especially as the Government cannot afford to run many colleges of its own and often runs these very badly with merely hireling second-rate Englishmen as teachers. And hence the futility of the feeble little attempts to check the constant spread of the desire for self-government that we see in the substitution of '*Cowper's Letters*' for Burke's political essays (Calcutta),[102] in the attempted suppression of English history from the B.A. curriculum (Bombay), in the prescription of namby pamby books of pure literature in the English course (Punjab) instead of anything intellectually stimulating, and in the refusal to develop a school of investigation and research in economics which Mr. Ratan Tata[103] actually offered to endow at Bangalore. The Government, having first wished the Indians to get educated (Macaulay),[104] then refused to do the work itself as being beyond the duties of Government (administrative nihilism), is now afraid of any intellectual development among the Indians because it finds that intellectual development always leads to a desire for self-government!

To come back to Fergusson College. Their only serious trouble was over Tilak. He was one of them, and gradually developed what might be called 'extremist' insurgent views. He, not content with the silent influence of an institution under such a brotherhood, wanted to make the College a centre of revolutionary propaganda. Gokhale fought this, in the interests of the College itself, on the 'larger expediency' line; and after some years of struggle Tilak and a few followers seceded. Naturally such a college, after such an episode, has been under Government suspicion; but apparently the Government can find nothing to take hold of and the educational work is so patently good, and the results are so marked, that the Government makes a considerable grant.

The other organisation centred at Poona is that of the Servants of India. This was founded by Gokhale when he left Fergusson College on completion of service, and is an attempt deliberately to train men for 'public service', either as teachers, as writers, as members of public bodies, as philanthropists, etc. These men are very carefully selected by Gokhale himself; they come on long probation; they are put through prolonged training under Gokhale; they are sent about India to see other parts; and the intention is gradually to form a body of trained and devoted men for any kind of public work. They get only a bare subsistence and they vow to serve as required for a long term (20 years?). The organisation has been going now for some seven years and the membership, of one grade or another, has reached nearly 50. It

is a proof of Gokhale's great wisdom and practical skill that he has
managed to steer this body through the troublous years that have
lately passed (1907–10) without giving the Government or the police
the slightest excuse for a prosecution. There is a branch at Madras and
others are in course of formation. But all the recruits must come to
Poona for their first three years, 24 months of which they spend under
the direct personal tuition and influence of Gokhale himself.

We naturally saw a great deal of Gokhale himself, both at Poona and
afterwards at Bombay, where he took no end of trouble to enable us to
see people. The more we know about him and his work the more highly
we appreciate him. About fifty years of age, a Chitpavan[105] Brahmin
apparently vaguely mystical in religion, he is a man of singular
sweetness of disposition, full of charm. He is remarkably well-read in
English history, economics and philosophy and even to some extent
keeps up with English novels. But what strikes us most is his political
sagacity and calm statesmanship. He is by repute an impressive speaker,
persuasive and convincing; and he seems to have a great deal of
political skill. He is evidently making a party of great and growing
influence in the Imperial Council; and though he is always outvoted by
the official Members, he is apparently building up a force of public
opinion outside amongst all sections of educated Indians (Muslims and
Parsees as well as Hindus), which the Government has to defer to.

He demurs in our suggestions for developing the forests, railways,
canals and Government workshops, on the ground that without
extensive further popular control, any such increase in Government
action would only be used against the Hindus. He is not even very
keen on getting more of the higher posts filled by Indians because he
says that without increased popular control and a change of spirit, such
Indian officials are (1) never put in positions of real power or authority,
(2) apt themselves to become anglicised or at any rate so timid as to be
even less favourable to Indian aspirations than the English, and (3)
almost bound by the nature of the case to be more rigorous in dealing
with Indians accused of disaffection than the English. Moreover, even if
all the officials were Indians, the present system, without popular
control, would still be evil. Hence, whilst not opposing simultaneous
examinations, etc., Gokhale aims persistently at popular control. He
puts his trust in popular education, steady pressure to increase the
power of the Legislative Councils, creation of local bodies, etc. But he
feels that a great deal must come from England. The Gov^t of India
won't move unless forced by England or by a Governor-General fresh
from England.

[BW→] In the course of conversation he g[SW: ave] us an interesting
account of the different schools of extremists. [SW: Tilak], of whom

Gokhale spoke with much admiration in spite of his bitter fights with him, desired to make English rule so d[SW: isagreeable] to the [SW: Rule]rs as to force them to make concessions and even perhaps to [SW: quit] the country. Like the South Wales syndicalists, he proposed to pursue the 'irritating strike'[106] — never to take part in anything that the British desired should be done and always to do what they disliked. From [SW: Gokhale's] account, Tilak was a shrewd politician in choosing his devices of irritation — he was, in fact, a sort of Parnell[107] of Indian nationalism. Then there was the Punjab school of extreme politicians — [SW: centring] round [SW: Lajpat Rai]. Lajpat Rai wanted eventually to drive the British out of India. But he recognised that this was wholly impracticable whilst the Hindus remained [SW: undisciplined,] under-educa[SW: ted] and divided. Hence he advised [SW: his] followers to throw themselves into social and educational work for the present, always keeping before their eyes the ideal of an independent India. In ultimate purpose he was perhaps more extreme than Tilak but in [SW: methods] he was more moral and practical — he would have denounced illegality until war could be openly declared and the Indians could fight to the finish. He did not believe in wringing reforms out of the British Gov^t. Finally, there were the Bengali extremists. These men were religious mystics — political assassination [SW: was] a righteous revenge on [SW: behalf of an] outraged religion — the [SW: British] were mere marauders whom the Hindu had to resist to the death — and this immediately. These [SW: were] in fact a distant echo of the worship of Kali[108] and the sacrifice of the 'White Goat' to the great goddess angered by the desecration of her country by impious foreigners.

Gok[SW: hale] himself believed in the self-education and self-discipline of the Indian people, and in persistent [SW: pressure] on English public opinion to grant self-government by instalments. He realises that these two complementary [SW: tasks are tasks] of supreme difficulty which can only be accomplished by lifelong devotion on the part of large numbers of Indian patriots. He looks to English public opinion as the ultimate [SW: arbiter] of the [SW: fate] of India, and he is perpetually revolving in his mind how to [SW: awaken] the conscience of England and how to bring it to bear on Anglo-Indian officialdom. Perhaps he is more optimistic about English [SW: opinion] and more pessimistic about Anglo-Indian [SW: opinion] than is quite justified. I asked him why cultivated Indians [SW: see] so little of intellectual Anglo-Indian society and he answered somewhat drily — 'where is it?' And certainly, we have found far more ca[SW: p]acity for sympathetic intellectual intercourse with cultivated Indians than with any of the English in India whom we have met; even the best of them, like Hope

Simpson and [SW: Hobart], sympathetic and sensible men, are hardly the intellectual equals of [SW: Gokhale] and the Fergusson College professors or of the staff of the *gurukula*. As for the ruck of the British Civil Service – leave alone the ordinary Army officers and the inferior administrative servants and the 'commercials' – they are too far below the highly-educated Hindu to find anything in common with him.

That is one of the great difficulties in our Government of India – a stupid people find themselves governing an intellectual aristocracy – the explanation being, as [SW: Gokhale] more than once remarked, that the *average man of the British race* is far superior to the *average man* of the Indian peoples. Until the average has been raised the aristocracy of India will be subject to the mediocrity of Great Britain – with the melancholy result of aloofness and disaffection on the part of the honourable Indians, and clever, servile duplicity on the part of the dishonourable Indians. Hence the mutual misunderstanding of Government House and the 'Servants of India'.

Whilst at Poona we met one breezy and sympathetic Englishman – [SW: Dr. Mann],[109] Principal of the [SW: Gov^t] Agricultural College. Mann is a Yorkshire [SW: radical] and nonconformist – with a strong Yorkshire [SW: accent] – a refined optimist whose pleasant manner and [SW: ob]vious ability and enthusiasm for his work has enab[SW: led] him to become almost one of the Poona nationalists, whilst keeping on the right side of the Government of India. He had been 8 years in India and [SW: confirmed] substantially all our views of the relations between the English and the cultivated Indians. Quite clearly he preferred the society of the 'Servants of India' to that of [SW: the Poona cantonment] – & as he is not what the [SW: Poona cantonment] would call 'a gentleman', he found no difficulty in avoiding the [SW: English].

His flourishing [SW: Agricultural College] was a remarkable contrast to the more pretentious establishment [SW: at] Lyallpur – there were many students and little plant instead of much plant and few students. After Waddington he was the most inspiring personality [SW: in] the Anglo-Indian Educational Service; and the contrast between the well-bred Waddington, with his distinguished manners, [SW: public school and university training and] sportsman's tastes, and the small and dowdy Mann, with his warm feelings and quick intellect, was coincident with the contrast between their respective tasks – the training of the Chiefs' [SW: sons] – destined to a life of leisure – and the education of the expert and the working landholder who will succeed in life according to [SW: his] industry [SW: & his brains] – [SW→] Mann had introduced the experiment of a vernacular class where cultivators' sons, knowing no English, could be taught how to be good agriculturalists. The boys we saw (aged 12–16) were sons of considerable holders, owning several hundred acres but cultivating it themselves with some hired labour. He had, by the way, incurred Government censure for too prominently taking part in an aggressive temperance movement which tried to 'picket' liquor shops.

[BW→] We are inclined to suggest that the Government of India should bring out first-rate middle-class men – the best type of elementary or science teachers rather than the leavings of the university world – unless they can afford to pay the salaries which would attract men of Waddington's standards. The hireling upper-middle class person who accepts a position in India because he cannot get one in England – and who is a hanger-on of the English Club – is a rotten element in Indian education. It seems the very best policy would be to train clever, well-bred Indians for the Educational Service; but *that* the Government will not do, for fear of sedition.

[SW→] There was staying with Gokhale an Indian I.C.S. (Bilgra-mi),[110] who was a District Judge in Bombay Presidency. He had been a wrangler at Cambridge (St. John's College). He was a determined nationalist more bitter in his complaints of the Gov^t than any we have met. He described to us case after case of unfair treatment of the Indian members of the I.C.S., how they were always presumed to be inefficient (unless they actually forced their capacity to notice) and how accordingly, any little mistake or fault was taken as proving it – how they were always sent to the most unhealthy districts irrespective of the fact that men from other parts of India suffered as much from the Bombay climate as the English: he himself was from the Punjab and he suffered acutely from the low-lying coast districts in which he nevertheless was invariably stationed, whilst the English had a monopoly of the healthier districts – how an Indian Collector was never trusted by the Gov^t, was always specially supervised by the Commissioner and always had an Englishman placed with him as Ass^t-Magistrate & as Ass^t-Superintendent of Police, who were relied on to keep him in order. As he said, such charges of partiality could not be proved: he could only assert that they were felt and that there were far too many instances to permit of any other interpretation. Without necessarily accepting as true *all* that he alleged, it is clear that there is much feeling that the Indian members of the I.C.S. are unfairly treated. Some have resigned (his own brother resigned from [the] post of Assistant Traffic Manager on the railways because he was given no responsible work and was put under a Eurasian of inferior official status); others remain on in bitterness and the total number does not increase. Add to this that some (like Ghosal) set themselves to become more English than the English & one can understand Gokhale's disbelief in anything like simultaneous examinations as a cure. Gokhale, by the way, in his solicitude for our comfort, had put it in the hands of Bilgrami as knowing English ways to see that we got food, etc., in every detail up to English standards of luxury.

We saw at Poona two other institutions, one an immense and surprisingly good girls' school run by the Deccan Educational Society (a Hindu voluntary trust) and officered (with one exception) by Indian teachers, mostly women but some men.[111] The headmistress was an Indian unmarried lady of great personality (aged 40?), highly culti-vated, speaking English perfectly, a native Christian by the way, governing her huge school and extensive mixed staff with perfect success, and withal, very attractive and charming. This seems to be the best Hindu girls' school in India; and here again these people, 'who are all talk', have shown very great executive capacity. The institution comprised (a) training college (b) primary school for practising purposes and (c) a high school – altogether I think some 800 pupils.

The other institution was a philanthropic working and training-home for Indian widows of sufficiently high caste to be forbidden to marry again. This was run by an ex-member of the Fergusson College brotherhood who was devoting the rest of his life to it. Here several scores of women of all ages were being taught to read and write and also, to some extent, trained to become teachers (all by men teachers, which seems wrong); and also taught to do weaving and various kinds of needlework. An extension was being built, destined to take in unmarried daughters whose parents wished to keep them unmarried until maturity, but who found it difficult to withstand the pressure if the growing girls remained at home. It was said that they would trust them to the widows' home in preference to the girls' high school because the former had a greater reputation for conservative orthodoxy.

We also saw a great Oriental scholar (Indian) whom European universities had delighted to honour with degrees, but no English university. He was getting old but was still active in his retirement, translating inscriptions, etc. He confirmed our impression that the *Arya Samaj* citations from the Vedas were not to be trusted. (He was himself *Prarthana Samaj*, the Bombay analogue of *Brahmo Samaj*.)

[BW→] Gokhale, the Fergusson College professor and the 'Servants of India', all took the modern historical criticism attitude towards the Vedas, and doubted whether the *Arya Samaj*, with the fanatical adhesion to the inspiration of the Vedas, would spread among educated Indians outside the Punjab. But they were warmly admiring of the spirit and work of the organisation. In fact, there is none of the detraction of 'other people's effort' among the Indian reformers – which is unfortunately common in England. Even towards the English official they preserve a kindly attitude and blame the inevitable tendency of alien rule rather than the individual. Moreover, most of them recognise that a certain measure of alien rule is necessary at present.

APRIL 10/15th [1912] TAJ HOTEL BOMBAY

On the eve of our departure! For the last five days we have been seeing the Indians to whom we have been introduced by Gok[SW: hale] – chiefly the leading Parsees – Petits,[112] [SW: Tatas][113] etc., with whom Gokhale seems on intimate terms. These millionaire financiers, merchants, and manufacturers are attractive, cultivated persons – enlightened and discreetly patriotic – the women attractive, good-looking, charmingly-dressed and highly-educated, and the men able and refined. They live in sumptuous palaces and bungalows with a plenitude of motors, and make frequent journeys to Europe. The [SW: Tatas] have [SW: houses] and flats in London and Paris and are completely cosmopolitan.

At these houses, we met one or two Europeans – the editor of the *Times of India* [SW: Stanley Reed][114] and his wife and one or two of the leading European commercial magnates – but no officials or Government House young men, partly no doubt because Government House is moving to the hills. A few wealthy and enligh[SW: tened] Muslims with their women out of *purdah*, and a few millionaire Hindus – complete the circle. The atmosphere is distinctly nationalist, though unenthusiastically loyal to the King Emperor and the imperial connection. There is a distinct resentment at the exclusiveness of the European society – the notorious exclusion of all Indians from the Yacht Club and the refusal of the Collector and other officials to return the calls of Indian magnates. Otherwise the relations seem far more friendly than in Calcutta and other great centres of population. Baronets abound [SW: especially amongst the Parsees]. Compared to other plutocracies these Indians are aristocratic in appearance, manners and cultivation; and far superior in [SW: personal] distinction to Government House or the English-Indian official world – not to mention the Anglo-Indian commercial man who is a very distinct commoner in body and mind.

One or two of the Parsees engaged in shipping and foreign trade spoke enthusiastically of the uprightness and honourable dealing of the larger Japanese firms. Their explanation of the contrary representation was that the Japanese had been so cheated by the Europeans that they retaliated in dealing with Europeans – and practised a lower standard of honesty deliberately as they thought such was the European custom!

We attended a meeting of the Municipal Council—partly because it was expected that there would be a heated debate on the Chairmanship for the ensuing year. J. Baptista [SW: a member of the Fabian Society], an able and ultra-progressive Indian Christian barrister[115] who had defended Tilak, had been nominated and had been promised the support of a large majority of the Council — had even been seconded by a leading English official. But Government House intervened, Sir G. Clarke actually sending for various members of the Council to persuade them to withdraw their support, and having ordered the English official to nominate a nonentity against Baptista. Gradually, as Baptista told us, he found his friends melting away under Government pressure. At the last moment he retired, as it was clear that he would be supported by a small minority [SW: only].

Another manifestation of what we should call improper Government interference was the drafting of rules and regulations by Sir G. Clarke for the discipline of all schools and colleges. These rules, which were printed in the agenda, were arbitrary and somewhat childish. The parents were to hand over the *whole* control of their children, in and *out* of school, to the headmaster of the school. No boy or youth was to attend *any* public meeting, to join any association, to subscribe to or collect any fund for any purpose whatsoever without the express permission of the headmaster — and so on. Here the Government got a distinct snub, the Council replying that the spirit of the rules had already been [SW: embodied] as far as practicable and desirable in their own regulations. [SW→] In the schools run by the district boards (that is, the rural schools) the Gov[t] had simply insisted on these rules being adopted.

We had several talks with the great leader of the municipality (he was just retiring from the Chairmanship) and of the Bombay University – Sir Phirozshah Mehta.[116] A very successful barrister, long the leader of the Bombay Bar, he had made himself leader of the two independent organisations of Bombay by sheer ability, persistence and public spirit. A Parsee by race and religion, he was in sentiment entirely nationalist, but he took his own line and preferred the organising of local centres of independent action to Gokhale's general political reforms. Perhaps he was too much concerned to have his own way and to score his little triumphs over the Government in local matters to be able quite enthusiastically to work for India at large. Thus, he was not in sympathy with Gokhale's Education Bill, holding that it was better to multiply university education and let it 'filter downwards'. He had had a terrific fight with the Government of India and Sir George Clarke over their proposed reforms of Bombay University, apparently resisting both the good proposals and the bad because these were one and all tainted with the evil that they tended to deprive the University of its independence and make it really an organ of the local Government. In the fight to maintain an independent senate he had failed, as the Government of India proceeded by statute which swept away the old, swollen and much-degenerated senate and replaced it by a smaller one (of 100), mainly nominated by Government. But Mehta threw himself energetically into the new senate and by sheer weight of argument converted the Government nominees, who were mostly well-chosen unofficial people.

The last fight had been over English history, which used to be compulsory for [the] B.A. The Governor, without actually avowing his reason that English history made for nationalism, tried to get it excluded except as a special study. Mehta failed to keep it compulsory but succeeded in keeping it in as an optional subject which any student can take. He was more successful with regard to the matriculation examination. This the Governor sought to make the University relinquish to the college, so that each college might make its own examination, fix its own subjects and set its own standard. So extraordinary a proposal required explanation and the only one we could get, on the Gov^t side, was that the existing univ^y matric^n examination was open to criticism, and that the Oxford and Cambridge colleges had their own entrance examinations — which, be it noted (though the Indians were not told this), are *over & above* what the Universities of Oxford and Cambridge require for their first examinations — not alternatives to these.

The real reason, so the Indians thought, was to get the control out of the hands of the senate, which in spite of its emasculation was still (under Mehta) obstinate and pretty independent, into the hands of the colleges which were still mainly under Government control (wholly so as regards medicine and engineering, predominantly so as regards science, and largely so as regards arts). Once the colleges could fix their own matriculation examinations, it was believed that the Government, in its new policy of restricting university education, would compel them to raise the standard of entrance, so as greatly to limit the numbers. Here Mehta beat the Government. By his passionate eloquence and tireless persuasion, he kept a majority even of the Government nominees, and Sir G. Clarke had just approved the new regulations, which fell far short of what he had asked for; and (as he told Sir P. Mehta), had approved them with great reluctance.

In all this contest with Bombay Univ^y, our impression is that Sir G. Clarke and the Gov^t generally, comes out very badly. It is not that the University did not need reform but that, in all the proposals for reform, the Government took the opportunity of withdrawing such autonomy as the University had previously been granted. It is not that the Governor interfered in the University, for as Chancellor he had a right to intervene and make proposals, but that he intervened as Governor and used all the influence of Government, legitimate and illegitimate, to carry his points, which he formulated without consultation with the University and pressed with bitter personal obstinacy. We cannot help feeling that it is a bad case of reaction, of taking back from the Indians opportunities for self-government which had actually been accorded to them.

We visited two of the Bombay cotton mills, one under the guidance of the proprietor, the other under that of the Factory Inspector whom the Government deputed to take us. They both had efficient English machinery in crowded and insanitary premises (one much worse than the other). In both it struck us that the shafting and moving parts were much less securely fenced than in Lancashire; and there is no Employers' Liability and (we are told) naturally frequent accidents. Both were under Indian management almost exclusively, though each had one Lancashire man, in one case as foreman and in the other case as weaving master.

In both the working day was 13 hours, less one hour for meals, with Sunday a holiday unless some Hindu festival was substituted for it. Both told us that other mills did a lot of 'cribbing time'[117] and that the factory inspection was very inefficient. There are only four Factory Inspectors in all India, all men, and Englishmen, apparently promoted from subordinate services (our man was from the Customs). There is no restriction on the hours of opening and closing − only on the hours worked by each operative − and as there is no requirement that half-timers should go to school and no provision for checking evasions, our Factory Inspector declared that it was practically impossible to get evidence that half-time boys were not putting in their free half-time there or elsewhere, and that women were not working illegal hours. The ventilation was extremely imperfect and dust and dirt abounded. In case of fire the mill would be a death trap. Both mills were making large profits and had never worked short time except in the famine years. Altogether we felt that, if the Indian mills had a grievance in being subjected to the excise duty, this ought not to be given up except as part of a bargain with the mill owners to accept a Factory Act to the latest Lancashire standard and [to] our own Workmen's Compensation Act.

The operatives were mostly recruited from the coast districts around Bombay, not from Bombay itself; and they are said to insist on frequently going home for longer or shorter periods on their private affairs. They came somewhat irregularly to work and there was a system of taking on temporary substitutes, a crowd of whom attended daily at the factory gates. There was said to be no scarcity of labour (though just now some extensive engineering works were somewhat competing for hands) and no organisation for recruiting in the country. The operatives were said to be very independent, shifting from mill to mill for the very slightest reason. They were paid only once a month. The methods of remuneration, terms and conditions were said to vary from mill to mill, there being no uniform rate or common rules, though naturally competition among the mills kept the terms fairly equivalent to each other. There was said to be no trade union though there were inchoate associations among the mill-hands for special purposes. Caste restrictions were said to be dying out and to be unimportant: the mills now contained people of all castes, high and low, and no objection was made. Piece-work was the rule, and usually, individual contracts, though in some cases a whole room would be on collective piece-work, the leading hands getting a (specified) larger rate than the others. The doffing boys[118] and the piecers[119] and the (few) mules[120] were always paid by the firm direct. There were a few mules but mostly ring-frames (all worked by men). The women only did such work as winding. The looms were worked by men, each minding two only. One of the firms employed no half-timers, declaring that it was impossible to prevent their tiring themselves out by working the other half, *sometimes actually at another mill.*

Both these mills were owned by Hindus. In one case, the father had started the mill some forty years ago and had been uniformly successful. The 1000 rupee shares were worth 2700 rupees. The company was virtually a family one, the family having three directors out of five. The family claimed to be *Kshatriyas,* or warriors, by caste.[121] The young proprietor, who took us over, was this year sheriff of Bombay. He had not been to England as his caste did not permit it, though they allowed voyages to Zanzibar, etc., and they would presently give way about England. The other mill belonged virtually to a *bunnia* family. It was far inferior in amenity.

This latter mill had its own dyeing and bleaching department, which we visited, and which only did work for other firms when it happened to have nothing to do. It had imported much German machinery for dyeing which was said to be in advance of English: also, the English machinery-makers were too obstinate: they would not make what they were told to make and thought they knew better! (Thus, though a screw-press was normally much superior to a lever-press, the latter was better for India, as the former got out of order in Indian hands.) Neither mill seemed to compete directly with Lancashire or Japan, making somewhat different products. One sold most of its yarn to dealers who supplied the Indian hand-loom weavers (one third of the total Indian consumption of cotton cloth is still made on hand-looms in the Indian factories and less than half is imported). Its cotton cloth was sold mostly in India & for Central Asia. The other mill sent its cotton cloth mostly to Zanzibar for East Africa.

The women at work were nearly all married, their husbands mostly also working in mills. A few were widows, but these mostly married again. No definite or reliable information as to morality. Altogether, the mills of Bombay are not a pleasing development. But they prove that the Indians, Hindus as well as Parsees, can successfully manage business enterprise on a large scale. We were told that $9/10^{ths}$ of the business of Bombay was in Indian hands, in contrast with Calcutta, where $9/10^{ths}$ is in European hands.

We went to Elephanta[122] in a Gov^t electric launch which Sir G. Clarke very kindly lent us, and we took with us a gentle and attractive Hindu friend of Gokhale, the Hon. Lallubhai Samaldas, who had been very attentive in looking after us, as well as another Hindu, the youthful chairman of the Standing Committee of the municipality. The latter was not interesting but the former, apparently a well-to-do commercial person, had been nominated by the Bombay Legislative Council and the University as a well-disposed, moderate person. This he was, but it is significant that his Gov^t nominee was a fervent admirer of Gokhale and essentially a nationalist and he had not hesitated to oppose Sir G. Clarke when he though he was wrong. He asked about the Fabian Society and expressed a wish to join. At his request S.W. saw his son, an attractive boy of twenty who had just taken his B.A. with distinction and was determined to join the Servants of India. The father did not altogether disapprove, but wished him to spend two years in his own business office and then to visit England and The London School of Economics before finally deciding. It is noteworthy that the boy of twenty had been married for two years to a girl now seventeen, but they have not yet commenced cohabitation.

We pass over the rest of our doings at Bombay – the Towers of Silence,[123] the drives along the seashore, the lunches and teas and receptions where we met the cultivated Parsee, Hindu and Muslims but scarcely any English, the stray English we saw at the hotel and elsewhere. We did not present various introductions to English people as there was little time to spare and we were tired. There is however just one more item to record. Ratan Tata (the second son of the Tata who started the great steel works and hydraulic electric works and the great Technical Institute at Bangalore) had wished to found and endow a corresponding institute for economic research. He had formulated this proposal & made a definite offer of a large sum to promote economic investigation and study in India. He wished to locate this at Bangalore alongside his father's Institute for Technological Research. He laid this offer before the Principal and council of the latter Institute, by whom the whole project was rejected lock, stock & barrel and the money refused! The ground of refusal was that any economic research was bound to be or to seem 'political', and likely to bring down on the Technological Institute Gov[t] displeasure. The refusal seems to have been accompanied by contemptuous references by the science men at Bangalore to the futility of any investigation into economic matters. And the Gov[t], far from encouraging Tata's desires or helping to get economic investigation started, has also thrown cold water on it. Hence Tata has let the matter drop. Meanwhile, he has made an offer to London University to endow an enquiry into the problem of destitution on which Miers[124] seems to have consulted Leonard Hobhouse[125] and Urwick,[126] and a draft scheme has been submitted to Tata (which his Manager, Padshah, gave S.W. in confidence, and on which S.W. wrote a long memo) which may lead to £1000 a year or so coming within the sphere of The London School of Economics.

Sir G. Clarke's own project of an institute or school of commerce, as to which he got out Lees-Smith[127] to lecture three years ago, seems to have made little progress. He has some promises of money, but he seems to be so pigheadedly obstinate on having his own way, so ungracious about other people's help and really so half-hearted about the project at all, that we doubt whether it will lead to anything. The fact is that he has become afraid of any kind of education! The sooner this worn-out, tired, saddened and embittered man goes home into retirement, the better. It is said that Lord Chelmsford[128] is to succeed him, which would be excellent.

ON THE 'HOMEWARD' SEA 16/25th APRIL [1912]

On a crowded ship, disturbed by three crying babies and two dogs in unpleasant moist heat which only the cool draughts of the incessantly-going fans make endurable, it is not easy to sum up India!

First may be noted the fact, whatever it may be worth, that the more we saw of India, the more we learned about the Gov[t] and the officials and the longer we lived among the people, *the graver became our tone* and the more subdued our optimism. At first, after China, India seemed hopeful. Great as were the difficulties they did not appear insurmountable. We could look with confidence on the future. I still think that the problems can be solved and that the future may be made bright. But as our acquaintance with the Indian bureaucracy has increased, and as we have more and more appreciated its alliance in the main with reactionary imperialism and commercial selfishness in England, we are less confident. Three months' acquaintance has greatly increased our estimate of the Indians, and greatly lessened our admiration for, and our trust in, this Government of officials.

Does this bureaucracy succeed in supplying a good Gov^t? Our impression is that the I.C.S. has succeeded fairly well in carrying out its ideals of Gov^t but its ideals are still those of 1840! Its conception of Gov^t is to put down internal war, brigandage and violent crime, decide civil suits and maintain order and, for the rest, to leave people alone. These things it has very fairly achieved and it is no doubt a great achievement to have done this for so huge a territory out of its own resources, with so limited a staff of English and with so imperfect a subordinate staff of Indians. Hence its self-complacency, and indeed, conceit, which is a serious obstacle to its learning anything or improving. There are shortcomings even in this limited realm. There is still a great deal of theft and extortion from poor folk; cattle-stealing, petty thefts on the railway, and even burglaries (*dacoities*) seem much more common than in Europe. Our law courts are honest and unbribable but they are by no means racially unprejudiced; the Magistrates commit many oppressions on poor and humble folk, largely because they do not regard their liberty as anything like so sacred as that of a white man; our procedure has encouraged an enormous amount of litigation and chicanery; its very excellence and rigour has greatly increased the evil power of the money-lender. It seems very doubtful whether a rural village, if it could give an opinion, would not rather be without our whole civil courts and civil procedure and without our criminal law – preferring its old way of dealing with its own cases in village *panchayats*.[129] It is nearly as doubtful whether it would not be well advised in so deciding.

[BW→] (S.W. has left off – yielding to the enervation of the midday heat and to the irritation of a screaming baby. I want him to sum up his impressions of the economics of the British dominions in India – of which I have, without due thought or knowledge, somewhat grave misgivings – more than misgivings as to past stupidity and plunder – and misgiving *questions* even about our present economic policy. Meanwhile, I jot down one or two impressions of the purely personal side of our contact with Indian life.)

First, there seems to be no typical 'Oriental' – no qualities that seem to be common to the Japanese, to the Chinese and to the Indians. There are of course *institutions* that are common to these three races, as compared to the institutions [SW: of the more advanced European communities.] The 'joint family', with its reverence for the parents' authority, its maintenance without question of even adult male members, its subordination of women and its community of property, still exists in Japan as well as in China and it is an equally common feature of Hindu and Muslim Ind[SW: ia.] The small cultivator and the small masters are characteristic forms of production throughout the Far East and India, as contrasted with the great industry and capitalist agriculture of so many of the western races and their colonies. There is even a certain community of religious experience in all these three countries — the Buddhism of Japan and China [SW: arising] in India and being [SW: in one sense] a mere offshoot of Hinduism. But after one has recited these obvious likenesses in social and economic structure, one comes to the deep-down unlikeness between the men and women of Japan, of China and of India respectively — an unlikeness which is certainly greater in the case of the educated Indians than the unlikeness of the Hindu Indian to the modern Italian and even to the Englishman.

The Japanese are a race of idealists, but these ideals are fixed and amazingly homogeneous and are always capable of being translated into immediate and persistent action. They are in fact perhaps the most *executive* race in the world — the most capable of discovering the means to the end — and the most self-contained and self-disciplined in working out these means, and therefore in attaining their ends. One sees in front of them the danger of becoming vulgarised by their success as practical men — of losing the substance of their ideal in the shadow of accomplishment.

About the Chinese, I do not feel competent to speak as I dislike them so heartily. But the very fact that they excite our dislike whilst the Japanese excite our almost partisan admiration and the Indians our real affection, shows how different the Chinese race must be, either [SW: to] the inhabitants of the great continent of India or [SW: to those] of the little island of Japan. What revolts [SW: us] in the Chinese is, on the one hand, the absence of the idealism of the Japanese and Indian races, [SW: and on the other, their present] lack of capacity for the scientific method and for disciplined [SW: effort] of the Japanese. There are doubtless qualities in the Chinese which we have not had the sympathetic insight to discover — in fact the Chinese do seem to be what all orientals are assumed to be, 'inscrutable'.

As for the Hindus, they strike us as an essentially lovable race. Unlike the Japanese and Chinese, they have the element of physical beauty — of fineness of feature, large shapeliness of stature and extreme spirituality and intellectuality of expression — they produce more aristocrats of body, mind, manners and bearing than either the Chinese or the Japanese. Then, the fact that the cultivated Hindu has more completely assimilated English thought and English literature whilst possessing a real knowledge of his own classics, gives him a broader base for intellectual intercourse with the cultivated Englishman. Like the Japanese, the Hindu is an idealist – but alas! for his political efficiency, his ideals are 'all over the place', and frequently he lacks the capacity to put them into practice – he can neither discover the means nor work at them with unswerving persistency. Then, the aristocracy of India is dragged down by a multitude of lower castes and lower races – embedded in a population which seems strangely childish in intellect and undisciplined in conduct. The perpetually-repeated commonplace of the Anglo-Indian official, 'they are like children – you must treat them as such', is ludicrous in its class insolence when you are thinking of the educated Hindu of higher caste, but probably statistically true about a great mass of the population of India – I say *statistically* true because if you treated them persistently as men they would probably 'grow up' to manhood. And yet, even in the hordes of humble Indian folk who crowd the third-class carriages you see a spirituality and a bright intelligence – sometimes a beauty and dignity which you altogether miss in the inhabitants of the Chinese village or of Canton.

And when you come to associate with the men who make up the *Arya Samaj* or the 'Servants of India', all your prepossessions as to the lack of self-discipline and persistent self-devotion, and even of executive force among Hindus, dissolve [into] a mere prejudice of which you become ashamed. But perhaps the most striking quality of the Hindus whom we have seen is their essential modesty – not so much a depreciation of *Things Indian* as compared to *Things European* – but the modesty of man against the universe. That terrible coarse-grained self-satisfaction and self-absorbed sensuality and self-conscious respectability – consciousness of God's own Englishmen as the king of the universe – which makes some good-hearted and capable English-men so horrid to live with or even to talk to, is not to be met with among Hindus. All humanity is a pitiful business to the philosophical Hindu – and the greatest one on earth is inferior to the humblest ascetic of the lowest caste on the straight way to final emancipation from the wheel of human desire. It is this quality of intellectual perspective that makes the Hindu a delightful and refined intellectual companion – whom one instinctively feels to be one's superior.

What strikes us as serious in the present state of feeling between the British ruler and the Indian ruled is the complete and almost fatuous ignorance of the bulk of British officials, of their essential inferiority in culture, charm and depth of intellectual and spiritual experience, to the Indian aristocracy of intellect. That means that as the Indian aristocrat grows in the power of self-discipline and executive force – and he *is* growing very rapidly, the cleavage will become wider and wider and co-operation between the actual alien governor and the potential native governor will become less and less possible. And as national feeling is bound to spread and intensify, the Indian aristocrat will have to work underground with the object of compelling the British ruler to relinquish his hold. If, on the other hand, the English would realise this new governing class – and would gradually take them into their confidence with a view to making them pair to the Government of India, then the British race might pride themselves on having been the finest race of schoolmasters, as well as the most perfect builders of an empire. The British Empire might endure until international law makes all empire a practical anachronism, though perhaps it would still remain as a much-loved sentimental tie embedded in an ancient name for certain far distant parts of this earth.

Travelling in India, associating with educated Hindus, observing the life of the common people, raises one long series of questions – questions which keep one's mind perpetually busy and always baffled at not finding any explanation or answer. Sometimes these questions relate to the relations between an alien government and a subject race, sometimes they concern the results of an economic policy prescribed by an individualist and materialist people on an essentially communal and religious race. But the one problem that has been before my mind – as an almost morbid obsession – is the problem of the religious life of Hinduism.

At the temples of Benares and at the *Magh Mela* of Allahabad, I was revolted by the incontinence of the popular religion – the strange combination of an almost hysterical and certainly promiscuous idolatry – with crude superstitions as to the physical results of 'God-propitiation' – and behind it all, the sinister background of revolting lasciviousness and gross exudity. This disgust reached its culmination in the grotesque lewdness of the Khajuraho temples, with their direct incitement to unnatural vice. Add to this the exhibitions of the life of the ordinary *sadhu*, with its self-indulgence, vagrant idleness and frequent hypocrisy and vice – or the equally na[SW: useous] imposition of the Brahmin family priest with horoscope and fortune-telling – and [SW: one] is reduced to a state of cynical doubt as to whether the most complete hedonistic-materialistic atheism would not be preferable to the religious experience of the Hindu people.

But this is only one side of the shield. [The other is] the vision of the austere and pious domestic life of the *purdah* ladies of Bhupendra Basu's household, with their [SW: unmeasured] devotion to husband and children, their industry and frugality, and, throughout the whole family life, the intense reverence of the younger to the elder, all qualities based on the Hindu religion. This vision relieves one's gloom, though possibly it does not make one more hopeful of the immediate progressiveness (in the western sense) of the Hindu race. With this almost fanatical idealisation of wifely devotion one might even see *suttee*[130] re-established in an 'India without the English'. Indeed, the rite of *suttee* ceases to appear barbarous if once you accept this atmosphere of pure idealism. If the body is a mere illusion, if the only reality is the spirit of devotional communion of wife with husband, then why retain the illusion — why not let the body dissolve in the flame of the funeral pyre? By this willing self-immolation, the reality endures — the spectators, far from taking part in a cruel custom, are witnessing the victory of the spirit of devotion over the physical fear of death. The only question that arises to the modern democrat is: why not a *suttee* for the widower as well as for the widow?

Another and more inspiring vision is that of the informal religious orders of [SW: social] service [SW: arising in modern India] — the teachers of the *Arya Samaj* educational institutions, or the members of the 'Servants of India' or of the 'Fergusson College'. Here the Hindu religion is combined with a sincere and powerful self-discipline, a self-discipline with the express object of maintaining the mind and body in the fittest condition for the most perfect service of the community. These orders seem preferable to the religious orders of western peoples in two remarkable features — complete freedom of thought and the normal domestic ties for all the members. Though the *Arya Samaj* has a definite doctrine and is almost fanatical in its propaganda of the Vedas, there seems to be no attempt to enquire into the particular faith of the individual member or to shackle him in any way in the expression of it. There is no authority that can determine what shall be the intellectual faith of the *Samaj*. It is an interesting sidelight that the only dispute that has arisen is not on the question of faith, but on the *practice* of meat-eating as against vegetarianism. 'You can *think* what you like so long as you *do* what is prescribed' is the universal attitude of the Hindu heresy-hunter. And when you pass from the religious sect of the *Aryas* to the Servants of India, you lose all trace of religious dogma — you are confronted with a religious order without any definite religion or even a definite metaphysics. The other great advantage of these modern Hindu orders is the absence of enforced celibacy for the adult men. The strictest chastity is prescribed for the boys and the most careful [SW: arrangements] are [SW: made] in the *gurukula* for the enforcement of it. But this chastity is with a view to 'greater virility' in adult life — a more perfect fulfilment of the duty of parenthood. Directly the man is adult he is expected to marry, and his wife and family are maintained in the same modest and abstemious way as he is himself. These two characteristics – freedom of thought and normal domestic life – are a real contribution to the institution of religious orders.

In estimating the net result of the religious experience of modern Hinduism, it is therefore essential to balance the superstition of incontinence of the Hinduism of the populace by a realisation of the new development – of the healthy, virile and free service of religious orders self-dedicated to the progress of the race. The only analogue in the European world is the Salvation Army, but that organisation is marred by the lack of broad culture or intellectual distinction. Moreover, the Salvation Army has the commonness inherent in an autocratic organisation dependent on the personality of one man.[131] One of the outstanding charms of Hindu religious organisation is in fact its impersonal character, its independence of any one personality, its free and untrammelled growth from the soul of the whole people. Indeed, the whole conception of service by an aristocracy of birth and intellect, for mere subsistence and within a democratically-managed community of social equals, is an entirely new idea to the western mind. If only the British official, with his insistence on high salaries, prestige, and elaborate arrangements for the pleasures of life, would recognise the existence within the Indian community of a moral and intellectual standard superior to his own, without necessarily desiring to imitate this standard. He might continue to assert the superiority of the British in other respects – without offending the susceptibilities of educated Hindu society.

A traveller, especially an elderly traveller, is liable to come back from his travels with his own general ideas confirmed. Observations of Hinduism in its baser and nobler aspects confirms my theory of the legitimate relation between the sphere of science and the sphere of religion. Most of the demoralisation of popular Hinduism arises from applying religious emotion to determine the *processes of life* – of seeking the help of the God in the illness of a child, in consulting the horoscope of a boy and girl prior to marriages and accepting the magic of priestly rites as the determinative factor in every act of life. On the other hand, in much of the popular religion there seems no kind of attempt to purify or exalt the purpose of life as displayed in nobility of human motive. In the worst forms of Hinduism the individual may be impelled by the most vicious desires, he may even murder and bear false witness without fear of religious ostracism, so long as he is true to the rites and ceremonies of his sect or caste. In his pantheon there are gods who will if duly propitiated help him to do evil things. In the lowest strata of Hinduism, superstition governs all the forms of conduct whilst the lowest animal impulses are permitted to determine the motives and even the substance of conduct. In the finest forms of Hinduism, we watch an almost perfect relation between religious emotion and intellectual life. Here all ratiocination is left free and untrammelled by religious dogma – you can think what seems to you to be true in any particular case. Religion concerns itself with the purity and nobility of your *purpose* in life – with the self-discipline which will enable you to maintain it intact. Even the control over your physical instincts which is enjoined is to be guided by a scientific knowledge of the laws of health and is to be varied and developed according to any new knowledge attained by scientific discovery. Hence, when we tried to explain our view of the relative sphere of science and religion to the professors of the *gurukula* and to Gokhale and the Servants of India, we found a complete and ready acceptance of our theory as the one which they had been themselves working out.

[SW→] What is to be said of the economic condition of the three hundred millions of Indians? It is an uncomfortable fact that it should not be beyond controversy whether they are better or worse off than a generation ago. The British official unhesitatingly says they are better off and alleges the rise in wages of his *syce* (groom) as proof. But as he will admit, prices have also risen enormously and the wages of the lowest grades of labour and those of the remoter places and the Native States, have gone up far less than those of the skilled domestic servants of the English. It is more to the point to assert that the average Indian now enjoys a great[er] variety of commodities than before; he is said to be visibly earning more and spending more. The general consumption of umbrellas and shoes, cigarettes and tea, gramophones and made clothes is demonstrably greatly increasing. On the other hand, serious nationalist thinkers declare that the cultivators are (outside Bengal) more impoverished than they were and therefore more easily brought into destitution by droughts, which are thereby made into 'famines' (for the famine of India is now only a 'money famine', a spasm of local 'unemployment' which might be weathered if the cultivator had his own savings to fall back upon). On the whole, I should infer that the average Indian both earns more and spends more, his standard of life has risen and is rising, and if he does not get rich, he at any rate gets a somewhat wider life.

What is more important is to consider the economic influences at work. Here the biggest factor is perhaps the Gov^t land revenue which (outside Bengal and Benares, etc.) is not a permanently fixed rental. Every thirty years – sometimes every twenty years – the Settlement Officer comes and looks at each village and (with all sorts of elaborate rules and safeguards) fixes, without appeal to any independent tribunal, *how much more* the cultivator shall pay for the ensuing term. Against this periodical 'skimming off the cream', R. C. Dutt and all the Indian nationalists declaim, and their objection has been supported by leading officials from time to time. But the India Office and the Government of India will not agree to concede a 'permanent settlement' on the sole ground that the Government cannot and need not forgo the continuous increase of the land revenue, especially in so far [as] this is of the nature of 'unearned increment'.

Now, on this point I am converted to the nationalist position. Safeguard as one may, the system comes essentially to that of the Irish landlord with his cottier tenants. It is worse, because the Gov^t is virtually in the position of a monopolist landlord. The cultivator has practically no option. He must have access to land and the Government fixes its terms. The Settlement Officer is admittedly driven to get all that (subject to the rules) he can. He is told to take all that the cultivator can spare over and above the limit (half the net assets) that the Government itself fixes. When the time for resettlement approaches, land goes out of cultivation, houses are let go into ruin, wealth is hidden, etc., in order to get a lower assessment.

All this comes essentially to the system that ruined Asia Minor, Korea, etc., viz., arbitrary taxation of those becoming wealthy. Only by the greatest care can the Government of India prevent its settlements being actually oppressive and productive of starvation. It seems clear that, notwithstanding all possible rules about exempting improvements, the continuous raising of the land revenue wherever there is improvement in yield cannot fail to discourage thrift, industry, enterprise, and even honesty in the cultivator. I conclude that, at whatever loss of future increases, the Government of India ought in one way or another to concede a permanent settlement to its cultivators – or (as Lord Ripon proposed), at any rate, make the land revenue vary only at intervals with the general price level. The *'unearned* increment' of agricultural land – apart from irrigation – reveals itself only in higher prices, and if this potential increase were retained by the Government it might well regard all the rest as due to the cultivator's efforts. The Government would be recouped (as has been the case in Bengal) by the growth in the other sources of revenue payable by a population which, *ex hypothesi*, has more wealth (e.g., licences, import duties, income tax, stamps, etc.).

Thus, contrary to my prepossessions, I come to regard the Permanent Settlement of Bengal by Lord Cornwallis in 1793 as a wise measure.[132] (The mere fact that the *zemindar* landlords oppressed their tenants has nothing to do with the 'permanence' or otherwise of their own state rent or land tax; they are not *more* apt to rack-rent their cottiers because their own head-rent is *not* increased! As a matter of fact, the same sort of legislative protection of tenants against landlords has been required in all the provinces.) Similarly, I am convinced that the evil of the state land revenue has been greatest where the state has dealt directly with the individual *ryot*, or small cultivator. He is, in Bombay and Madras, not in the least like a peasant proprietor. He is an Irish cottier under an all-powerful absentee landlord. It is hard to resist the evidence that he has been much oppressed by the Government. He ought to be given the 'Three F's' at once — fixity of tenure, fair rents and free sale — and the same status should be given to the actual cultivators elsewhere, both as against their landlords and as against the Government land revenue demand.

One other measure is required, viz., credit legislation. The peasant cultivator needs to be protected against the usurer and against himself in the way of borrowing, by an extensive 'homestead law', which should prevent his holding and his cattle as well as his plough, etc., being seized for debt, or even mortgaged, or (as the Punjab law has it) even sold to anyone not being a cultivator. But this is to injure his power of borrowing. Supply this by a ubiquitous system of co-operative credit societies which the Government itself might well supply with all the capital needed, thus using its own credit to enable them to lend at low rates for legitimate purposes.

The Gov^t of India (and the India Office which has been even worse than the Viceroys) clings to the growing land revenue and pursues an extremely faint-hearted economic policy — partly out of ancient prejudice, but chiefly because the Government is horribly *poor*. Its revenue is small and precarious and the customary sources of English Chancellors of the Exchequer are closed to it. The Hindu joint family system stands in the way of death duties and increases the difficulties of an income tax. The consumption of popular luxuries is so small that no great sum can be got from alcohol, tea, tobacco, etc. English opinion won't permit any increase of the import duties against English goods. Under these circumstances, we suggest a bold policy of Government exploitation — taking into Government hands all the railways, developing the 240,000 square miles of forest by Government paper mills, match factories, timber trade, etc., and perhaps starting Government tobacco works and spirit distilleries. The I.C.S. is aghast at this and even Gokhale does not approve, because, to the nationalists, the position is rather as it was to the *laissez-faire* Liberals a century ago. To the Indians, the Government is a hostile force and they are loath to see it expand in any way. This cripples them in political programme because they are always urging retrenchment.

[BW→] To resume my disjointed notes on Hinduism. What is the value of all that religious expression that is covered by the term yoga — that self-study and contemplative concentration of thought to which

Hinduism & Buddhism attach such immense importance, with its coincident aspiration towards a complete suppression of human desire and of the greater part of human faculty? In our *Industrial Democracy* we defined the desire for liberty as the striving after an increase of human faculty and desire, a state of liberty as the maximum of desire and faculty among all the members of a given society. Our western ideal is in fact the fullest possible development of human faculty among the whole people – assuming that we agree as to what constitutes the fullest development both in quality and quantity.

But it is clear that the ideal is wholly antagonistic to the eastern ideal of restricting activity and assiduously cultivating a state of mind which seems to us to resemble blankness. Was there ever any justification for the practice of yoga – has any progress in the development of human personality been attained by it? Quite clearly the modern Hindu religious order, unlike the ancient *sadhu*, either eliminates yoga (as in the case of the Servants of India or the professors of Fergusson College) or subordinates it as a part of mental and physical discipline, whilst insisting on the obligation of each individual to develop all the faculties of body and mind for the service of humanity. I had hoped that our journey to the east would have enlightened this fundamental question, but I come back as mystified as ever. Mrs. Besant's coquetry with yoga, and the sight of the *sadhus* who are supposed to practice it, leave me in a state of cold scepticism – testifying to my continued ignorance of what may be behind this old world wisdom.

ON THE IONIAN SEA MAY 5th 1912

We were somewhat bored by our eight days' visit to Cairo – not for any lack of kindness or interest in our hosts – the Maurice Amos's[*sic*][133] and the Elgoods[134] – but because we were filled up with sightseeing, had made no arrangements to see any Egyptians and were really thinking over the problems that await us at home. Egypt seems like a pale reflection of India – a sort of mongrel East – with all the defects and with none of the virtues of Hindu and Muslim Indian civilisation. But then, we were staying with British officials and seeing exclusively other British officials – not a single Egyptian did we see in our stay at either house.

No one had a good word to say of the Egyptian – except that Elgood and some others sentimentalised over the idyllic industry of the *fellah*,[135] without attributing to him anything but the most primitive devotion to himself and his family. The educated Egyptian was wholly worthless! We asked everyone that we came across whether there was any movement in Egypt similar to the *Arya Samaj* or the Servants of India. Elgood said that there was a movement among the younger Muslims to emancipate themselves from both the religious bondage of Islam and the humiliating presence of the English – but he implied that this was a mere desire of the average sensual man to get rid of what prevented him indulging in sensuality and corrupt dealing. But then we knew that we should have heard exactly the same thing about India if we had not access to the Indians as well as the British officials.

There was more interest in Maurice Amos's criticism of the present governmental arrangements.[136] The British officials, whether Judges or 'Advisers', were there as half-timers – drawing good salaries but always checked in the quantity and quality of their work by incompetent Egyptians with a low standard of effort and doubtful morality, who were nominally their superiors. We are not really training the Egyptian to self-government, we are merely propping them up – alternating the policy of doing their work for them with that of sitting still and winking at their manifold defalcations. Eldon Gorst[137] had emphasized the policy of sitting still, and had reduced the country to semi-anarchy by ordering the English not to interfere, and leaving the Egyptian officials to pursue their nefarious ways. Kitchener[138] was reversing this policy and giving orders right and left. But he was doing it as the lonely autocrat equally indifferent to the British Adviser and the native Minister – except that he felt he must attend to the susceptibilities of the 'natives' more than to those of his fellow citizens.

Maurice Amos was really in favour of deposing the Khedive[139] – a wholly evil man, cruel and corrupt – and taking over the whole Government, training natives as subordinates, promoting them when fit, and gradually giving the Egyptian people the power of popular control. The state of Egypt seems a sort of half-way house between the complete control of the Malay States and the occasional intervention of the British Resident in a Native State in India – complicated, of course, by the sovereignty of Turkey and the jealousies of the European powers. The central figure seems to be the evil personality of the Khedive – corrupt in public and private life alike. 'If we were to retire he would be dead in a week' was the opinion of the British official. As it is, no one is responsible for the good government of Egypt and the development of Egyptian character. By our financiers and our engineers and our police, we have enormously increased the material prosperity of Egypt. It seems more doubtful whether we have added one iota to her moral and intellectual development. At least, this is the impression left on our minds by talking with the British official.[140]

Notes

1. *Mss Diary*, Volume 31.f.1. The volume opens with the entry, in Sidney's hand, 'Peshawar 4/6th'.

2. J. A. Richey, M.A., Indian Educational Service, Director of Public Instruction, North-West Frontier Province and Baluchistan, from 1911.

3. From the Arabic *kutub*, meaning a place where writing is taught.

4. In 1911 it was estimated that there were some three million Christians in India.

5. Cf. J. S. Mill, *The Subjection of Women* (London, 1869): 'What marriage may be in the case of two persons of cultivated faculties, between whom there exists that best kind of equality, similarity of powers and capacities with reciprocal superiority in them – so that each can enjoy the luxury of looking up to the other, and can have alternatively the pleasure of leading and of being led in the path of development – I will not attempt to describe.'

6. Alfred Ollivant (1874–1929), author of *Owd Bob, the Grey Dog of Kenmuir* (London, 1898) and other books.

7. A fiercely independent Pashtun tribal people whose territory straddles the Khyber Pass, from the eastern spurs of the Safed Koh to the borders of the Peshawar district of present-day Pakistan.

8. Lieutenant Maurice Hubert Bickford (b. 1887), Indian Army, Double Company Officer, 38th Dogras, from 1908.

9. Pierre Loti (1850–1923), French travel writer and romantic novelist.

10. Lieutenant-Colonel Sir George Roos Keppel (1866–1921), ICS, Chief Commissioner and Agent to the Governor-General, North-West Frontier Province from 1908, and subsequently Member of the India Council, London. Keppel's wife is said to have been a mistress of Edward VII.

11. Later Sir J. L. Maffey, who was to become Private Secretary to the Viceroy, Lord Chelmsford, Commissioner of the N.-W. Frontier Province and, in 1926, Governor of Sudan.

12. J. A. Spender (1862–1942), Liberal journalist and biographer of H. H. Asquith.

13. Evelyn Berkeley Howell, ICS, appointed 1899, Deputy-Commissioner, Punjab, who later saw service at Baghdad.

14. A Muslim, Pashto-speaking tribal people of south-eastern Afghanistan and what is today north-western Pakistan, famed for their martial traditions.

15. The Hindu spring festival of Holi, in light-hearted mood akin to All Fools' Day, contrasts sharply with an annual religious drama performed by the Shiite Muslims of Persia and North India (present-day Pakistan) on the tenth day of Muharram, the first month of the Muslim year. The 'solemn' event commemorates the slaying (by a rival faction) of Husayn ibn Ali (c. 629–80), son of the fourth Caliph, Ali, by his wife Fatimah, daughter of Muhammad the Prophet, founder of Islam. The Shiah, as distinct from the majority Sunnah Muslims, regard the family of Ali as the only true heirs of Muhammad. Since the Muslim calendar is based on a year of twelve months, each beginning approximately at the time of the new moon, the named months do not remain in the same seasons but retrogress through the entire seasonal year every 32½ solar years. It was thus that the Hindu and Muslim religious observances had happened to occur at the same time two years before the Webbs' visit to Peshawar.

16. *Joshua*, ch. 2.
17. Viscount Alfred Milner (1854–1925), journalist and civil servant, British High Commissioner in South Africa at the time of the Boer War. Milner's young Oxford admirers in South Africa were known for their common subscription to his robust imperialist ideas.
18. Founded by the British in 1892 at Lyallpur (now Faisalabad), one of several such settlements, part of a strategy of creating newly-irrigated areas and colonising them as a means to relieve pressure of population on the land, as well as to raise revenues and to generate surplus food and exportable crops.
19. Frederick William Knaggs Yeoman, India Public Works Department, appointed 1886, Executive Engineer, Punjab, from 1897.
20. The Royal Indian Engineering College, Cooper's Hill.
21. J. H. Barnes, Principal, Agricultural College, Lyallpur.
22. Frank Edwin Gwyther, India Public Works Department, appointed 1881, Superintendent Engineer, Punjab, from 1908.
23. Robert Tyndall Gibbs, India Telegraph Department, appointed 1886, Director of Telegraphs, East Bengal and Assam, from 1910.
24. Sir William Ramsay (1852–1916), Professor of Chemistry at University College London from 1887–1912 and winner of the Nobel Prize for Chemistry in 1904.
25. The tombs of Emperor Jahangir.
26. Patrick Dalreagle Agnew, ICS, appointed 1887, Divisional Judge, Punjab, from 1910.
27. See 'Lahore 29th Feb^y–3rd March 1912' (at page 270).
28. *The Tribune*, begun in 1881, an influential nationalist newspaper in the Punjab.
29. Gopal Singh Chowla, M.A., Professor of Mathematics, Government College, Lahore.
30. *Unani*, meaning 'Ionian' or Greek, remains today the predominant traditional system of medicine amongst the Muslims of Pakistan and North India. Like the Hindu *Ayurveda* and *Siddha* systems of healing, *Unani* emphasises holistic diagnosis and treatment. All three are now supplemented by modern biomedical science throughout South Asia.
31. Named after Sir C. U. Aitchison, Lieutenant-Governor of the Punjab, 1882–87. The foundation stone for the College was laid in 1888 by Lord Dufferin.
32. Brij Indar Singh Bahadur (b. 1896), who had succeeded while still a child, in February 1906.
33. J. R. Cornah, M.A., Punjab Education Department, who was Assistant-Principal, Aitchison College, Lahore, in 1912.
34. Hon. John Cornwallis Godley (1861–1946), Indian Educational Service, appointed 1904, Director of Public Instruction, Punjab, 1907–17.
35. G. A. Wathen, M.A., Indian Educational Service, Professor, Government College, Lahore.
36. Sydney Buxton (1853–1934), Viscount Buxton, was a Radical politician and President of the Board of Trade in the 1910 Liberal Government of Herbert Asquith.
37. Justice Shah Din (1868–1918), a Judge on the Punjab Chief Court and the first President of the Muslim League in the Punjab.
38. See 'Hardwar 24/26th Feb^y [1912]' (at page 262).

39. See 'Lahore 29th Feb^y – 3rd March 1912' (at page 266).
40. Bertrand Nigel Bosworth-Smith, ICS, appointed 1896, Assistant-Commissioner, Punjab, from 1897.
41. Ajit Singh (d. 1947), revolutionary journalist and associate of Lala Lajpat Rai, who like him was deported briefly to Mandalay for his part in protests against Government agrarian policy during 1907. Out of sympathy with the political direction of the INC, Singh was to leave India, first, as the Webbs presently indicate, for Persia and Constantinople, before settling permanently in South America.
42. Armed gang-robbery, from the Hindi *dakaiti*.
43. Resident Magistrate.
44. A Muslim victory tower in red sandstone and white marble, dating from the twelfth century and rising in five stories to a height of 288 feet.
45. Humayun, or Nasir-ud-din Muhammad, reigned as Mughal Emperor from 1530–40 and again from 1555–6. His domed tomb has a garden with paths and water courses in four squares (*charbagh*) with the tomb in the middle, whereas at the Taj Mahal the tomb is placed at one end.
46. John Ruskin (1819–1900), Victorian author and artist. The sublimely opinionated Ruskin's *Seven Lamps of Architecture* (1849) and his classic *Stones of Venice* (1851–53) were influential in the Gothic revival of his day.
47. Alma Latifi, ICS, appointed 1901, barrister and author, Assistant-Commissioner, Punjab, from 1903.
48. Charles Mowbray Dallas (1861–1936), ICS, former Lieutenant-Colonel, Indian Army, who was from 1911 Commissioner at Delhi.
49. Henry Cecil Beadon, (1869–1959), former Major, Indian Army, who was from 1909 Deputy-Commissioner and Settlement Officer at Delhi.
50. C. F. Andrews, author of *The Renaissance in India: Its Missionary Aspect* (London: Church Missionary Society, 1912).
51. St. Stephen's College, a Christian institution founded in 1882 and at the time affiliated to the Punjab University.
52. Hindu College, founded in 1899, which was to be incorporated in the new University of Delhi in 1922.
53. From the Persian *zanana*, meaning woman, signifying the secluded quarters for women in a high-caste Hindu household. 'Zenana work' was akin to social work in the Western sense, its aim to propagandise modern medical knowledge and other progressive ideas among the women inmates.
54. Reverend Canon S. S. Allnutt, M.A., Cambridge Mission at Delhi.
55. Lieutenant-Colonel Herbert Lionel Showers (1861–1916), British Army, Resident at Jaipur from 1910, and at Nepal from May, 1912.
56. Sir Sawai Madho Singh Bahadur (1861–1922).
57. Nawab Mamtaz-ud-doula Muhammad Sir Faiyaz Ali Khan, KCIE, CSI.
58. Member of a Hindu soldier caste claiming descent from Kshatriyas.
59. The entry for Adaipur (Udairpur in original) is given as it appears in the holograph diary, before the 'Ajmere' entry for '19–21st M^{ch} 1912' (see page 305).
60. *Tanga* (Hindi), a light two-wheeled vehicle.
61. Which may or may not have been the case, since the Maharana Sir Fateh Singh Bahadur of Adaipur (1849–1930) was notorious for avoiding contact

with India's British rulers. When he resigned under pressure from the British in 1921, he was replaced by a more compliant Maharaja Kumar.

62. Lieutenant-Colonel James Levett Kaye (1861–1917), Indian Army and Foreign Department, Government of India, who was Resident at Mewar from May, 1911.

63. Ajmer, as it is now generally known.

64. Charles Waddington (1865–1946) was Principal of Mayo College, Ajmere from 1903 to 1916.

65. Har Bilas Sarda (1867–1955), an *Arja Samaj* social reformer for many years Municipal Commissioner at Ajmere. Sarda is also the 'voluble Pleader' subsequently alluded to as the author of *Hindu Superiority: An Attempt to Determine the Position of the Hindu Race in the Scale of Nations*, (Ajmere, Scottish Mission Industries, 1917).

66. Sir Swinton Jacob (b. 1841), Indian Army and India Public Works Department, whose service included that of Public Works Secretary to the Agent to the Governor-General for Rajputana at the time Mayo College was built.

67. Maharaja Lieutenant-General Sir Pratap Singh Bahadur, *gaddi* of Idar, who in 1911 had become Maharaja Regent at Jodhpur on the death of his nephew, Maharaja Sardar Singh.

68. German for 'a companion or escort'.

69. The great attraction of Mount Abu, which rises to 3800 feet. The older of the two finely-carved marble temples, surrounded by high hills, dates from the eleventh century and is amongst the most complete examples of a Jain temple.

70. The Achilgarh group of statues and temples is situated some five miles distant from Dilwara.

71. Sir Elliot Graham Colvin (1861–1940), ICS, appointed 1880, Agent to Governor-General, Rajputana, from 1905.

72. Reginald Peacock Barrow, ICS, appointed 1883, Commissioner, Bombay, from 1909.

73. The Indian Association was founded in 1876 with the aim of promoting Hindu-Muslim accord and providing a common forum for the political aspirations of all Indians.

74. The *Prarthana Samaj*, founded in 1867.

75. Sir Chinubhai was the grandson of Ranchhodlal Chhotalal, founder of the Ahmadabad Spinning and Weaving Company in 1858, and the son of the founder of the Ahmadabad Ginning and Manufacturing Company, dating from 1876.

76. That is, thirteen hours less an hour for meals in summer, and twelve hours less an hour for meals in winter.

77. Harold Liscombe Painter, ICS, appointed 1894, Junior Collector, Bombay, in 1912.

78. Godhra.

79. Jyotsnanath Ghosal was the son of Rabindranath Tagore's sister Swarna Kumari. He had joined the ICS in 1895 and when the Webbs met him was Joint Collector and Political Agent at Bombay.

80. The ironic allusion is to the principal character in J. M. Barrie's 1902 dramatic fantasy *The Admirable Crichton*. The Earl of Loam, his family and

one or two friends are wrecked on a desert island, where the butler, 'the admirable Crichton', proves himself a man of infinite resource and power, far superior to the rest of the party.

81. Public Works Department.

82. There seems to have been a slight confusion on the part of the Webbs here. The *nyaya mantri* or Dewan of Baroda at the time was Bihari Lai Gupta (1849–1916), ICS – until his retirement in 1907 a High Court Judge at Calcutta – and not the J. N. Gupta who wrote *Life and Work of Romesh Chunder Dutt* (London, 1911). Dutt (1848–1909) was President of the Indian National Congress for 1899 and Prime Minister of Baroda in 1909.

83. Adarji Mernosji Masani, B.Sc.,M.A.

84. Doctor of Science.

85. A. B. Clarke, B.A., Principal, Baroda College.

86. Maharaja Gaekwar Sir Sayaji Rao III (1863–1939).

87. Whether by inadvertence or design, the Gaekwar had caused a sensation at the Delhi Durbar when, upon formal presentation to the Emperor King, he was observed not to be wearing the sash of the Star of India. The breach of protocol was only exacerbated by the Gaekwar's turning his back on their Royal Highnesses on exiting. An apology was forthcoming to the Viceroy and printed in *The Times*; but the incident provided an occasion for allegations in the London press about the Gaekwar's sympathy for political extremists in Baroda.

88. 'Feby 17/19th Gwalior' (see page 253).

89. Literally non-Aryans, thus signifying all those not light-skinned.

90. Sir George Clarke (1848–1933) was Governor of Bombay from 1907 to 1913, when he was created Baron Sydenham of Combe.

91. Henry Venn Cobb (1864–1949), ICS, appointed 1883, Resident at Baroda from 1908.

92. Charles Norman Seddon, ICS, appointed 1889, Settlement Commissioner, Baroda, from 1904.

93. Reginald Edward Enthoven, ICS, appointed 1887, Senior Collector, Bombay, from 1910. He subsequently returned to London to serve as Controller of the Department of Import Restrictions at the Board of Trade during the First World War.

94. William Henry Clark (1876–1952) was Secretary to the Board of Trade and to the Chancellor of the Exchequer from 1908–10, and thereafter, served in India as Member for Commerce and Industry in the Governor-General's Council.

95. Later Sir Claud Hill, who was a Member of the Governor-General's Council from 1915–20 and, upon retirement from the ICS, became heavily involved in the Red Cross.

96. Maharaja Kumar Shri Ranjitsinhji, Jam Saheb of Nawanagar (1872–1933), who was subsequently a member of India's delegation to the League of Nations.

97. As Inspector-General of Police in Bengal from 1891–1900, Henry had introduced the finger-print system for identifying criminals, a system, at his instigation, subsequently adopted by Scotland Yard.

98. The Servants of India Society had been founded by Gopal Krishna Gokhale in 1905, its aim the training of a nationwide network of recruits committed

to Indian self-government, living modestly and dedicating themselves to programmes of social reform.

99. Pune.
100. Built in 1884, the College contained accommodation for 800 students.
101. Surendra Nath Banerjea (1848–1925), educator and political reformer, was the founder of Ripon College, Calcutta.
102. A complete edition by Thomas Wright of the letters of William Cowper (1731–1800), poet and stylist, had appeared in 1904. The Webbs' point is that whereas Cowper bore no overt political message, the political essays of Edmund Burke (1729–97) did. Though famously opposed to the French Revolution, Burke had supported the American colonists in the American Revolution, and had led a parliamentary fight to impeach Warren Hastings for 'oppression, maladministration and corruption' when he was Governor-General of India. Burke's positions on the issues of his day might thus be thought a source of potential embarrassment to the imperial rulers of India.
103. Ratan Tata (1871–1918), Bombay business man. See also the Bombay entry below.
104. Thomas Babington Macaulay (1800–59), historian and Whig statesman. As legal adviser to the Supreme Council of India in 1834–37, Macaulay had played a leading role in founding the Indian educational system, arguing in a famous Minute for the adoption of an English rather than an 'oriental' curriculum.
105. A highly esteemed caste of (blue-eyed) Brahmins from Maharashtra from whose ranks a large number of early Indian nationalist leaders were drawn.
106. The reference is to the circumstances surrounding an epidemic of strikes in Britain in 1911–12, outstanding amongst which were those involving the transport workers, the railwaymen, and most dramatically the miners – some million and a half of whom left the pits in early 1912 in response to calls from a leadership influenced by direct-action syndicalist ideas originating in the United States and continental Europe.
107. Charles Stewart Parnell (1846–1891), Irish politician and leader of the movement for Irish Home Rule in the late nineteenth century.
108. In Hindu worship, the one God, Brahma, has three manifestations: as *Brahma* the creator, *Vishnu* the preserver, and *Siva* the destroyer and reproducer. *Kali, Siva's* wife, is especially associated with his terrible qualities and must be propitiated by sacrifices.
109. Dr Harold Hart Mann (b. 1872), agricultural chemist, had joined the Department of Agriculture, Bombay, in 1907, and in 1911 became Principal, College of Agriculture, Poona.
110. Syed Husain Bilgrami, ICS, who had served on the Governor-General's Legislative Council and the Council of India, 1907–09.
111. Originally the Poona Sanskrit College, The Deccan College was housed in a large Gothic-style building dating from 1864, designed by Captain H. C. Wilkins, RE, and largely paid for by the College's founder, Sir Jamsetjee Jeejeebhoy, the first Parsee baronet.
112. An establishment Bombay family of manufacturers and merchants, descendants of Sir Dinshaw Petit (1823–1901).
113. Jamsetji Nusserwanji Tata (1839–1904) was the founder of a family-based industrial empire that remains one of the largest in India.

114. Stanley Reed (1872–1969) had been editor of the *Times of India* since 1907.
115. Joseph Baptista (1864–1930), first President of the Indian Home Rule League and eventual Mayor of Bombay.
116. Sir Phirozshah Merwanjee Mehta (1845–1915), President of the Indian National Congress in 1890 and for long a dominant figure on Bombay's political scene.
117. The duplication or imitation of a competitor's wares without acknowledgement.
118. Or 'doffers', workers who remove the full bobbins or spindles.
119. Or 'pieceners', whose job it was to keep the frames filled with 'rovings', or cotton drawn out and slightly twisted, and to join together the ends of threads which broke.
120. The operator of a type of spinning-machine (from the general term for the machine itself).
121. The Hindu caste system originates in the Vedic division of society into three *varnas* or 'colours', *Brahmins* or priests, *Kshatriyas* or warriors, and *Vaishyas*, merchants or agriculturalists – to which came to be added the *Shudras* or servants.
122. A small island in Bombay harbour famed for its ancient cave carvings of Shiva.
123. The whitewashed Towers, associated with Parsee funeral rites, number five in all, with the largest 276 feet round and 25 feet high. The first Tower of Silence was erected in 1674.
124. Sir Henry Miers (1858–1942), Principal of the University of London, 1908–15.
125. Leonary Trelawny Hobhouse (1864–1929), sociologist and political theorist, Professor of Sociology at The London School of Economics and a long-standing friend of the Webbs.
126. Edward J. Urwick (1867–1945), Professor of Social Philosophy at the University of London.
127. Hastings Bertrand Lees-Smith (1878–1941), Liberal and later Labour Party MP, who had been associated with Ruskin College, Oxford from its foundation in 1899.
128. Frederic J. N. Thesiger, afterwards Viscount Chelmsford (1868–1933), whom the Webbs had known on the London School Board and the London County Council, Viceroy of India from 1916–21, and First Lord of the Admiralty in the first Labour Government.
129. The *panchayat* was a traditional institution of local government in India predating the arrival of the British, its membership consisting of respected elders whose rulings were accepted as representing the will of the collectivity.
130. From the Sanskrit *sati*, the former Indian custom of a widow burning herself, either on the funeral pyre of her dead husband or soon after. The practice was abolished by the British in 1829.
131. 'General' William Booth (1829–1912), founder of the Salvation Army, succeeded by his son, William Bramwell Booth (1856–1929), who was eventually compelled to retire by demands for a more democratic system of leadership.
132. As Governor-General of India, Lord Cornwallis (1738–1805) had in 1793 effectively established a class of Indian landlords in Bengal with rights of

transfer and inheritance, approaching the matter with the preconceptions of a Whig gentleman in order to make a Permanent Settlement of the land revenues. The flaw in the arrangement was that while the rights of the *zemindar* were thus assured, those of the under-proprietors and occupying cultivators were not, and in consequence the land often fell under the control of rack-renting middlemen.

133. Sir (Percy) Maurice Amos (1872–1940), who was Judge of Cairo's Native Court of Appeal, 1906–12.

134. Lt-Col. Percival George Elgood (1863–1941), at the time Financial-Secretary to the Egyptian Army.

135. An Egyptian peasant.

136. From 1882 to 1936 the British were the *de facto* rulers of Egypt. At the time of the Webbs' visit there was a Legislative Council, composed of nominees of the Khedive and native members elected by provincial assemblies, as well as a General Assembly. But these had only an advisory power, and real authority, resting ostensibly with the Khedive, was in fact exercised by British Advisers to all the native officials. These Advisers were themselves accountable to the British Consul-General.

137. Sir John Eldon Gorst (1861–1911), Consul-General in Egypt, 1907–11.

138. Horatio Herbert Kitchener, 1st Earl Kitchener of Khartoum (1850–1916), who had succeeded Gorst as Egypt's Consul-General in 1911. Secretary of State for War in the First World War, Kitchener was lost with most of the hands when HMS *Hampshire* was sunk *en route* to Russia in 1916.

139. Abbas Hilma II, who was Khedive from 1892–1914.

140. End of *Mss Diary*, Volume 31.f.174.

Appendix

The National Committee for the Break-up of the Poor Law marked an important transition on the part of the Webbs from a strategy of attempting to 'permeate' the British political elite behind the scenes, to one of openly 'propagandising' their reformist views before a much wider audience. While founded in 1909 specifically to publicise their *Minority Report on the Poor Law*, the Committee soon attracted the interest of middle-class supporters concerned about poverty in a more general sense – and thus the subsequent change of name to 'The National Committee for the Prevention of Destitution'. *The Crusade*, the Committee's organ, appeared monthly under the editorship of a young Fabian, Clifford Sharp, during the National Committee's brief heyday, from February 1910 – February 1913. Its successor, announced in its final issue, proved to be a more durable journal. It was *The New Statesman, A Weekly Review of Politics and Literature*, instigated by the Webbs with Sharp as its first editor. While in Asia, Beatrice had sent letters to Sharp and others at the National Committee headquarters in Norfolk Street describing their experiences, with the suggestion that they be copied and circulated among others in London. In addition, the Webbs sent three articles – on Canada, Japan and China – the last two of which are reproduced below. Loose in Volume 30 of Beatrice's holograph diary are seventeen folio sheets in Sidney's hand, a preliminary draft of the Japan article, beginning 'Not full impressions – only greetings from afar.'

'The Social Crisis in Japan'

We do not presume, in these words of greeting from afar to the members of the National Committee, to give any full or detailed account of our impressions of Japan.

Who could adequately describe the extraordinary charm of that wonderful country, which we have found far more beautiful than we had ever imagined? Japan is wonderful for its profusion of picturesque mountains, which are scarcely even mentioned in England; wonderful in its primeval forests of giant *cryptomerias*; wonderful in the ubiquitous intensity of the cultivation of its irrigated plains, out of which the hills always rise so abruptly, and which are surprisingly rich in rice and mulberry and beans and millet, with here and there maize and tea and grapes and oranges; wonderful in its ancient palaces, with their wealth of carving and painting, and in its multifarious temples, embowered in groves of immemorial trees; wonderful, indeed, in the charm of its ancient civilisation. If anyone is tired of the complexity and ugliness of modern industrialism, we can imagine no holiday so complete and so restful as a walking tour in Japan away from the ports and the very few inland places in which the tourists and missionaries congregate. We shall never forget our own ten days' walk in the August sunshine, with clothing reduced to a minimum, and luggage in the basket that one coolie could carry, from Nikko to Nagano, over mountain passes up to 7000 feet above sea level; through forests, climbing up to the very tops of these heights; with a semi-tropical vegetation full of new delights to European eyes; by rushing rivers and silent lakes and bubbling waterfalls; along the narrow paths connecting the innumerable villages with each other; past countless shrines and tombs and temples of century-old piety; across endless smiling plains of rice in little patches at different levels a few inches higher or lower than each other to permit of irrigation; and through one populous village after another, each with its own individuality but always swarming with babies, and really seeming at last to differ from all the rest of those seen throughout the day, chiefly in its totally unrememberable name!

But Japan is not all country. Large towns of fifty to a hundred thousand inhabitants, of which European geographies do not give even the names, are numerous, each with its schools and temples and manufactories; and there are also half a dozen giant cities as large as Manchester and Liverpool (but oh, how different!), with palaces and castles and sights [and not] the slightest fear of molestation by man or beast. Then, it is a country in which everyone seems always to be travelling — immense concourses of pilgrims and holiday-makers and business people are everywhere on the move — so that everywhere there is accommodation and provision for travellers' needs. Add to this that the common lump of men are, in Japan, perhaps more civilised than those in any other country that we have seen — clean, elaborately well-mannered, common schooled if not educated, kindly and polite to a degree that leaves far behind the English labourer, town or country — whilst the officials and rich men are eager to be friendly to the wandering Englishman; and it does not need any special introductions to make travelling pleasant. But the traveller makes a great mistake who, through shyness or modesty or mere lack of foresight, does not provide himself with pilgrim's scrip in the form of letters or introduction of one sort or another. They are easy to get, they are almost always effusively honoured on presentation, and they add enormously to the charm and interest of travel. We have ourselves lived so entirely with the Japanese officials, statesmen, bankers, professors, priests and business men to whom we brought or obtained introductions, that we have had hardly any time to see the European and American residents.

But this sort of travel involves getting hold of a good interpreter. We were fortunate through friends in engaging, actually before we left the steamer, an interpreter of education and refinement to whom, in our two months' intercourse, we have become personally much attached, and by means of whose skill we have been able to conduct long intellectual discussions with our Japanese friends, on all sorts of subjects, from economics to Buddhist philosophy, from agriculture to art. And all our expenses in Japan, including first-class travelling and this interpreter, have come easily within twenty-five shillings per day for each of us.

Now, of Japan today there are two aspects, the old and the new, agriculture and manufactures, the country and the town. Of the charm of rural Japan we cannot speak too highly. Imagine an intelligent and essentially *civilised* population of millions of families, settled in closely contiguous villages, on fertile plains, between picturesque mountain ranges from which descends abundant irrigation water; each family with its own series of plots of highly cultivated and copiously irrigated garden land, on which, by incessant hard labour, minute care and abundant manuring, huge crops of rice, millet, beans, mulberry, maize, buckwheat and barley are raised under the sub-tropical sun; the families often owning as well as cultivating their little plots, which hardly ever exceed in extent the amount cultivable by the members of the families themselves, so that there is no class of agricultural wage labourers; or, if not themselves the owners, being tenants on a customary rent of about one half of the rice crop, and enjoying, in practice, virtual fixity of tenure; and, whether owners or occupiers, having often been in occupation of the same land for five or ten generations. Where non-cultivating landlords exist, having numerous tenants, the relationship seems to be one of friendly mutual co-operation, the landlord exercising a sort of paternal supervision and direction of the village affairs, and obtaining, as rent, such proportion of the rice crop as the harvest allows. And intermingled with these millions of agricultural families – often coincident with them – there exist apparently no less numerous families of petty handicraftsmen and retailers, supplying all the household wants of the countryside. In short, rural Japan represents the perfection of *la petite culture* and *la petite industrie*. In no country of Europe or America that we have seen is there so large a proportion of the population in the position of being their own masters, owning themselves the instruments of production, working for their own profit, occupying their own little houses, worshipping at their own family shrines, and consuming very largely the products of their own labour. Here, at any rate, is the proprietary state, with the family group as the economic unit, which Mr. Hilaire Belloc finds so attractive. And certainly, nowhere is this society more alluring than in rural Japan.

Whether such a social order could, in the twentieth century, ever be created anew – whether, even in rural Japan, it can long be maintained in existence – we need not now discuss. What must be noted are several concomitants not usually remembered, which rural Japan forces on our attention. In the first place, it is a community of superstitions of all sorts, wedded to the old ways, with a tremendous blinding force of national sentiment. Perhaps as the other side of this feature, this community of small peasant cultivators are practically devoid of political democracy. Absorbed in the incessant toil that their fields and handicrafts demand, their horizons bounded practically by their family, or at most their village concerns, these thriving millions of rural families are plainly incapable of organising, controlling, criticising or even intelligently comprehending the large enterprises characteristic of a community of the size of twentieth century states. What disables such a community from wide political interests, and from that active personal participation in movements having no direct bearing on their family concerns – and it is these that make effective political democracy possible – is not merely the incessant toil in which their lives are spent. It is also the fact that (as with the indoor domestic servant and the working mother of a young family) there is no division of their lives between work and leisure. They have no working hours. Their work is never done. From waking to sleeping they are never free from its presence, never able to take their minds off its perpetual insistence on an endless series of petty details in which their own personal concern is paramount and all-absorbing.

In western industrialised states, these two new classes furnish the material for political democracy. We have the growth, on the one hand, of an intellectual proletariat of teachers, clerks, lawyers, doctors and journalists – in Switzerland the hotel keepers – with leisure to think; and on the other hand, of a class of hired artisans and labourers in whose lives the hours of work, few or many, are sharply marked off from the rest of their lives, so that their waking day is not wholly taken up with an endless series of petty personal affairs requiring all their thought. In a universally proprietary state of agricultural peasants and petty retailers, the railway and postal service and telegraphs and telephones, the conservancy of the rivers, the construction of main roads, the organisation of an educational system from the kindergarten to the university – not to mention international relations, the army and the navy – inevitably become, if they are to exist at all, the sphere of an expert bureaucracy, without any effective supervision or control from the people at large. For a community of tiny peasant occupiers and petty handicrafts-men, scattered over the countryside, the only alternatives are to confine the state to the small size contemplated by Aristotle and Rousseau, like the forest cantons of Switzerland, forgoing such essentially large enterprises as railways and universities; or to leave all the public affairs transcending the family and the village to a bureaucracy outside and above the village life.

The latter is the position of rural Japan. The Government officials seemed to us as a class admirable. They were everywhere on the most friendly, intimate terms with all classes. They appeared to be taking the keenest interest in their work and eager for the public welfare; to be full of intellectual curiosity about it, open-minded and curiously unprejudiced. But they were (and were recognised to be) so superior in knowledge and ability to the rural population that what they did and decided was practically beyond all effective check or criticism. We do not see how, in a rural community of small cultivators and handicraftsmen – if it is to have large enterprises at all – such a bureaucratic administration of these enterprises can be avoided. In the twentieth century state, peasant cultivation and rural handicrafts are, to the extent that they make up the community, incompatible, beyond the affairs of the family and the village, with effective political democracy. This, at any rate, is our comment on rural Japan.

And the country-side of peasant cultivators and petty retailers inevitably creates its own destruction. With cultivation already pushed to its maximum of intensity, and with every inch of ground in use on which rice will grow, the village finds itself unable to provide a livelihood for the natural increase of its population. If famine is not to ensue, the surplus of boys and girls must swarm off; and in Japan, as elsewhere, they swarm off to swell the huge cities in which the modern machine industry and capitalist production on a large scale is both creating and demanding a wage-earning proletariat.

And this brings us to the other aspect of Japan, with its surprising and rapid development of a native capitalism, reproducing, with minute accuracy, all the features of the industrial England of 1790–1840. Japan has already a million factory operatives, in some 20,000 factories – not to speak of extensively-worked mines of coal and copper, oil-fields and petroleum refineries as hideous as anything in the United States, and huge capitalist exploitations in timber, fisheries, merchant shipping, and what not. In the cotton and silk mills we found young girls (as young as 9 or 10) and women working (night shifts along with day shifts) for over eighty hours per week, with no Sunday rest, and practically no holidays. We found these girls sometimes working (for such hours) in unsanitary processes which in England are confined to men, and are even then largely mitigated in their evil influences by extremely short shifts. We found the hands (just as in the Lancashire of 120 years ago) collected by recruiting agents from all parts of the country – even children of 9 or 10 – separated from their families, and boarded and lodged in the employers' own premises, to which (under normal circumstances) they were practically confined — if, indeed, they have any time or energy left for anything but working, sleeping and eating.

Until last year there was absolutely nothing in the nature of a Factory Act, and no restriction on the will of the employers as to the conditions of labour. There was not (and still is not) any effective registration of children liable to attend school; there is no power legally to compel attendance; and moreover, tens of thousands of children of school age are actually exempted from attendance on the ground of poverty. Even now the Factory Law of 1910 resembles rather the English Factory Acts of 1819 and 1833 than a twentieth century law; and some of its prohibitions (as of night work for women) do not come into force for fifteen years. And whilst some of the factory managers are philanthropic men, desirous of doing for their thousands of operatives the best that they can — just as England had its Peels and Gregs and Marshalls and Ashworths — and accordingly, some of the boarding houses are swept and garnished, and there are flowers and amusements and benevolent tuck-shops where the operatives can buy what they want without leaving the compound, the system remains in all its hideousness. The girls, contracted away by their parents, or entrapped by alluring offers of wages, looked sullen, apathetic, and discontented. It was complained by the employers that they seldom stayed on after their three years contract service, and that they took every excuse for leaving before the term expired, so that the mill had to be perpetually breaking in new hands. Finally, it was asserted everywhere that nothing would induce a girl living in the city where the factory was situated (and therefore knowing what the life was like) to become a factory operative. Similarly unrestricted conditions of employment prevail in the coal and copper mines, and in the oil-fields, where the men seem to be much as were the English coal-miners a hundred years ago. And these and similar industries are increasing in Japan by leaps and bounds.

We saw something of the conditions of existence of the poorest quarters of the great cities; and naturally, we found them pretty nearly as bad as they could be. The Japanese Government has had too much to do, in its amazing task of taking three centuries of social evolution in a stride of forty years, to undertake much in the way of town sanitation, the prevention and treatment of disease, or proper housing requirements. And the Japanese central Government has not yet learnt how to call to its aid, in administration as well as in finance, the indefinitely expansible force of local self-government. In its eagerness for efficiency, the Japanese Cabinet has adopted a bureaucratically-controlled and minutely-super-vised system of local administration, partly German and partly French in its structure; and has failed, as yet, to learn from England how to create really independent centres of local initiative and local administration, which would relieve it of some of its gigantic task.

The education system is a strange mixture of universal provision and nominal compulsion, with a practical failure to ensure universal attendance; in some places fees are charged in the poor districts, whilst the richer districts have free schools; there is a system of elaborate secondary schools, pretentious and very imperfect, but no provision for enabling the poorest children, however clever, to take advantage of them. There is no general provision for the prevention and treatment of disease, and (in spite of apparently endless charity on the part of the very poorly remunerated doctors, and various charity hospitals as they are called) the death rate is half as much again as in England; with tuberculosis and infantile disorders fatally prevalent; and with the children growing up, untreated, with all sorts of eventually disabling complaints. How quickly the alert and open-minded Japanese bureaucracy will realise the precipice down which capitalist exploitation (by Japanese capitalists, be it noted, not foreigners) is hurrying the nation, we cannot estimate; whether they will be clever enough to jump to a systematic application of the policy of the national minimum in sanitation, education, leisure and subsistence, by which, as English experience teaches us, the country can alone be saved, as they have jumped to other things, no one can foresee; finally, whether without the driving power of a politically-active democracy, the bureaucrats will be able to overcome the resistance of the capitalists (who declare that they are producing the wealth without which Japan cannot make good its position as a first rate power), we do not pretend to judge. The moment is, for Japan, perhaps the most critical in its whole national history; and it is one of extraordinary interest to the instructed observer.

Of destitution in Japan, in the comprehensive sense in which we now use the term, there is already no lack; but it naturally takes different forms from those to which we are accustomed. As in England, however, the greatest number are those who are sick and destitute of medical attendance. The amount of preventable disease, of unnecessary disablement and of premature old age and death is costing Japan today more even than its gigantic naval expenditure or its war debt. The lack of any systematic and complete public health organisation, which would actually prevent the occurrence of much disease; and of a public medical service (including hospitals) to supply appropriate treatment at the earliest stage, when alone it is really preventive, constitutes, at the present, the most glaring failure of the Japanese Government to bring the nation abreast of the ideals of western civilisation.

An almost equally extensive section of destitution is represented by the children. A large proportion of the children of Japan are suffering severely from the want of the necessaries of healthy child life. There is very little public provision for orphans or abandoned children; in the absence of any supervision of child birth and infancy, the infantile death rate (in spite of universal breast feeding) is very high, implying much infantile disease; as the children do not go to school until 6 or 7, the period during which they escape all inspection or supervision is much greater than in England; and even during the school years there is no systematic provision for ensuring that they are medically attended to. No doubt the Japanese family achieves a great deal: but in the slums of Osaka and Nagoya — even in the mountain villages that we passed through — the family system cannot in the absence of systematic medical inspection and provision, prevent the development and dissemination of tuberculosis and enteric, nor save the children from *sequelae* of neglected measles. The child destitution of Japan, in this all-important particular, is of course not to be compared with that of most Eastern nations — there is no such glaring child neglect as is seen in the streets of Cairo, or even in those of Calcutta — but what Japan pretends to, and what the world now expects from her, is civilisation of a high Western standard.

Of the destitution of the aged we saw little in Japan. In this particular the nation sets an example to all Europe, and perhaps leads the world. The family system makes it a matter of course for the aged to be provided for as honoured guests in the families of their descendants. There must be some not thus provided for; and Tokyo has a general mixed workhouse not essentially different from a typical Scottish poorhouse. But the problem is mitigated by the grim fact, not in itself creditable to Japanese administration, that extreme old age is rare. Men and women become old at 50 or 60; and those of 70 or 80 seem very much less common than in Europe. Japan escapes old age pauperism partly because the neglect of health in early life prevents there being many aged.

Able-bodied destitution, or unemployment, appears also to be rare. Whether this is to be ascribed to the still great prevalence of the hand industry, to the people still having practical access to the instruments of production, to the family system or to the lower standard of subsistence, we cannot determine. Certainly, an able-bodied man, even if he indulges in *sake*, seems always able to earn the extremely minute sum on which he can live from day to day. There used to be local famines from failure of crop. There are now periods of stress owing to a rise in the price of rice; and a system of poor relief is on the point of springing up. The Tokyo poorhouse, already mentioned, is a semi-philanthropic, semi-municipal enterprise of a generation old, but still an exception. We came across, however, in other places, spasmodic distributions of rice by the public authorities, in order to keep people alive. In Osaka, the second city of the Empire, they were just on the point of establishing a municipal Department of Poor Relief, to deal with all classes of the destitute − once more preparing to repeat the English mistake! The Japanese Government has a great opportunity of avoiding the administrative blunder, which has given England the mournful heritage of a huge pauper class, by refusing to create any special organisation for the relief of destitution as such. It can, if it chooses, arrange for each section of the destitute to be dealt with on preventive lines by the public authority charged with dealing with that section of the population (the sick, the children, the mentally defective, etc.), and thus avoid the creation of any class specifically pauper, with all its demoralising tendency to increase and to become a permanent burden on the community.

But the greatest blot on the civilisation of Japan is its treatment of women. We do not here mean simply the subjection of the wife to the husband, a position compatible with a very real equality in practical life, and one which we need not here discuss. But the subjection of the wife in the family is one thing: the subjection of the young woman to the factory owner, the *geisha*-master, or the licensed quarter is quite another. Japan is trying the most extraordinary experiment on the health and character of its whole population: and an experiment, as it seems to us, fraught with the greatest possible danger. There may be something to be said for taking about 40 per cent of all the young men and making them serve for two years in the army; with results good and bad, on health and character, which are evidently considerable. What is remarkable, and, we think, peculiar, is that in Japan a very large proportion of its young women − a proportion which seems to run up to something like 20 per cent, and in some places much higher − are also passed into bondage for a term of years. There is the annual recruitment under contract of the million of factory operatives. There is the not inconsiderable annual recruitment − virtually sale by the parents − of girls to be trained as *geishas*. And there is the still darker shadow of the passing into the almost hopeless bondage of the licensed quarter (which exceeds in horror and cynical bestiality anything that we could have imagined) of literally thousands of young girls every year. This subjection of the girls of the nation to a period of what is really involuntary servitude, under conditions making neither for health nor for character, is of ominous portent. It is not the way to bring up the mothers of a great race. And it is, for the most part, a new evil which it is quite possible to stop. We cannot believe that if it is allowed to continue Japan can permanently make good its position among the great world powers.

But, in such a period of transition, it is unlikely that anything, good or bad, will long remain unchanged. In our own analogous period of transition – in England of 1790–1840 – social conditions were, so far as we can judge, considerably worse than in the Japan of today. Japan today has the advantage, which England a hundred years ago had not, of facing its problems with an instructed and highly intelligent civil service, and with the mass of the common people, in their own way, essentially civilised. It has the further advantage over the England of a century ago – perhaps even over the England of today – of being open-minded, eager to learn, and intellectually modest. It has before it the results of a century of experiment by other nations; and in social organisation, as in military and naval matters, it may well learn to improve even on those whom it takes as models. In short, it is a land full of hopefulness. We believe it is still the Land of the Rising Sun.

The Crusade, Vol. III, No. 1, January 1912

'China In Revolution'

We had not contemplated a 'China in Revolution' as part of our holiday experiences; and though this has occasionally added to the excitement, it has a little detracted from the equanimity of our travels. The scanty, alarmist telegrams that we saw in the Japanese newspapers during September and October made us afraid that we might not be able to visit China at all; or that, if we got into Peking, we might not be able to get out again! But Mukden was quiet; the railway to Peking was running smoothly; the Revolutionary forces were a long way off; and the British Consul-General saw no reason why we should not proceed. But as we neared Peking we passed trains packed to overflowing with terrified Chinese – trains packed in a way that we had never seen before – with every carriage filled to overflowing, so that there was no more standing room; men riding on the roofs; men, women and children crowding the platforms at either end of the American carriages; and men and boys clinging to the sides, sitting on the steps, and even standing on the buffers. These were fugitives from Peking, fleeing in blind terror from something – they knew not what: it might be a massacre of the Chinese by the Manchu soldiers; it might be a massacre of the Manchus by a Chinese uprising in Peking; or it might be an outbreak of the starving mob of the great capital, in which no life would be secure, and no house safe from incendiary fires.

We found the same panic during our ten days at Peking. As a matter of fact, nothing untoward did happen at Peking; and in the three weeks that have since elapsed, nothing has happened to justify the panic. But it went on unabated. Every day the trains leaving the capital were filled with fugitives. More than a hundred thousand people are said to have fled from Peking. We found the University, the colleges, and even the elementary schools, either closed because their students had fled, or else diminished to such tenuity that the classes numbered only three or five students. Our own friends among the younger Chinese officials were themselves placing their families in security, and running off to Tientsin now and then in a renewed panic; or else lingering in other cities rather than return to their duties at the capital. The two foreign hotels in Peking were filled to the roof with the wives and children of Manchu and Chinese dignitaries who had been placed there for safety; and even princes and officials did not disdain to come in secretly at night, lest their houses should be burnt before morning. One great Chinese noble, a highly placed official to whom we had a letter of introduction, invited us to lunch at our own hotel, explaining that his own palace was in the hands of the builder for repairs! As a matter of fact, he was hiding (with his four wives and a wagon-load of valuables) in the compound of a French banker within the Legation Quarter, whence he sallied forth furtively in the middle of the day to put in an appearance at his office.

Peking was, in fact, full of alarmist news (nearly always untrue), and of 'camp rumours' of the most exciting kind (which always proved to be baseless). Every day we heard that the rising (of the Chinese against the Manchu dynasty) was definitely fixed for the coming night. Nearly every day we were told on good authority that the little boy Emperor, with the Prince Regent, the Prime Minister and the Court, were to flee that night, in the long string of native carts that were already packed with their possessions, to Mukden, to the recesses of the most western province, or to Jehol, beyond the Great Wall, in the deserts of Mongolia. What was interesting to us in this universal panic was its revelation of Chinese character, the capacity for almost hysterical fear, and the estimate put by the Chinese themselves both on the probable brutality of their compatriots and on the incapacity of any conceivable Chinese Government, whether Manchu or Revolutionary, to protect the harmless, unoffending citizen against the worst manifestations of barbaric warfare.

Yet, from first to last of our glimpse of Peking, the duly-constituted governmental authorities were in full force and activity. Every street had its post of Manchu soldiers, ostentatiously armed with ball cartridge; the gaily-uniformed Chinese police, bearing loaded rifles, were everywhere in the fore; and ten or twenty thousand Manchu troops were encamped around the Forbidden City, their tents filling the vacant spaces between the inner and outer walls of the Imperial City. Meanwhile, so far as the tourist was concerned, everything went on as usual. We, like other foreigners, went all over the densely-peopled city in the universal 'ricksha', visiting the sights or lunching and dining with friends; penetrating into all the recesses of the Chinese City or the Tartar City; and coming home at midnight under the stars through the silent streets, without insult or molestation. We even had a couple of days' excursion a hundred miles into the interior, making the usual trip to the Ming tombs and Great Wall and the Nankow Pass without any danger. The Legation professed to be quite unalarmed so far as foreigners were concerned. But they were quietly taking a few precautions. The number of their armed guards was increased, and these were kept on the alert. Troops were accumulated at Tientsin and other conveniently near ports. A few soldiers were lent at night to Roman Catholics and other large missions, in the depths of the Tartar City; and in the case of the American missions, rifles and revolvers were served out to the missionaries by the American Legation, in order that they might be able if necessary to defend themselves and their converts from attack.

Meanwhile, more by the absence of resistance than by reason of their own strength, the Revolutionary forces were steadily overrunning all the rest of China. At Peking we had less real news than London heard day by day in the cablegrams. But city after city 'went over', usually quite quickly – even Shanghai and Canton and Tientsin. Province after province declared itself independent or neutral (the delightfully vague Chinese language left it uncertain which was meant); Viceroys and other officials left their posts; everybody put up something purporting to be the Revolutionary flag (often with eighteen stars on a red or blue field, intended to signify 'The United States of China'); no more tribute was remitted from the provinces to the Court at Peking. Presently there was (as at Shanghai and Canton) a general cutting off of pigtails (the pigtail being the three-centuries-old mark of subjection to the Manchus), any hapless wight who hesitated finding himself insulted and mobbed, and summarily docked of his queue by whatever chopper or knife came handiest to the mob. In city after city the prisons were opened; every sort of male person, whether convict or brigand or pirate, was enlisted in the Revolutionary army, decorated with a white rag armlet, and given a rifle, a bright new revolver and a beltful of ball cartridges to play with; and here and there we used to read of indiscriminate fighting, promiscuous looting, and cases of piracy in the rivers. Trade, it is needless to say, came to a standstill. Out of all the eighteen provinces and three hundred millions of people, the Imperialist troops hold only Peking and Nanking, with the railway line from Peking, through Paotingfu, towards Hankow. It is at Hankow and Nanking that the only real fighting has taken place; and at this moment the issue is still undecided.

Unfortunately, it was exactly to Paotingfu and Hankow and Nanking that we had intended to proceed on leaving Peking, so that the indecisive fighting, the successive capture and recapture of Hankow, and the burning of that city, with the consequent complete interruption of the passenger traffic, were both interesting and inconvenient to us! In the end we were driven, in order to keep our engagement in Calcutta, to join the crowd of fugitive Chinese fleeing to Tientsin, just gaining standing room in the train, crowded as already described, by favour of the English guard, who turned out to be an enthusiastic member of the I.L.P. and subscriber to the *Labour Leader*; and whose fraternal intervention proved of more practical use in the terrified mob than all the efforts of a high Chinese dignitary from the Ministry of Railways who had come down to the station to befriend us.

By this time, practically the whole Empire had slipped away from the Manchu dynasty; millions of men outside Peking and Nanking have been cutting off their pigtails; no compensating success of the Imperial troops is reported; and whether the Imperial Humpty-Dumpty can ever be set on the wall again – that wonderfully picturesque, high wall that encircles the yellow-tiled roofs rising out of the mass of green foliage that characterises the million-peopled Peking – seems extraordinarily doubtful. It is, for the first time in three hundred years, more than a revolt; it is a popular revolution. Nor is it against any particular measure, nor any new or exceptional oppression, that all China is revolting. From end to end of China the people want simply to get rid of their existing Government, with its ubiquitous corruption and amazing inefficiency and futility. The leaders of the revolution, like the rank and file of its adherents, declare their intention of entirely clearing out the Manchu dynasty, and with it the Manchu troops and the Imperial throne; and of setting up a federal republic on the model of North America, Mexico or Brazil, under the title of The United States of China.

It must be remembered in this connection that the eighteen provinces of China – not to speak of Manchuria, Mongolia and Turkestan – are each of them as large as a European state, and contain on an average something like twenty millions of people. What is more important still is that they, for the most part, speak languages unintelligible to each other; and they have been for centuries accustomed to separate laws and customs, separate treasuries and taxes, and practically distinct administrations. Each has had its own autocratic Viceroy or Governor; and each has now its own Provincial Assembly. When we remarked to one of the Revolutionary leaders that a federal republic for one quarter of all the world's inhabitants was the most difficult of political organisations to construct, he replied that 'all great achievements were difficult; but the Chinese would be equal to the task'. He said, however, that it was only in outward form that they intended to imitate the United States; and that he much preferred the English cabinet system of responsible government. He eagerly accepted the suggestion that the Australian Commonwealth Act supplied a convenient model, with merely the substitution of a President for a Governor-General. But the Australian Constitution includes women's suffrage. It would indeed be curious if the women of China find themselves in possession of the vote before the women of England!

What are we to think of the capacity of the Chinese, and of the prospects of a peaceful reorganisation of that great Empire? We cannot pretend, from our mere five weeks' glimpse of only half-a-dozen cities, to anything like an independent judgement. But we have seen something of not a few prominent Chinese men, young and old, high and low. We have read diligently the testimony and the experiences of missionaries, travellers, business men, consular agents, and diplomatists of more than one nationality, some of whom have lived in China all their lives. And we have lost no opportunity of questioning and cross-examining any number of such persons from Mukden to Canton. As the outcome we impart our views to our fellow members merely as the irresponsible first impressions of two unbiased observers.

We record, to begin with, an almost universal testimony of those who have lived among the Chinese that they 'like' them, and think well of them. We are always assured that they are a 'great' people, full of potentialities. The Chinese, to judge from what is said of them, are honest, industrious, sober, docile – and you presently realise that your informant is thinking of them as house-servants! As a matter of fact, the Chinese have so little of what the Norwegians or the Bavarians call honesty, that every growing crop must be watched continuously night and day to prevent it from being stolen; whilst in every form of internal trade false weights and measures and counterfeit coin are employed and looked for as a matter of course. You are told that they are peaceful, law-abiding, frugal, thrifty and skilful – and you find that what is referred to as the untiring industry of the millions of petty cultivators, anxious only to be let alone in their rice fields. So far are the Chinese from being peaceful and unaggressive that highway robbery with violence, murder and piracy are extremely rife; whilst as for 'law-abiding', it is admitted on all hands that no Chinese person ever dreams of obeying a law merely because it is a law, or indeed, of obeying any new or unaccustomed law whatsoever, if it can possibly be evaded.

But the European in the Far East is not, as a rule, thinking of these things. Of any vision of the Chinese nation as an organised, civilised state on a par with other civilised states, to be judged by the same standards and weighed in the same balances, the English resident in China has not a glimmering. When he realises that what you are asking is whether the Chinese are at all equal in their social or political capacity or in their industrial or commercial achievements to the English or the Americans, or even to the Spanish or the Portuguese, he will sometimes quite angrily resent the idea that a 'coloured' people can ever be admitted into the comity of civilised nations. And you presently realise that what the European in the Far East likes in the Chinese is not their virtues, still less their intellectual capacity or practical achievement, but their virtual admission of their inferiority to himself – their docility as servants; their willingness to content themselves with the position of clerks or coolies under European Managers; their cession to the Europeans of all the organisation of foreign trade; all the international banking; all the management of ships and railways and telegraphs and post offices and customs; all the direction of mines and manufactures; and, in short, all the positions of profitable 'exploitation'.

Moreover, you are not long in discovering that this universal profession of 'liking' for the Chinese character, and of admiration for the Chinese capacity – which never, by the way, leads to any real social intimacy, even with the Europeanised Chinese – is only by way of contrast with the Japanese, who are universally disliked in the Far East. It is not so much that the Europeans actually love the Chinese as that they emphatically do not love the Japanese! And though the Europeans do not analyze their own feelings, we hazard the opinion that their dislike of the Japanese proceeds fundamentally from the fact that the Japanese, unlike the Chinese, *claim to be regarded as equals, and to be treated as the equals of all other nations*; and are making good their claim, in war and in peace, in army, navy and civil administration, in literature, science and art, in international banking and shipping, in internal manufactures and foreign trade. To be faced by this determined assertion of co-equality by a 'yellow' race, and to feel themselves now and again actually beaten by the Japanese (as is happening to the English and American and German business men in the Far East) is gall and wormwood to the Europeans, and even more to their wives. And, by contrast, the Chinese, who put forward no such claim to equality, and who (if they speak English and come at all into contact with Europeans) take up a position of conscious inferiority in all that the European regards as important in life, seem an agreeable and a 'like-able' [*sic*] race.

If, however, we abstract ourselves from this subjective influence, and consider the Chinese objectively, in the dry light of scientific inquiry, we find them a striking example of arrested development. A biological analogy may help to make the position clear. The highly-developed insect has gone very far, but it is along a line in which further progress seems to be impossible. The lowly vertebrate may be less highly developed, but has greater potentialities. The Chinese have perhaps pushed to a high point in the virtues of the self-regarding individual producer; the little cultivator in his paddy field is perhaps as industrious, as skilful in his own hereditary business, as frugal, as sober, and as faithful to his own standards as any human being in the world. Moreover, he is, by long family training, courteous and even polished – with an unreasoning respect for literature. The Chinese artisan, money-changer, shopkeeper, merchant and banker, seems to us to have, in a very high degree, qualities and capacities analogous to those of the rice-growing peasant.

These blue-clad three hundred millions, whether rural or urban, are bound together in a 'family system' which (as it is *piquant* to be told by Christian missionaries) is the most potent obstacle to any progress. Moreover, they display a capacity for combination in guilds and secret societies of all sorts. Beyond this, they seem incapable of constructing any social organisation, either commercial or governmental. The Chinese Empire – even the Chinese city or the Chinese province – can hardly be said to exist as an organism. The family system and the guild comprise all that really exists in China in the way of social organisation. Beyond these two imperfect developments of social life, the rice cultivator or the shopkeeper has nothing but, on the governmental side, a horde of officials who rob him; and, on the business side, a crowd of foreign bankers and merchants who exploit him. The whole Chinese nation reminds us, in fact, of a race of ants or bees of gregarious habits, but incapable of organisation of the ant-hill or the hive. They show us, indeed, what *Homo sapiens* can be if he does not evolve into the social organism.

If in the same dry light we ask what signs of capacity the Chinese exhibit, we find a remarkable phenomenon, for which our sociologists should be invited to account. The Chinese, we are told, used to be a 'great' people. They certainly built up a civilisation of their own, inadequate as we may think it, at a time when our own forefathers were painted savages. They made inventions and discoveries which Europe painfully worked out a thousand years later. They had a highly evolved and very extensive literature, however little we may today find in it to satisfy our intellectual curiosity; and an art in painting and carving which has, in its own handicraft way, never been surpassed. They gave civilisation, art and letters to the neighbouring peoples, even to Japan. They were able to construct a social organisation and an administrative system which, however imperfect we may now reckon it, has, unlike those of Babylon and Nineveh, Egypt and Judaea, Greece and Rome, at least endured. All this, we freely admit, entitles them to be regarded as one of the 'greatest' nations of the past. It is not merely that, in marked contrast with Japan, China has shown no capacity for adopting western learning. *It has shown, so far as we can discover, no capacity for anything.*

Let us begin with intellectual things. For a hundred years or more no Chinese person seems to have written an original book on any serious subject whatsoever. Even the flow of commentaries on the ancient classics, and of ephemeral poems in classical style, appears practically to have stopped. Apart from a few translations, some doubtful novels, and mere journalism of no lasting worth or intellectual dignity, we cannot learn that, from one end of the three hundred millions to the other, China is in this generation producing anything whatsoever. Experts tell us that the same is true in painting and porcelain, in bronzes and carving – there has been no good work for at least a century. There has certainly been no revival in religion and metaphysics. The race has, in the meantime, been accomplishing nothing in political or social administration, or in manufactures or international finance. They have accomplished nothing in law or in philosophy. They have done no better in war than in the pursuits of peace.

The Chinese are commonly said to be unrivalled in business; and they are certainly skilful enough at keeping a shop or a money-changer's office. But we could not learn that the Chinese had come to the fore, even in their own country, in any of the more highly evolved forms of business enterprise. Unlike the Japanese, we do not find them organising and managing extensive lines of passenger steamers (there is one small Chinese line, which was established by Americans and is now officered by Englishmen); they direct no railways; they develop no mines; they administer no banking or commerce on anything like an international scale; indeed, after many inquiries, we do not feel sure that, in all China, there exist more than a handful of Chinese business firms that have risen above the status of the local store or bank, in such as a way as to have branch establishments in other cities than those in which their principals live. And even in their own staple products, their incapacity stands revealed. We were told that the quality both of the tea and the silk has, in the past generation, markedly deteriorated, owing to faulty cultivation, careless preparation, and fraudulent packing. Certainly, the net result seems to be, as one thoughtful Chinese put it to us, that China, as a whole, is, so far as can be estimated, actually producing less year by year, even of material products; and that the nation is really poorer today, in wealth as in everything else, than it was a century ago. To sum up, this so-called 'great' race, whose capacity is so much extolled by those who profess to admire them, and whose reputed achievements in the distant past claim our respect, is today, by all the available evidence, capable of nothing! Its sole achievement in the past few centuries is that it has endured. But persistence or endurance or survival is, as every biologist knows, no proof of quality or excellence. A race, like a species, may endure and survive by reason actually of its low quality; and may, in fact further degrade in surviving (*vide* the Esquimaux, and all the parasites).

We cannot here even hazard a suggestion as to the causes of the sterility or decadence which seems to have fallen on the Chinese people. But we realise, as we never realised before, the imminence and the gravity of 'the Yellow Peril'. Not that this peril bears any resemblance to the absurd bogey that is usually meant by that phrase. Europe needs have no apprehension that its civilisation will be endangered, or its military supremacy imperilled, by a nation, however numerous, which is wholly lacking in intellectual or practical capacity. It is a strange delusion that millions can effect what brains cannot. Numbers, without capacity, are only an added impediment. Nor is the danger one of economic competition. It is a fundamental truth that no country need ever be afraid of a low-waged nation: it is the relatively high-waged nations like the United States and Germany – and just in those industries in which they pay the highest rates – that England finds its most dangerous competitors. No lowness of wage will ever make Chinese labour cheap – even if it were by cheapness of labour, and not by productive capacity, that nations industrially thrive. All such apprehensions of China are born only of economic ignorance. The real Yellow Peril is the moral and intellectual decadence into which this vast Empire has fallen; the helpless incapacity of its people to create even a decent social organism; their failure to develop the vast natural resources of their country, which are perhaps as extensive as those of the United States; their abject inability even to train their rivers so that agriculture (and with it foreign trade) may not be disastrously interrupted. The serious evil that China does us is not to undersell our artisans, but to lower the tone and coarsen the fibre of the European in the Far East. 'This living with inferior races' – meaning races whom we think inferior – 'is a terrible business', records one intelligent observer.

But the Yellow Peril is graver still. China lies, like a stranded whale bearing the costly ambergris, before the greedy eyes of the civilised powers; tempting them, almost beyond their powers of resistance, to an armed intervention, and a scramble for annexation, which is only too likely to light the torch of European war, in the course of which (as markedly happened in Germany in the seventeenth and to all continental Europe in the eighteenth century) our own civilisation and morality may retrograde to a lower level. The best defence against this real Yellow Peril is the elevation and training of the Chinese themselves. Those are doing more to ward off from Europe what would be an incalculable disaster who are helping the Chinese to raise themselves. The new schools and colleges of the Chinese Government, the educational and medical work of the missionaries, the instruction of Chinese students abroad, all the efforts that are now being made to improve Chinese administration – everything that tends to raise China from its humiliating degradation before the Western powers and to restore to the educated Chinese their national self-respect – is tending to diminish the Yellow Peril that we have reason to fear. The new Government University at Hong Kong, which Sir Frederick Lugard is organising for the use of all South China, may prove in this way, if given time, a more potent bulwark of the West than either tariffs or battleships.

It is from this standpoint and in this sense that the present revolution is full of hope. Whether the decrepit and decadent China of today can pull itself together, and take the same sort of new start that Japan has taken, is, however, more than doubtful. And as for the Yellow Peril that is so commonly feared by those destitute of economic knowledge – the victorious industrial competition of three hundred millions of docile yellow men living on twopence a day – all that need be said is that if this would be a peril to Europe, which we do not ourselves believe, it cannot possibly come into existence as a peril until the really existing Yellow Peril, that of decadent, incapable, helpless China exciting the greed of the world, has passed away.

The Crusade, Vol. III, No. 3, March 1912

Index